I mean high praise for *Territoriality and Hospitality* when I say that Lamin Sanneh himself would have thoroughly relished this collection of essays presented in his honor. The wide range of topics and scholarly approaches would certainly have appealed to his versatile mind, which was always open to fresh insights. He would have welcomed the thoughtful and erudite essays collected here on the intimate connections that so often link Christianity and Islam. This is a very rewarding collection.

Philip Jenkins, PhD
Distinguished Professor of History,
Institute for Studies of Religion,
Baylor University, Texas, USA

Lamin Sanneh was a true pioneer, reflecting his ancestral legacy as a *Soninke* or *Sarakhole*, as we say in Wolof. The *Soninke*, or *Sarakhole*, people were builders of ancient African empires such as Ghana and Mali. They are people who challenge both mental and physical boundaries, even if it causes discomfort for those who prefer to hold on to tradition. Sanneh was no exception to this characterization. He pushed religious boundaries in his quest for truth and his intellectual absence is deeply felt.

Mbaye Bashir Lo, PhD
Associate Professor of the Practice of Asian and Middle Eastern Studies,
Middle East Studies Center,
Duke University, North Carolina, USA

Territoriality and Hospitality

Langham
GLOBAL LIBRARY

Territoriality and Hospitality

Christian and Muslim Perspectives

John Azumah and Cheikh Anta Babou

© 2024 John Azumah and Cheikh Anta Babou

Published 2024 by Langham Global Library
An imprint of Langham Publishing
www.langhampublishing.org

Langham Publishing and its imprints are a ministry of Langham Partnership

Langham Partnership
PO Box 296, Carlisle, Cumbria, CA3 9WZ, UK
www.langham.org

ISBNs:
978-1-83973-757-2 Print
978-1-78641-072-6 ePub
978-1-78641-073-3 PDF

John Azumah and Cheikh Anta Babou hereby asserts their moral right to be identified as the Author of the General Editor's part in the Work in accordance with sections 77 and 78 of the Copyright, Designs and Patents Act 1988.

All rights reserved. No part of this publication may be reproduced, stored in a retrieval system or transmitted, in any form or by any means, electronic, mechanical, photocopying, recording or otherwise, without the prior written permission of the publisher or the Copyright Licensing Agency.

Requests to reuse content from Langham Publishing are processed through PLSclear. Please visit www.plsclear.com to complete your request.

Scriptures marked (NIV) are from the Holy Bible, New International Version®, NIV®. Copyright © 1973, 1978, 1984, 2011 by Biblica, Inc.™ Used by permission of Zondervan.

Scripture quotations marked (ESV) are from The Holy Bible, English Standard Version® (ESV®), copyright © 2001 by Crossway, a publishing ministry of Good News Publishers. Used by permission. All rights reserved.

Scripture quotations marked (RSV) are from Revised Standard Version of the Bible, copyright © 1946, 1952, and 1971 National Council of the Churches of Christ in the United States of America. Used by permission. All rights reserved.

Scripture quotations marked (NRSV) are from the New Revised Standard Version Bible, copyright © 1989 National Council of the Churches of Christ in the United States of America. Used by permission. All rights reserved.

Scripture quotations marked (NKJV) are from the New King James Version (NKJV). Copyright © 1982 by Thomas Nelson, Inc. Used by permission. All rights reserved.

British Library Cataloguing-in-Publication Data
A catalogue record for this book is available from the British Library

ISBN: 978-1-83973-757-2

Cover & Book Design: projectluz.com

Langham Partnership actively supports theological dialogue and an author's right to publish but does not necessarily endorse the views and opinions set forth here or in works referenced within this publication, nor can we guarantee technical and grammatical correctness. Langham Partnership does not accept any responsibility or liability to persons or property as a consequence of the reading, use or interpretation of its published content.

Contents

Foreword xi

Introduction 1
    John Azumah & Cheikh Anta Babou

Leaving Home: A Biographical Note 7
    Kelefa Sanneh

Lamin Sanneh, Historian of Hope 13
    Joel A. Carpenter

Opening Keynotes

1   Comparative African Reflections on *Ekklesia* and *Umma* 29
    John Azumah and Lamin Sanneh

2   Jihad Contested 43
    Exploring Islamic Pacifism in West Africa
        Cheikh Anta Babou

3   *Summoned from the Margin* 55
    Territoriality and Conversion in the Life and Thought of Lamin Sanneh
        J. Kwabena Asamoah-Gyadu

4   God's Hospitality and the Idolatry of Territoriality 75
    Rowan Williams

5   "God Is Not Your Train Driver; nor Your Soccer Mascot" 83
    Otherization, Tribalism, Territorialism, and Creation of the Transcendent in Our Image
        Farid Esack

Biblical and Theological Themes

6   Territoriality and Hospitality in Our Understandings of Salvation . . . 99
    Daniel A. Madigan

7   Islam and the Secular State 111
    Reflections on the Work of Abdullahi Ahmed an-Naʿim
        David Marshall

8   Muslim Minorities in Non-Muslim Lands 121
    A Comparison of the Suwarian Tradition with the Approach of Tariq Ramadan
        F. Peter Ford, Jr.

9   "Translatability and Nontranslatability" 139
    Bible, Qur'an, and Land in Northern Nigeria, 1913–1915
        Caroline Seed

10 "The Kingdom of God Is Like a Mustard Seed" 161
    Reconsidering the Nature of the Kingdom in a Post-Christendom World
        Martin Accad

11 Separation without Marginalization 173
    Church, Mosque, and State in the Political Theology of Lamin Sanneh
        Joshua Ralston

Historical and African Perspectives

12 Territoriality, Xenophilia, and Xenophobia 195
    Religious Change in the West African Sahel and Savannah
        Patrick Ryan

13 Beyond Exclusivism 211
    Exploring, Engaging, and Expanding Interreligious Hospitality in Yorubaland
        Akintunde E. Akinade

14 African Christianity and the Religious Question. 223
    Pentecostalism and Indigenous Religions
        Elias Bongmba

15 *Pulaaku*: The Fulani Notion of Land and Hospitality 239
        Haruna Yussif Mogtari

Contextual Perspectives

16 The Pacifist Hijab 255
    Typologies of Religious Co-existence Amongst Muslim and Christian women in Madina Zongo
        Kauthar Khamis

17 Reimposing *Dār Al-Salām* and the Kingdom of God in the
   Indonesian Context 269
   A Detour from Geopolitical Territorialization to
   Religioethical Conversation
   Ferry Y. Mamahit

18 The Akan Cognate Bonds, Indigenous Hospitality, and Christian-
   Muslim Relations in Ghana. 285
   Cosmas E. Sarbah

19 Pig Feet in Madina's Multireligious and Multi-ethnic Zongoscape,
   Toward Hospitality 301
   Afterlife of Trotter Barrels
   Rashida Alhassan Adum-Atta

Summative Note

20 Land, Grief, Justice, and the (Ir)relevance of Hospitality 321
   A Christian's Theological Reflection on Issues Arising out of the Papers of
   the Conference on "Hospitality and Territoriality"
   Ida Glaser

Contributors. 343

Foreword

There are a significant number of great human beings in the world; there are fewer great scholars; and there are even fewer great scholars who are great human beings. Lamin Sanneh was one of those rare individuals.

Born during WWII in a remote corner of the world on MacCarthy Island (now Janjanbureh Island) in the Gambia, Lamin captured the story of his life in the title of his autobiography: *Summoned from the Margin: Homecoming of an African* (Grand Rapids: Eerdmans, 2012). He understood his career as a call from God that took him from one of the smallest countries in the world to some of the world's most prestigious universities where he ascended the academic *cursus honorum*. At the same time, he never forgot his roots or his family: Africa was always home.

One of eleven children born into an ancient royal African family, Lamin became convinced by reading Helen Keller's *The Story of My Life* that education and faith should be the north stars of his life (*Summoned from the Margin*, 17–18). As a Muslim with intellectual promise, he began his education at Armitage High School, a competitive boarding school on his home island. Following graduation, he moved to Banjul, the capital of Gambia, and worked. While there, he converted to Christianity, more specifically to Methodism since Methodist missionaries had first settled MacCarthy Island. He later became a Roman Catholic. He never forgot his roots in Islam and studied both Christianity and Islam, and became – in my estimation – the leading authority on Islam and Christianity in Africa, especially in West Africa.

He came to the US to attend an HBCU in the South during the sixties but had such a poor experience that he left and moved north to Union College in NY, receiving his BA in history. He went to England for graduate school, earning a MA from the University of Birmingham and a PhD from the University of London in Islamic history. He later received honorary doctorates from the University of Edinburgh and Liverpool Hope University.

His faculty career spanned the same three continents as his education. He began at the University of Ghana (1975–1978) and then reversed the sequence between England and the US by serving on faculties first at the University of Aberdeen (1978–1981), then Harvard University (1981–1989), and finally Yale University (1989–2019) where he was the D. Willis James Professor of World

Christianity at Yale Divinity School. Throughout his career, he continued to move back and forth among the three continents with temporary or honorific appointments. He had a lifetime appointment at Clare Hall, University of Cambridge (1996–2019), and was an Honorary Professional Research Fellow at the School of Oriental and African Studies, University of London (1997–2019). He also had temporary appointments at the Centre for the Study of Islam and Christianity, Ibadan, Nigeria (1969–1971); Fourah Bay College, the University of Sierra Leone, Freetown (1974–1975); San Francisco Theological Seminary (summer of 1987); and the Library of Congress, where he was the John W. Kluge Chair in the Countries and Cultures of the South (2004–2005).

Lamin was a prolific author: he wrote or edited or co-edited twenty books and monograph-length essays and composed well over 200 articles and chapters in scholarly venues. *Translating the Message: The Missionary Impact on Culture* (Maryknoll: Orbis, 1989; 13th printing 2002; 2nd ed., 2009), may be the work that had the greatest impact. In his explanation of how Christianity had become a global religion, Lamin argued – counter to the prevailing view that missionaries had been fronts for colonization – that Christianity needed to be translated and understood in native languages – a point that was not lost on missionaries. This was, however, more than linguistic translation, it was also cultural or what he called "the radical pluralism of culture": Christianity had to adapt to the local culture. In this way, Christianity respected rather than repudiated local culture. Perhaps the best illustration of this is Africa where Christianity has exploded in recent decades. While there are different causes, it is almost universally acknowledged that it was the adaptation of Christianity to native African religion, especially the connection between the Holy Spirit of Christianity and the spirit world of indigenous African religions, that has led to its rapid embrace by Africans. It is not the western Christianization of Africa, but the Africanization of Christianity.

The impact of this work and Lamin's other work on Christian missions – e.g., *Whose Religion is Christianity? The Gospel Beyond the West* (Eerdmans, 2003; trans. into German, 2013), *Disciples of All Nations: Pillars of World Christianity* (Oxford, 2008), and *The Wiley-Blackwell Companion to World Christianity*, co-edited with Michael McClymond (Wiley, 2016) – has been enormous. Lamin teamed up with Andrew Walls at the University of Edinburgh to host the Yale-Edinburgh Conference which rotates from one institution to the other on a bi-annual basis. The pair have led the transformation of their discipline from Christian missions to World Christianity. Lamin succeeded Kenneth Scott Latourette in the D. Willis James chair at Yale. Latourette was unambiguously one of the world's experts on Christian missions. Lamin not only enhanced what Latourette had helped to build, but transformed the discipline – a feat that few holders of academic positions can claim.

Two other works of Lamin are worthy of note. *Abolitionists Abroad: American Blacks and the Making of Modern West Africa* (Cambridge: Harvard University Press, 1999; selected for review in *The New York Review of Books*), tells the story of how freed enslaved persons returned to Africa to uproot the source of slavery by attacking the African chiefs who were capturing and selling Africans. The work extended the story of abolition to Africa. It was a way for Lamin to reach from his new home to his original home.

Beyond Jihad: Pacifist Impetus in Muslim West Africa and Beyond (New York: Oxford University Press, 2016), tells the counter-intuitive – at least to many of us in America – tradition of Islamic pacifism in West Africa. Written after 9/11 and the fallout that came in its wake, it was a sober reminder not to form prejudices about religious traditions about which we know far too little.

Lamin was my colleague and friend. We were all shocked by his sudden death at the age of 76. I am deeply grateful that John Azumah has launched the Lamin Sanneh Institute and that the twenty scholars in this volume have reflected carefully on the issues that Lamin addressed. I am also grateful that Kelefa has written about his father. Lamin was an exceptional writer, a quality that he passed on to Kalefa who has perhaps exceeded his father in this regard. As important as the work of Lamin's was, it is even more important that it has served as a stimulus for others to continue to reflect on the same major issues. The great French literary critic Paul Valery once wrote: "A true artist is not one who is inspired, but one who inspires others." These essays attest that Lamin was a true artist.

Gregory E. Sterling
The Rev. Robert L. Slack Dean and The Lillian Claus Professor of New Testament,
Yale Divinity School, Connecticut, USA

Introduction

John Azumah & Cheikh Anta Babou

In February 2020, The Sanneh Institute was launched with an inaugural academic conference – entitled "Territoriality and Hospitality: Christians and Muslims Sharing Common Space" – that convened a group of global scholars dedicated to and inspired by Lamin Sanneh's legacy. The conference was a call to reflect on the divine mandate to be custodians of space and spheres and of God's command to share these. The theme of territoriality reflected the view that tensions between Christians and Muslims mainly have to do with the question of who has oversight over this space and who has access or can be allowed into it. Obviously, this space or territory comes with resources. This theme also assumed that people of faith in both Christian and Muslim communities would be in agreement that all space and spheres belong, ultimately, to God.

The focus on hospitality was meant to draw attention to the teachings in both traditions on stewardship, custodianship, and the related divine injunctions in both traditions, especially with regard to the sharing of space. In particular, the African continent has often demonstrated that the harmonious coexistence of Christians and Muslims, even within families, is rooted in African traditions of hospitality. Such themes of tolerance and accommodation were central to Sanneh's own life and work, some of which explored the accommodation of incoming traditions like Christianity and Islam by the host indigenous African religions. But with different faith communities vying with each other for territory amidst increasingly limited resources, Christian and Muslim scholars are called upon in this volume to reflect from the teaching of their respective traditions on sharing common space.

This book is a collection of select papers presented during this inaugural conference. Written primarily by African scholars, these contributions address the questions, assumptions, and concerns of Christians and Muslims on the continent of Africa with regard to shared public space. The volume is complemented by reflections from Western, Middle Eastern, and Asian perspectives, addressing issues germane to the majority or non-Western world, including the role of indigenous traditions and religious actors as key players in a shared public space. Furthermore, the contributions are interdisciplinary, constructive, and dialogical, and are written by distinguished Christian and Muslim scholars as well as by junior scholars. At their core, the chapters expose the divisions, fault lines, and potential for conflict across the world's two largest faiths and also point to inherent resources and values as possibilities for harmonious engagement in shared public spaces.

This introductory section includes a personal reflection by Kelefa Sanneh – son of the late Professor Sanneh – who offers glimpses into the personal and professional journey of a father and scholar. Joel Carpenter's reflection traces Sanneh's intellectual and academic journey as a missions historian and his distinguished contribution to the field of World Christianity and the pacifist Islamic tradition in West Africa. The rest of the volume is then organized around four main sections. The "Opening Keynotes" starts with a piece on the *ekklesia* and the *umma*, reworked by John Azumah from notes of the last academic lecture given by the late Professor Sanneh at the planning conference of the institute in Accra in December 2018. The chapter undertakes a comparative exploration of the nature and mission of *ekklesia* and *umma* and the theological and scriptural imperatives in both traditions to engage with each other.

Cheikh Babou then picks up on one of Sanneh's favorite themes: the history of the spread of Islam in West Africa and the place of militancy and pacifism in West African Islam. Babou contends that when the history of Islam in Africa is examined from a *longue duree* perspective, it becomes clear that instances of jihad and militancy are the exception rather than the rule. Islam spread across sub-Saharan Africa through peaceful means as it was carried by traders, clerics, and saints. He argues that if the history of Islam in West Africa is considered beyond the jihad narratives, we can discern a deep-rooted tradition of quietism, hospitality, and pacificism in African Islam.

In the next piece, Kwabena Asamoah-Gyadu uses territoriality and conversion as lenses to reflect on Sanneh's autobiography and on what Sanneh's conversion experience teaches us about the tensions related to territoriality and hospitality in matters of faith and Christian scholarship. The section also includes the two keynote addresses delivered at the official inaugural event of The Sanneh Institute: the first by Rowan D. Williams, former Archbishop of Canterbury, and the second by Farid Esack, a professor at the University of Johannesburg. These chapters are transcribed from the oral presentations delivered at the inauguration. In his opening address, Williams argues that the error of historic Christianity lies in the idea that there is, in some sense, a native Christian territory that has to be extended. In contrast, he argues that the church exists to say to the entire world, "This is the sphere of God's action, and God's grace, and God's love." God does not have to fight for space because God is not a reality like us, alongside of other realities. God is the supreme, unique, undefended source of all things, needing no protection from us or from anyone else. Farid Esack's address underscores that both Christian and Muslim traditions are guilty of creating God in their own respective images. Esack calls for a reexamination of our prejudices and biases, particularly those of Muslims – in light of the greatness of Allah, who cannot be reduced to human efforts at domestication and territorialization.

Under the "Biblical and Theological Themes" section, Daniel Madigan reflects on Sanneh's spiritual and intellectual journey and makes the point that Sanneh continually tried to break down the idea that Islam and Christianity are separate, exclusive territories. In speaking of Sanneh's conversion, Madigan intimates that Sanneh does not suggest an abandonment of Islam and an emigration away from it but, rather, a recognition in Christ of a deepening and an expansion – "a stupendous breakthrough" of that same *missio Dei* that he already recognized at work in the Islam into which he had been born and within which he "came to God as a moral, ethical, and eschatological reality."[1]

David Marshall, in his essay, discusses the work of Abdullahi Ahmed an-Na'im, a Sudanese Muslim scholar, with particular attention to an-Na'im's arguments for the necessity, on Islamic grounds, of a secular state. Marshall focuses on key aspects of an-Na'im's thought and offers comments on his proposals as well as some reflections from a Christian perspective. In an-Na'im's work, Marshall finds an impressive account of the "difficult negotiations" involved for Muslims, Christians, and others as they work out how to share the spaces in which we live alongside each other in God's world.

Peter Ford, in his chapter, undertakes a comparative exploration of the Suwarian clerical tradition and the thought of Tariq Ramadan in the quest for an Islamic theological grounding for Muslim minorities living in non-Muslim lands. Ford argues that the situation of Muslim minorities living under non-Muslim systems of governance – which are often informed by a secular ethos – is a fact of life that has deep roots in Muslim scholarship and is increasingly critical in a progressively globalized world.

In the next chapter, Caroline Seed discusses another important theme in Sanneh's scholarship: the translatability and nontranslatability of the scriptures within Christianity and Islam. Seed relates the theological positions of the

---

1. Sanneh, "Muhammad," 169.

two religions on their translatability to the understanding of the concept of territoriality in the early period of Christian mission in northern Nigeria.

Martin Accad's chapter revisits the "mustard seed" metaphor of the kingdom of God through a hermeneutic of hospitality. Accad argues that the increasingly dissolving lines of a so-called Christian culture in our post-Christendom world is a blessing to be celebrated rather than a phenomenon to grieve over.

Joshua Ralston engages the church, mosque, and state in the political theology of Lamin Sanneh. In dialogue with the thought of Ahmed an-Na'im, Ralston argues that a major strength of both Sanneh's and an-Na'im's approaches is that their arguments for the separation between state and church or mosque are based on religious reasons and are for the benefit of religious practice.

The "Historical and African Perspectives" section includes chapters that draw lessons from the past and from different contexts. Patrick J. Ryan, SJ, assesses religious change in the West African Sahel and Savannah region, contending that contemporary forms of xenophilia and xenophobia throughout West Africa cannot be understood apart from pre-Christian and pre-Muslim conceptual notions of territory, earth shrines, and rulerships. Ryan's view is that the interplay between these three elements is critical to understanding and assessing the complexity of Christian-Muslim relations today.

Within the broader discourse of the "interfaith industry," Akintunde E. Akinade asserts that Yorubaland provides creative paradigms and templates for contemplating interreligious discourse as it relates to ethics, solidarity, and human wholeness. Akinade discusses the meaning and parameters of interreligious hospitality and the "dialogue of life" and examines how the twin issues of justice and societal transformation can contribute to expanding the discourse in Yorubaland.

Elias K. Bongmba discusses the place of African indigenous religions and religious pluralism at a time when Christianity in Africa is experiencing significant growth. In particular, Bongmba focuses on Pentecostalism's disdain, disregard, and denigration of indigenous religions. Through narratives on the continent and the diaspora, he assesses prevailing Pentecostal attitudes and practices and suggests that, paradoxically, these practices represent a return to precolonial assumptions and attitudes. He then probes prospects for religious pluralism in Africa by examining African ideas about hospitality as a way of fostering respect for different religions.

In Haruna Mogtari's chapter about the Fulani people, he argues that these people have been largely misunderstood, marginalized, and blamed for perpetuating the farmer-herder conflict throughout West Africa. It is within the scope of this Fulani custom that Mogtari, using the Bible as the hermeneutical tool, examines the concepts of territoriality and hospitality. Consequently, he concludes that the Fulani recognize that to achieve a balance between the resources of land and livestock, human beings have a responsibility to care for and preserve God's creation.

In the final section, which deals with "Contextual Perspectives," Kauthar Khamis examines hijab as a source of religious tolerance, pacifism, and conflict in Madina Zongo (Accra, Ghana) – a territory dominated by Muslims but also inhabited by Christians and adherents of African traditional religion. Drawing on the experiences of young Muslim women in Madina Zongo, Khamis discusses the use of the hijab and its implications in a shared public space.

Writing from the Indonesia context, Ferry Mamahit contends that the notions of *dar al-islam* and *dar al-harb* have limited scriptural basis and are, therefore, irrelevant and nonnormative. So, too, the concept of Christendom, the Christian counterpart of this binary territorial concept. Instead, Mamahit proposes an alternative – namely, the qur'anic idea of *dar al-salam* – that conceives, constructs, and promotes the religious-ethical ideal for a context such as Indonesia.

From a Ghanaian perspective, Cosmas E. Sarbah focuses on Akan lineage groups that have embraced Christianity and Islam, contending that church and mosque life have not supplanted the old indigenous foundations of society with new ones – either political or religious – due to the strength of cognate bonds in both Christian and Muslim communities' lineage members.

Another Ghanaian scholar, Rashida Alhassan Adum-Atta, asserts that religion is not merely connected with doctrine and faith or modes of worship and rituals but extends to other mundane daily interactions. The centrality of religion in day-to-day interactions is no more evident than at the Madina market, a multireligious and multiethnic space in Accra, Ghana, where people "bargain their religious identity." Using food and foodways as her central foci, Adum-Atta engages interreligious narratives of Christians and Muslims in relation to their identity formation and their relationships across religious boundaries.

The book ends with Ida Glaser's summative note, which seeks to integrate the different perspectives and themes explored in the various papers. Glaser pushes back against the impression created that territoriality is a fundamental problem to which proper hospitality offers an important solution. She argues that territoriality is not in itself the problem and that hospitality – important as it may be for Christian-Muslim relations in any context – is not in itself an answer to territorial tensions. Reading Genesis 1–11, Glaser contends that, properly understood, territoriality and hospitality are not opposing but complementary concepts. Therefore, the reflections in the summative note eloquently brings the book to an appropriate close.

Bibliography

Sanneh, Lamin. "Muhammad, Prophet of Islam, and Jesus Christ, Image of God: A Personal Testimony." *International Bulletin of Missionary Research* 8, no. 4 (1984): 169–74.

Leaving Home:
A Biographical Note

Kelefa Sanneh

Like most kids, I was not particularly interested in what my dad did for a living. In 1981, shortly after my fifth birthday, our family moved from Scotland to America when my father took what was supposed to be a temporary job at Harvard. I remember saying goodbye to my Scottish friends and telling them that I'd be back in a year. I didn't know anything about the tenure track or the hiring practices of Harvard Divinity School, and I don't remember a family discussion about where we would be living. But sometime during that year, it became clear that we weren't going to be returning to Scotland.

Not long after I arrived in America, I remember realizing that the world of my parents was a foreign place. My father came from an obscure country called the Gambia – and not, as I would sometimes have to explain, Zambia or Ghana. And my mother came from a less obscure and much more notorious country called South Africa. For one year, we lived at the Center for the Study of World Religions on the Harvard campus, among neighbors were visiting scholars from all over the planet, many of whom were generous enough to contribute local dishes to the annual Christmas party. After that we moved to the next-door suburbs of Arlington and Belmont, where our neighbors were much less exotic. Like many immigrant kids, I developed a fascination with everything American. I wanted to fit in, although later I came to accept and even enjoy the idea that I would always be a bit of a misfit wherever I went.

I'm not sure that my father would have ever described himself as a misfit, and yet his life and work reflected both his restlessness and his search for home. In his memoir, *Summoned from the Margin: Homecoming of an African*, he writes about his boyhood in Georgetown, an island town that is now known as Janjanbureh. I heard some of these stories as a boy, and when he talked about swimming in the river and keeping an eye out for aggravated hippos, it sounded like a movie: I could scarcely understand how he had moved from that world to the suburban American world I knew. In the book, he describes his boyhood as a series of leavings: leaving home to attend Armitage, a strict boarding school on the island; leaving Georgetown to study in Banjul, the country's capital; leaving Gambia for college in America, graduate school in Beirut and London, and then a career as a historian and teacher on three continents.

Perhaps the most consequential of my father's many leavings was his leaving Islam for Christianity when he was a teenager. In his memoir, he describes his conversion in both intellectual and emotional terms, as a theological wrestling match but also an instinctual journey. "I got up from my knees with the feeling that I was waking up on a new day," he writes, describing the moment when he finally "yielded" and prayed. He adds, "I could speak about it only in terms of new life, of being born again."[1] That moment shaped the rest of my father's life: he went on to become a profoundly influential scholar of both Christianity and Islam. But his conversion to Christianity was not the end of his spiritual journey. He writes movingly of his lifelong search for a church home – a search that led him, later in life, to the Catholic Church. "I had finally come home," he writes, while also conceding that "this home was not a peaceful place."[2] The Catholic Church that he joined was being jolted by scandals and debates, and yet he was inspired by its vision of a truly inclusive church. "In its current resurgence outside the West," he writes, "Catholicism is poised to play a major role in the demand for a new design of society based on the dignity of human beings as human beings, not simply as consumers or as subjects of the state."[3]

Readers of my father's memoir may have noticed that his careful attention to the complexities of human society extended to the institution that became his intellectual home. "Academic dynamics can be very similar to those of the polygamous household in which I grew up," he writes.[4] And it wasn't until he had left Harvard for Yale and I had left home for college that I first thought about what it must have been like for my father to become a scholar and encounter his fellow scholars in America and around the world – and what it must have been like for those scholars to encounter *him*. He wrote fondly about his experiences at Harvard Divinity School, although he also made it clear that he sometimes felt like an outlier, not least because of his intellectual (and personal) commitment to Christianity. Surrounded by professors and students of "world religions," he came to feel that "many colleagues assumed

---

1. Lamin Sanneh, *Summoned from the Margin: Homecoming of an African* (Grand Rapids, and Cambridge: Eerdmans, 2012), 102.
2. Sanneh, *Summoned*, 252.
3. Sanneh, *Summoned*, 259.
4. Sanneh, *Summoned*, 226.

that Christianity is too Western, its cultural forms too European, to be included under the rubric of a world religion."[5] This determination to take Christianity seriously as a "world religion" was central to his work and to his life, setting him apart from a wide range of skeptics who suspected that African Christianity, in particular, was not truly Christian, or not truly African.

He published his first book, *West African Christianity*, in 1983; it emphasizes the importance of "local African agency," to make the point that Christianity in Africa, as elsewhere, was in some sense homegrown.[6] Twenty years later, in 2003, he published *Whose Religion Is Christianity?*, which is structured as a series of questions and answers that are designed to help casual readers rethink their assumptions about how and why Christianity spread. "[T]he Western guilt complex hinders us from acknowledging the role of local agents in the story of the planting of the church in Africa," he writes.[7] By then, he had moved from Harvard to Yale, where he had been named the D. Willis James Professor of World Christianity and Professor of History in 1989. (At that time, I was just starting high school, which meant that I was old enough to understand that a chaired professorship was a big deal but young enough not to understand much more than that.) In 2008, he published *Disciples of All Nations: Pillars of World Christianity*, the first in a planned series of books documenting the ongoing "worldwide Christian resurgence," written by scholars all over the world.[8] Part of what drew my father to the topic, I think, was the pleasure he took in defying the secularists who had been predicting – or, rather, assuming – that the world was inevitably growing less religious and, in particular, less Christian.

When new acquaintances asked what my dad taught, I usually said that he was a historian of religion. But when I wanted to be provocative, I would explain that his basic position was anti-anti-missionary – in other words, he was eager to complicate the simple stories that people sometimes liked to tell about narrow-minded missionaries fanning out across the globe, across the centuries, to convert whichever indigenous people lacked the strength or foresight to resist. Missionaries, in fact, had played an important but complicated role in his own conversion. In Banjul, he had been surprised to discover that the local churches seemed uninterested in baptizing him and that

---

5. Sanneh, *Summoned*, 237.

6. Sanneh, *West African Christianity: The Religious Impact* (London: C. Hurst & Company, 1983), xiv.

7. Sanneh, *Whose Religion Is Christianity?: The Gospel Beyond the West* (Grand Rapids, and Cambridge: Eerdmans, 2003), 35.

8. Sanneh, *Disciples of All Nations: Pillars of World Christianity* (New York: Oxford University Press, 2008), xix.

the missionaries seemed to regard potential converts like him less as prizes than as threats. My father wrote that "the mission schools active in the town officially abjured even the desire to convert Muslims," explaining that this policy reflected political considerations: "missions were allies of the colonial government's policy of support for Muslim institutions."[9] He distilled his thesis into one of his most widely read books, *Translating the Message: The Missionary Impact on Culture*, which was first published in 1989 and reprinted numerous times since then. In that book, and in books and papers he published since then, he wrote about Christianity as a disruptive and destabilizing force. Since Christianity embraced local language and local customs, it had an "ability to assume and to transform the culture it encounters, with the risk of being itself culturally overtaken."[10]

When I think about my dad, I think about him disappearing into his study, which gradually filled up with books, papers, and letters from a growing cadre of admiring students and fellow scholars. He was an incorrigible keeper of things, which had a tendency to accumulate in piles wherever he worked. At one point, he seemed to be maintaining three different offices in our Connecticut home: his original office upstairs, his new and expanded office in the basement, and his makeshift office in the family room, where he would often work to the sound of a televised soccer match or a cable news debate. My father attended a never-ending series of conferences, from which he would often return with complaints about the food and enthusiastic reminiscences about the scholars he had met – although, if I am being honest, there were times when it was the other way around.

Over the years, I slowly realized just how influential my father had become, and I learned that lesson anew after his sudden death in 2019, at the age of seventy-six or approximately seventy-six. (He had always maintained that he was not sure exactly when he had been born, since the assignment of a birth date had been a rather casual process back in Janjanbureh in 1942, if it actually was 1942.) In those strange and sad months, it was heartening to hear from friends and acquaintances and admirers worldwide, who sent emails and letters, eulogies and farewells. Some people had been moved by his lifelong engagement with Muslim scholarship, which, my father felt, was too often simplified by both scholars and politicians: especially after 9/11, many people were eager to show that Islam was inherently hostile to the Christian world,

---

9. Sanneh, *Summoned*, 95.

10. Sanneh, *Translating the Message: The Missionary Impact on Culture, Revised and Expanded* (Maryknoll: Orbis Books, 2009), 99.

or else easily compatible with it. Others drew inspiration from *Abolitionists Abroad*, a book published in 2000 about the formerly enslaved people who traveled to Africa at the end of the eighteenth century on a Christian mission to end the slave trade. (I used to tell him that maybe one day, an intrepid producer would find a way to turn it into a feature film.) Still others remembered him as a teacher of extraordinary erudition and extraordinary patience, an organizer of conferences and initiatives, a mentor, a collaborator, a sounding board, a dining companion, or a friend.

In my house, of course, he was Gramps, a devoted husband and father, and the delighted grandfather of two boys who loved him, and a third one – my nephew – that he never got to meet. My mother, my sister, and I know how pleased he would be to see that the conversations he initiated are continuing in this volume and beyond. And perhaps he would hope that in faraway and not-so-faraway corners of the globe, budding scholars might have the opportunity to encounter his words and to start thinking about their own intellectual journeys – their own leavings and their own searches for home.

Lamin Sanneh, Historian of Hope[1]

Joel A. Carpenter PhD

Lamin Sanneh (1942–2019) exerted a profound influence on the study of Christianity in Africa, and beyond that, on the study of Christianity worldwide, past and present. Sanneh introduced some striking new lines of conversation into the history of African Christianity, and for the emerging field of world Christian studies he became, as Andrew Walls put it, an "architect of the discourse."[2] Indeed, the influence of Sanneh, Walls, and other Africanists was so strong on world Christian studies that at least one recent attempt to reframe it began with critiques of its being skewed toward Africa.[3] Sanneh's interests and inquiries became world-ranging, but Africa was at the center of his attention.

Sanneh's personal story is quite amazing. He made his way from a remote, up-river town in the Gambia to become a distinguished member of one of the world's greatest universities. He converted from Islam to Christianity as a teenager, after years of interrogating his schoolmates and teachers about the nature of God and of God's ways and will in the world. When he decided for Christianity, he recalled, it was because of the Incarnation, of God's coming down to be with us in our suffering and to deliver us.[4] Yet unlike most converts, Sanneh never pushed away hard against his legacy faith. Indeed, he found much to admire in Islam, and he was widely admired by Muslim leaders.

---

1. Originally published as "The Writings and Legacy of Lamin Sanneh," in *The Palgrave Handbook of Christianity in Africa from Apostolic Times to the Present*, ed. Andrew Eugene Barnes and Toyin Falola (Cham, Switz.: Palgrave Macmillan, 2024), 97–106.

2. Andrew Walls, "Tribute of a Colleague and Co-founder," *Journal of African Christian Biography* 4:2 (2019): 10.

3. Joel Cabrita, David Maxwell, and Emma Wild-Wood, eds., *Relocating World Christianity: Interdisciplinary Studies in Universal and Local Expressions of the Christian Faith* (Leiden: Brill, 2017), 2–3.

4. Lamin Sanneh, *Summoned from the Margins: Homecoming of an African* (Grand Rapids: Eerdmans, 2012), 90–91.

The abiding questions of Sanneh's long career as a historian of African religions came out of these formative experiences and the questions they raised. What is distinctive about West African Islam? How are we to understand the massive movement in Africa toward faith in Jesus Christ? And what does that movement reveal about how Christianity has made its way as a movement, both in Africa and across the globe?

Sanneh began university-level studies in the 1960s, just as independent African states (and their universities) were emerging, and "African studies" began to take off as a field of inquiry in the West. He completed his bachelor's degree in history at Union College in New York State in 1967, then earned a master's degree in Islamics at the University of Birmingham (England) in 1968 and then studied Islamics for a year at the Near East School of Theology in Beirut. He followed that with a PhD in Islamic history at the University of London in 1974. Sanneh's dissertation was on the Jakhanke Muslim clerics, in which he revealed a 600-year tradition of Muslim piety and mission that was not, he insisted, founded upon *jihad* (militant struggle). In his reading and travels, Sanneh had been taught the centrality of jihad for Islam, but this understanding did not resonate with the Islam that he learned and practiced in the Gambia.[5] He was thus able to look across the grain of this field of inquiry and come to fresh and surprising conclusions. This contrarian approach became a main feature of Sanneh's work, and it fueled his originality.

Sanneh's first five years or so of publications give no hint that he would re-set the discourse of African Christian history, or that he would have much to say about that field at all. As he traversed through brief teaching assignments at Fourah Bay College of the University of Sierra Leone and the University of Ghana, his publications were almost entirely about West African Islam.

Sanneh was hired in 1978 to teach as an Islamist in the religious studies department at the University of Aberdeen, but not long after starting there, he fielded a surprising request. His department's specialist in African Christianity would not be on hand to conduct a course on Christianity in West Africa, and Sanneh was asked to teach it. In his struggle to organize the course, Sanneh discovered a striking fact: Christianity spread across West Africa primarily by African initiative. Conventional wisdom, both in African history and in African religious studies, was that European missionaries brought Christianity to the continent and urged it on the people, and that as such it was a form of false consciousness, reinforcing and in turn propped up by colonial power. Sanneh recalled a conference held on Christianity in Africa at the University

---

5. Sanneh, *Summoned from the Margins*, 197–205.

of Ghana in the mid-1970s, where the main thrust was that the faith would die out in post-colonial Africa. But those predictions did not match what he was seeing on the streets while he taught in West Africa. Christianity was growing rapidly and taking on an ever more African character in the absence of the Europeans.[6]

Sanneh's idea of "African agency" was not a novel one among the historians of African Christianity at the time that his first book, *West African Christianity*, appeared.[7] Indeed, it came at the high tide of interest in the "African independent churches," whose rise and rapid growth throughout much of the twentieth century attracted major scholarly attention.[8] Sanneh, however, was showing his peers that even the old, mission-founded churches had been built upon the efforts of African catechists and evangelists, and that the most important work that the foreign missionaries did was translating the Bible into African languages. As time went on, and with vernacular Scriptures in hand, African Christians read themselves into the great biblical drama and made Christianity their own faith. They accepted it on their own terms as they found answers to their own religious questions. As colonial influence waned, even the old mission churches were becoming more African.[9] So, in Sanneh's first book-length publication, we see two main themes of his life work emerging: African agency in the spread of Christianity, and the "translating" of Christianity into African cultures.

Sanneh had been encouraged to develop these ideas by his colleagues at Aberdeen, especially the historians Adrian Hastings and Andrew Walls. Walls was teaching about Christianity's "translatability" in his seminars,[10] and Sanneh readily picked up on the idea, which as an Islamist he found particularly striking. Certainly, he saw the ways in which West African cultures had assimilated Islam, but the Christian idea that translation was at the heart of the Gospel made Christianity much more amenable to cultural appropriation than was Islam. Sanneh continued to work on this theme after he moved to Harvard

---

6. Sanneh, *Summoned from the Margins*, 216–217.

7. Lamin Sanneh, *West African Christianity: The Religious Impact*. (Maryknoll: Orbis Books, 1983).

8. Adrian Hastings, "African Christian Studies, 1967–1999: Reflections of an Editor," *Journal of Religion in Africa* 30:1 (2000): 32–34.

9. Sanneh, *West African Christianity*, xii–xiv, 242–246.

10. Walls, Andrew. 1996. *The Missionary Movement in Christian History: Studies in the Transmission of Faith* (Maryknoll, N.Y.: Orbis Books), 26–42; Kwame Bediako, *Christianity in Africa: The Renewal of a Non-Western Religion* (Edinburgh: Edinburgh University Press; Maryknoll: Orbis Books, 1995), 61. 157.

Divinity School in 1981, and he brought out a major tour de force on the topic eight years later, *Translating the Message: The Missionary Impact on Culture*.[11] Sanneh swept through all the centuries of Christianity's existence to show that the faith was translated into the deep cultural terms of one people after another, and indeed that translatability has been the driver of Christianity's worldwide spread and lasting impact. This book had a stunning effect on the study of Christianity's history. It laid out a new paradigm for understanding the faith's universality, one that immediately seemed more satisfying than focusing on the history of missionary efforts or the rise of national churches. Alongside Andrew Walls' *The Missionary Movement in Christian History* (1996), Sanneh's *Translating the Message* had an immensely formative effect on the rise of world Christianity as a concept and as a field of inquiry.

Sanneh stayed in close contact with his colleague and mentor, Andrew Walls, and in 1992 they formed a network to encourage the historical study of Christian missions and of world Christianity. The Yale-Edinburgh Group was essentially an e-mail list and directory of scholars who were actively engaging this field. Members participated in annual themed conferences, held in alternate years at Yale Divinity School, where Sanneh had moved in 1989, and at the New College of Edinburgh University, where Walls had moved in 1986. This informal network has continued to grow, and it now has more than 900 registrants in its directory. The annual meetings continue, and now in hybrid form they attract participants from around the world.

The theme of the first Yale-Edinburgh meeting in 1992 was "From Missions to World Christianity," and in effect it was announcing a paradigm shift in a field of inquiry. Just as African history had long been preoccupied more with the colonizers than the Africans themselves and now was making vigorous moves to correct that astigmatism, the study of the spread of Christianity, in Africa and worldwide, was also shifting from a preoccupation with European and North American missionaries to a focus on new indigenous movements and ancient traditions in the rest of the world.

Andrew Walls had been teaching such things since the mid-1970s, and his arguments for the salience of non-Western Christianity were bolstered by the pioneering work of David Barrett, whose *World Christian Encyclopedia* documented the fact that most Christians lived outside of Europe and North

---

11. Lamin Sanneh, *Translating the Message: The Missionary Impact on Culture* (Maryknoll: Orbis Books, 1989).

America.¹² Yet Walls' influence at the time was hampered by the scattered nature of his publications. It was not until the mid-1990s that some of his most important essays and articles appeared in book form in *The Missionary Movement*. But with Walls as networker and organizer, and Sanneh's *Translating the Message* providing a fresh approach to the historic rise of world Christianity, this field of inquiry took off.¹³

During his first decade at Yale, Sanneh co-led the Yale-Edinburgh group and advised grants officers at the Pew Charitable Trusts, which were providing major support for new research and scholarship on world Christianity. Sanneh also became an important adviser for the Overseas Ministries Study Center (OMSC), which had moved to New Haven in 1987 and became the convening center for two Pew-funded programs to support research on world Christianity. Sanneh also published two follow-on books to *Translating the Message* that explain and defend his approach to religion and culture: *Encountering the West: Christianity and the Global Cultural Process*,¹⁴ and a brief recap and expansion of some of its arguments, *Religion and the Variety of Culture: A Study in Origin and Practice*.¹⁵

Focusing on African examples in these books, Sanneh explained at more length what he meant by the "translatability" of the Christian message and the cultural effects that followed on the translation of the Bible into African mother tongues. Scholars had focused much attention on the intentions of Western missionaries and paid too little attention, he thought, to the actual outcome of their efforts, particularly in the indigenous reception and appropriation of Christianity. He put forward some dramatic examples in Ghana and in South Africa of people finding in Christianity the means to resist the negative effects of colonialism and to develop a richer and deeper cultural awareness.¹⁶

But Sanneh did not stop there. He was concerned that African scholars of religion and culture like himself were being handicapped in their attempts to evoke the full meaning of religion's cultural role. European post-Enlightenment

---

12. David B. Barrett, *World Christian Encyclopedia: A Comparative Survey of Churches and Religions in the Modern World, A.D. 1900–2000* (Oxford: Oxford University Press, 1982).

13. Dana Robert, "Naming 'World Christianity': Historical and Personal Perspectives on the Yale-Edinburgh Conference in World Christianity and Mission History," *International Bulletin of Mission Research* 44, no. 2 (2020): 111–128.

14. Lamin Sanneh, *Encountering the West: Christianity and the Global Cultural Process* (Maryknoll: Orbis Books, 1993).

15. Lamin Sanneh, *Religion and the Variety of Culture: A Study in Origin and Practice* (Valley Forge: Trinity Press International, 1996).

16. Sanneh, *Encountering the West*, 73ff.

assumptions separated religion and culture and in effect rendered religion as irrelevant, a false consciousness, and a dependent variable with little or no formative or motive power in culture. Sanneh would have none of it. This was a view of reality that was much too thin for African consciousness, and he was not about to engage in methodological atheism to meet the expectations of the North Atlantic scholarly realm. He defended theological analysis of culture because a philosophy of culture devoid of moral commitments and the acknowledgement of spiritual forces was effectively useless to engage African life, and indeed life more universally.

Sanneh was not alone in this quest. African scholars were beginning to recover from the horrific declension of African university life in the 1980s and early 1990s and were busily carving out approaches to their disciplines over against the norms and expectations of the Western academy. Perhaps most famously, V. Y. Mudimbe, the Congolese poet and philosopher, wrote in *The Invention of Africa* that Western Africanists still controlled the idea of Africa and made it part of the Western neocolonial imagination.[17] Mudimbe's work helped to spark a postcolonial interpretive frame for studying the African past and present.[18] African Christian scholars were wading into the fray as well. Ezra Chitando, for example, recounted the tense debates between European and African religion scholars. The Europeans insisted that one must study religion "non-confessionally," leaving one's beliefs and commitments to the side, while Africans said that this was an artificial and stultifying way to study religion.[19]

Within Christian theology per se, African scholars were arguing that post-Enlightenment materialism had put Western theologians back on their heels and made them less likely to acknowledge the work of spiritual forces in the world. Kwame Bediako thought that Western Christian theology had become weak and thin and was lacking the "power of God unto salvation" (Rom. 1:16) that Africans were seeking.[20] Sanneh was sounding off, then, on a theme that a growing chorus of African Christian scholars were taking up. They insisted on

---

17. V. Y. Mudimbe, *The Invention of Africa: Gnosis, Philosophy and the Order of Knowledge* (Bloomington: Indiana University Press, 1988).

18. Paul Tiyambe Zeleza, "African Universities and African Studies," *Transition* 101 (2009): 128–132; Thandika Mkandawire, "The Social Sciences in Africa: Breaking Local Barriers and Negotiating International Presence," *African Studies Review* 40:2 (1997): 28–34.

19. Ezra Chitando, "African Christian Scholars and the Study of Traditional Religions: A Re-evaluation," *Religion* 30 (2000): 392–396.

20. Kwame Bediako, "The Emergence of World Christianity and the Remaking of Theology." *Journal of African Christian Thought* 12:2 (2009): 53.

the unity of religion and culture, the presence of spiritual forces within human affairs, and the necessity of making moral and spiritual judgments as scholars.[21]

On another front, Sanneh was circling back to look at West African Islam. He published his dissertation on the Jakhanke Muslim clerics in Senegambia,[22] and then three books on Islam engaging the state and other religious believers (mostly Christians), both in West Africa and in Great Britain.[23] At a time of rising concern because of the growth of radical Islamist movements, Sanneh held up the example of pluralistic and tolerant West Africa. Christians and Muslims commonly lived together there, often within extended families; they did not see each other as engaged in a winner-take-all contest.

The main sources of concern among both Muslims and many Christians, Sanneh argued, were the attempts to impose a secular state that would rule without regard to religion. That posture was simply unacceptable for Muslims, and it struck Christians, too, as stilted, and artificial. The better choice, he counseled, was a more positive pluralism in which each faith brought their values to public affairs while seeking common ground and guarding others' right to practice faith freely. The state, moreover, should affirm religions' contributions to the public good and support plural religious public engagement rather than trying to expel religion from the public square. Sanneh saw his work in interfaith relations as a divine calling, something that the Almighty had uniquely situated him to do. He found ways to be helpful on the ground as well as in the study, such as participating in the Programme for Christian-Muslim Relations in Africa (PROCMURA, f. 1959), and accepting appointment to the Vatican's Commission for Religious Relations with Muslims.

As if all these matters were not enough to engage, Sanneh also wrote a remarkable piece of transatlantic history, *Abolitionists Abroad: American Blacks and the Making of Modern West Africa*.[24] He had thought for years about the North American freed slaves that settled on the coasts of Liberia and Sierra Leone, having written a senior undergraduate thesis on the subject and then

---

21. Ogbu Kalu, "Clio in A Sacred Garb: Telling the Story of Gospel-People Encounters in Our Time." *Fides et Historia* 35 :1 (2003): 29–39.

22. Lamin Sanneh, *The Jakhanke Muslim Clerics: A Religious and Historical Study of Islam in Senegambia* (c. 1250–1905) (Lanham: University Press of America, 1989).

23. Lamin Sanneh, *Piety and Power: Muslims and Christians in West Africa* (Maryknoll: Orbis Books, 1996);
Sanneh, *The Crown and the Turban: Muslims and West African Pluralism* (Boulder, CO: Westview Press, 1997); and Sanneh, *Faith and Power: Christianity and Islam in 'Secular' Britain* (London: SPCK, 1998).

24. Lamin Sanneh, *Abolitionists Abroad: American Blacks and the Making of Modern West Africa* (Cambridge, MA and London: Harvard University Press, 1999).

having encountered Andrew Walls' avid interest in it too. In a dramatic and compelling narrative, Sanneh showed that the freed American slaves who came to West Africa were not just the castoff victims of North American prejudice. They were evangelical abolitionists who publicized the antislavery cause internationally at the same time they were establishing Christian republics on African shores and suppressing the slave trade at its source: in the hands of African chiefs. Thus, Sanneh joined the movement among black historians to turn the history of antislavery on its head. It was not just a predominantly white movement, mounted largely by elite spokesmen. It was also a story of black initiative and agency, based on an anti-structural social argument fueled by evangelical revivalism. The black abolitionists challenged the privilege and power of those who felt justified in making their fortunes by exploiting black people. If that weren't enough to convey in one book, Sanneh also showed that these transatlantic black revivalists and reformers laid the groundwork for African Christian nationalism, based on universal human rights and hope for a better future.

After 2000, Sanneh's attention increasingly focused on the broader realm of world Christianity. While throughout the 1990s, the Yale-Edinburgh group was busy making the shift from studying foreign missions to studying world Christianity and producing dozens of path-breaking works in this field, the idea of Christianity's rise as a world religion had not captured much public attention. Then the topic gained extraordinary publicity because of historian Philip Jenkins' arresting best-seller in 2002, *The Next Christendom*.[25] Sanneh and others had produced the great wave of evidence that Jenkins cited in his work, and they took some satisfaction from the growing publicity for their field. They were not overjoyed, however, by the approach that Jenkins took in presenting their work. Jenkins suggested that non-Western Christianity was tending to come out as conservative, even reactionary, and it might well present a threat to the liberal world order.

Sanneh was encountering similar concerns in conversations with students and colleagues in New Haven and out on the lecture circuit, so he decided to address the questions he was fielding in *Whose Religion is Christianity?*[26] In a delightfully informal, Q&A format, Sanneh imagined an interlocutor who is a liberal minded, thoughtful Northerner who was a bit disturbed at the way

---

25. Philip Jenkins, *The Next Christendom: The Coming of Global Christianity* (New York: Oxford University Press, 2002).

26. Lamin Sanneh, *Whose Religion Is Christianity? The Gospel Beyond the West* (Grand Rapids: Eerdmans, 2003).

Christianity was turning out in the rest of the world. While emphasizing that most Christians live in a world where miracles do happen and transcendence is an everyday way of life, Sanneh also stressed that these Christians live constantly with religious pluralism and have a love of freedom. Some critics thought that Sanneh was a bit too sanguine about world Christianity's prospects regarding such matters, but Sanneh presented a compelling case for a Christianity that was not bowing down to modern secularism and had a hard-won right to be heard.

Sanneh's next book-length work, *Disciples of All Nations*, was his entry into a growing industry of attempts to capture the story of world Christianity.[27] Sanneh's treatment covered Christianity since early times by anchoring the narrative to eight "pillars," or definitive themes and episodes in the faith's development and spread. One such theme was empire, and it examined the ways that Christianity both engaged the Roman Empire and was shaped by it. So too with other themes, such as Islam; the transport of the faith via European empires to the New World; the rise of the successive pietist, revivalist, Pentecostal, and charismatic neo-Pentecostal movements; and a striking finale: China. Throughout, Sanneh showed Christianity to be a profoundly embedded religion, engaging traditions and cultures at deep levels wherever it went.

Disciples of All Nations was heralded as the first of a series that Sanneh would organize for Oxford University Press: Oxford Studies in World Christianity. Three other works have appeared in the series, Todd Hartch, *The Rebirth of Latin American Christianity* (2013); Alan Anderson, *To the Ends of the Earth: Pentecostalism and the Transformation of World Christianity* (2014); and Chandra Mallampalli, *South Asia's Christians: Between Hindu and Muslim* (2023). Sanneh took special delight in meeting with his series' advisory board, hosted by OMSC, and brainstorming new authors and titles. The series made a very fruitful start but does not appear to be continuing in Sanneh's absence.

Throughout the final decade of Sanneh's life, he spent increasing amounts of time and energy engaging African affairs, especially where church, academy and public life intersected. With the help of an energetic and entrepreneurial project partner, Michael Glerup, director of the Center for Early African Christianity, Sanneh hosted several consultations for African Christian leaders regarding religious freedom and religions' contributions to the health of African society. These meetings followed the themes that Sanneh had laid out in his books on Islam, public affairs, and Christian-Muslim relations back

---

27. Lamin Sanneh, *Disciples of All Nations: Pillars of World Christianity* (New York: Oxford University Press, 2008).

in the 1990s. They were pleas for constructive pluralism and for the Christian churches and their thought leaders to develop a more robust public theology. Sanneh argued that religious leaders, according to Afro-barometer surveys, were the most trusted class of leaders on the continent, and it fell to them to work more concertedly for the public good. These meetings resulted in a public statement, the "Accra Charter of Religious Freedom and Citizenship," published in 2011 in the *International Bulletin of Missionary Research*.[28] Thereafter, Glerup assisted Sanneh in setting up a "Program on Religious Freedom and Society in Africa" housed in the Macmillan Center for International and Area Studies at Yale University.

What promises to be a more enduring legacy of Sanneh's concern for constructive religious pluralism is the Lamin Sanneh Institute, opened in 2020 at the University of Ghana. The institute exists to equip and resource "religious leaders, scholars, academic institutions and wider African society through advanced inquiry." It will foster both scholarly research projects and more popular conferences and workshops on inter-religious relationships and religions' public role and responsibilities. The institute has an initial focus on West Africa but hopes eventually to range more widely across the continent and to foster inter-continental exchanges as well. Sanneh was on hand for a major planning conference in late 2018, shortly before his passing. The Sanneh Institute, directed by the Ghanaian theologian John Azumah, is off to an ambitious start with major research funding for a study of the pacifist tradition of Islam in West Africa. This project was inspired to a great extent by Sanneh's final book, *Beyond Jihad: The Pacifist Tradition in West African Islam*,[29] in which he revisited the Sufi-inspired West African Muslim tradition and showed how it spread by persuasion, patient witness, and cultural accommodation.

While teaching a summer faculty seminar at Calvin College in 2008, Sanneh told me that he was writing his memoirs, something that his children had urged him to do. The result, four years later, was *Summoned from the Margin: Homecoming of an African*.[30] This eloquent, touching book operates on a variety of levels; it is at once a personal memoir; a conversion and pilgrimage story; a journal of travels, projects, people and places; and an intellectual excursion. It shows how Sanneh's lineage as a Muslim from up-river Gambia

---

28. "Accra Charter of Religious Freedom and Citizenship," *International Bulletin of Missionary Research* 35:4 (October 2011): 198–201.

29. Lamin Sanneh, *Beyond Jihad: The Pacifist Tradition in West African Islam* (New York: Oxford University Press, 2015).

30. Cited above, footnote 3.

and his life encounters since then have fed into his highly original and often gently contrarian scholarship. The story portrays a boy and young man with an insatiable intellectual appetite who repeatedly impressed people who had the power to advance his education. They granted him opportunities to learn from a generation of brilliant Western scholars who built the contemporary study of Islam, Christian-Muslim relations, comparative religions, and Christianity in Africa. His intellectual biography since those early years has been one long narrative of his putting the perspective gained from his life to work as he looked across the grain of conventional wisdom and reached new conclusions. Sanneh was gifted with a relentless critical curiosity, a genial confidence in his own ability to discover new things, and a vastly different cultural vantage point from most Western scholars. These traits enabled him to see things that others did not see.

So, when a generation of venerable scholars of Islam, both secular Westerners and Islamic intellectuals, posited *jihad* as the fundamental driver of Muslim spirituality and mission, Sanneh pointed to a compelling alternative in West African Islam. When it was common knowledge that Christianity was a foreign imposition in Africa and a handmaiden to European imperialism, Sanneh showed that whatever the motives and prejudices of the missionaries, their translation of the Bible into African mother tongues empowered Africans to accept Christianity on their own terms and to make it their own faith. Christianity then became a foundation for their critique of colonialism and their vision for a more just society.

And when the common historical memory of abolitionism was as a white person's movement, led by social elites, Sanneh showed the outsized influence of Black former slaves, transported to West Africa from North America. They established Christian republics on the coasts of Liberia and Sierra Leone, publicized their anti-slavery arguments, and made their case on evangelical Christian grounds. By these means they attacked the structures of privilege and power that made white people assume that slavery was acceptable and that enabled African rulers to exploit the vulnerable. Not only that, but these African Americans also laid foundations for African nationalism. *Abolitionists Abroad* was one of Sanneh's most powerful contributions to a historiography of African agency and creativity, not just of African victimhood.

Sanneh was of course more the scholar than the activist, but he volunteered his energy and expertise to the fields of Christian-Muslim relations and Christian democratic public theology for Africa. The Sanneh Institute at the University of Ghana promises to sustain this legacy and extend it far beyond Sanneh's personal reach.

And finally, Sanneh helped to shape world Christianity as a concept and a field of study. Christianity has become a predominantly non-Western religion, regarding where most of its members reside, where its patterns of growth are most dynamic, and where its on-the-ground vitality exists. Lamin Sanneh showed, with great originality, how a new narrative of Christian history should read – in Africa first but far beyond as well.

Bibliography

"Accra Charter of Religious Freedom and Citizenship." *International Bulletin of Missionary Research*, vol. 35, no. 4 (2011), 198–201.

Barrett, David B. *World Christian Encyclopedia: A Comparative Survey of Churches and Religions in the Modern World, A.D. 1900-2000*. Oxford: Oxford University Press, 1982.

Bediako, Kwame. 1995. *Christianity in Africa: The Renewal of a Non-Western Religion*. Edinburgh: Edinburgh University Press; Maryknoll: Orbis Books.

———. "The Emergence of World Christianity and the Remaking of Theology." *Journal of African Christian Thought*, vol. 12, no. 2 (2009), 50–55.

Cabrita, Joel; David Maxwell, and Emma Wild-Wood. *Relocating World Christianity Interdisciplinary Studies in Universal and Local Expressions of the Christian Faith*. Leiden: Brill, 2017.

Chitando, Ezra. "African Christian Scholars and the Study of Traditional Religions: A Re-evaluation." *Religion* vol. 30 (2000), 391–397.

Hastings, Adrian. "African Christian Studies, 1967–1999: Reflections of an Editor." *Journal of Religion in Africa* ,vol. 30, fasc. 1 (2000), 30–44.

Jenkins, Philip. *The Next Christendom: The Coming of Global Christianity*. New York: Oxford University Press, 2002.

Kalu, Ogbu U. "Clio in A Sacred Garb: Telling the Story of Gospel-People Encounters in Our Time." *Fides et Historia*, vol. 35, no. 1 (2003), 27–39.

Mkandawire, Thandika. "The Social Sciences in Africa: Breaking Local Barriers and Negotiating International Presence." *African Studies Review*, vol. 40 no. 2 (1997), 15–36.

Mudimbe, V. Y. *The Invention of Africa: Gnosis, Philosophy and the Order of Knowledge*. Bloomington: Indiana University Press, 1988.

Robert, Dana. "Naming 'World Christianity': Historical and Personal Perspectives on the Yale-Edinburgh Conference in World Christianity and Mission History." *International Bulletin of Mission Research* 44, no. 2 (2020), 111–128.

Sanneh, Lamin. *West African Christianity: The Religious Impact*. Maryknoll: Orbis Books, 1983.

———. *Translating the Message : The Missionary Impact on Culture*. Maryknoll: Orbis Books 1989, rev. ed. 2009.

———. *The Jakhanke Muslim Clerics: A Religious and Historical Study of Islam in Senegambia* (c. 1250–1905). Lanham: University Press of America, 1989.

———. *Encountering the West: Christianity and the Global Cultural Process*. Maryknoll: Orbis Books, 1993.

———. *Religion and the Variety of Culture: A Study in Origin and Practice*. Valley Forge: Trinity Press International, 1996.

———. *Piety and Power: Muslims and Christians in West Africa*. Maryknoll: Orbis Books, 1996.

———. *The Crown and the Turban: Muslims and West African Pluralism*. Boulder: Westview Press, 1997.

———. *Faith and Power: Christianity and Islam in "Secular" Britain*. London: SPCK, 1998.

———. *Abolitionists Abroad : American Blacks and the Making of Modern West Africa*. Cambridge, MA and London: Harvard University Press, 1999.

———. *Whose Religion Is Christianity? The Gospel Beyond the West*. Grand Rapids: Eerdmans, 2003.

———. *Disciples of All Nations: Pillars of World Christianity*. New York: Oxford University Press, 2008.

———. *Summoned from the Margins: Homecoming of an African*. Grand Rapids: Eerdmans, 2012.

———. *Beyond Jihad: The Pacifist Tradition in West African Islam*. New York: Oxford University Press, 2015.

Walls, Andrew. *The Missionary Movement in Christian History: Studies in the Transmission of Faith*. Maryknoll: Orbis Books, 1996.

Walls, Andrew. "Tribute of a Colleague and Co-founder." *Journal of African Christian Biography* 4, no. 2 (2019), 10.

Zeleza, Paul Tiyambe. "African Universities and African Studies." *Transition* 101 (2009), 117–135.

Opening Keynotes

1

Comparative African Reflections on *Ekklesia* and *Umma*

John Azumah and Lamin Sanneh

Beyond the Differences

A rather remarkable picture staring the observer of religion in Africa in the face concerns how, when Africans seem to be disenchanted with politics, they flock to religion in ever increasing numbers – over 520 million today compared to 60 million in 1965. What explains this striking picture? How do we account for religious fervor in the midst of diminishing trust in political and economic prescriptions of governments?

Africans' trust in religion is occurring in the ferment of political disruption, which seems to suggest that there may be a tacit connection between the two, with the failures or shortcomings of the political system leaving people inclined to turn to religion in their search for deeper meaning in life. Stress and disappointment can weigh on the conscience and inspire the quest for meaning and purpose with the realization that the pursuit of power on its own does not call forth the best of our instincts or inspire us to dream and work for our own good and that of others.

Government enforcement cannot compel moral progress or deal with the failure of conscience; only strength of mind and spirit can align the will with the dictates of a virtuous, generous life. The dysfunctions of power are symptoms of a deeper alienation in the spiritual life. All the weapons of war cannot arm fear or insecurity, but love conquers all things and never ends (1 Cor 13:7–8). Power is temporal and finite, and force is not assurance enough.

Engaging spiritual values in a multifaith context should provide a foundation as well as guideposts that focus on religion as an institution of civil society.

Some of the nagging questions in African societies concern how to apportion loyalty between God and Caesar and how to determine the appropriate balance between the political community and the moral community, between the use of power and the dictates of conscience and spiritual virtues, and between the duties of citizenship and the obligations of faith. Is human destiny subject only to state jurisdiction or does it belong, finally and ultimately, with loyalty to our common destiny as members of the human family? Does being a citizen of civil society affect our position as those who are subject to the Creator? Can we be religiously faithful without mutual obligations as one another's neighbors? Is Christian charity merely the sentimental residue of piety or is it a necessity of society, a rule of belonging to one another and a demand for self-inquiry? Is the Muslim zakat – the obligatory tithe – simply a rite of self-acquittal? Or does it belong with the spiritual challenge involved in possessing and sharing, a symbol of the truth that God is the true giver and we the privileged stewards of the divine mercy and munificence?[1]

"Habits of the heart" in terms of individual goodness and personal integrity are social values required for humanizing politics and making living in society worthy of a moral purpose. We are intended for each other for reasons far deeper than those of casual companionship. Spiritual power does not compel compliance with what is merely fashionable; rather, it quickens the moral will for discovery and engagement. Instinct conforms with our reactive nature; spirit pries and "searches all things, even the deep things of God" (1 Cor 2:10 NIV).[2] If people are not persuaded that there is a future worth possessing for the sake of peace and solidarity, they will see no purpose in trying to stop the flames of extremism and division from spreading. Human potential cannot be encrypted and reduced to living for the here and now. G. K. Chesterton challenges complacent self-sufficiency with the call to humility with the words, "How much larger your life would be if your self could become smaller in it." As between Muslims and Christians, being partners in the moral quest and the inquiry requisite to it requires investing in a common future. Partnership

---

1. 9:71; 22:42; 70:19–27; 98:3–4. One verse speaks of the giving of self and possessions as a symbolic anticipation of the divine felicity: 9:112. On the institution and administration of zakat, see de Zayas, *Law and Institution*, 23–24. For a Christian reflection, see Cragg, *Call*, 149–51.

2. Templeton, *Possibilities*, 164–65.

should model mutual openness and hospitableness. If you are too quick to judge people, says Mother Teresa of Calcutta, you have no time to love them.

For emerging societies in Africa, the civil institution is indispensable to diversity and tolerance; without it, it is hard to conceive of a flourishing community life and personal integrity. It takes the hearts and minds and voices of all concerned to fully grasp the hopefulness in that challenge. Civic engagement is more than just valuable for nation-building. Nation-building emphasizes unity in the means pursued to achieve it; in matters of conscience, however, the emphasis lies with the process involving diversity of views and functions based on persuasion. In spiritual matters, unity as a goal resides in the purpose. The political conception of unity is based on power as the instrument to achieve it, while in the moral and spiritual view, unity concerns our destiny in terms of the Creator's purposeful design. In the political conception, undertaking a task requires employing uniform and centralized measures; in the moral scheme, the means are many and exist to serve a unified transcendent purpose – namely, to honor our diverse gifts as intended in the purpose of an all-wise, all-knowing Creator.[3] The merit of multifaith engagement, therefore, lies in the plural perspectives of the traditions involved and their expanded capacity for humility and curiosity in the other. It is to these perspectives that we now turn as we examine the concepts of *ekklesia* and *umma* in Christianity and Islam.

Ekklesia and Society

A Christian society – founded on the basis of free association and free agency – represents the diversity of gifts and experiences whose combined influence helps in character formation and a flourishing life. The roots of such a society go back to the origins of the faith. As a matter of regular practice, the early Christians gathered in the church as a Christian society in microcosm, "knit together by common religious profession, by the unity of discipline, by the bond of a common hope."[4] The church's treasure chest was not made up of purchase money, as of a religion that was on sale. Rather, its funds came from small, individual donations as each member was able and had the means to contribute; and there was no compulsion since this giving was voluntary. And the money was not spent on feasts, drinking bouts, or eating houses; instead, it was used to support and bury the poor, to supply the wants of destitute

---

3. For a variation of this description, see de Tocqueville, *Democracy*, 369.
4. Schaff, *Latin Christianity*, 57–59.

orphans, and to help the elderly who were housebound, those who had suffered shipwrecks, those who were prisoners because of their faith, and so on.

From their celebration of the Eucharist, Christians went out not as troops of mischief-makers but as people duty bound to care for their modesty and chastity as if they had been at a school of virtue rather than at a banquet. As Tertullian said, "Whatever it costs, our outlay in the name of piety is gain, since with the good things of the feast we benefit the needy."[5] Pope Leo XIII described the motives of almsgiving in a similar way, saying that it fosters the obligation of mutual service. "There is no one so rich as to have no need of anyone else; none so poor that he cannot do his neighbor some good turn; it is human nature that we should confidently ask for and charitably afford assistance one with another."[6]

We are not just political animals; we are also moral persons with an inalienable affinity with God's intention that we should have life and have it abundantly (John 10:10). We affirm that our oneness in God is fulfilled in our diversity, that we are fellow human beings – even if not of one tribe, ethnicity, race, nationality, creed, or fellowship – and that we are bound to one another in our joys and afflictions even though our situations and circumstances may be vastly different (Acts 17:24–28). In this case, the sum of our unequal parts is indeed commensurate with our moral whole. Our moral nature makes for our nearness to our Creator in whose image we are created, and our social nature brings us close to one another; and both are God's will for our well-being. The will of God is that our imperfections should goad us to strive for a higher end; in the meantime, these imperfections make society necessary. Grace is able to transform our imperfections in incremental stages as we learn the art of mutual charity and forbearance. Community is the logical outcome, and there is no community without the sharing of common space – whether physical or virtual. There can be no community without hospitality.

St. Paul dwells at length on the body as a moral metaphor for society, with the many diverse parts and functions serving one common object when all the parts and functions are gathered and consecrated in service to God and to our fellow human beings.[7] Like the family, society flourishes by virtue of – and not in spite of – its uneven, unequal, and diverse character in order that we should have the same care for one another that St. Paul requires. With their own interests, believers should, nevertheless, be of one mind where it concerns

---

5. Tertullian, *Apology*, https://www.ccel.org/ccel/schaff/anf03.iv.iii.xxxix.html.
6. Pope Leo cited in Cahill, *Framework*, 551.
7. Romans 12:4–8; 1 Corinthians 12:4–31.

the example of Jesus. "Let each of you look not only to his own interests, but also to the interests of others" (Phil 2:4 ESV). Particular attention is required for the care of those members less able to look after themselves. The "parts of the body which seem to be weaker are indispensable, and those parts of the body which we think less honorable we invest with the greater honor, and our unpresentable parts are treated with greater modesty" (1 Cor 12:23–24 RSV). It makes little difference to the truth of our being part of society when some declare that they do not belong, clinging to individualism: "For the body does not consist of one member but of many. If the foot should say, 'Because I am not a hand, I do not belong to the body,' that would not make it any less a part of the body" (12:14–15). The tendency toward individual self-exaltation cannot dispense with our mutual need of one another, thanks to a common Creator. Freedom, as an attribute of God and with its social and spiritual aspects, is value-laden with a moral teleology; it expands and flourishes by the duty we owe to our Creator and to our fellow citizens, regardless of creed, race, or gender, as people made in the image and likeness of God.

In his reflections on the subject, Tawney makes some acute observations concerning life in the spiritual dimension.[8] To say that the individual is responsible, that no one can save their brother or sister, and that the whole meaning of religion is only the converse of the soul with its maker is all too true – yet not true enough. From this way of thinking, it is easy to slip into the notion that society is without responsibility, that we cannot help each other, and that the social order and its ramifications are not the scaffolding by which human beings may climb to greater heights, thereby reducing society to something removed, foreign, dispensable, and unimplicated in the life of the spirit. Instead, society becomes detached from the quest for wholeness and fulfillment and is viewed as a subterfuge to ensnare the soul. This is how pride can insinuate in the will stubbornness to resist being open to learning and to new information. It is treacherous to imply that the spiritual life has nothing to contribute to our corporate life.

It happens so often in the annals of human endeavor that, in the midst of inertia, resignation, and complicity with falsehood, a person or a movement will emerge to gather the thwarted dreams of a dispirited group of people and offer hope and endurance to stiffen the resolve for change and a new orientation. The monasteries in early and late antiquity performed such a quickening role in the aftermath of the fall of the Roman Empire; Augustine's "City of God" stood guard for restraint and morality amid the crisis of Rome's unraveling and

---

8. Tawney, *Religion and the Rise of Capitalism*, 57–69.

exposed the corroded power that substituted hedonistic egotism (*amor sui*) for love of God. The eighteenth-century evangelical awakening was a lightning rod for the antislavery campaign by whose agency new forms of community and moral example were created.

In the same vein, the missionary enterprise – as the precursor of the decolonization process – became the unwitting catalyst of indigenous cultural renewal; the civil rights movement spearheaded by Martin Luther King Jr. and the struggle by many against apartheid in South Africa plucked out of the fire of racial terror the lukewarm embers of the long struggle for racial justice to stir the national conscience; and the life and death of Oscar Romero awakened a complacent and complicit church in Central America to commit themselves to fixing an unjust and disordered world.

The transformative turning points of meaningful change have occurred by such means as these, subtle and indirect, with a sprinkle here and a sprinkle there joining to make a torrent. The crucial question is this: What accounts for these unsuspecting turning points and for the paradigmatic individuals who plucked courage and initiative out of the general lethargy? The early stirrings of spiritual awakening and civic engagement in Africa showed a people poised at a historical crossroad; and the direction the future took depended on the choices the leaders made. To grasp the new opportunities, leaders had to choose between progress and inertia, between innovation and stagnation, for which vision and character were indispensable.

An incident that took place in Freetown in the nineteenth century is instructive. There was a proposal by missionaries and colonial officials, including the bishop and the governor, to fund the Anglican mission in West Africa using government funds. But Sir Samuel Lewis (1843–1903) – the distinguished son of an Egba Yoruba receptive – firmly opposed this proposal, saying that it was not a government's place to favor any one particular religion or denomination to the exclusion of others. He stated his willingness to support the mission out of his own pocket – a principled stand given the fact that, though a devout Christian, he was not an Anglican. He was ready to gladly bear his personal share of the cost of upholding the principle that religion must be free of governent funding if it is to be true to its calling, even while Christians such as himself continue to play an important role in government for the good of all society.[9]

Lewis insisted that a Christian society – such as Freetown was aspiring to be – had a duty to prevent government from playing religious favorites

---

9. Hargreaves, *Life of Sir Samuel*, 18–19, 63, 71–72.

and sowing seeds of jealousy and division. Christians must live by what they preach and should lead by moral example and fairness, not by the magistrate's favor. No claim of entitlement could justify Christians turning the state into a church, which would be the ruin of the church. For all its many failures and limitations, including being faulted for adopting a patronizing attitude toward hinterland populations, Freetown – as a Christian experiment – could nevertheless claim notable achievements, if critics would relent. Lewis showed that the value of religious open-mindedness does not preclude commitment to religion; on the contrary, it assumes and requires it. A Christian society is a safeguard and witness of the faith, not of government patronage with strings attached. This attitude is not charity to the non-Christian other but, rather, true to Christian teaching.

Because of their proximity to power, missionaries did not give much thought to this African understanding of the basis of a Christian society. Instead, they trusted in a wage-based economy. Christian observance would be the by-product of a higher standard of living and, in any case, would involve nothing more onerous than a voluntary, perfunctory weekly church attendance. Officials took their eyes off the fact that they were aiding and abetting the shrinking of civil society by deferring to political economy to establish a Christian jurisdiction. Nevertheless, adding a halo of ethical sanctification to the appeal to economic expediency does not turn it into a spiritual truth.

It is regrettable that the idea of a Christian society along these lines was not broached whereby Africans could build on it on the basis of local experience and background helpful to its possibility. There were tantalizing pointers close to home that offered support for the idea, but these were overlooked – partly because the initiative lay in the hands of subordinate Africans rather than in those of missionary officials and partly because Africans were eventually diverted to the nationalist cause whose focus was political, not religious or social. Unfortunately, these nationalist causes continue to beset many nation-states, including African ones, to the detriment of harmonious interreligious coexistence.

Yet, African initiatives were proliferating in many places, invoking parallels with medieval European religious models such as the xenodochia, which were originally set up in the fourth century for the care of widows, the poor, the homeless, foundlings, and the indigent.[10] In the course of translating the Bible, African leaders paused as they came upon the term *philadelphia*, which was not understood as superficial brotherly love but as the ethics of empathy,

---

10. Cahill, *Framework*, 23.

compassion, honor, humility, philanthropy, equality, and community – things they felt were missing in their interaction with the missionaries. The followers of Simon Kimbangu of the Congo established fellowship groups that called themselves *Kintwadi*, meaning "the brotherly community." Similar groups elsewhere adopted the name *philadelphia* to emphasize this corporate, caring understanding of Christian love: the Filadelfia Church of Africa, the African Sixth Church of God of Philadelphia, the Divine Love of Christ Church, the Luo People of Love, the African Brotherhood Church, and the Christian Brotherhood Church. This movement of social amelioration "introduced onto the African scene and forcibly drew attention to a new quality of corporate Christian life and responsibility, a new *koinonia* (sharing) of warmth, emotion and mutual caring in the Christian community, together with a new philanthropy towards all."[11] *Caritas nimia*[12] – love's bargain – united a scattered fellowship to fuel a spiritual movement for the common good of the whole of society.

Umma and Society

The Qur'an presents the *umma* in the specific ethnic, linguistic, and traditional sense it had acquired among the ancient Arabs until Muhammad gave it a distinct moral meaning and invested it with the seal of revealed teaching. This transformed the *umma* from being simply the ad hoc aggregate of civil elements of Muslims, Pagans, Jews, Christians, and others living under a single dispensation into a community of faith, disciplined by worship and faith practice and assembled under the Prophet of Islam's leadership (3:104, 110; 17:23–40).

The *umma* emerged as part of the structure of Muslim faith and practice; and drawing on Scripture and jurisprudence, the *umma* has continued to exercise a major influence in the formation of community and character. By assuming individual responsibility for the duties and obligations of faith (*fard ayn*), Muslims gave religion a civil character, with personal conscience a rule of discernment: *innama al-amal bi-n-niyah* – "it is the intention that confers moral merit on a deed." The regimen of daily worship and the annual rites of the lunar calendar gave shape and momentum to the *umma* as Islam's cumulative spiritual heritage. That heritage continues to provide a transcending

---

11. Barrett, *Schism*, 169.

12. The title of a poem by Richard Crashaw (d.1649), the Catholic poet who was a contemporary of Milton.

moral norm for ethnicity, race, and citizenship, just as it did for ancient Arab ideas of kinship, tribe, and tongue. Ibn Hanbal – a ninth-century Iraqi jurist, theologian, and ascetic – is cited by a nineteenth-century Muslim scholar to the effect that in Islam, "the brotherhood of *iman* (faith) precedes that of blood."[13] Blood is thicker than water, except when it is consecrated water.

In describing the *umma*, the Qur'an initially notes its diverse ethnic, linguistic, and religious usage among the ancient Arabs before turning to its religious meaning. It is as such that the *umma* became the focus of divine revelation. To each *umma* among the religions, God sent a prophet or an admonisher to guide the people on the right path, but with mixed results as each prophet or admonisher was attacked and rejected as a liar (6:42; 7:47; 13:30; 16:34, 63; 23:44; 29:18; 35:24, 42; 40:5). The divine message was then directed to the company of the righteous, also called *umma*, of the *ahl al-kitb* (people of the book) – that is, Jews and Christians (3:115; 5:66; 7:159, 168, 181; 11:48).

Muhammad faced challenges and resistance when he sought to bring his message to his Arab contemporaries in Mecca for whom the *umma* was a closed kin-based unit relying on ethnic chauvinism. As with the *umam* (pl.) of other prophets and messengers, the Arab *umma* met him with resistance, mocking him and accused him of lying (23:34–36). In Medina, however, Muhammad once gave the *umma* a defining religious standing, transforming it from being simply an ad hoc aggregate of unorganized elements of Muslims, Pagans, Jews, Christians, and others living under one temporal dispensation into one united in faith and worship under his spiritual stewardship (3:104, 110; 17:23–40).

In this new spiritual understanding, the *umma* was beholden primarily and ultimately to God; as a historical community, it was bound to Muhammad by virtue of his office as prophet and admonisher (88:20). The *umma* was witness of Islam's religious message as distinct from a political message. It stamped the *umma* as a moral community rather than a national, ethnic, or tribal association, a fact that distinguished the spread and expansion of the religion beyond the Arab heartlands.[14] Muslims would ultimately be defined by religious and ethical rules and conduct, not by political jurisdiction (3:104, 110). Worship of the

---

13. The emir of Hausa, Alfa 'Umar b. Muhammad al-Hausi, thus cited Ibn Hanbal to affirm solidarity with fellow believers against the multiplicity of ethnic and tribal fragmentation he knew in Africa. Willis, *Path of God*, 73.

14. Marcello Pera, a senior European statesman and a former president of the Italian Senate, made a polemical point about Islam that attacked the *ummah* as a political institution: "A free parliament is better than a great *ummah*; a political and electoral struggle better than a *jihad*. Citizenship is better than *dhimmitude*." Pera, *Why We Should*, 111.

one God, with the Ka'ba as the *qibla* – the orientation for prayer – defined the *umma*'s practice and identity. The spread and influence of Islam and, with it, the *umma* are a function of the religion's moral teachings free of ethnic or national aspirations. The *umma* is comprised of all who profess the faith or are within reach of the Islamic *dawah*. It is the crucible of formation, giving the *umma* its moral cosmopolitan character.[15]

In time, two conceptions of the *umma* converged to emphasize its spiritual nature: the anticipated *umma* of those who are invited (*umma al-dawah*), as a foreshadowing of the *umma* of those who have responded to the call to faith (*umma al-ijaba*). The whole of humanity – regardless of national, social, or racial status – is embraced in this accumulative ethical view of community and identity. By rejecting the extremes of ethnic and national chauvinism at one end of the spectrum and an imperial destiny as *siyasah dunyawiyah* at the other, the *umma* exerted a transcending moderating influence on the civil order. "If there is one quality distinguishing above all others the legislative work of the Prophet of Islam it is the quality of moderation. 'Truth lies in the middle'" (*khayr al-umur awsatiha*).[16] Muslims are assured, "Thus have We made you a middle community" of moderation (*kadhalika ja'alnakum ummatan wasatan*) (2:137).

God established the bounds of human habitation for sustenance of life (13:9–10; 18:20; 54:49). All creation and all empires are by God's prerogative (7:53, 158), and they stand and abide at his bidding (30:24). No country or group of countries may annuitize to themselves the mind of God, any more than any individual or group can commandeer the air we breathe. As the Qur'an declares, God's hands cannot be tied by human presumption (5:69). On the contrary, God gives good things to human beings with unstinting generosity (2:167). In other words, God is generous in hospitality.

The *umma* has flourished in a great diversity of cultures and circumstances, often despite considerable political obstacles and internal conflicts.[17] The *umma* witnesses to the fact that their religion is a living reality in the lives of Muslims regardless of political or national jurisdiction. Muslims are summoned to reflect on this question: "How do you think God will know you when you are in His presence – by your love of your children, of your kin, of your neighbours, of your fellow creatures?" (*Mishkat al-Masabih*). The Qur'an enjoins believers to commit to the pursuit of justice and kindness: "Verily, God commands you

---

15. Khadduri, *Islamic Law of Nations*, 10.
16. Russell, *Muslim Jurisprudence*, xiii.
17. For the Chinese case, see Stewart, *Chinese Muslims*, 36–42.

to be just and kind" (16:90). The Qur'an assures believers that each of them have a goal toward which they strive and a direction to which they turn rather than to which they are made to turn against their will (*li kulli wijhatun huwa muwallíha*) (2:144). Believers are constrained "to compete with one another in righteous deeds" (*fa istabiqu khairat*) (23:61). "Wherever you are, God will bring you all together" (2:148), the Qur'an declares, indicating how the *umma* is united in diversity, location, and individual disposition as part and parcel of God's sovereign design for human society.

The story of al-Baydáwí (d.1316), the renowned Qur'an exegete, illustrates this rather well. His teacher, Muhammad b. al-Kathitá'í, who was mentor of the Mongol sultan 'Aghá b. Hulagu (d. 1283), recommended al-Baydáwí to the sultan's patronage for a judgeship, using these remarkable words: "This is an excellent learned man who requests a share with Your Lordship in hell; I mean he bids you grant him the length of a prayer rug in the Fire, namely, the chair of judgeship." Political favor is moral quicksand and may be embraced at personal moral risk. For his part, al-Baydáwí, when he found out, was scandalized by the solicitation on his behalf and proceeded forthwith to "divest himself from his ambition and retired from the world,"[18] so fearful was he of staining his moral character by so close a proximity to power.

The ethical character of society is a collective safeguard. For Muslims, religion is not simply about dispensing generic courtesies and platitudes that come and go by popular fashion. Rather, religion summons the community of nations (*umam*) to an ethical task: What is our moral obligation before God to call on fellow human beings to do good and to forbid wrong? What is the role of civil society in discharging that responsibility? Islamic religious scholars responded that, in the final analysis, these questions are matters of conscience and the spirit.

Citing the Jesuit paleontologist Teilhard de Chardin, Sir John Templeton asks, "Does the astonishing creativity of the world and of ourselves within it signify a sphere of possibility that might flourish were we to consider humbly what our role could be in a quest to comprehend and follow sublime purposes?"[19] Appreciating the potential of the Muslim *umma* and the Christian *ekklesia* for lessons about community and hospitality will open our eyes to new truths and provide a criteria for measuring progress in "the sphere of the spirit" (2:89). This approach will place the interaction between and among religions and religious groups within the dynamic process that Templeton calls

---

18. al-Baydáwí, *Lights of Revelation*, 44–47.
19. Templeton, *Possibilities*, 41.

"cosmogenesis." This is a process that will bring us to the humble realization that the record we have amassed so far, while admirable, still falls far short of the "over one hundredfold more spiritual information" yet to be uncovered – the subtitle of Templeton's *Possibilities*.

This should take us beyond interreligion as an organized end in itself to interfaith encounter as discovery and mutual curiosity; it should, in the words of Jaroslav Pelikan, inspire us to affirm religion "as the living faith of the dead" rather than "as the dead faith of the living."[20] An African proverb says that the darkest place is under the candlestick. This conveys the sense that in both the religious and secular fields, dogma erected to defend the truth can obscure the truth it exists to illuminate, just as blinders on a horse can shut out the wider angle of its vision or a canal, in a reversal of its purpose, diverts the water it is there to channel.

Mamadou Dia – a pioneer Muslim elder statesman of Senegal, who exchanged the role of politician for qur'anic scholar – says that the true "return to God" involves embracing the *umma* as a spiritual force rather than as a fossil.[21] In other words, this involves taking the *umma* as "the living faith of the dead" rather than as "the dead faith of the living." Dia's is a bold challenge to Muslims and others to think of the *umma* not simply as privileged monopoly of a calcified code but as spiritual stewardship of God's sublime purposes for community and creation. It evokes the famous Sufi saying to the effect that religion was formerly a reality without a name, but now it is a name without a reality. It is what happens when spiritual life becomes arthritic from the stockade of rules that drain religion of its vital, quickening spirit. For a remedy to this problem, spiritual discovery and adjustment of perspective are indispensable.

Meanwhile, a new dawn of possibilities are breaking out on the near horizon, set to awaken us to the measure of our full potential. St. Paul speaks to this spiritual impulse that has animated and steered creation from its birth and in whose light believers are slated to discover "sublime purposes" of life and existence. In consequence, "we ourselves, who have the first fruits of the Spirit, groan inwardly as we wait for adoption as sons, the redemption of our bodies. For in this hope we were saved" (Rom 8:23–24 RSV). In patient humility, the apostle counseled how we should recognize that the present order is not complete and that what we are is so much less than what our destiny

---

20. Pelikan, *Vindication*, 20.
21. Sanneh, *Beyond Jihad*, 262.

holds for us, which is why we must wait with eager anticipation for the time when faith will be consummated (Rom 8:18–25 RSV).

The Summons

To amend Templeton's question, with specific regard to new possibilities of progress for humanity, when is the blossoming time for multifaith engagement in Africa? The task ahead concerns how Muslim and Christians in Africa can unite to initiate a long-range trend in which they do not hinder or inhibit development and change but, rather, inspire and shape the forces of peace and progress by their willingness to learn with and from each other about the high purpose of the divine wisdom. According to an African proverb, when you have not reached your destination, you never get tired. The Spirit beckons us today to raise our expectations: "I tell you, lift up your eyes, and see how the fields are already white for harvest" (John 4:35 RSV).

Bibliography

Barrett, David B. *Schism and Renewal in Africa*. Nairobi: Oxford University Press, 1968.
Baydáwí, Anwár al-Tanzíl al-. *The Lights of Revelation*. Translated and edited by Gibril Fouad Haddad. Manchester: Beacon Books & Media Ltd, 2016.
Cahill, E. *The Framework of a Christian State: An Introduction to Social Science*. Dublin: M. H. Gill & Son, 1932.
Cragg, Kenneth. *The Call of the Minaret*. 3rd ed. Oxford: Oneworld, 2000.
Hargreaves, J. D. *A Life of Sir Samuel Lewis*. West African History Series. London: Oxford University Press, 1958.
Khadduri, Majid, tran. *The Islamic Law of Nations: Shaybání's Siyár*. Baltimore: Johns Hopkins University Press, 1966.
Pelikan, Jaroslav. *The Vindication of Tradition*. New Haven: Yale University Press, 1983.
Pera, Marcello. *Why We Should Call Ourselves Christians: The Religious Roots of Free Societies*. Translated by L. B. Lappin. New York; London: Encounter, 2011.
Russell, Alexander David, and 'Abdullah al-Ma'mún Suhrawardy, eds. & trans. *First Steps in Muslim Jurisprudence, Consisting of Excerpts from Bákúrat al-Sa'd of Ibn Abí Zayd*. London: Luzac, 1906, repr. 1963.
Sanneh, Lamin. *Beyond Jihad: The Pacifist Tradition in West African Islam*. New York; Oxford: Oxford University Press, 2016.
Schaff, Philip, ed. *Latin Christianity: Its Founder, Tertullian*. Vol. 3 of *Ante-Nicene Fathers*. Grand Rapids: Christian Classics Ethereal Library, 2004.
Stewart, Alexander. *Chinese Muslims and the Global Ummah: Islamic Revival and Ethnic Identity among the Hui of Qinghai Province*. New York: Routledge, 2016.

Tawney, R. H., *Religion and the Rise of Capitalism*, with a new introduction by Adam B. Seligman. New Brunswick; London: Transaction Publishers, 1998.
Templeton, John. *Possibilities: The Humble Approach in Theology and Science*. West Conshohocken: Templeton Foundation, 2000.
Tocqueville, Alexis de. *Democracy in America*. New York: Random House, 1994.
Willis, John Ralph. *In the Path of God: The Passion of al-Hajj 'Umar: An Essay into the Nature of Charisma in Islam*. London: Frank Cass, 1989.
Zayas, Farishta G. de. *The Law and Institution of Zakat*. Edited by A. Z. Abbasi. Kuala Lumpur: The Other Press, 2003.

2

Jihad Contested

Exploring Islamic Pacifism in West Africa

Cheikh Anta Babou

Introduction

Jihad has become a metonym for Islam, and Islamic Africa is no exception. The historiography of Islam in Africa is dominated by studies of militant movements. True, it was believed that Islam emerged in sub-Saharan Africa through jihads that removed syncretism and heterodoxy. Studies of jihad and Muslim state-building were then seen as a way of inscribing African Islam into the broader history of the religion of Islam, if not into global history. Recently, one prominent historian of Africa observed, "If we examine the age of revolutions as a unifying feature of history in the world of Western Europe and the Americas, we need to understand the age of jihad in West Africa in the same period."[1] I contend that when we look at the history of Islam in Africa from a *longue durée* perspective, it becomes clear that instances of jihad and militancy are the exception rather than the rule. Carried by traders, clerics, and saints, Islam spread across sub-Saharan Africa through peaceful means. When we move from the high politics of Muslim warriors and state-builders and focus on the work of Muslim entrepreneurs and organic intellectuals who ran qur'anic schools, built networks of disciples, maintained mosques, and provided services to ordinary Muslims and clients, we can discern a deep-rooted tradition of quietism, tolerance, and pacifism in African Islam.

---

1. Lovejoy, *Jihād in West Africa*, 7.

The Many Faces of Jihad in Islamic History

Jihad has meant different things to different Muslim communities across space and time. Its meaning has never ceased changing right down to our own day. As historian Michael Bonner argues, "If it [jihad] ever had an original core, this has been experienced anew many times over."[2] The changing meanings of jihad have more to do with the conditions of Muslim societies in specific contexts than with the scriptures.

It is possible to distinguish something that could be called classical jihad. The exercise of this form of jihad can be located in the period 624–661 CE. This era in Islamic history coincided with the rule of Prophet Muhammad (in Medina) and the Four Rightly Guided Caliphs. During this period, jihad was a practice rather than a formal ideology. There was no formal doctrine of jihad. Nevertheless, ideas about jihad from this era could be distilled from the Qu'ran, the biography or hagiography of the Prophet, the Hadiths, and the *maghazis* (books of wars). From these texts – sometimes written two centuries after the events they narrate – it is possible to distinguish a few principles that later served as the foundation of a classical doctrine of jihad that was formulated during the Abbasid Caliphate from the eighth century CE.

But before discussing these principles it is important to consider the etymology of the word "jihad" and its presence in the Qu'ran. The word "jihad" means struggle, striving, or persevering. The basic connotation is an endeavor toward praiseworthy aims for the betterment of the community through one's wealth, one's voice or jihad of the tongue, or one's intellect or jihad of the pen. Jihad also connotes the struggle to tame one's carnal soul – this is the greater jihad of the Sufi. The root of the word "jihad" (*jahada*) appears forty-one times in the Qur'an under different meanings that relate to generosity, gift-giving, and almsgiving. There are ten instances where the word relates directly to war.

From 610 CE – when Prophet Muhammad received the first revelations in Mecca – to 622 CE – when he migrated to Medina – he only waged what one might call jihad of the tongue. The qur'anic verse that, for the first time, authorized the use of violence to defend the nascent Muslim community was revealed in Medina in 624 CE. It reads, "Leave is given to those who are fought because they were wronged – surely God is able to help them – who were expelled from their habitations without right, except they say 'Our Lord is God.' Had God not driven back the people, some by the means of others, there had been destroyed cloisters and churches, oratories and mosques, wherein God's name is much mentioned" (Q. 22:39–41).

---

2. Bonner, *Jihad in Islamic History*, 4.

From this verse, and other related sources, one may conceive of classical jihad as a defensive war. Fighting this jihad required following an ethic of war rooted in the Qur'an and Hadiths that determine the leadership and nature of the fighting force, the enemy, the rule of engagement, the treatment of the spoils of war, and the conditions for making peace. Legitimate jihad should be led by the caliph or imam (Shia), at the head of an army of volunteers who were motivated by their salvation and the protection of the Muslim community. The killing of the elderly, women, children, priests, or noncombatants is prohibited.

As Islamic dominion expanded outside Arabia and clashed with Byzantium and the Persian Empire, and as the leadership shifted to powerful dynasties, the nature of jihad changed. While some principles – such as the protection of the "People of the Book" and the goal of defending the land of Islam – remained, jihad was increasingly used to further the imperial ambitions of rulers who were more interested in accumulating power and wealth. Classical jihad gradually gave way to fighting practices that were not different from those of the enemies that the Muslims confronted.

The expanding Muslim empire created new conditions and challenges that required continuous revision and rethinking of the meaning of jihad. In many regions of the land of Islam, including North Africa, but especially South and Southeast Asia, Muslim rulers were a small minority ruling large populations of non-Muslims. Competing Muslim dynasties fought each other, sometimes in the name of jihad. Governing an empire required a professional and salaried standing army and logistics that could not rely on the original notions of volunteerism, gift-giving, and generosity in the name of God.

Jurists debated the legitimacy of jihad fought by legitimate or illegitimate rulers. To weigh the lawfulness of their actions, they scrutinized the motivations, character, and piety of those who called for jihad. These debates loom large in the history of Islam in Africa in the nineteenth century – when Abdul Kader tried to mobilize reluctant Algerian Sufis against the French colonial invasion – and in West Africa, when Usman dan Fodio and Alhaj Omar Tall waged jihads against Muslim rulers they accused of corruption and hypocrisy.

In our own time, in the context of rising militancy and Islamist violence in the name of jihad – against Muslims and non-Muslims alike – debates about the legitimacy of jihad of the sword continue to rage among Muslims. A recent Gallup poll asked Muslims worldwide to define jihad in one word.[3] Personal definitions of jihad ranged from affirming commitment to working hard, achieving one's goals in life, assisting others, and struggling to achieve a noble

---

3. See Esposito, "Islam and Political Violence," 1070.

cause. Small minorities in four Muslim countries – Iran, Indonesia, Pakistan, and Turkey – reported sacrificing their lives for the cause of Islam. Muslims who gave such responses are likely to affirm the legitimacy and urgency of jihad against those whom they label the new crusaders in the West and their allies in the Muslim world who, they believe, are bent on destroying Islam and spreading Western values and culture. The best representatives of this group are the Salafi jihadis. They claim that jihad is the sixth pillar of Islam or the missing obligation for Muslims and that it is no longer a collective duty (*fard al-kifaya*) fulfilled by volunteer fighters as during the time of the Prophet but an individual duty of all Muslims (*fard al-ayn*). Osama bin Laden's fatwa declaring war on the West is a good illustration of this way of thinking:

> In compliance with God's order, we issue the following fatwa to all Muslims: the ruling to kill the Americans and their allies – civilians and military – is an individual duty for every Muslim who can do it in any country in which it is possible to do it, in order to liberate the al-Aqsa Mosque [Jerusalem] and the holy mosque [Mecca] from their grip, and in order for their armies to move out of the lands of Islam . . . This is in accordance with the words of Almighty God, "and fight the pagans all together as they fight you all together," and "fight them until there is no more tumult or oppression, and there prevail justice and faith to God."[4]

Liberal Islam and the Ideology of Jihad

In contrast to bin Laden and like-minded promoters of jihad, there are those I call liberal Muslims, who reject the lawfulness and legitimacy of jihad after Prophet Muhammad. Liberal Muslims are mostly interested in exploring scriptural prescriptions and proscriptions to lay the foundation of a tradition of secularism, tolerance, and nonviolence in Islam.[5]

Exploring the relationship between religion and the state, liberal Muslims argue that Prophet Muhammad was a warner and not a warden and that Islam supports the separation of church and state. This argument is endorsed by Islamic thinkers such as the fourteenth-century Tunisian scholar Ibn Khaldun, who wrote, "Since the Qur'an emphasizes a just society rather than an ideological state, the form the state takes is not mandated . . . [Muslims]

---

4. Esposito, 1073.
5. For more on Liberal Islam, see Kurzman, *Liberal Islam*.

should regard the Qur'an as a moral edifice rather than a code of laws."[6] Contemporary scholars such as Ira Lapidus and Lamin Sanneh are of the same opinion. Lapidus observes that from the tenth century, in the Arab-Muslim Empire, "religious and political life developed distinct spheres of experience, with independent values, leaders, and organizations."[7] Sanneh argues that "the idea of revealed law in Islam is predicated on God as law-giver and ruler of the universe. Human affairs belong in the realm of the created order while religion has its foundation in the transcendent will of God."[8]

Mahmoud Mohamed Taha, the Sudanese thinker and activist who was accused of heresy and executed in 1983, offers the most original interpretation of the separation of religion and state in Islam.[9] Taha argues that the Qur'an contains a double message – one that was delivered to Muhammad the Prophet in Mecca and another that was destined for Muhammad the earthly ruler in Medina. He suggests that the second message, aimed at earthly governments, ceased to be valid after the death of Muhammad and that only the first message, intended for the pure prophet in Mecca, has universal validity and should remain as guidance to Muslims until the end of time. The underlying argument in this interpretation is a rejection of the validity of jihad of the sword in the post-prophetic era and a refutation of the idea that seventh-century Medina is a model Islamic state offered to Muslims at all times and in all places as promoted by Islamists.

By disentangling religion from the state, liberal Muslims are able to articulate an ethics and practice of conversion that rejects coercion and emphasizes tolerance and gradualism. There is evidence for this way of thinking in the Qur'an and the Hadiths. For example, the Qur'an states, "There should be no compulsion in religion. Truth stands out clear from error. Whosoever rejects Evil and believes in God hath grasped the most trustworthy hand-hold, that never breaks." Other relevant quotes include, "Say . . . I worship not that which you worship, nor will you worship that which I worship, and I shall not worship what you are worshipping. To you your religion and to me my religion" and "If your Lord had willed it, all the people on the earth would have come to believe, one and all."

Liberal Muslims' emphasis on tolerance and patience echoes their rejection of extremism. They evoke qur'anic condemnation of *ghulluw* (excessiveness),

---

6. Quoted in Kurzman, *Liberal Islam*, 19.
7. Lapidus, "Separation," 364.
8. Sanneh, *Beyond Jihad*, 17.
9. See Taha, "Second Message," 273–83.

tanattu (going beyond the limit in utterance and action), and *tashdid* (strictness, austerity), and they emphasize qur'anic calls for moderation. They reference Qur'anic verses such as "Do not exceed the limits of your religion" (Q. 4:171) and Hadiths such as "Beware of excessiveness in religion. [People] before you have perished as a result of [such] excessiveness."[10] They remind people of the Prophet's characterization of Islam as a religion of the middle ground or *deen al-wasati*.

For liberal Muslims, jihad should be understood in the context of *dawah*, which is a call to natural reason through study, reflection, and contemplation. They argue that divine revelations are apprehended through investigation, demonstration, and free choice. There should be no power but reason, no coercion except through argument.

A Tradition of Islamic Pacifism in Sub-Saharan Africa

Despite the scholarly fascination with jihad, I am suggesting that the trajectory of Islam in sub-Saharan Africa is more reflective of the values of liberal Islam than militancy. The teachings and practices of Al-Hajj Salim Suwari – the founder of the Suwarian tradition of Islam – and the Sufi leader Shaykh Ahmadou Bamba – founder of the Muridiyya Sufi order in Senegal – offer apt illustrations of the connections between liberal Muslim thinking and a tradition of pacifism and nonviolence in sub-Saharan Africa.

Al-Hajj Salim Suwari spent the earlier part of his life in Massina, in the current Republic of Mali.[11] This is a region located in the heart of the Sudanic empires of Mali and Songhai, exposed to the influence of Timbuktu, Jenne, and other centers for the production and diffusion of Islamic knowledge in medieval West Africa. None of Al-Hajj Salim's writings seem to have survived, but information gleaned from local hagiological texts in Arabic and local languages can help sketch his biography. There is no scholarly consensus about when he lived but, as suggested by historian Ivor Wilks, the early sixteenth century seems plausible. Al-Hajj Salim is described as a highly learned and pious Muslim, who made the pilgrimage to Mecca numerous times. Sources refer to him as Imam and *wali Allah* (friend and neighbor of God) and leader of the Jakhanke or Juula community. Al-Hajj Salim's teachings were instrumental in the construction of the identity of a diaspora of Juula traders and scholars

---

10. See Yusuf Al-Qaradawi, quoted in Kurzman, *Liberal Islam*, 196.
11. For the history of Al-Hajj Salim Suwari, I rely on Wilks, "Juula," 93–117, and Sanneh, *Beyond Jihad*, 85–94.

that spanned West Africa, including lands such as Ashanti that were governed by non-Muslims. Building on the works of Wilks and Sanneh, who offer the most complete scholarly reconstruction of the life and influence of Al-Hajj Salim Suwari, it is possible to outline the most salient dimensions of his thoughts and teachings.

Al-Hajj Salim's teachings represent the foundation of a pedagogical tradition among the Juula that has resisted the test of time; indeed, his teachings continue to shape behavior even today. These teachings primarily concern the issues of conversion, religion, and the state, the relationships between Muslims and non-Muslims, and jihad. As we have seen, liberal Muslims continue to be preoccupied with these same questions.

Al-Hajj Salim taught that unbelief was the result of ignorance rather than wickedness. Echoing al-Kanemi – who used the same argument against the Sokoto Jihadists later in the nineteenth century – Al-Hajj Salim argued that it is God's will that some people remain in the state of ignorance longer than others. True conversion, in his view, will occur only when God wills it. Therefore, coercing people to convert is tantamount to refusing to accept God's design for the world. Al-Hajj Salim condemned jihad of the sword against unbelievers as an unacceptable method of conversion. For him, recourse to arms is permissible only in self-defense when the very existence of the Muslim community is threatened by unbelievers.

Regarding the relationship between religion and the state, Al-Hajj Salim taught that Muslims may accept the authority of non-Muslim rulers, and even support such a rule, so long as this enables them to live their life in accordance with their religion. For him, non-Muslim government is preferable to non-government. Ahmadou Bamba, the founder of the Muridiyya in late nineteenth-century Senegal, used a similar argument in a fatwa he wrote in 1910 to condemn jihad waged by the Mauritanian cleric Ma al Aynayn against the French in Morocco.[12]

Al-Hajj Salim inspired a pedagogy of conversion based on patience and exemplary behavior. This pedagogy requires Muslims, wherever they live, to embody the highest values and ideals so that they represent attractive examples for people to emulate when, according to God's will, the time for conversion arrives. Finally, Al-Hajj Salim emphasized the central role of education to ensure that Muslims keep the observance of the law free from error.

---

12. See Archives Nationales du Sénégal, Dossier Ahmadou Bamba, folder no. 3, 19 December 1910.

Al-Hajj Salim Suwari's teachings were preserved and disseminated through networks of scholars and teachers linked by "isnads" or chains of authority. These scholars carried the legacy of Suwari Islamic tradition through half a millennium. Wilks notes the resilience of Suwari teachings even when its disseminators were persecuted by jihadis who condemned them because of their opposition to warfare and their willingness to accommodate non-Muslim rulers, including European colonialists.[13]

It is possible to discern an epistemological kinship between liberal Islam, the Suwari Islamic tradition, and the thought and practice of Shaykh Ahmadou Bamba, the founder of the Muridiyya of Senegal. Jonathan Bornman provides evidence of a direct link between Jakhante clerics, bearers of Al-Hajj Salim's teachings, and Shaykh Ahmadou Bamba and describes the different ways in which Bamba's teachings and practices align with Suwari traditions.[14] Bamba was a Sufi, but I am suggesting that although most liberal Muslims do not refer to Sufi Islam, and even though Al-Hajj Salim lived at a time when institutional Sufism had very little influence in sub-Saharan Africa, these three Muslim traditions share a similar ethic and theology. Sufi theology offers the most compelling articulation of a pacifist and nonviolent tradition in Islam.

Perhaps one of the most salient features of Sufism is the distinction between the worlds of *batin* (the hidden, internal) and that of *zahir* (the manifest, external). The Sufi's emphasis on *batin* has important theological and organizational implications. Perhaps the most consequential of these implications is the suggestion that God can be known through means other than the divine revelations enshrined in the Qur'an. Because the world of *batin* does not lend itself to discursive scrutiny, Sufi theology tends to favor a universalist perception of religion that emphasizes sameness rather than the differences that an exoteric and legalist reading of Islam would encourage. This is what Engineer explains when he writes that "when God is comprehended intellectually, theological differences arise but when He is approached devotionally, everything dissolves into His Being and differences are wiped out."[15] Devotional approaches to God do not eliminate differences; indeed, Sufi rituals can be, and often are, a source of division. But the kind of divisions created by this devotional approach tend to be less contentious because they are legitimized through "esoteric" and, therefore, untestable knowledge. I am

---

13. Wilks, "Juula," 108.
14. Bornman, *American Murids*, 30.
15. Engineer, *Sufism*, 3.

arguing that the world of *batin* represents a universal spiritual canvas that provides space for the expression of diverse religious traditions.

In their quest for closeness to God, one of the greatest rewards that Sufis long for is the acquisition of *ma'rifa* or gnosis. *Ma'arifa* is knowledge beyond the book that God gives to whom he wishes, particularly to those who have succeeded in befriending him (*wali Allah*). *Ma'arifa* is experiential knowledge that is acquired through *ilham* (inspiration) or *kashf* (unveiling). *Ma'rifa* is, therefore, unmediated knowledge that escapes the strictures of nature and the human intellect. It is always received in a state of altered consciousness. For Sufis, the immediacy of this knowledge gives *ma'rifa* a certain superiority over other forms of religious knowledge mediated by the senses or reason. *Ilham* and *kashf* are the tools through which the Sufi unveils the hidden meanings of the Qur'anic texts and, in so doing, gains religio-theological openness.

Ma'rifa allows Sufis to reach beyond scripture-bound knowledge, denoting the view that basic truth can be expressed in several religions. This pluralistic theological positioning explains why Sufis tend to stress the connection between Islam and other religions. This logic has brought some Sufis, such as Jalal al-Din Rumi and the medieval Andalusian Sufi, Ibn Sabin, to mitigate the claim of Islamic monopoly over the knowledge of God and to consider the possibility that divine truth can also be found in other religions. Such theological innovations are only possible because of the unmooring of Islam from rigid legalistic structures and the Sufis' emphasis on God's immanence and the possibility of personal and individual relationship with him.

Sufis are able to make the theological synthesis and cultural compromises that explain their spiritual agility because they have always strived to maintain their autonomy from the state. Ghazali's affirmation that the best ulama are those who do not know and are not known by the sultan offers the best illustration of the Sufis' suspicion of state power.[16] Ghazali enjoined ulama to avoid violence and combat unjust rulers through the tongue and the pen and if these weapons should trigger violence and chaos to hold contempt against them in their hearts.

But most Sufis favored escapism, sometimes choosing a peripatetic lifestyle, taking their message to remote places away from the center of power or to lands where the influence of the state was weak. In doing so, they have

---

16. Al-Ghazali. *Ihya ulum al-din*, https://caliphate1.com/2021/05/08/imam-ghazali-on-the-ulama-of-the-hereafter-the-teachers-of-falsehood-and-avoiding-rulers/. Accessed February 5, 2024. Ghazali had a major influence on Ahmadou Bamba who refers to him as the Master.

enjoyed the freedom to model their religion in conformity to their idiosyncratic inspirations, defying the conformism of ulama and their state sponsors.

Ahmadou Bamba was one of those charismatic Sufis who founded his own community in Senegal in the late nineteenth century. Like Sufis who preceded him, Bamba drew inspiration from Sufi theology and philosophy to model his community. Two key concepts provide the philosophical underpinning of pluralism in the Muridiyya: *maslaha* and ecumenism.

The word *maslaha* refers to the common good. The aims of *maslaha* are fivefold: the preservation of religion, the preservation of life, the preservation of reason, the preservation of one's descendants, and the preservation of property. We can understand, then, that any action taken that does not contradict the principles of Islam but protects the public good is *maslaha* and, therefore, should be encouraged. I have already indicated that historically Sufi scholars have been critical of unjust rulers and have warned against the corrupting potential of power, but they have also been careful to avoid creating situations of chaos and violence where the lives and property of Muslims may be put in jeopardy. Some of these scholars even agreed that tyranny is better than anarchy and civil strife.

In line with this thinking, Shaykh Ahmadou Bamba distrusted both the Wolof rulers of precolonial Senegal and the French colonizers, but he also criticized the Muslims who waged jihads of the sword against them. He charged that those who chose violence to bring about social change were being motivated by greed and power and argued that they achieved nothing apart from hurting the Muslims they intended to protect. For Bamba, the greatest jihad is the jihad of the soul: that is, the struggle to overcome one's spiritual flaws. He believed that so long as Muslims were granted unfettered freedom to practice and promote their religion, they should be able to live in peace under whatever rulers God had chosen for them. Decoupling Islamic identity and just rule, he hinted that one does not need to be under the authority of a Muslim ruler or under the rule of shari'a to live the life of a good Muslim.

Ecumenism constitutes another founding principle of pluralism in Bamba's thought and practices. Bamba's ecumenism reflects Sufi universalism, as discussed above, and is rooted in his *iman* (faith) and the Sufi idea of the unity of creation. This belief suggests that all human beings originated from one soul, that God endowed humanity with reason so that humanity can distinguish between good and evil, and, further, that God has made it humanity's duty to recommend what is good and discourage what is forbidden. Because human beings are, in God's eyes, the single beings entrusted with reason and intelligence, they are *khalifat ul Lah fil ard* or God's representatives on earth.

So, whether a person is a Christian, a Muslim, a Jew, a Buddhist, or a pagan, they all belong to the same family – the human family – and they are all *khalifat ul Lah fil ard*.

The ecumenism of Cheikh Ahmadou Bamba is further reflected in his interactions with people of other faiths as well as in his relationships with fellow Muslims. It was logical that Bamba's absolute trust in God should also translate into openness of mind and religious tolerance. He repudiated the wholesale condemnation of people because of their beliefs and used forgiveness as therapy against violence. Returning to Senegal after more than seven years of exile in Equatorial Africa – a sentence unjustly meted out to him by the French colonial rulers of Senegal – he proclaimed that he had forgiven all his enemies for the sake of God.

Conclusion

When we think of Islam as an African religion – and not as a religion of Arabs or converts – and of African Muslims not as mere imitators but as intellectual innovators, it is possible to unearth what scholar Ousmane Kane calls the "African Islamic library."[17] I am suggesting that the most important contribution this library makes to the history of Islam – particularly in our time when Islamist violence is spreading across Africa – is an Islamic ethic rooted in pluralism, tolerance, and nonviolence. Although the battle against violent Islamist extremism is not only about ideas, it is important for scholars and policymakers alike to pay serious attention to local quietist African Islamic traditions that, in my view, constitute the most effective tools for combating radical Islamism on the continent.

Bibliography

Babou, Cheikh Anta. *Fighting the Greater Jihad: Amadu Bamba and the Founding of the Muridiyya of Senegal, 1853–1913*. Athens: Ohio University Press, 2007.

Bonner, Michael. *Jihad in Islamic History: Doctrines and Practice*. Princeton: Princeton University Press, 2006.

Bornman, Jonathan. "American Murids: Muslim Proponents of Nonviolence Open Alternative Conversations about Islam, Jihad and Immigration." PhD diss., Oxford Centre for Mission Studies/Middlesex University, 2020.

Engineer, Asghar Ali. *Sufism and Communal Harmony*. Taylor: Printwell, 1991.

---

17. Kane, *Beyond Timbuktu*, 39.

Esposito, John L. "Islam and Political Violence." *Religions* 6 (2015): 1067–1081.
Ghazali, Abu Hamid al-. *Ih'yà ouloûm ed-dîn; ou Vivication des sciences de la foi*. Edited by G. H. Bousquet. Paris: Besson, 1955.
Kane, Ousmane O. *Beyond Timbuktu: An Intellectual History of Islamic Africa*. Cambridge: Harvard University Press, 2016.
Kurzman, Charles, ed. *Liberal Islam: A Source Book*. Oxford: Oxford University Press, 1998.
Lapidus, Ira. "Separation of State and Religion." *International Journal of Middle Eastern Studies* 6 (1975): 363–385.
Lovejoy, Paul E. *Jihād in West Africa during the Age of Revolutions*. Athens: Ohio University Press, 2016.
Sanneh, Lamin. *Beyond Jihad: The Pacifist Tradition in West African Islam*. New York; Oxford: Oxford University Press, 2016.
Taha, Mahmoud Mohamed. "The Second Message of Islam." In *Liberal Islam: A Sourcebook*, edited by Charles Kurzman, 270–284. Oxford: Oxford University Press, 1998 .
Wilks, Ivor. "The Juula and the Expansion of Islam in the Forest." In *The History of Islam in Africa*, edited by Nehemia Levtzion and Randall L. Pouwels, 93–117. Athens: Ohio University Press, 2000.

3

Summoned from the Margin

Territoriality and Conversion in the Life and Thought of Lamin Sanneh

J. Kwabena Asamoah-Gyadu

This article reflects on the relationship between evangelical conversion and what that experience teaches us about the tensions relating to territoriality and hospitality in matters of faith and Christian scholarship. In the biblical material, a classic example of this development is the conversion of Paul, where his encounter with Christ led the apostle to write epistles on various aspects of the Christian faith; and thirteen of the twenty-seven books of the New Testament have traditionally been attributed to him. Paul, who described himself as an apostle to the Gentiles, took advantage of his status as both Roman and Jewish to emphasize that in Christ, the walls of hostility between Jews and Gentiles were broken down (Ephesians 2:14–16).

Paul's words to the Galatians make it clear that the faith into which people convert has implications for territoriality and hospitality:

> As many of you as were baptized into Christ have clothed yourselves with Christ. There is no longer Jew or Greek, there is no longer slave or free, there is no longer male and female; for all of you are one in Christ Jesus. And if you belong to Christ, then you are Abraham's offspring, heirs according to the promise. (Gal 3:27–29 NRSV)

The following reflections are based on Lamin Sanneh's autobiography, *Summoned from the Margin: Homecoming of an African*. My thesis is that Sanneh, in this autobiographical work, gives us more than personal memoirs; that is, the contents consist of more than stories on childhood, personal growth and development, education, social life, religious experiences, and career path and choices. This chapter attempts to reflect on some key themes in Sanneh's memoir, with the aim of showing the kind of issues that have come to be of concern to world Christianity as the faith continues its inexorable shift from the northern to the southern continents.

We find in Sanneh's exposé an example of a gradual but radical conversion of the crisis-type, in which an individual is confronted with the truth of Christ during crisis, and how that experience subsequently culminates in a calling to Christian witness through scholarship. In the process, we learn about how faiths such as Christianity and Islam constitute religious territories and create boundaries; and we also learn about the challenges associated with these developments in terms of hospitality as a critical virtue of religious inclusivity.

I knew Lamin Sanneh personally – as a senior academic colleague, friend, and inspirer. Sanneh's Christian faith played a critical role in his scholarship. This observation is critical to our reflections on his autobiography. We are accustomed to theologians and missiologists who handle their disciplines in the same way that others teach secular subjects in secular university settings. Sara J. Fretheim, who has studied Bediako – a man who, in many ways, has a similar profile to Sanneh – has noted that African Christian scholars are best understood within the "historical continuum" from which they have emerged.[1]

In particular, when we look at the works of many African scholars, we tend to encounter a different approach to Christian scholarship. Bediako was an example of the sort of African theologian and churchman in whose career faith and scholarship constantly engaged with each other in the public sphere. While pursuing his doctoral studies in French literature in France during the 1980s, he converted from atheism and turned his attention to theology. In *Theology and Identity* – his published PhD thesis – Bediako writes that from the dawn of his conversion experience, he felt the need to seek clarification on how the "abiding Gospel of Jesus Christ" related to questions of culture and how this relationship may be enhanced without injury to the integrity of the gospel.[2]

---

1. Fretheim, *Kwame Bediako*, 11.
2. Bediako, *Theology and Identity*, xi.

Lamin Sanneh: A Spiritual and Intellectual Journey

Lamin Sanneh begins by outlining the motives for writing his life's story. He notes, "This book is about my spiritual and intellectual journey and tracks the path of my career from its unlikely beginnings in a traditional African Muslim society to its eventual culmination in the world of academia."[3] What do we learn about Islam, Christianity, and territoriality in a context like the Gambia, where Muslims are in the majority? In what senses does the conversion of Sanneh from Islam to Christianity amount to a shift in religious territory, and what does his encounter with Christianity teach about religion and hospitality?

Sanneh attempts to unpack the words of his book's title, pointing out that the word "summoned" captures the feeling of encountering a religion – in this case, Christianity – to which he had never given much thought: "Only in hindsight could I see a purpose in coming to embrace it. The summons turned out to be real, even though it had been only a faint awareness at the time. It felt like being awakened."[4]

Sanneh uses the expression "margin" in his book title to refer to the fact that, in the Gambia, he had been nurtured by the Islamic faith, a religion that eclipsed Christianity on every level. Islam was thus the center of Sanneh's universe; Christianity was marginal. The religious territory, then, belonged exclusively to Islam, and this meant that the success of any conversion experience was predicated on how hospitable Muslims were prepared to be:

> There was no church in town when I was growing up; I had never seen a Bible in my life; I had never heard anyone teach or preach about Christianity; there was no mention of Christianity in the books we read at school. There was not a single missionary in my town that I knew of. The known history of the Mandinka, my people, is for the most part the history of Islam among them . . . More than a thousand years of Islamization had contributed to making Christianity virtually invisible among us.[5]

In other words, rather than being a faith from which he was converted to Christianity, we could speak of Islam as the religious territory in which Sanneh was nurtured. The words of Paul capture Sanneh's self-description as one summoned from the margin:

---

3. Sanneh, *Summoned from the Margin*, 19.
4. Sanneh, 19.
5. Sanneh, 19.

> Consider your own call, brothers and sisters; not many of you were wise by human standards, not many were powerful, not many were of noble birth. But God chose what is foolish in the world to shame the wise; God chose what is weak in the world to shame the strong; God chose what is low and despised in the world, things that are not, to reduce to nothing things that are, so that no one might boast in the presence of God. (1 Cor 1:26–29 NRSV)

Foolishness, weakness, lowliness, and being despised are the chief characteristics of those who come from the underside of history. It is the reason Bediako chose the word "surprise" to describe the development of Africa as a major Christian heartland, something that the world completely missed when the missionary movement convened at Edinburgh in 1910. The weak and the lowly are literally summoned from the margins by God in order to prove the divine ability to use people of little, marginal, or no consequence, to accomplish consequential and monumental things.

Evangelization through Missionary Education

Religion, education, politics, and territoriality have intersected most frequently in Gambian history during the colonial period. The importance and implications of the evangelization through missionary education policy that was pursued by the historic mission denominations across nineteenth-century Africa ought not to be taken for granted. That policy, prevalent across Africa, accounts in part for the current aggression that Islam is beginning to demonstrate within these geographical regions. It prepared Africans to serve in the public sector, especially in the immediate postcolonial era. The Christian spiritual disciplines and liturgical practices of prayer, Bible study, and singing hymns were always part of the process. Christian baptisms and confirmation frequently took place in secondary boarding schools, and many unchurched students had been denominationalized by the time they completed high school education.

In countries like Ghana, Sierra Leone, and Nigeria, it was, until fairly recently, impossible to find a high-ranking official serving as a public or civil servant, or even in political office – sometimes including people of other faiths – who had not trained in a mission school. The reason the leadership of Africa's public and political offices have mostly been Christian is because of the Islamic resistance to educating their children through Christian mission schools. Sanneh writes of Georgetown School as representing a significant initiative by a young church "undaunted in exercising its missionary warrant." How was this "missionary warrant" understood? It was conceived of as "raising the quality of life of future leaders of church and society and transmitting the gospel in partnership with local agency."[6] The government of the Gambia became involved in rehabilitating the school because "it needed the students of the schools to man the offices of the state."[7] Indeed, it was through education that many Africans would be summoned from the margins of society to play leading roles as teachers, doctors, nurses, engineers, and technocrats, serving their nations at both the national and international level.

In that respect, Sanneh's experience was not atypical. This is where the intersection between formal education and territoriality regarding the relationship between Christianity and Islam needs to be interrogated. The Muslim community did not see education in terms of opportunities for the development of the nation but, rather, as a Christian attempt to dominate the public sphere, eclipse the Islamic faith, and, most significantly, indoctrinate young Muslims against the faith of their ancestors. In the Muslim imagination, these are the strategies of infidels, and so, not surprisingly, Muslim resistance proved impossible to overcome in the government's attempt to rehabilitate the Georgetown School. In fact, Sanneh observes that his father, Ousman (or Suti), denounced him for accepting employment in the transport office of an "infidel colonial administration."[8] To mitigate the backlash from the family's unhappiness with Sanneh's choice, his father refrained from sending his children to the Western school, which was seen by the Muslims as "a promoter of unbelief" and a means of "atheistic propaganda."[9]

The tensions between Islam and Christianity within the context of education is further evident in what Sanneh says of Armitage, the government Islamic boarding school where he had received part of his education:

> Intended as a magnet to overcome the resistance of chiefs to infidel colonial rule, Armitage succeeded in attracting the sons of chiefs, which was why my father allowed me to enroll there, instead of sending me to the Methodist Boys High School in Bathurst, where he was certain they would take me moral captive.[10]

---

6. Sanneh, 7.
7. Sanneh, 7.
8. Sanneh, 8.
9. Sanneh, 8.
10. Sanneh, 9.

The moral captivity to which Sanneh refers relates to the kind of formal education that became indistinguishable from religious conversion. Today, some people refer to this kind of institutional conversion as proselytizing, which aptly fits the expression "homecoming" in the title of Sanneh's autobiography. He uses this term as a metaphor for pilgrimage in the sense of "coming home" to faith in God and describes how this faith went on to shape his life and work as a Christian scholar. In other words, Sanneh wrote on world Christianity as a critical insider.

Sanneh reflects on how his qur'anic schoolteacher, unable to do anything about Western-style formal education, continued to hope that training in the Qur'an would help overcome the "moral corrosion" of the Western school. Sanneh quotes his teacher as saying, that "at the Western school they teach you the infidel tongue so that men may speak without speaking the truth." This teacher's words suggests that he was sneering at what, with the arrival of Western forms of education, he thought might take away his competitive advantage in education.[11] In the Qur'an school, the goal of education was to make people genuinely and thoroughly Islamic, which had the consequence of fostering religious territoriality. In the Western school, the philosophy was to prepare children for future roles in the public service, something that the Muslim leadership of the time failed to understand.

Amid the challenge posed by Western-style education, Sanneh quotes his own Muslim father as taking the position that religion must rout infidel delusions. On the broader attitude to the Western school, Sanneh notes, "Our Muslim town had long resisted Western schools as a cesspool of infidel corruption. School bewitches children and feeds them with the illusion that self is supreme. School makes you big-headed so you think you don't need God or tradition."[12] In a sense, by turning its back on colonial education, Islam seemed to have inadvertently "shot itself in the foot" by ceding territorial control of the public service to the Christian fraternity.

Religious Formation and Territoriality

After his conversion, Lamin Sanneh did not become an isolated Christian; rather, he leveraged his Islamic background not only to study Islam but also to develop the dialogical relationship between Christians and Muslims. Given the absence of any encounter with Christianity in his childhood, Sanneh could

---

11. Sanneh, 40.
12. Sanneh, 40.

easily have become a "territorial Muslim" – that is, a radical fanatic for whom taking the life of an infidel would have amounted to the execution of the will of *Allah*. This is how Sanneh came to appreciate the importance of the Qur'an in his childhood:

> Literature of any kind was scarce in my childhood, which reinforced the position of the Qur'an as the paradigmatic book, its holy character proof that books were oracles of the enlightened spirit. I remember seeing the pages of the Qur'an gathered in a skin cover, tied with a red ribbon, and carried with reverence. A small crowd would gather when someone opened the book to read it. That was how I thought books in general were treated.[13]

There is a line in the first chapter of Sanneh's autobiography, *Summoned from the Margin*, that I think, captures that with which we came to associate Sanneh, namely, a scholar in religion who was a religious scholar. In this line, Sanneh notes how his various readings and travels made him feel "increasingly drawn into accounting for the religious contribution to a humane engagement with the world."[14] He concludes from this desire to account for the religious contribution to human development as driving his academic interests in the study of Scripture and translation.[15] Whether on the basis of our difference or our common humanity, he championed the notion that mutually deciphering other cultures is the answer to alienation because of its capacity for mutual recognition.[16]

Language and Territoriality

Lamin Sanneh pays tribute to the African family and communal environments in which he was nurtured. What did this nurturing environment look like? Sanneh describes it in the following way: "The African child lives in a close, crowded world, a world teeming with faces and sounds and movements that the child learns to decipher eventually into recognition and affirmation, each smiling face a lighted clue in the growing shape of knowing and belonging."[17]

---

13. Sanneh, 20.
14. Sanneh, 21.
15. Sanneh, 21.
16. Sanneh, 21.
17. Sanneh, 26.

Sanneh's qur'anic schoolteacher significantly influenced his formation. The incessant corporal punishment was obviously detested, but the excuse for inflicting such pain on children in the school was attributed to the need to learn the holy scriptures. The reception of language – in this case Arabic – as "sacred and absolute" and the fact that the vernacular was unfit for "faith and worship" and, therefore, less esteemed, is a key childhood observation. The Qur'an was not only written in a sacred untranslatable language, but the words contained in it also carried sacred, almost magical, power on the lips of those who knew how to recite the appropriate verses.[18]

Sanneh's thesis on the relationship between language and religion is well laid out in *Translating the Message*. In that work, he talks about how the reality of God supersedes culture. Christian mission was a barrier against cultural immobility because, through translation, "it challenged the idea of culture as the arbiter of the truth of God."[19] Sanneh's early impressions of Arabic as a holy language are worth quoting at some length:

> Even the little we understood made us realize that Arabic was special; that the words had a holy reputation and a sacred personality; that they never changed or aged; that we suffered for offending against them, for soiling them, and for tripping over them. We stood condemned for failing to master the sacred word but were amply rewarded for memorizing the tone and sound.[20]

For those who have attended Sunday school, the experience would have been a bit different. Although children were encouraged to memorize a few Bible verses, the approach to those who were slow was often, relatively speaking, a little gentler and more empathetic than the experiences of Muslim children. What one would have typically learned were stories of how Jesus expected children to be good to their friends and honor their parents. The Bible was a translated version of an original manuscript, and there were vernacular versions for those children who were not in school because they served as domestic helpers in homes. The Bible was certainly a holy book, but its contents were not written in any sacred language. Even within the same Sunday school, there would not only have been different versions of the Bible but also versions in local languages for those not accustomed to reading in English.

---

18. Sanneh, 4.
19. Sanneh, *Translating the Message*, 37.
20. Sanneh, *Summoned from the Margin*, 39.

Conversion, Mother Tongue, and Mission

Lamin Sanneh was a very careful and skilled writer. His formative years as a young African on a quest for meaning interpret what later became his academic preoccupation. This is an essential part of what his autobiography offers. The inferiority of the mother tongue was inflicted on Africa by colonialism and Western education. Colonial rule, Sanneh notes, "inserted the Western world into Christianity's missionary endeavor more as a costly, complicating irritant than as an advantage."[21] In European hands, Christianity nearly degenerated into a political project in which missionaries often created the erroneous impression that Christianity as a faith was itself European. This attitude, Sanneh explains, was considered detrimental to colonial rule because it offended local sensibility and made converts harbor the idea that they were equal with the colonialists.[22]

In spite of these difficulties, Sanneh credits missionaries with the courage to develop written forms of indigenous languages, and thereby making the Bible available in "infidel tongues." In his words:

> It stumped me that, in spite of its relative disadvantage as an undocumented language without any literary works to its credit, the mother tongue should attract the interest and devotion of missionaries who made it the language of scripture – something Muslim agents will never dream of doing.[23]

Local African languages were unknown beyond their own cultural contexts. Without written literature to advertise and promote them and without any organized means of transmission, many local languages were heading toward extinction. However, as Sanneh later proves, the translation of the Bible into vernacular languages prevented Christianity from suffering a moribund fate. The religious territoriality of Islam viewed language quite differently:

> The idea of language as God's gift is odd in respect of the mother tongue, because the God in question is none other than Islam's God, who shut the door on it. To be religious required listening to God in the revealed language, and that demoted the mother tongue to the religious black market of juju and nocturnal rituals . . . It is not possible to conceive a divine role for the vernacular against the

---

21. Sanneh, 168.
22. Sanneh, 168.
23. Sanneh, 216.

transcendent Arabic, thus making worship a ban on the mother tongue.[24]

Sanneh laments that the elevation of Arabic into the realm of the sacred language of Allah made his mother tongue look "mundane and vain."[25] His teachers, he notes, had little sympathy for those who were weak in Arabic because it was, in their view, the perfect, preordained language.[26] Indigenous tongues were redundant; yet it was through the "tones and sounds" of his mother tongue that thoughts of God formed in Sanneh's imagination.[27] In other words, if, in Islam, Arabic was a critical mark of religious territoriality, in Christianity, that mark was nonexistent on account of the translatability of the scriptures. According to Sanneh, translatability of the Bible "dissolves all false, obstructive claims of exclusion, superiority, and inferiority, and in their place relied on interpretation for sense and meaning."[28]

The routine nature of the religion, the total disregard for the religious other, and the violent reactions to those who fell "out of line" when it came to observances pushed Sanneh to reflect on his options with regards to piety. The deep-seated and heartfelt spiritual hunger – the virtual thirst for the presence of God – that has often led to his internal quest for a more fulfilling spiritual encounter. The following experience that Sanneh recounts in his book may lead us to conclude that he was a man who longed for something a bit more real, something close to what the psalmist yearned for when he wrote, "As the deer pants for streams of water, so my soul pants for you, my God" (Ps 42:1 NIV).

> I heard St. Anselm whispering: "Woe is me, one of the poor children of Eve, far from God, what did I set out to do and what have I accomplished? What was I aiming for and how far have I got? What did I aspire to and what did I long for? O Lord, you are not only that than which nothing greater can be conceived, but you are greater than all that can be conceived." I could hear pursuing footsteps at night, as if my thoughts could walk.[29]

---

24. Sanneh, 67.
25. Sanneh, 67.
26. Sanneh, 71.
27. Sanneh, 67.
28. Sanneh, *Translating the Message*, 110.
29. Sanneh, *Summoned from the Margin*, 68.

Lessons for World Christianity

In these reflections, I have tried to demonstrate that Lamin Sanneh was not writing a simple biographical portrait. Rather, he used his life story – beginning with his difficult childhood and his growth within the Islamic faith – to narrate how God, presumably working by his Spirit through a combination of people, circumstances, and experiences, made him into a world Christian scholar. He uses a particular methodological approach in which he reads the progression of life's experiences in his childhood into his scholarship. The book title was perceptively chosen – for this is a story of being literally "summoned from the margin" and placed at the center of world Christianity. The timing was significant on account of the fact that Sanneh's life unfolded at the same time that Christianity was making its proverbial shift from its former heartlands into its new centers in the non-Western world. So what specific lessons on world Christianity can we discern in Sanneh's life story?

First, there are different types of conversion and conversion experiences. From an African Christian perspective, people convert when they change their religious orientation, completely abandoning a previous faith and embracing a new one. Thus, Christian evangelization since the colonial era has meant a turning away from traditional African religions of one sort or another; this turning is tantamount to a virtual renunciation of unhelpful, irrelevant, or even senseless faiths in order to embrace another faith. In more than a few cases, people may already have been members of a church when they were obliged to renounce certain religious habits and moral failings that were deemed inconsistent with the teachings of the Bible. In such cases, conversion would have been more like a transition from being a false or dubious Christian to becoming a truer and more honest one. In other words, these radical conversions could signify anything from change of religious affiliation to making the transition from being a nominal or carnal Christian to becoming a more serious and spiritual one.

Second, as we learn from the writings of Andrew F. Walls, the history of the two great missionary faiths suggests a contrast in their methods of expansion. Islam seems largely able to retain its allegiance in the places where it has spread, whereas Christianity often demonstrates recession in one place before undergoing accession in another. Walls notes that this recession and accession of Christianity in history does not seem to jeopardize God's saving action in relation to humanity.[30] Walls does not necessarily have individual conversions in mind when he makes these observations. Nevertheless, it is

---

30. Walls, *Cross-Cultural Process*, 29.

easy to see how Sanneh's story of conversion – which took place within a predominantly Islamic context and is about a man who eventually made his mark both in his native country and in the West, where the faith had been in recession – could be interpreted as a sign of God choosing people from the underside of history in order to establish his purposes among the powerful.

Sanneh was "summoned from the margin" by God who made it possible for him to study and work in such ivy league institutions such as Yale and Princeton and through that exposure, prepared him to serve as a leading voice in the study of world Christianity in the twentieth century and beyond. The Yale-Edinburgh Group on World Christianity, established by Walls and Sanneh in the early 1990s, is a symbolic testimony to Sanneh's commitment to and influence on the study of world Christianity in the world today. At the Group's inauguration in 1992, Sanneh presented a background paper titled "From Christendom to World Christianity." This was about a decade before I joined the Yale-Edinburgh Conference, but as I reread the paper recently, a particular paragraph that talked about what scholars ought to be doing with respect to the study of world Christianity, caught my attention. Sanneh wrote that the Christian missionary movement was born within the context of the loss of Christendom and the European territorial unity that religion once assumed. Christian mission, he notes, developed as the extension abroad of the successful separation of religion and territory and, thus, of the understanding of religion as a matter of individual persuasion and choice. The missionary movement proved that religion could be separated from European territorial identity and succeed – if not in the hearts of the transmitters, then certainly in those of the receivers.[31]

Third, the effects of translation of the Christian scriptures are evident in Sanneh's life story. The incarnation itself, Walls notes, constitutes a "massive act of translation," in which the Word became flesh and dwelt with humanity. Walls's words explaining the implications of the incarnation for translation and world Christianity are worth quoting in full:

> Christian faith must go on being translated, must continuously enter into vernacular culture and interact with it, or it withers and fades. Islamic absolutes are fixed in a particular language, and in the conditions of a particular period of human history. The divine Word is the Qur'an fixed in heaven forever in Arabic, the language of the original revelation. For Christians, however,

---

31. Sanneh, "Christendom to World Christianity," 6.

the divine word is translatable, infinitely translatable. The very words of Christ himself were transmitted in translated form in the earliest documents we have, a fact surely inseparable from the conviction that in Christ, God's own self was translated in to human form.[32]

The untranslatability of the Qur'an and the inferiority of the mother tongue are treated at length in Sanneh's autobiography. Sanneh says that the fact that Christianity is a "translated religion" places God – and not religious traditions – at the center of the universe of cultures. For the purposes of Bible translation, the implication is that "all languages have merit and are necessary, yet none is indispensable in its particularity."[33] Perhaps one place to discern this truth is on the day of the Pentecost, when people assembled from "every nation under heaven" and heard the "mighty acts of God"(Acts 2:5 ESV) proclaimed in their own languages by the enabling power of the Holy Spirit. For Sanneh, the Bible translation project made Christianity into a means of "indigenous empowerment."[34]

Fourth, Christianity presents a personal dimension to faith in which conversion is critical. Lewis R. Rambo and Charles E. Farhadian identify seven general steps that people usually follow on the road to conversion. A number of these steps are evident in Sanneh's journey as he transitioned from engagement with an untranslatable Qur'an to an embrace of a God who was translated as the Christ of Christianity. The second stage within these steps is the potential convert's crisis in the quest for meaning. The two authors define crisis as "disordering and disrupting experiences that call into question a person's or group's taken-for-granted world."[35] External or internal factors could trigger the sort of crises that set in motion the personal quest for meaning in life.[36] In Sanneh's case, the external factors include the sort of Islamic faith that he was brought up to believe. The internal catalysts for conversion include illness as well as existential questions about the purpose of life, the desire for transcendence, and apostasy.

An important stage in Rambo and Farhadian's process is what they describe simply as "quest" or "searching for salvation."[37] Here, the authors talk about

---

32. Walls, *Cross-Cultural Process*, 29.
33. Sanneh, *Translating the Message*, 110.
34. Sanneh, *Summoned from the Margin*, 217.
35. Rambo and Farhadian, "Converting," 25.
36. Rambo and Farhadian, 26.
37. Rambo and Farhadian, 27.

the various ways in which people respond to the crises of their lives as they seek to reorient themselves toward that which will bring needed fulfillment. An important feature of the quest for salvation is the motivational structure of the quest, which might involve emotional, intellectual, or religious reasons.[38] The next three stages are described as encountering new options, creating new identities, and making a new commitment – that is, consolidating new spiritual orientations. All these stages in the conversion process are evident in one way or another in Sanneh's journey toward Christianity.

The sixth stage – commitment – is particularly instructive because it is at this point that the new convert makes a decision as a demonstration of status change. From here, "converts experience a sense of surrender, a 'giving in' to the religious option, that often gives rise to feelings of relief and liberation."[39] I find the use of the word "surrender" to describe the commitment stage critical for what seemed to have transpired in Sanneh's life. He proceeds to capture his conversion in terms of *dankeneya* (surrender) – a word that connotes "faith-filled certainty" – and draws out the implications as follows:

> On that day the boundary between these two worlds merged to compel a decision for faith and trust. It produced the state of mind for which the word *dankeneya* is most apt: a providential process that brings one to encounter with unshakable truth. The calm waves echoed the absence of any duress in the call, only that truth should make me free.[40]

Fifth, Sanneh searched for a church that was willing to baptize him into his new faith. In the eyes of his friends and family, he had chosen a path that would forever be considered an affront to Islam. In his words, "I was raised to value the truth that was not owned by any tribe, class, or rank, making me aware that truth was not our possession alone."[41] He notes that in "surrendering" himself to the God of the Christian evangel, "I was also acknowledging the goodness and kindness of others as so many material tokens of God's unfathomable and unstinting generosity, and the fact evoked grateful memories of old associates, and a lively hope for new beginning and commitments."[42] Conversion, rather than becoming a means to territorial squabbles with those with whom he used

---

38. Rambo and Farhadian, 27.
39. Rambo and Farhadian, 31.
40. Sanneh, *Summoned from the Margin*, 102.
41. Sanneh, 104.
42. Sanneh, 103.

to share the Islamic faith, turned out to birth within him a new hospitality in which, as he notes, "my respect and appreciation of Muslim friends had never been more heartfelt."[43]

What has not been understood in the perception of Christianity, particularly by Muslims, is that the territoriality of Islam and that of Christendom are not so dissimilar. In religious terms, Christianity is no longer an empire in the same way that Islam continues to be associated with political governance in the Arab countries, for example. In spite of the questions provoked in Sanneh's mind concerning the credibility of Christianity, Islam's inability to deal with and answer these questions drew him closer and closer to conversion.[44] Sanneh writes that Jesus, the slain founder of Christianity, "had risen from the grave and was threatening to pursue me in my thoughts."[45]

In the end, it was a personal solidarity with Jesus as the suffering servant of God – and not necessarily with Christianity – that brought Sanneh to the Christian faith. Starting from the violent and cruel crucifixion of Jesus, the big question that confronted him was what Jesus's death had to do with personal faith:

> The fact that I was driven to ask for God's mercy for the tragedy of Jesus meant that I could not do so credibly from a remote, uncommitted position. It required personal proximity, in fact personal solidarity with the enmity that targeted Jesus precisely because it was enmity against God. If the enemies of Jesus sinned, we had all sinned. Their guilt was ours too.[46]

Religious conversion of the kind that Sanneh describes here usually has implications for territoriality and hospitality. For Muslims, Christian missions functioned as a shield against defections from Islam to Christianity.[47] Muslim parents were also reluctant to enroll their children in mission schools for fear that they would be converted. Religious territories between the two faiths – Christianity and Islam – were guarded quite jealously by each. Consequently, the transition that Sanneh made in converting to Christianity implied courting martyrdom.

---

43. Sanneh, 103.
44. Sanneh, 93.
45. Sanneh, 97.
46. Sanneh, 100.
47. Sanneh, 95.

Sixth, Sanneh's autobiography contains lessons on territoriality and hospitality. The last of the seven-stage process of conversion is described as "consequences" – that is, "assessing the effects of converting."[48] Religious conversion is a process, not an event. Writing about the pre-conversion process, Sanneh notes, "In my fumbling steps I came to realize that there was a sure road to fellowship with God and I should take it without hesitation and without deviation."[49] The use of the expression "road" to capture the journey evokes images of traveling toward something new, a new set of religious truth-claims that might prove a bit more fulfilling and reassuring than one's previous territory. The Akan of Ghana often say that "the traditional healer who undertakes the task of care prior to the hiring of a new one ought not to be damned." The philosophy of this proverb is that the traditional healer, regardless of competence, at least succeeded in keeping the patient alive. Lamin Sanneh left Islam, but he did not damn his religious ancestors. His conversion became an ongoing process of transformation in which the convert immersed himself in the teaching and practices of the new faith.

Within these memoirs – wherein we have sought to assess the dual issues of territoriality and hospitality in Sanneh's conversion – we encounter him not only seeking baptism but also looking for literature that was supposed to explain to him some of the critical teachings of the new faith. Christianity must necessarily be understood apart from the denominations that represent it. The lack of hospitality on the part of some denominations clearly led Sanneh to question the love of Christ that these churches professed. Whereas "Muslims honor and celebrate their converts as trophies of faith . . . Christians take their converts as charitable ration with a pinch of shame."[50] The defective hospitality of denominations was evident in the unwillingness of first the Methodists and then the Catholics to willingly embrace a young Islamic convert: "My conversion was beginning to feel like managing an ecumenical hedge fund, with the Protestants and Catholics agreeing to share the risks of accepting a convert from Islam but neither being willing to take them on alone."[51]

That was then; but the denominational uncertainties and tensions have continued even in postcolonial Africa, where virtually all denominations are now in the hands of Africans. The inability of the churches to sincerely cooperate and work together has turned the ecumenical project into a marriage

---

48. Rambo and Farhadian, "Converting," 32.
49. Sanneh, *Summoned from the Margin*, 101.
50. Sanneh, 105.
51. Sanneh, 108.

of convenience; and since the majority of Christians live in non-Western contexts, it is becoming even more burdensome for churches to work together.

Conclusion

In his autobiography, Sanneh takes his readers through an array of themes and issues, ranging from territoriality and hospitality in conversion to perceptions of Christianity in Islamic thought. From his own initial attitude as a skeptic of Christianity, his embrace of the faith propelled him to a lifetime career in Christian-Muslim scholarship.[52] Sanneh himself confesses that, for several reasons, Christianity initially made only "a superficial impression" on him. One of the internal tensions for him was in the area of language. Unlike the sacred Arabic, Christianity did not seem to possess a "revealed language."[53] The religious functionaries of Islam, including his Arabic schoolteachers, worked to deliver Christians from "error and blindness."[54] The stringent form of the Islamic school that he knew made Christianity seem like "weak stuff" by comparison.[55] However, Sanneh grew to appreciate the critical importance of translating the message and argued that Christianity's uniqueness as a missionary religion was its transmission without the language of the founder of the faith. In Sanneh's words, "It is as if the religion must disown the language of Jesus to be the faith Jesus taught."[56]

The church in the West, as Sanneh was to discover, was in decline. Sanneh describes his experience of encountering, as a new Christian, "old crumbling churches and empty, ornate cathedrals" as being "unsettling."[57] We usually speak of Christian decline in the West in terms of numbers, but in the America that Sanneh encountered in the early 1960s, it was the faith itself that had been debased and secularized. Thus, in the American public sphere, "Jesus Christ" and "God" had become common swear words and terms like "sacrifice" and "cross" had acquired secular meanings.[58] Western society was turning increasingly secular and, to his dismay, Sanneh also encountered segregation – to put it bluntly, the church was inhospitable for racial reasons. He describes

---

52. Sanneh, 88.
53. Sanneh, 88.
54. Sanneh, 88.
55. Sanneh, 89.
56. Sanneh, 222.
57. Sanneh, 116.
58. Sanneh, 128.

one such experience: "One Sunday a group of us students marched to a nearby United Methodist Church to participate in the worship, but the stewards there refused to seat us, and we left without incident."[59]

Today, those who are keeping Christianity alive in Western contexts are people we have described as coming from the underside of history. Non-Western Christians are making Christianity relevant and compelling in the former heartlands of the faith, even beyond its immigrant confines. That is only one part of the story of Christianity as a non-Western religion. The discipline of world Christianity itself has become one in which non-Western scholars are now staking an important claim.[60]

All the scholars we mentioned earlier as scholars in world Christianity are connected to Lamin Sanneh in one way or another. The autobiography *Summoned from the Margin* can only serve as an inspirational work for those of us who are interested in the development of Christianity as a non-Western religion. Sanneh points to the fact that present and future prospects of the church have changed the equation between the claims of the West with regard to cultural superiority and post-Western developments of indigenous initiatives in religion.[61]

This has implications for the future of the faith as we seek to respond to the questions of territoriality and hospitality in the study of religion. World Christianity as a field of academic study is unlikely to be the same without Sanneh's continued contribution to our knowledge of this nascent, vast, still-developing, and exciting field of scholarship. That is to say, it is impossible to study world Christianity today without some reference to Lamin Sanneh's impressive legacy in this field.

Bibliography

Bediako, Kwame. *Theology and Identity: The Impact of Culture upon Christian Thought*. Oxford: Regnum, 1999.

---

59. Sanneh, 132.

60. For example, Nimi Wariboko of Boston University, Afe Adogame of Princeton Theological Seminary, Jehu H. Hanciles of Emory University, Akin Akinade of Georgetown University, and Jacob Olupona of Harvard University constitute only a representative list of Africans who are teaching and researching world Christianity in some of the most prestigious Western institutions.

61. Sanneh, *Summoned from the Margin*, 265.

Fretheim, Sara J. *Kwame Bediako and African Christian Scholarship: Emerging Religious Discourse in Twentieth-Century Ghana*. African Christian Studies Series. Eugene: Wipf & Stock, 2018.

Rambo, Lewis R., and Charles E. Farhadian. "Converting: Stages of Religious Change." In *Religious Conversion: Contemporary Practices and Controversies*, edited by Christopher Lamb and M. Darrol Bryant, 23–34. London; New York: Cassell, 1999.

Sanneh, Lamin. "From Christendom to World Christianity." Background Paper to Yale-Edinburgh Conference at the Yale University Divinity School/Overseas Ministries Study Center, 26–28 March 1992.

———. *Summoned from the Margin: Homecoming of an African*. Grand Rapids; Cambridge: Eerdmans, 2012.

———. *Translating the Message: The Missionary Impact on Culture*. Rev. and exp. ed. Maryknoll: Orbis Books, 2009.

Walls, Andrew F. *The Cross-Cultural Process in Christian History: Studies in the Transmission and Appropriation of Faith*. Maryknoll: Orbis Books, 2002.

4

God's Hospitality and the Idolatry of Territoriality

Rowan Williams

I had the privilege of knowing Lamin Sanneh as a friend. He was a generous supporter and someone who contributed greatly to the discussions of my own Anglican Church as well as to the wider agenda of building confidence and trust between Christian and Muslim communities worldwide. It is perhaps some tribute to his memory that I find I continue to use his writings regularly in my own teaching in Cambridge and London.

I begin with some reflections on certain aspects of Sanneh's writing and research that are relevant to the subject of this consultation on the themes of territoriality and hospitality. The first of these is the strong focus in his writing on understanding that the center of gravity in global Christianity is no longer where it has historically been – namely, in the West and the North. This is one aspect of appreciating the global character of Christian presence as it now exists, not as it has often been seen. In addition, we should attend to Sanneh's specific research on the ways in which communities that have become Christian, especially in Africa, have taken different approaches in how they speak about God.

For example, did newly Christianized communities use their own language, literally, to speak of God or did they borrow names for God from missionary bodies and cultures? In other words, when the Christian faith arrived in cultures that were historically strange to European travelers, did those Christian cultures see themselves as dominant? Or did they see themselves as guests who were learning to speak and not simply talking others into silence? Sadly, part of the history of Christian mission in Africa and elsewhere has often been talking other people into silence rather than listening and learning how to speak.

I would say that those two themes in Professor Sanneh's work highlight those of our conference, specifically with regard to Christianity, and I shall turn in a moment to some thoughts about their implications for interfaith conversation. First, we Christians in the global North are being invited to learn and relearn that we are no longer the dominant partners in a master-servant relationship. "Christendom" – the idea that there is a territory belonging to Christians in the world, which has to be extended as a kind of empire – is thankfully a notion belonging to the past. The Christian message and the Christian presence, cannot be an empire; it cannot be an exercise in domination, whereby the boundaries of a Christian territory are steadily pushed out until they involve control of the entire globe.

If we have learned anything in the last century or so of reflection on the history of colonialism, we have learned that the association between Christianity and colonial power has not served the integrity of Christians or the well-being of anyone else. So the second major issue comes into focus. In relation to the willingness of missionaries to learn new languages, we are reminded of a theme very dear to Professor Sanneh's heart – that "hospitality" is about learning to *receive* hospitality as well as learning to *give* it. This is a grace that involves learning to be a guest as well as learning to be a host, and this learning to be a guest entails respect and gratitude toward those who are making space in their home for you. I will return to both these themes a little later in these reflections.

But let me pause for a moment concerning the question of "territory": why and how it matters and why we have to think very critically about it. I said that one of the errors that Christianity has historically been prone to is the idea that there is, in some sense, a native Christian territory that has to be extended. This is something rather different from sharing the Christian message universally, something that has, uncomfortably, more to do with an idea of universal control, dominance, and hegemony.

This theme was addressed in a very unusual and striking way by one of the great Christian theologians of the twentieth century – Dietrich Bonhoeffer, a German theologian who resisted the Nazis.[1] Bonhoeffer was imprisoned for his complicity in the plot to assassinate Adolf Hitler and, eventually, executed

---

1. Geffrey B. Kelly, F. Burton Nelson, and Dietrich Bonhoeffer. 1995. A Testament to Freedom: the Essential Writings of Dietrich Bonhoeffer. Revised edition. ed. (San Francisco, Calif.: Harper SanFrancisco).

in a German prison camp shortly before the end of the Second World War. In some of his last writings, Bonhoeffer himself speaks of the danger of a territorial mindset. Of course, he says, the Christian church occupies a space in the world. You can certainly see where Christians are on Sunday mornings. One hopes that they are at worship. Yet the church does not exist in order to take up space in the world, to say, "This is Christian territory." The church exists to say to the entire world, "This is the sphere of God's action and God's grace and God's love." The church exists not in order to say something that flatters our assumptions about power and privilege, reassuring as that may be to its own members. The church exists to say something challenging and transforming for the entire world in which it is located. So, the church should never be preoccupied with defending its boundaries – as if it were a kind of nation-state in danger of invasion – and it should never allow its energies to be consumed in this defense of territory. And why is that?

Bonhoeffer says it is something to do with the very nature of God. God does not need to carve out some part of the world in which he is sovereign because God is sovereignly present by his freedom and his grace in every part of his creation. God does not have to fight for space because God is not a reality like us, alongside other realities. God is the supreme, unique, undefended source of all things, who needs no protection from us or from anyone else.

This insight regarding the connection between the nature of God and the nature of the Christian community rests upon the crucial insight that God is not simply "one of us." God is not simply a very large reality, compared with whom we are a very small reality. God belongs to another order of reality altogether. God is the source of all that is, depending on nothing but himself. To understand this is to understand something of how idolatry works. Idolatry is the identification of God with some part of the world, with an image of the Divine, with myself, my needs, my priorities, or with the well-being of a nation or a culture. To identify God with any of these ideas – and there are many more examples – is idolatry. This, I would say, is where the Christian and Muslim agendas coincide very significantly. One of the greatest contributions made by Islam to the religious history of the world is the central insistence that idolatry must be avoided at all costs – the insistence that to confuse God with what is not God is the beginning of all error and all evil.

This is an area where the Christian and the Muslim can heartily agree. God is who and what God is. And we must, at all costs, avoid confusing God with what God is not, which is to reduce God to our own level. When we embark on this program of reducing God to our level, one of the things that can very easily happen is that we become territorial. That is to say, we assume that the reality of God is essentially bound up with my reality, the reality of my culture, the reality of my class, or the reality of my race. I identify God with what is not God. I assume that it is through my defense of my nation, my culture, my class, or my race that I defend God. If this evolves to become our collective reality, the world is more and more deeply trapped in irreconcilable conflict because by associating God with my own interest, my own territory, my own psychology, or my own imagination, I give to that territory, that psychology, and that imagination a divine character – an absolute character that does not belong to it.

So perhaps that is one way of beginning to think about the themes for our conference. We are territorial and defensive about our territory to the extent that, consciously or not, we are idolatrous – identifying God with ourselves, our interests, and our agenda. Looking back at the history of Christian missionary engagement outside the historic territories of Christendom, we can often see that identification at work. And, I dare say, there are parallel stories to be told about the expansion of Islam.

But what if we resist idolatry? What if we step back from this very seductive and attractive idea that God might be identical with us and our interests? Then we learn to see and to imagine our human world and the non-human world rather differently. Instead of beginning with the question, "Where are the boundaries, on the other side of which is darkness and godlessness?" perhaps we should begin by claiming that the entire world has been received and welcomed into the hospitality of God. It has been called into being, called into the presence of God. That is one way of understanding what creation itself means – a world is summoned into being, into the presence of God, and invited into love, into joy, and into fullness. So, in resisting the temptations of idolatry and territorial anxiety, can we imagine afresh the world around us, a human world around us, full of things and persons invited into being by God? When I begin to see my human neighbor as somebody who has received the divine invitation, to see my human neighbor as somebody who has been called into being, into the presence of God, then, I would venture to say, I see them very differently. The human "other" is no longer simply a stranger and a threat. The human other is the guest of God.

And the material world that we inhabit, instead of simply being a storehouse of resources that we can use as we please to make ourselves comfortable, comes to be seen as invited into being by God and called into God's presence so as to live and to flourish. When I see the world around me as invited into being by God, once again, I view it differently. I see it as carrying the creative word of God. I see it as responding to God's invitation to reconciliation and joy. So what I am suggesting is that when we are released from idolatry and from the territorial obsessions that go with it, what begins to happen is a transfiguration of our sense of the world around us. We see what is around us and who is around us in terms of God's hospitality and God's welcome.

For the Christian, this is expressed uniquely and fully in the way in which Jesus of Nazareth invites, receives, and welcomes all those persons and things around him, to bring to them the transforming love of God. That is a theme which I believe we should be discussing and exploring together as persons of faith. All of us – Christians, Muslims, and others – believe in a God who is not part of the world but, rather, invites the world into his presence. To the extent that we believe this, we can share and develop a transforming vision of our world. We can say to the world around us that we refuse to accept the terms of exclusion and fear, which are so common in this world. We can, together, nourish a vision of reality that is fundamentally generous and welcoming. That, of course, means the exercise of hospitality to one another.

I deliberately did not begin with that idea of hospitality to one another, important though it is, because I think it is crucial to ground the notions of welcoming and hospitality into our understanding of God's very activity. We are hospitable and seek to welcome one another because we ourselves have been welcomed. We have been invited into the Divine Presence. "Receive one another," says St. Paul in Christian scripture, "just as Christ also received us" (Rom 15:7 NKJV). The receiving, the drawing into the presence, begins with God's act. And we are called to reflect that in our relations with one another.

Hospitality, then, rests on the very nature of creation. Both as created human beings and as persons of specific and explicit faith, we are to live in the truth of that hospitality and live out of the reality of God's welcome. Therefore, we are to seek to welcome one another. While this may sound straightforward, as we all know, it is not. Every society seems to operate, at least to some extent, by the energy of fear. Every human society we know is permeated with anxiety about the stranger – someone who is perceived as compromising my integrity, fighting me for my resources, and undermining my identity. Therefore, I have to keep the doors tightly shut and the walls very high.

Both Christianity and Islam are faiths with a universal perspective. Both believe that there is some reconciled peaceful existence that is proper to all human beings, not just to one nation or one culture. This means that both faiths have a universal horizon, which is always going to make life uncomfortable in a world of small and anxious states and societies. In this context, as people of faith, our business is to engage the assumptions I have just been discussing with the following question: Why are we afraid of the other? Why is it that we retreat and isolate? When we encounter the stranger, why is it so hard to believe that our own identity and reality is so deeply secured in the gift and invitation of God that we do not have to be afraid of its demise? To put it very simply, it will take more than a stranger to undermine my identity because my identity is called into being by God; and so is the stranger's. Whatever conflicts and difficulties we encounter on the way, that is the reality that underlies everything and spells out the work we have to do together. And this is not a particularly welcome message in an anxious world.

At present, in countless countries throughout the world, the voices of fear and anxiety are prevailing. In the last decade or two, we are seeing a fairly steady movement toward higher levels of self-protection and higher levels of suspicion and hatred toward the stranger. Conflicts and inequalities that many of us thought had been dealt with decades ago have returned in full force and with great violence.

If anyone is disposed to have a simple confidence in human progress, I suggest a close study of international politics in the last decade. We are not becoming more welcoming and more friendly or less suspicious and less anxious. This is a time when conflict and pressure on resources is leading to unprecedented numbers of displaced persons in our world. We do not need reminding that, at the present time, there are almost certainly more displaced persons on the face of the globe than ever before. These millions of people who are away from their homes and their countries because of poverty, disease, or open conflict are urgently in need of hospitality.

In my country, the United Kingdom, we have had, in the last few years, repeated controversies about how we should deal with migrants. Again and again, we have had an embarrassingly thin and unsatisfactory response from the government on this subject. Yet what is remarkable is that, at a grassroots level, many people in the United Kingdom and elsewhere continue to be inclined to take the risk of welcome, the risk of hospitality toward the stranger.

Two weeks ago, I was at Cambridge, attending a meeting to discuss various aspects of the refugee challenge in the United Kingdom. The most effective presentation came from a Jewish woman in Cambridge, who told the story of how she had responded to an invitation from a refugee charity to take a Syrian migrant into her home. The Jewish woman recounted how, at first, she had met her Syrian Muslim refugee guest with great trepidation and great uncertainty. She went on to describe the friendship that had developed between them and the way in which her guest had transformed her understanding not only of Islam but also of her own Jewish identity and, even more, her human identity.

And she spoke of how this Syrian guest later went on to find a home and a place in British society.

It is an unusual story but not a unique one. It is a story that reminds us that the attitudes of anxiety, hatred, and suspicion are not the only ones possible for human beings. There is potential for mutual transformation in hospitality: I discover more about myself as I learn more about a guest, and I learn more about my host as I understand how to be a guest. These realities are possible once we break through the prison of what I have been calling idolatry – the identification of myself, my agenda, my literal physical territory, and my culture with the divine and the absolute. God alone is God. What makes that good news for us is that none of us has to try to be God, to stand in God's place. Consequently, none of us has to defend ourselves as if we were defending God.

Thus, perhaps, from some of those insights that were so dear to Professor Sanneh's heart, you will see a kind of broad moral vision that emerges for our work together as people of faith. As we reflect on the nature of our God, we learn something about how to resist idolatry. As we resist idolatry, we learn something about the nature of creation. God, who owes us nothing, has, of his free love, summoned reality into life. All of us are guests of God. As we learn how to be guests of God and subjects of God's welcome, we learn how to see one another in that light – as invited by God – and to view the world itself as invited into being. We learn that our own agenda – the craving for security, for example – is not something we have to pursue at the cost of our human neighbors or at the cost of the earth in which we live.

The unhappy paradox of the last few years is that the resurgence of anxious and defensive attitudes toward the other – the stranger – has occurred at the precise time we have become aware, more than ever before, of how intricately interdependent our world is. The recent COVID-19 pandemic reminds us that disease pays no attention to political or social boundaries. Disease knows no boundaries; neither does environmental degradation.

The environmental crisis is no better at reading maps than pandemic disease. The economies of the world are linked together as never before; and despite the myths that are propagated in some high places, it is impossible, in the long run, for one society to be secure and prosperous while others fail and decline. In this world we all inhabit, the good of each and the good of all are much more obviously interconnected than we might have suspected even a century ago. Through the reality in which we live – the reality of environmental degradation, pandemic disease, poverty, violence, and other crises – this world we live in is teaching us, in a most unwelcome way, some important theological truths.

At present, the challenge we face as a human family is whether we are willing to learn those lessons and to allow ourselves to be taught by these crises something about the necessity of freeing ourselves from idolatry, freeing ourselves from territorial obsession and the myth of self-sufficiency, and freeing ourselves from a dangerous picture of the world in which we imagine that your suffering has nothing to do with me and that my prosperity has no impact on you.

In the Gospel of Luke, when the rich man in hell prayed that help would be sent to his surviving brothers, Abraham famously said, "They have Moses and the prophets. Let them listen to them" (16:29 NABRE). In other words, through Moses and the prophets, as well as through all the history of revelation, we have received from God the truth set before us. We have the truth about the nature of creation and the truth of being invited into the free love of God. We have the truth of our interconnectedness set before us in various ways – the truth that none of us lives or dies alone.

Yet we repeatedly choose to turn aside from that revealed truth and take refuge in the myths that we find more comfortable. Therefore, the effects of our untruthfulness and our idolatry come back to us in the form of medical and environmental crises, political instability, and many other issues that we now face. We have not listened to Moses and the prophets. Can we now listen to the call of a global crisis and recover once again the sense that we are, all of us – including our material world – guests of the divine love, called to show hospitality to each other in the name and power of that divine love?

In these difficult times, the foundation of The Sanneh Institute is a sign of hope and a reminder that we do not have to be prisoners of our mythology. Faith can still break through the prisons that have been central in our reflections today. My prayer and my hope for The Sanneh Institute is that it may do full justice to the memory of an unusual, creative, and, in every respect, great scholar and believer, and that it may have the impact it deserves on a world so desperately in need of liberation from the fantasies of self-sufficiency and division – a world in need of recovering the good news of God's welcome and the strength and freedom to share that welcome with one another.

5

"God Is Not Your Train Driver; nor Your Soccer Mascot"

Otherization, Tribalism, Territorialism, and Creation of the Transcendent in Our Image

Farid Esack

Bismillahi al-Rahman al-Rahim

(In the Name of God, the Gracious, the Dispenser of Grace)

Greetings and My Context

I greet you with the universal greetings of Islam, *Assalamu 'alaykum warahmatullahi wabaraka tuh*. "peace be upon all of you."

Our interreligious encounters are often filled with platitudes. We speak with a specific language of decorum and fraternity. But underneath this language lie several little demons that have buried themselves in the backs of our heads. Occasionally, when our societies feel threatened, those little demons come to the forefront. At present, we are seeing this painfully and vividly manifested in India, with the rise of Hindutva,[1] with its dreadful consequences for Muslims

---

1. According to Aloysius (1994: 1452), "Hindutva as a communalism of vertically constructed communities is the dominant [Hindu] caste's response to the emergence of the Indian version of 'class-struggle.' Setting up the two religious monoliths [Muslim versus Hindu],

and Christians. You can see it in many parts of the world where neighbors have lived close to one another for years. Then something strange but very human occurs. Moved by something as as small petty personal dispute or a significant ongoing and unsettled consequences of a long denied colonial occupation all indications of neighbourliness vanish overnight. Neighbors completely forget whom they lived next to for decades, with whom they broke bread throughout their lives, with whom they collectively survived under and stood in solidarity against the *zamindār* (Hindi for "feudal lord").

I am a South African, I am a Muslim, I am a male, and I am a believer like all of you. I am a human being. I share this planet and this continent with you. I am in Ghana, the land of Kwame Nkrumah (1909–1972), a country that inspired so many of us on the rest of the continent in our own struggle for liberation and freedom against colonialism.

I stand in front of you with dirty hands, with hands that are sullied. I am also a citizen of a country, a part of Africa whose inhabitants have been guilty of one of the most hateful crimes against human beings – the crimes of xenophobia against dark-skinned Black Africans and other darker-skinned foreigners, particularly Pakistanis and Bangladeshis. Normally described as "xenophobia," an irrational fear of foreigners, in South Africa it is not exactly about a fear of foreigners. All sections of South African society welcome White people from Britain, Poland, and the United States. So, this is the shame and stigma I bear as a South African. I cannot come to this event held in the heart of Africa as a mere victor of the liberation struggle or as a veteran of the interfaith movement that fought for our country's freedom.

Nevertheless, sullied as my hands may be, I struggle to speak my truths to myself, my compatriots, and my fellow Muslims. It may sometimes appear as if this were easy for me, but I am good at putting on an act; it is never easy to speak these truths.

In a narration of the Prophet Muhammad (peace be upon him), he is reported to have said *Qul al-haq, wa law kana murrah* (speak the truth, though it is bitter). Yet, very often, it is not the truth that we are particularly interested in; rather, we want to hear the speaker do us proud as Muslims for he is representing "our side" in front of "these other people." We do not want to be embarrassed or shamed. The demands of truth-speaking, however, my dear brothers and sisters, are somewhat different.

---

thus, is intended to cover up and suppress the growth of the class-like formations that have threatened the traditional solidarity in modern history.

Lamin Sanneh and His "Treacherous" Departure from the Muslim Train Compartment

I speak as an invited guest at this conference today. However, let me also add that I have never considered it my primary personal, religious, or scholarly task to make everybody feel comfortable. Let me now address the elephant in the room – an awkward and even bitter one for a Muslim.

In the video introducing the Lamin Sanneh Institute Inaugural Lectures, there was a brief comment about Professor Lamin Sanneh's conversion to Christianity. This volume is published to celebrate the life and work of one of Africa's great sons, whose vision is now to be continued in the form of The Sanneh Institute. *But* he was one of us; he *was* a Muslim, and he walked away, and we have not quite forgiven him; we have not quite dealt with it.

But what about Lamin Sanneh in his fullness – as an intellectual, a scholar, and the world's leading expert on Christianity and Islam in Africa? What about the man who challenged the Eurocentrism of much of Christian scholarship and wrestled profoundly with his Muslim faith? What about Sanneh, who, until his death and in all his works, continued to exhibit a deep respect for Islam and who cherished his Muslim parents and his Muslim upbringing? Lamin Sanneh always remembered his indebtedness to the home he came from:

> Having converted from Islam to Christianity, he never lost his profound respect for the religion of his upbringing. The zeal of a convert often brings contempt for the faith left behind, but not so with Lamin. He never lost his appreciation for how seriously his education in Islam encouraged him to take matters of faith, and he never lost his ability to cherish the insights of the religion of his ancestors. Here was someone who could be firm in his beliefs while respecting and appreciating those who disagreed with him and wanted him to return to Islam. He loved them, and that fact shone through in his scholarship.[2]

Nevertheless, this African giant could not let go of the deep feeling in his heart and mind, in the deepest part of his soul, that Islam and adherence to it did not fulfill his own deepest yearnings. It must have been an enormously painful choice for Sanneh, but he could do none other if he wanted to lead a life authentic to the voice of his inner self. His wrestling and agony in matters of faith are reflected in his letter to Professor John Azumah, whose mentor and

---

2. David Bratt, "Remembering Lamin Sanneh (1942–2019)," *Eerdword: The Eerdmans Blog*, 8 January 2019, https://eerdword.com/remembering-lamin-sanneh-1942-2019/.

teacher he was and who is the man responsible for setting up this gathering and The Sanneh Institute.

> When I was thwarted in my wish to study theology and be ordained, I went through a terrible period of confusion and doubt. It was like a sickness in which I wondered whether God really wanted me. I started to emerge out of that hole when I saw that I could offer my training and scholarship as a small tribute to the God of Jesus, with Muslims within hearing distance.[3]

Despite all that painful agonizing discernment, Lamin Sanneh decided to get off the train compartment of Islam and board another compartment – that of Christianity. This is a serious and challenging issue for believing Muslims. It is difficult, even dangerous, to generalize about any religious community, let alone one that comprises more than a quarter of the world's population and spans the earth from New Zealand to Alaska. But I do want to venture into two related generalizations. First, it is extremely difficult to get a Muslim to change his or her religion. Second, Muslims rarely – if ever – forgive anyone who abandons Islam. As individuals – and even as communities – we may abandon Islam in our practice, character, and ethics, but exiting with an announcement for all the other passengers on the train to hear is simply not done. In South Africa, we would say, "*Sies*! This is just not on!" And the truth is that our extreme discomfort – to put it mildly – with someone exiting the Islamic faith, appears to have categorical qur'anic support. In the words of the Qur'an,

> As for those who reject faith after they accepted it, and then go on adding to their defiance of Faith, never will their repentance be accepted; for they are those who have gone astray. (Q 3:90)

Increasingly, Muslim scholars are finding ways to reinterpret earlier texts and judgments to bring Islamic law in this regard closer to the contemporary

---

3. See [n.a.], "Lamin Sanneh, Christian Convert From Islam & Gambian Scholar Who Shaped Contemporary Discourse Around African Missions, Dies at 76," *Black Christian News Network One*, https://blackchristiannews.com/2019/01/lamin-sanneh-christian-convert-from-islam-gambian-scholar-who-shaped-contemporary-discourse-around-african-missions-dies-at-76/. Re-published from CT Editors, "'Remembering Lamin Sanneh, the World's Leading Expert on Christianity and Islam in Africa," *Christianity Today*, January 8, 2019, https://www.christianitytoday.com/news/2019/january/lamin-sanneh-died-world-christianity-islam-africa-yale.html.

appreciation of human rights, invoking a key qur'anic text – "There is no compulsion in religion" (Q 2:256) – to justify their position.[4]

Lamin Sanneh: Scholar and Abiding Friend of Muslims and Islam

I want to draw your attention to some aspects of Professor Lamin Sanneh's life and his contribution to Muslim-Christian relations and Christian and Islamic studies. This giant, who, when he passed our horizons as Muslims, we switched off the lights so that we may not see him and be reminded of our hurt when he stepped out of our train compartment.

I have not been a serious scholar of the works and contributions of Lamin Sanneh. However, I did have the opportunity of meeting this regal and scholarly giant, along with his wife, Professor Sandra Sanneh, at a small reception at Yale University when I went there for a job interview some twenty or more years ago. I have read his magnum opus – *Summoned from the Margin: Homecoming of an African* – which tells "the story of Lamin Sanneh's fascinating journey from his upbringing in an impoverished village in West Africa to education in the United States and Europe to a distinguished career teaching at the Universities of Yale, Harvard, Aberdeen, and Ghana" (back cover description by Eerdmans, the publisher).

Walls describes Sanneh as a scholar who "has added to the sum of our knowledge, transformed understanding with illuminating comparisons, and widened debate by insights from different disciplines" and "has advanced the study of both Christianity and Islam in Africa with major works; he has also advanced understanding between Christians and Muslims in active relationships." Walls goes on to describe Sanneh as a "visionary, man of faith, scholar, teacher, writer, architect, motivator, networker, dear friend and pillar of our fellowship."[5]

---

4. In Islam, the crime of apostasy – abandonment of Islam by a Muslim – is called, *riddah* or *irtidad* and the apostate is called a *murtad*. Although the terms "*riddah*" and "*irtidad*" are technically applied to apostasy by word and deed, social and legal abandonment by deed is regarded as far more egregious. Definitions of *riddah* and the punishment for the crime varies extensively in classical Islamic law. A number of Muslim countries include *riddah* and punishment for committing in their penal codes. Implementation of punishment, usually the death penalty, is extremely rare. The cases are often the subject of interventions by Western countries who also offer political asylum to the alleged apostates. For a detailed discussion on freedom of religion and apostasy in Islam, see Saeed and Saeed, 2004.

5. Andrew F. Walls, "Professor Lamin Sanneh: In Memoriam," Centre for the Study of World Christianity (Edinburgh), 8 January 2019, http://www.cswc.div.ed.ac.uk/2019/01/professor-lamin-sanneh-in-memoriam/.

"When I asked how he found time to write so much," says Esther Acolatse, he simply said, "Because I'm afraid one day I'll be asked by God to give account of how I have used my time. I want to be able to bear up under the question."[6] Joel Carpenter says,

> Lamin was as celebrated a scholar of Islam as of Christianity. His masterwork in this field is his most recent, *Beyond Jihad: The Pacifist Tradition in West African Islam* (2016). Lamin came up with these and other significant insights because he had the unique ability to ask fresh questions, to look across the grain, and to be a genial contrarian. He was a brilliantly original scholar.[7]

Sanneh's *Beyond Jihad: The Pacifist Tradition in West African Islam* (2016) reflects his commitment to serious and generous scholarship. Despite his conversion to Christianity he still insisted that Islam was primarily a religion of peace. Contrary to the common notion in the west that the major reason for the spread of Islam was its military conquests, he argued that its spread was due to its emphasis on peace. Upon the book's release, and in the context of the global war on terror, he warned, "The only thing worse than being the target of religious extremism and violence is the forsaking of the very values and ideals that violent extremists find so abhorrent."[8]

There are not nearly enough consequential Muslim references to Sanneh's work in Islamic scholarship. While this is partly because of Sanneh's exiting from Islam, it is also partly due to our self-containment because of which we often refuse to take on others' contributions to human understanding or our understanding of religiosity.

So, we have this elephant in the room. On the one hand, the Qur'an is very clear: *La ikraha fi al-din* (there is no compulsion in religion) and, on the other, there are clear denunciations of those who choose paths other than that of Islam. When dealing with our texts, there is a tension between the demonization and the celebration of the religious other. However, this is also awkward for many Muslims in societies where our presence is being challenged, particularly with the rise of Islamophobia in the West. We have

---

6. Esther Acolatse, quoted by Katharine Q. Seelye, "Lamin Sanneh, Scholar of Islam and Christianity, Dies at 76," *New York Times*, 11 January 2019, https://www.nytimes.com/2019/01/11/obituaries/lamin-sanneh-dead.html.

7. Quoted in "Remembering Lamin Sanneh, the World's Leading Expert on Christianity and Islam in Africa," *Christianity Today*, 8 January 2019, https://www.christianitytoday.com/news/2019/january/lamin-sanneh-died-world-christianity-islam-africa-yale.html.

8. Harrison Smith. "Lamin Sanneh – Pioneering Historian who Studied Christianity's Spread Dies at 76," 2019.

become pretty good at demanding all kinds of freedoms from other societies in which we find ourselves. At the same time, in countries where we are in the majority, not only are we theologically unable and unwilling to provide the same rights that we demand for ourselves in the new dominantly Western or Christian societies we live in but, often, from a political standpoint, we flatly refuse to do so. As Muslims we deny all sorts of fundamental human rights to people who live in our societies. We demand spaces in the trains that belong to others but refuse to let them get on when the trains belong to us.

Train Compartments, Seating, and the Territorialization of the Transcendent

I have referred to getting on and off a train a few times. That was not incidental. I want to use the analogy of a train to look at some of the issues concerning how we live in the world with each other and to consider the question of territoriality and hospitality, which is the central theme of our conference and of this book.[9]

The curious thing about traveling on most European trains, especially in the north, is that once passengers get on the train, the first thing they usually do is to find a seat – but not just the one that they sit on. If two adjacent seats are empty, they usually opt for the aisle seat and place their bags on the window seat. In most other situations, people typically choose a window seat because of the view, but these travelers choose the aisle seat in order to block any newcomer who wishes to occupy in that empty window seat. These travelers settle in only after they have carved out this space on the train. In doing so, they are free from potential invaders. Their bags act as objects of familiarity. While the presence of their bags may may provide some form of psychological comfort in a new space, they also act as barriers to block the foreign invader who may want to occupy what they now imagine to be their expanded space.

I have observed, in the European countries I have visited, that even when the train is full, a typical response is to remain glued to your mobile phone or headphones, blocking out the sounds around you, pretending that nobody needs the seat. And if they do need one, you remain unaware of it and so, it is not your problem. You keep hoping that this person getting closer and closer to your seat will go away and inconvenience another person – "not me!" He

---

9. Much of this analogy used in this keynote address was used in a previous conference presentation and published in German. See "Skepticism and Certainty," 258–74. The analogy is used as an anchor, and the different points drawn from it do not necessarily fit together.

or she can go to another compartment and walk the length of the train, but I will not remove my bag to give him or her a seat.

Now, of course, that traveler has no legal authority, or any authority for that matter, to occupy another seat. They have only paid for one seat. This scenario stands in sharp contrast to what happens in many parts of Africa or Asia, where it is not only considered exceptionally impolite to claim any space beyond your own but where sharing your seat with a second person is regarded as a common courtesy. There, if the earlier occupant of a seat makes no move to shrink his body and if the newcomer were to be told *Jagah nahin hai'* (Urdu for "There is no space"), the occupant would likely be rebutted with *Dil mai jagah hona chaihi hai!* (meaning, "There should always be a place in the heart!"). There are many times when the hearts are so big but the physical space is so limited that thousands are forced to make the journey either hanging on for dear life to the door handle with the wind embracing their bodies or perched on top of the train roofs, where they risk falling from mercifully slow-moving trains. Overcrowdedness resulting from large-heartedness has led to many a train crash, dispatching travelers to an earlier-than-scheduled encounter with their Lord and the beginning of their first stage of life in the hereafter.

Human beings created in the image of God are entities that go beyond just the biological that is driven by the survival instinct. A human being is not just a thing but a *mensch* – a person deeply aware of his or her personhood and also aware that this is intrinsically interwoven with the personhood of all others. *Ubuntu* is the term we often use in South Africa to refer to the notion that "I am a human being because you are." My humanness is relational, and I exist because you exist. Your *menschlichkeit* – your humanness – implies that when the train gets full, the human being will remove the bag on the seat.

In our "territorialization" or tribalization of God, we create an entity because of our need for comfort – forgetting that while our religious texts promise to provide us with solace, they do not promise to fulfill our hunger for power. This bag on the seat next to you also serves as your prison wall, a barrier between you and the other passenger that you do not want next to you. Inside your prison, you are afraid to open yourself to the smells of a foreigner or a stranger, to a noisy talker, or to somebody whose beliefs you may not like. You sit surrounded by your bag, and, in this case, you have got your God with you. You carry your God with you in your bag; you imprison your God, and, so, your God is now quite literally defined by all your baggage – your baggage as a male person who thinks that you live in authority over women; your baggage as a White person who thinks that you have to bring civilization to all the world; your baggage as . . . whatever. In reality, of course, it is not God who suffocates but our understanding of God that suffocates us and denies people around us territory. The passenger is no longer a being created in the image of God but God is created in the image of the passenger. This God is no longer *Akbar* (the Eternally Greater than); instead, He is a Muslim God, a Christian God, a bigot's God. He is a homophobe's God, a male God, a God who hates the Jews, Catholics, Muslims, Ahmadis – whoever is your favorite enemy of the day or of your generation.

Let me use a soccer analogy to make my point. Suppose Ghana plays Nigeria tomorrow, and you pray to God to give Ghana victory over the Nigerians. In that case, God becomes a little mascot dressed up in a Ghanaian flag to help us against the Nigerian enemy. Do we seriously think that God had anything to do with this border separating Ghana and Nigeria?

This is the madness of the territorialization our own faith, but more so of the territorialization of God. God becomes a Ghanaian. *Inna shirka la zulman azīm'* (this association with God is a terrible crime).

We see the logical conclusion of this theological trajectory of territoriality in what has been happening recently in Malaysia, where the Malaysians enacted legislation that the Chinese or the Hindus may not call God "Allah." However, the Chinese have been calling God "Allah" in the Malaysian language for many years, for centuries. In Pakistan, in the last thirty years or so, Muslims no longer say *Khuda hafiz'* but only *Allah hafiz'* because *khuda* is somebody else: the Persian God, or the Christian God; they say, "**Our God is a Muslim**."

God's Land for God's Chosen People

We confuse Christ's witness with a demographic game: Can we increase our numbers? How many people do you have? And it becomes a battle. We use numbers as a guise for being "commissioned" and then conflate this with the notion of being a chosen people; then comes the idea of a chosen land for a chosen people. In the Apartheid era, the White people had the Flag Anthem sung at all solemn national religious events.

> *Ons nasie se grondbrief van eiendomsland,*
>   *Uitgegee op gesag van die Hoogste se hand.*
> Our nation's deed of land ownership,
>   Given on the authority of the Hand of the Highest.

In other words, this announces that God gave us (that is, the White people) the land of South Africa, which is the confinement of God to a "chosen people." We also observe this attitude in the case of political Zionism in Israel. The whole Zionist idea is based on the notion that God has promised this land to the Jews. God is not only reduced to a real estate agent but, worse, to a dishonest, arbitrary, and tyrannical lord baron, a god who is reckless in his disregard for those like the indigenous South Africans and the Palestinians who have lived on that land for centuries. This was a God who parcels out land to his chosen as if these lands were registered in a twentieth-century title deeds office – all at a time thousands of years ago when national boundaries were vague – a vagueness that allows us to desire endless expansion – claiming an endless amount of seats on ever-expanding compartments.

God's People: *Din* and *Dayn'*

The question of territory and religion also hinges on language. For example, what does *din* (usually translated as "religion") mean in the earliest Arabic sense? It means "debt" and refers to the debt human beings owe to God – a debt settled by a lifelong commitment to obedience and responding to God's call. Thus, your religious life is a fulfillment of your indebtedness to God in awareness that you are in a state of returning to God, and your current responsibility and ultimate accountability is to him. This *din* is a transaction entered into with a transcendent being who is beyond your imagination or your conceptualization of this being.

How have we come to religionize *din* solely as organized religion? We now talk about faith as Baptists, Anglicans, Presbyterians, or Episcopalians; likewise, you have the Muslims, the Sunni Muslims, and the Shi'a Muslims. We interpret *din* entirely in the sense of a constructed train – trains like those in the Apartheid era, which had separate carriages for people of different ethnic groups, all of these socially constructed according to the White bureaucracy's definition.

In taking the word *din* away from its root *dayn'* (meaning "debt" – that is, indebtedness to the transcendent), we transfer it into a group, a class, or a club. In doing so, we simply do not care where our journey should lead us. Instead, we start worshiping our train compartments, turning them into golden calves. Moreover, even as we are unable or unwilling to make space for those whom we believe are – at some level – legitimate passengers, we still cannot find a place for them next to us. Just consider for a moment the way mainstream Sunni Muslims cannot find a seat for Shi'a Muslims, let alone smaller sects, on the Islam train. So, other than conflating the train with Destiny, we all alleviate our own statuses to being the sole owners of the train.

We must ask, "Who is this God, and what is his relationship to *din* and accountability?" The Qur'an describes this God as *Akbar*. However, this *Allahu Akbar* is wrongly translated as "God is the Greatest." The correct translation is "God is the eternally Greater Than"; God is more significant than our theological constructs or religious labels.

Pre-Seated Passengers: Understanding Ourselves

The entry of others on the train should be a moment for us to reflect on who we are. Our sense of self should never be so sedimented, so solidified, that we are unable to imagine our encounter with other passengers leading to the enrichment of ourselves and our society.

Leaving aside the more dramatic stories of the Spanish Inquisition, the Christian Crusades, the barbarous history of colonialism, and the unspeakable crimes of the Nazis in the Holocaust, we have other, more positive, narratives – for example, the enriching influence of Greek philosophy on Muslim culture; the Muslim contribution to science, physics, and maths, which became the foundation of much of the technological advancement of Western civilization – and also led to the construction of the first trains; the Jewish obsession with learning, which, even though its impulses might have been primarily the study of religious texts, led to an invaluable contribution to the intellectual development of Europe in numerous fields.

Our challenge as Muslims, once we have found a place on the Western train, is whether we are going to replicate the behavior of those people on the train and prevent others from coming onto the train in the way that they have prevented us from doing so. Are we are going to use the same kind of bigoted theology that they have used? Are we going to bring our baggage on the train, place it on the seat or seats next to us, and use it to prevent others from getting a seat?

Ownership or Stewardship? Where Is This Train Headed?

There are several further seriously challenging issues in this train analogy that I want to raise directly related to religion. As the Luxembourg authorities show us, with their free tickets for public transport, we are all guests on this train. All of us are guests of God – *wa illallahi turja'u al-umur, wa ilayhi 'l-maser* (to God is the return, to God is the journeying). When Muslims die, the first thing we say is *inna lillahi wa inna ilayhi raji'un* (we come from God, and unto God we are returning.) The text does not read "We *are going* to return to God" but, instead, "We are in a state of returning to God." God is the objective of a believer's life, and while this returning is not intended to be a path filled with thorns, neither is it one that we are expected to adorn with golden calves. We cannot carve out space to accommodate our unlimited fear of others or our greed that seeks to occupy more space than allocated to us or to consume beyond our needs.

The desire for a comfortable journey is only legitimate to an extent because comfort, if undefined and unrestrained, can be hugely problematic and has implications for others – not only for passengers, but also for ourselves and the only earthly home that we have ever had. There are even more significant challenges – beyond those of coexistence within our shared world – that reduce the crisis of territorialized compartment seats on the train to a primary school bun-fight over who gets to play first in the relatively small playground.

Where is this train headed? Other than the limited stops along the way, the train is heading for a crash because the drivers are sitting there with blinkers on. The environmental challenges of climate change and global warming stare humankind in the face – even as we have placed blinkers over our eyes. We are fighting over territory. Dear brothers and sisters, soon there will be no territory left at all for our children to inherit. Let me rephrase this: Soon there will be no children to inherit the earth. The earth will survive – about that, there is no doubt – but if we remain on our current trajectory, it is inevitable that humankind will be destroyed.

There is an urgent need to apply the brakes on our contestations for more territory and deal with our relationships with our home and with other sentient beings with whom we share this planet. The crisis we are facing has to do with where this train is going.

The question is not merely one of our own survival. Our survival depends on the survival of the other, just as the survival of the human race depends on the survival of the ecosystem. We have gone beyond the saying "No man is an island, entire of itself" to declaring that "no entity is an island unto itself." A vague and sentimental attachment to my clan, my religious group, my territory, or my community will not see us through this tough challenge that we are facing. There are many ways of dying. There is, however, only one way to live. And that is through discovering what the self and the other are really about, understanding how much of the other is reflected in us, and finding out what it is that we have in common in the struggle to create a world of justice and dignity for all the inhabitants of the earth.

In the words of Lamin Sanneh, "We are being summoned from the margins."

Bibliography

Aloysius, G. *Nationalism without a Nation in India.* New Delhi: Oxford University Press, 1997.

Esack, Farid. "Who Will I Allow on to the Train – and Enable to Sit Next to Me?" In *Freiheit im Angesicht Gottes – Interdisziplinare Position zum Freiheitdiskurs in Religion und Gessellschaft,* edited by Milad Karimi and Amir Dziri, 223–34. Freiburg: Kalam Verlag, 2015.

Kamali, Mohammad Hashim Kamili. *Freedom of Expression in Islam.* Cambridge: Islamic Texts Society, 1997.

Kunnummal, Ashraf, and Farid Esack. "Traveling Islamophobia in the Global South: Thinking Through the Consumption of Malala Yousafzai in India." *Journal for the Study of Religion* 34, no. 1 (2021): 1–25.

Saeed, Abdullah, and Hassan Saeed. *Freedom of Religion, Apostasy and Islam.* Burlington: Ashgate, 2004.

Smith, Harrison. "Lamin Sanneh – Pioneering Historian who Studied Christianity's Spread Dies at 76." https://www.washingtonpost.com/local/obituaries/lamin-sanneh-pioneering-historian-who-studied-christianitys-spread-dies-at-76/2019/01/13/9974781c-1747-11e9-8813-cb9dec761e73_story.html, 2019.

Biblical and Theological Themes

6

Territoriality and Hospitality in Our Understandings of Salvation

Daniel A. Madigan

I have not had any experience of Africa's territory south of the Sahara; nor, sadly, have I had the opportunity to experience its hospitality. Therefore, my exploration of the two themes of our conference will keep mostly to the realm of theology – particularly as the themes bear on our understandings of the religious other, especially on the question of the salvation of the other.

In his writing, Lamin Sanneh continually tried to break down the sense of Islam and Christianity as being separate, exclusive territories. The way he speaks of his conversion does not suggest an abandonment of Islam and an emigration away from it but, rather, a recognition in Christ of a deepening and an expansion – "a stupendous breakthrough," he calls it – of that same *missio Dei* that he had already recognized at work in the Islam into which he was born and within which he "came to God as a moral, ethical, and eschatological reality."[1] Sanneh bids Christians recognize in Muslims not competitors but fellow pilgrims.[2] Bishop Kenneth Cragg, one of the most venerable modern figures in Christian reflection on Islam, once remarked, "Our discussions of God are not domestic matters. Indeed, it is fair to say that where theology is the concern there are no outsiders."[3] That is to say, we are all in this together. Pilgrims do not control territory; as pilgrims, we are all in this together, and

---

1. Sanneh, "Muhammad," 169.
2. Sanneh, *Summoned from the Margin*, xiv.
3. Cragg, "Islamic Reflections," 103.

we have to rely on the help of others. We journey in the hope of enjoying the hospitality of God, who draws us to himself.

In this brief treatment of our themes, I hope to draw from our twin foci of territoriality and hospitality some lessons for Christian theology of religions, in particular for Muslim-Christian understanding. However, let me begin with a few geographic and political observations that might set up the theological question more clearly.

Even after the many declarations of independence during the last century, and even this century, Africa has not yet fully emerged from the depredations inflicted on it by the imperial powers who, from ancient times, have carved up its territory and despoiled its wealth. The human rivalry that played out on a global scale in the history of empires – and still does so today in forms sometimes less bloody, though perhaps even more oppressive – continues on a smaller scale between nations, tribes, language groups, and ethnicities; between herders and farmers; between military and civilians; and, in some places, between Muslims and Christians. One of the principal symptoms of this pandemic of human rivalry that has affected the world since time immemorial is the struggle for territory.

People often speak of the African continent as if it were a battleground between Islam and Christianity. Measurements of territory are taken, percentages of adherents estimated, historical rates of conversion calculated; and, based on these figures, a judgment is rendered about the strength, the appeal, the adaptability, or even the *veracity* of one tradition or the other. Sometimes, this judgment is even used to predict the outcome of what is seen as a worldwide struggle between our two traditions – quantify Islam and Christianity in Africa, we are told, and you will be able to predict the future global triumph of whichever is the "true religion."

This insinuation of demography into theology is perhaps even more damaging to human community than a geopolitical sense of territoriality. It gives rise to what we might call "soteriological territoriality" – the tendency to think of salvation as a matter of order and control, of authority and borders, of insiders and outsiders. We can recognize the strength of this notion of territoriality in both our traditions – for example, in the ideas of *dar al-islam* and *dar al-harb* or in the appeal to verses like Q 3:35: "And whoever desires a religion other than Islam, it shall not be accepted from him, and in the hereafter that person shall be one of the losers."

Among Christians, from as early as the third century, the strongly territorial maxim *extra ecclesiam nulla salus* (outside the church no salvation) has held sway – and for many, it still expresses the final word on the subject.[4] It is a saying that seems to have originated with and been further strengthened by a number of North African thinkers in the third century CE, beginning with Origen of Alexandria (d. 254) and, particularly, Cyprian of Carthage (d. 258). It is crucial to note that these early writers who adopted this idea that there was no salvation or safety outside the church lived at a time when Christians were still a persecuted minority. They used this maxim only in reference to other Christians whom they considered heretics and schismatics.[5] Given that the unity of the church was understood to be a unity of love, such people were judged to be guilty of a grave sin against charity. It was only later, as the Roman Empire became officially Christian, that the idea that there is no salvation outside the church was explicitly applied to pagans and Jews – by writers such as John Chrysostom (d. 407) in the East – and, later, to Muslims as well. The operative assumption was that the gospel had been proclaimed everywhere in the known world and, therefore, anyone who refused to accept it must be culpable of rejecting the divine call.

Returning to North Africa, *extra ecclesiam nulla salus* was given a harsher tone when used by Augustine of Hippo (d. 430) against the Donatists. However, it is worth remembering that the *extra ecclesiam* doctrine, which seems to have such a holier-than-thou air about it, was being invoked against the holier-than-thou Donatists – people who had separated themselves from a church they saw as morally and spiritually flawed because of the failure of some of its leaders to stand bravely against the persecutions of Diocletian in the fourth century. Thus, as used by Augustine, *extra ecclesiam* represented not a preening self-righteousness but, rather, the call to an ecclesial solidarity that does not scorn human weakness. Some of Augustine's harsher views on the question were not retained by the mainstream of later Christian tradition. However, the general assumption that all those who had freely chosen to remain outside the church had forfeited the possibility of salvation was retained.[6] Another North African bishop, Fulgentius of Ruspe (d. 533), expressed this conviction in the strongest possible terms, exhorting his readers to "most firmly hold and

---

4. For a fuller treatment of these matters, see Madigan and Sarrió, "Thinking Outside the Box," 63–119. See also Ruokanen, "Pre-Conciliar Catholic Views," 11–34.

5. In this respect, it is not unlike the sayings attributed to the Prophet of Islam about *fitna* and those who separate themselves from the *ummah*: "Whosoever removes himself from the *jamāʿa* by the space of a single span, withdraws his neck from the halter of Islam" (*Sunan Abii Dawud*, Book 35, No. 4740) and "Whoever dies after being separated from the *jamāʿa*, dies as people died in the *jahiliyya* – the time before Islam (*Sahih Muslim*, Book 20, No. 4555).

6. Sesboüé, *Hors de l'Église*, 67.

by no means doubt, that not only all pagans, but also all Jews, and all heretics and schismatics who die outside the Catholic Church, will go to the eternal fire that was prepared for the devil and his angels."[7]

In both our traditions, Muslims and Christians have often seen themselves as custodians – sometimes almost as owners – of the "territory" of salvation, maintaining the order we believe God commands, controlling the borders and limits we believe God sets, and enforcing the conditions God has imposed. At times, when religion has been united with political power, this has often meant forcing the outsiders to come within the confines of our religious "territory"; at other times, it has meant excluding and abandoning them as altogether beyond any possibility of being saved.

A major blow to the idea that everyone outside the church is damned came with the discovery of the Americas, with the voyages of exploration that took European Christians around the globe. Suddenly "outside" appeared as big, if not bigger, than "inside." If it were true that everyone was expected to believe in Christ in order to be saved, how could it possibly be the case that God would have left the bulk of humanity ignorant of his will for so long after the coming of Christ?[8] The groundwork for an answer to that question had already been laid by Thomas Aquinas (d. 1274).[9] In order to soften the condition of an *explicit* belonging to the church, Thomas appealed in two ways to what might be considered *implicit* belonging. First, he proposed that faith in God's providence *implicitly* included faith in everything that pertains to God's saving plan, including Christ as the one mediator of salvation. Second, he developed the idea of an *implicit* desire for baptism, that is for membership of the church. An *explicit* belief in God and a desire to do whatever God willed *implicitly* contained the desire to enter the church by baptism – even if that person had never heard of either Christ or the church.

The conversation developed over the succeeding centuries and – although it has never entirely been disavowed by the Roman Catholic Church in which it developed – it is clear that the old adage "outside the church, no salvation"

---

7. Fulgentius of Ruspe, *De fide seu de regula fidei ad Petrum* n. 80, quoted in Sullivan, *Salvation*, 43.

8. In his *Fayṣal al-tafriqa*, Ghazali considers a parallel problem from the Muslim side: what was the fate of those who did not embrace Islam? He admits that he held out hope that "most of the Christians of Byzantium and the Turks of this age will be covered by God's mercy," either because they lived so remote from Muslims that they would never even have heard the name of Muhammad or because, even though they might have heard of him, they only knew that he was said to be false prophet. These two groups will be excused for their failure to embrace Islam. See Jackson, *Boundaries*, 126.

9. Aquinas, *Summa Theologica*, IIIa q. 68.

has effectively been, we might say, "pensioned off." It is not at all difficult to find authoritative statements to the effect that there is indeed salvation outside the church. For example, in 1990, Pope John Paul II, writing about the missionary mandate of the church, had this to say:

> Since salvation is offered to all, it must be made concretely available to all. But it is clear that today, as in the past, many people do not have an opportunity to come to know or accept the gospel revelation or to enter the Church. The social and cultural conditions in which they live do not permit this, and frequently they have been brought up in other religious traditions. For such people salvation in Christ is accessible by virtue of a grace which, while having a mysterious relationship to the Church, does not make them formally part of the Church but enlightens them in a way which is accommodated to their spiritual and material situation. This grace comes from Christ; it is the result of his Sacrifice and is communicated by the Holy Spirit. It enables each person to attain salvation through his or her free cooperation.[10]

One way out of the rather territorial understanding of salvation – with its insiders and outsiders, and its clear boundaries – has been to exercise what we could call a kind of soteriological hospitality. Instead of condemning people as outsiders, we shrink the "outside" and treat most people as though they are honorary insiders. This is a common move in religiously plural situations, particularly in the West. It has become part of the culture in many places, and it seems to be a requirement of good citizenship to acknowledge the believing other as somehow "one of us." We recognize this move being made in other situations as well. Many Christians do this, as we have seen, by telling good people that they effectively belong to the church – even if those people do not particularly *want* to belong. It is thought to be high praise to say of some Muslims that they are "more Christian than we are." In doing so, however, such Christians are implying that what someone actually says they believe about God does not really count and that what they are *unknowingly implying* is a belief in Jesus Christ as savior. To use the technical term from the Roman Catholic tradition, we are saying they have "implicit faith."

Muslims do this in a slightly different way but with similar effect by telling people that they are *muslims* with a small *m* – that is, they are people who, in a generic way, submit to God. Or they are told that since, in qur'anic terms,

---

10. John Paul II, *Redemptoris Missio*, §10.

they "believe and do good works," they belong to the community of believers and can be considered to be in good standing with God.[11] These attempts at inclusion are not always welcomed by those who are thus included.[12]

The proponents of such inclusive theologies see themselves as being very hospitable and overcoming the exclusivism that has traditionally characterized our religions. However, they do not always recognize that even hospitality can be an exercise of power since the hosts effectively claim the territory as their own and expect guests to comply with certain conditions. Above all, the guests are expected to show gratitude for having been included and to behave politely, knowing their place.

Another alternative to the hegemonic territorial approach is a pluralist approach,[13] which takes two major forms. The first approach, hoping to avoid conflict, isolates difference and particularity into separate territories – a kind of balkanization. Although proponents of this approach think of themselves as very generous and accommodating, in the end, people are allowed to be themselves only in isolation; they can shape their own religious, cultural, and political space according to their beliefs but must not impinge on others. The second pluralist approach usually avoids being territorial, but it does so at some cost. A favorite image invoked by the pluralists is of religions as the differing paths people take going up the same mountain – paths that will all eventually lead them to the same sought-after summit. However, we are not simply travelers greeting one another briefly as we cross paths, exchanging tales of the adventures of our separate journeys. Rather, we inhabit together a single human ecosystem. A pluralist society cannot simply be a society with a patchwork of separate religious communities, like individual states, each with its own separate understanding of the divine and the human, each with its sovereign independence and the right not to be questioned. We share one human ecosystem. What one person or group believes about race or about slavery or gender or ethnicity or war and peace, or health and well-being has

---

11. This pairing of terms is regularly used in the Qur'an. See, for example, Q 2:82; 5:9; 7:42; 10:9; 18:30; 19:96; 29:7; 42:26.

12. Here I am using the rough threefold division that has become commonplace in discussing theologies of religion: exclusivism, inclusivism, and pluralism. This schematization, which was initially proposed by Alan Race (see Race, *Christians and Religious Pluralism*), was given more complex development, particularly by Paul Knitter (see Knitter, *Introducing Theologies*), and examined most searchingly by Gavin D'Costa (see D'Costa, *Theology and Religious Pluralism*, and D'Costa, *Christianity and World Religions*).

13. The major figure in the development and defense of pluralist theologies of religion has been John Hick. See Hick, *God Has Many Names*; Hick, *Religious Pluralism*; Hick and Knitter, *Myth of Christian Uniqueness*.

an effect on all society. We do not live isolated human lives. Because our beliefs affect everyone, we have to be accountable to one another.

Most of us now recognize that with regard to the state of our natural environment, we have both a right and a duty to call each other to account for the ways we live – how we drive and fly, where we smoke, the ways we generate power, mine and drill, produce food, and dispose of our waste. Similarly, we have a right and a duty to call each other to account for the ways we treat one another – the attitudes we adopt, the way we speak to one another, the injustices in which we are involved, sometimes unknowingly, and our respect of the rights of others who have a claim on us.

This calling to account is certainly not just a case of the majority ruling or the traditional culture of dictating to others. Majority cultures and religions are only too ready to challenge minorities and newcomers. The majority's culture is presumed to be universal. They reject difference as unnatural and as a threat, and they tend to respond to criticism and questioning with a love-it-or-leave-it arrogance. However, the majority is just as much in need of challenge as anyone else, which is also something we have learned from our reflection on the environmental crisis. Dominant cultures have to be open to challenge and change as a result of encounters with different insights into the nature of human relationships. Such engagement with each other is a long and complex process that requires patience and humility. A pluralism that simply separates or denies difference rather than engaging with it sells short our common humanity.

These questions remain: Is there a way of avoiding altogether the rivalry that comes from being territorial? Is there a way of understanding hospitality that does not involve owning and controlling a territory into which we invite others under certain conditions?

As Muslims and Christians, our shared fundamental belief in God as creator should make us constantly alert to the fact that we are guests in God's space. Humanity has a long history of laying claim to what really belongs to God and treating it as our own. Even though our very existence is a gift of God, we begin, quite early in life, to convince ourselves of the grand lie that we are self-sufficient and self-made. We carve up God's earth and pretend to be its proprietors. We mark out religious spaces and define them as the space of salvation, the safe space, the space that we control on God's behalf. "Religion" is always at risk of becoming just one more instrument of human rivalry, particularly when it maps onto territory. We see this increasingly in the so-called culture wars and identity politics of traditionally Christian-majority areas like Europe and the United States. Perhaps one sees it in parts of Africa as well.

The meaning of being guests in God's space could be expressed using the qur'anic concept of mutual satisfaction: "God will be well-pleased with them and they will be well-pleased with Him."[14] One says of the great figures of Islamic tradition who are now deceased, "*Raḍiya Allāhu 'anhu* [or *'anhā*]" – by which one expresses the hope that God may be pleased with that person. This mutual satisfaction is augmented with an image of divine hospitality in gardens prepared for the faithful, "wherein they will abide forever" (Q 9:100). This eternal enjoyment of God's gracious hospitality is referred to as "the supreme triumph," and those who enjoy such hospitality are described as *al-muflihun*, the successful (Q 58:22). One is reminded of the song of the angels at the announcement of the birth of Jesus: "Glory to God in the highest, and on earth peace among those with whom he is pleased [εὐδοκίας]" (Luke 2:14 ESV), words echoed later on by the divine voice who declares Jesus the Son in whom "I am well pleased [ἐν σοὶ (ἐν ᾧ) εὐδόκησα]" (Matt 3:17; 17:5; Mark 1:11; Luke 3:22).

We could also think of the qur'anic notion of "turning" (*taba, tawba*, and *tawwab*). God turns toward us, and believers are turned toward God.[15] It is a question of *orientation* rather than territory – the question is not what space we are occupying but what direction we are facing. For a Christian, it is what Paul calls being "in Christ." Being in Christ is not a synonym for being in Christendom. In Jesus Christ, God definitively turns toward the world in love even though the world may continue to turn away. In Jesus Christ, humanity is turned definitively toward God.

However, to be turned toward God is also to participate in God's turning toward the world that God loves. Again, even though Christians speak of this as being "in Christ," it is not a question of marking out an exclusive space or controlling access to it; rather, it is a question of two inseparable orientations – one toward God, in response to God's love, and the other toward the world, as an expression and extension of God's love. To be "in Christ" is certainly to be situated with relation to that historical event in which Christians see God and humanity turned toward one another in a defining way. Yet we might almost say that this is a situatedness that does not take up space and does not jostle for position or try to push others out. Salvation, in this context, is not so much

---

14. Q 9:100. See also Q 58:22.

15. The noun *tawba* is usually translated "repentance." However, this word is also applied to God's eliciting and acceptance of human repentance. Thus, there is a mutual turning to one another. *Al-Tawwab* is a name of God – often translated as titles like the "Oft-Returning" or the "Acceptor of repentance."

being in a defined "rescue area" but, rather, being oriented in love. In Greek and Latin – the languages in which Christians first discussed these questions – the words for "salvation" (*salus* and *soteria*) were also the words for "health" and "healing" not only for "rescue." To be saved is to be in a healthy or, perhaps even better, a *healed* relationship with God and with the rest of God's creation.

Recognizing this truth frees us to acknowledge that there are people who, despite inhabiting a different religious "territory" or wearing a different religious "label," are oriented the same way as we try to be. They are oriented to what Christians would call the reign of God or the kingdom of God. Although such people might not recognize this truth themselves, an attentive Christian eye will not be able to deny that they are *de facto* configured to the humanity of Christ – whether in their suffering of injustice without retaliating, in their patient forgiving, in their constant concern to heal, in their gracious generosity, in their humble service, or in their willing obedience to God. They are oriented and configured not by creedal propositions or religious laws but by their flesh-and-blood living. After all, flesh and blood was the language, if we can call it that, in which Christians believe God chose to express God's Word – God's self – in a defining way in our history. Flesh and blood is, if you like, the sacred language of Christianity; in Jesus, we hear and see and touch God's Word (1 John 1:1) that is expressed in a flesh-and-blood life like our own. The only way we, in turn, can truly proclaim that Word is in that same flesh-and-blood language. We have heard that truth, and we try to remain attuned to it and, in turn, to speak it. Therefore, we will also be able to recognize others who have heard the Word because we hear them "speaking" it in their own flesh-and-blood living. Lamin Sanneh constantly challenged Christians to recognize in the generosity, humility, courage, loyalty, modesty, and humility of Muslims – all qualities based on imitation of the Prophet – something of the same impetus and energy of God that Christians would say was at work in a preeminent way in Jesus Christ.[16]

The important difference between this recognition of a common orientation and the supposed hospitality of an inclusivist view is that here we do not set ourselves up as the hosts. We are fellow pilgrims, recipients of God's hospitality, neither of us controlling the space but both of us positioned and oriented by God. We do not minimize what we hear as only being *implicit* in the propositions to which other believers subscribe. Rather, we recognize and resonate with what is being said *explicitly* in their body language. Christian

---

16. For a presentation of the various writings in which Sanneh explores this theme, see Tieszen, "Muhammad as a Signpost," 133–42.

theology has long been convinced that even prior to the coming of Christ, there were those who knew and witnessed to his truth. Experience teaches us that after Christ's coming, too, there are people who show that they know that truth in their very flesh even though they do not or cannot associate it with the name of Jesus. Perhaps the difficulty they experience in linking what they know of the truth of divine love and mercy with Jesus, the crucified one, is a result of the way Christians have turned the cross of Christ into a battle standard where territory is at stake – whether in medieval crusades or in contemporary culture wars. We have used Jesus to mark out a privileged territory rather than allowing him to orient us toward the reign of God that he preached and that he inaugurated in his own living.

Bibliography

Aquinas, Thomas. *Summa theologica*. Translated by Fathers of the English Dominican Province. New York: Benziger Brothers, 1911–1925.

Cragg, Kenneth. "Islamic Reflections in Contemporary Theology." *Duke Divinity School Review* 31 (1966): 99–112.

D'Costa, Gavin. *Christianity and World Religions: Disputed Questions in the Theology of Religions*. Chichester: Wiley-Blackwell, 2009.

———. *Theology and Religious Pluralism: The Challenge of Other Religions*. Oxford: Blackwell, 1986.

Hick, John. *God Has Many Names: Britain's New Religious Pluralism*. London: Macmillan, 1980.

———. *Problems of Religious Pluralism*. London: Palgrave Macmillan, 1985.

Hick, John, and Paul Knitter, eds. *The Myth of Christian Uniqueness: Toward a Pluralistic Theology of Religions*. Maryknoll: Orbis Books, 1988.

Jackson, Sherman A. *On the Boundaries of Theological Tolerance in Islam: Abū Ḥāmid al-Ghazālī's Fayṣal al-tafrīqa bayna al-islām wa al-zandaqa*. Studies in Islamic Philosophy 1. Karachi: Oxford University Press: 2002.

John Paul II. *Redemptoris Missio: On the Permanent Validity of the Church's Missionary Mandate* (1990). http://www.vatican.va/content/john-paul-ii/en/encyclicals/documents/hf_jp-ii_enc_07121990_redemptoris-missio.html.

Knitter, Paul. *Introducing Theologies of Religions*. Maryknoll: Orbis Books, 2002.

Madigan, Daniel A., and Diego R. Sarrió. "Thinking Outside the Box: Developments in Catholic Understandings of Salvation." In *Religious Perspectives on Religious Diversity*, edited by Robert McKim, 63–119. Leiden: Brill, 2016.

Race, Alan. *Christians and Religious Pluralism: Patterns in the Christian Theology of Religions*. London: SCM, 1983.

Ruokanen, Miikka. "Pre-Conciliar Catholic Views On Non-Christians." In *The Catholic Doctrine of Non-Christian Religions according to the Second Vatican Council*, edited by Miikka Ruokanen, 11–34. Leiden: Brill, 1992.
Sanneh, Lamin. "Muhammad, Prophet of Islam, and Jesus Christ, Image of God: A Personal Testimony." *International Bulletin of Missionary Research* 8, no. 4 (October 1984): 169.
———. *Summoned from the Margin: Homecoming of an African*. Grand Rapids; Cambridge: Eerdmans, 2012.
Sesboüé, Bernard. *Hors de l'Église pas de salut: histoire d'une formule et problèmes d'interprétation*. Paris: Desclée de Brouwer, 2004.
Sullivan, Francis A. *Salvation Outside the Church? Tracing the History of the Catholic Response*. New York: Paulist, 1992.
Tieszen, Charles. "Muhammad as a Signpost for Fellow Pilgrims: Lamin Sanneh and Christian Appreciation of the Prophet's Biography." In *The Christian Encounter with Muhammad: How Theologians Have Interpreted the Prophet*, 133–42. London: Bloomsbury, 2021.

7

Islam and the Secular State

Reflections on the Work of Abdullahi Ahmed an-Naʻim

David Marshall

In this essay, I will discuss the work of Abdullahi Ahmed an-Naʻim – a Sudanese Muslim scholar who has taught law at Emory University, USA, for many years – with particular attention to his arguments for the necessity (on Islamic grounds) of a secular state. I will first focus on key aspects of an-Naʻim's thought before offering some comments on his proposals and some reflections from a Christian perspective.

A key point in an-Naʻim's formation is that he was a devoted disciple of the controversial thinker Mahmoud Mohamed Taha. Taha was committed to the ideal of Muslims and non-Muslims living together as equal citizens of the same state. But he believed that it was not possible to achieve that goal so long as Muslims accepted the traditional approach to the Qur'an, which accords to the second stage of the Qur'an (what we could call the Medinan paradigm) final authority over the first stage (the Meccan paradigm). Taha argued that Muslims must admit frankly that because the Medinan paradigm requires Muslims to fight non-Muslims and come to power over them, it is not compatible with the equal rights of all human beings. So, Taha proposed a radical solution, which, as far as I am aware, is unique in the history of Islamic thought.

Taha argued that rather than the Medinan paradigm, it is the Meccan paradigm – in which Muhammad lived peacefully (for his part, anyway) alongside unbelievers, having received no command from God to rule over them – that is the heart of the Qur'an, its eternal message, with abiding authority.[1] The Meccan parts of the Qur'an teach the equality of all people.[2] What then did Taha say of the Medinan parts of the Qur'an? He regarded them as having been genuinely revealed by God but only as a temporary measure that was required by the challenges of establishing Islam in a hostile environment. In Taha's view, the fullness of God's purpose was for the Meccan paradigm to be established, and the time was now right for this to happen. Taha's bold approach sought to overturn the traditional Islamic theory of abrogation (*naskh*), and he was explicit about the need for this revolution. He did not diplomatically ignore or tinker with the Medinan paradigm; instead, he insisted on a principle of reverse abrogation that elevates the Meccan paradigm to a position of greater authority than the Medinan paradigm. Crucially, this move is a way of setting to one side the requirement in Medinan passages that Muslims should fight non-Muslims and come to power over them. This reverses the traditional Muslim approach to the Qur'an – in which, when there are contradictions in its practical teachings, the later Medinan verses abrogate or supersede the earlier Meccan parts. Thus, it has been the Medinan paradigm that has had the decisive role in shaping Islamic practice, including Islamic political theory. For teaching these ideas, Taha was executed in 1985 by the Sudanese authorities as an apostate – that is, one guilty of having abandoned Islam.

Following Taha's execution, his movement was banned, his books were burned, and advocating his views became a capital crime. An-Naʿim left Sudan the same year and, thereafter, developed his scholarly career in the USA. In 1990, he published *Toward an Islamic Reformation*, which gives a lucid account in English of the complex, mystical ideas that Taha had written in Arabic. An-Naʿim's book has much in common with other modernist or reformist Muslim works, at least in terms of the kind of social order that is being advocated. What makes it unique is its use of Taha's approach to reform based on reverse abrogation and its argument that modernist reformists were generally avoiding the elephant in the room – that is, the fact that democracy, the secular state, human rights, international law, and so on were all completely incompatible with the Medinan paradigm and the principles of shariʿa derived from it. An-

---

1. For Taha's exposition of these ideas, translated from Arabic into English by an-Naʿim, see Taha, *Second Message*.

2. Though beyond the focus of this essay, it is interesting to note that Taha argues that, in contrast to the Medinan paradigm, the Meccan paradigm upholds the equality of men and women as well as of Muslim and non-Muslim. See an-Naʿim, *Islamic Reformation*, 52.

Na'im criticizes the superficiality and evasiveness he sees in much of modernist Islam's engagement with the Qur'an. He argues that Islam is compatible with pluralist, tolerant, democratic societies, but only if Muslims deal honestly with the different paradigms of political power within their scripture.

How were an-Na'im's ideas received? Western academic circles showed considerable interest – see, for example, the foreword to an-Na'im's book by John Voll of Georgetown University. But even among reform-minded Muslim scholars, there has so far been little evidence of willingness to embrace the key idea of reversing the theory of abrogation. However attractive, and indeed urgent, one might find an-Na'im's vision, it is nevertheless important to grasp why Muslims might reject it. From the beginnings of Islam, Muslims have understood the Qur'an in a clear, linear way that by the end of the Medinan period works through to Muhammad's triumph. The triumph of Islam in Medina has therefore typically been seen by Muslims as Islam's God-given glory and not just a temporary arrangement required by the circumstances of that time. Islam came to bring to the world the harmonious and just order decreed by God. The Medinan polity was Muhammad's crowning achievement, and it cannot be edited out of Islam.

Years later, in 2008, an-Na'im published another book, *Islam and the Secular State*. Here, he pursues the same essential goal as in the earlier book – offering Islamic grounds for the secular state – but even though he makes clear his continuing preference for the methodology proposed by Taha, he now turns to other arguments.[3] His memorable opening sentence reads, "In order to be a Muslim by conviction and free choice, which is the only way one can be a Muslim, I need a secular state."[4] An-Na'im emphasizes that his project is profoundly religious. He is not asking Muslims to abandon their religion in order to live equally with non-Muslims in secular societies. Rather, he argues that it is only in a secular state that Muslims are free to be Muslims voluntarily and, therefore, sincerely. From the very first paragraph, an-Na'im stresses that he is not opposing shari'a but, rather, arguing for the proper context for its free observance, which, he says, "cannot be coerced by fear of state institutions or faked to appease their officials."[5] The alternative – which is living under pressure to conform to Islam – "promotes hypocrisy . . . which is categorically and repeatedly condemned by the Qur'an."[6] So, here, an-Na'im offers religious

---

3. An-Na'im, *Islam and the Secular State*, 2.
4. An-Na'im, 1.
5. An-Na'im, 1.
6. An-Na'im, 4.

arguments for the secular state, emphasizing that true religious practice must be marked by freedom, sincerity, and the avoidance of hypocrisy. It is notable that these are arguments that focus more on the conscience of the individual believer than on the cohesion of the believing community.

Muslims who argue for the creation of Islamic states tend to understand secularism in one simple way as the exclusion of religion from public life. In contrast, an-Naʿim insists that secularism does not have to be like that. He acknowledges that while there have been authoritarian secular states – like Ataturk's Turkey – there is also the kind of secular state that is not hostile to religion showing itself in public life and even acting as a motivation in politics. This kind of secular state acts as an honest broker, negotiating between different religions and preventing any one religion imposing itself over others. Islamist attacks on secularism tend to engage in simple (one might say, simplistic) black-and-white polemics in which secularism is nothing but godlessness, with which Muslims cannot compromise.[7] In contrast, an-Naʿim frequently admits that his project is complex and involves challenging negotiations. In particular, he touches on the "difficult distinction between the state and politics," arguing for the separation of Islam and the state but not of Islam and politics.[8] Along with Christians and others, Muslims will inevitably be inspired by their religion to seek to influence politics. But they must not – as Islamists would generally encourage them to do – seek to take over or control the state in the name of Islam.

An-Naʿim also argues that serious study of the history of Islam supports his case over against that of Islamist promoters of the Islamic state. An-Naʿim recognizes that although religious and political authority were combined in one person in Muhammad's case, this was a unique, unrepeatable occurrence. Ever since Muhammad, Islam has involved a difficult negotiation between individuals and institutions expressing religious authority and individuals and institutions expressing political authority, with of course some crossover. So, for an-Naʿim, the kind of difficult negotiation of the place of religion in a secular state that is necessary in the modern world is simply a continuation of what Muslims have always had to do. In contrast, he insists, along with many other commentators, that the idea of an Islamic state is something genuinely

---

7. For a selection of relevant texts by Sayyid Abu l-Aʿla Mawdudi (1903–1979), an extremely influential Islamist thinker, together with a brief introduction and commentary by Abdullah Saeed, see Marshall, *Tradition and Modernity*, 115–32. A PDF of this volume, which also includes an-Naʿim's essay "Freedoms of Speech and Religion in the Islamic Context" can be downloaded from https://berkleycenter.georgetown.edu/projects/the-building-bridges-seminar.

8. An-Naʿim, *Islam and the Secular State*, 4.

new in Islam; this political concept is not part of the Islamic tradition and, ironically, in view of Islamist contempt for the West, derives mainly from modern European ideology, with sinister fascist undertones.[9]

I turn now to some comments on an-Naʿim's thinking, starting with some reflections from a general perspective before turning to questions that might arise for Christians engaging with his ideas.

An-Naʿim may be right about his ideal of Muslims living faithful lives in secular states having better grounding in Islamic history than the Islamist vision of the Islamic state. However, it is natural to ask how his arguments are being received today. Even though *Islam and the Secular State* was published only fifteen years ago, it is worth reflecting on whether any discernible pattern has emerged in recent years that indicates the direction in which the nations of the Muslim world are moving. In his book, an-Naʿim offers case studies of secularism and Islam in three different contexts: India, with Muslims as a minority in a secular state, and Turkey and Indonesia, which are states with Muslim majorities and different kinds of secular traditions.[10] Back in 2008, an-Naʿim appeared cautiously optimistic about the prospects for the flourishing of the secular state in Turkey and Indonesia. At that time, President Erdogan seemed to be achieving a reasonable balance between allowing religion more of a role in public life and respecting Turkey's secular traditions. I suspect that most observers who shared an-Naʿim's hopes at that time have felt growing disappointment about developments in the years since then, not just in Turkey and Indonesia but also, for example, in Malaysia and Pakistan, where the Islamization of the state has advanced. In such contexts, Christians and other non-Muslims, as well as some Muslim minorities, are under increasing pressure.

However, pessimistic observations of this kind could be criticized for taking far too short-term a view of history and overlooking the long and tortuous processes of political development in, for example, the nations of Europe. We should also beware of concluding that recent movements away from secular principles in nations such as Turkey or Pakistan are all related to issues internal to Islam. There is not enough space here to ask the important balancing question of whether the pattern is different, and perhaps more encouraging, elsewhere in the Muslim world, recognizing that any grand overarching theory in this field is likely to break down at certain points. Furthermore, we must acknowledge developments outside the Muslim world, noting, for example, that India, too, has recently been moving toward greater identification of the

---

9. An-Naʿim, 7.
10. An-Naʿim, chs 4–6.

state and the dominant religious tradition – in its case, Hinduism – resulting in increasing pressure on its religious minorities, particularly Muslims. Muslim minorities also suffer in other contexts. In some Western nations, too, liberal secular ideals are under pressure and on the retreat; and in many parts of the world, religious minorities are feeling increasingly vulnerable. Globally, there is a growing reluctance to engage in the "difficult negotiations" that An-Naʿim describes as the core work of secular states. Developments in the Muslim world must be seen both in terms of debates within Islam but also in the wider global context.

Keeping in mind the context of the Muslim world today as we consider an-Naʿim's passionate defense of the compatibility of Islam and the secular state, it is hard not to see a clear contrast between the likely progress of the two different approaches he has developed to promoting the case for the secular state among Muslims. With regard to his most controversial idea, reverse abrogation, at present, it is hard to see this approach gaining significant support among other Muslim thinkers. In contrast, it is easier to see the possibility of progress being made by his other arguments, as set out in *Islam and the Secular State*. In An-Naʿim's own mind, it is the radical approach of reverse abrogation that will enable Muslims to get to the heart of the religious questions that they must ultimately address if they are to achieve genuinely Islamic resolution of the challenges they face. For now, however, it is easier to see the appeal of an-Naʿim's other arguments, emphasizing "conviction and free choice," particularly to younger Muslims who are disillusioned with experiments in the Islamization of society and who demand a political order in which they are free to be or not to be Muslim – as they choose and in the ways they choose.

It is also worth noting here that the debate around Islam and the secular state to which An-Naʿim has contributed is not just a simple contest between views such as his and Islamist ideas of the type mentioned earlier. For example, Michaela Quast-Neulinger has explored the striking contrast between An-Naʿim's enthusiastic support for the secular state and liberal citizenship with Talal Asad's "severe critique of liberal citizenship as an exclusivist mechanism, particularly hostile against Muslims in Europe."[11] An interesting new argument in this field insists that Muslims should not be striving for any version of the modern nation-state, whether Islamic or secular, because the nation-state per se is a modern development that is profoundly at odds with fundamental principles of Islam and, arguably, is on its last legs anyway. Wael Hallaq and Ovamir Anjum have both argued powerfully that Muslims should look neither

---

11. Quast-Neulinger, "Believing and Belonging?," 167.

to Mawdudi nor to An-Naʿim for guidance but, rather, should aim for a quite different political reality – the revival of transnational Islamic governance uniting all Muslim-majority societies. Anjum expresses this vision explicitly in terms of a call for a renewed caliphate.[12] It would be fascinating to be a fly on the wall at a seminar involving a discussion between Hallaq, Anjum, and an-Naʿim of their different visions for the future of Islam.[13]

I conclude with some reflections on An-Naʿim's work from a specifically Christian point of view, looking first at his approach to the contrast between the Meccan and Medinan paradigms. In some of his writings, Anglican bishop and scholar of Islam Kenneth Cragg (1913–2012) argues that Muslims today should prioritize Mecca over Medina; and at least on one occasion, Cragg expresses support for the approach of Taha and an-Naʿim.[14] This is an understandable Christian response. After the long centuries of Christendom, a fairly broad, though not universal, Christian consensus has emerged around a somewhat similar argument that has been variously expressed in different strands of the Christian tradition. Christians now tend to accept that when Christianity is imposed by force, or even just by social pressure, this involves a corruption of the faith, at the heart of which stands the revelation of God in the crucified and risen Jesus. Coercion cannot truly serve the purposes of that kind of Christlike God and cannot ultimately bring about the kind of human flourishing willed by such a God.[15] So, when Christians read a proposal for Muslim engagement with politics that prioritizes Muhammad the powerless Meccan preacher over Muhammad the powerful Medinan prophet, statesman, and warrior, they sense a resonance with their own convictions and are tempted to say, with Cragg, "Amen to that!" However, Cragg has been robustly criticized by Muslim scholars for seeking to Christianize and depoliticize Islam by commending

---

12. Hallaq, *Impossible State*; Anjum, "Who Wants the Caliphate?," Yaqeen Institute for Islamic Research, 31 October 2019.

13. There are many other intra-Muslim discussions related to the debate around Islam and the secular state which it has not been possible to explore here: for example, the relationship between the categories of "*dhimmis*" and "citizens," and the development of a "*fiqh* (jurisprudence) of minorities" relevant to Muslims living as minorities in, for example, Europe.

14. Cragg, *Am I Not Your Lord?*, 215.

15. The point is made famously in the Vatican II document *Dignitatis Humanae*, 11: "In the end, when He completed on the cross the work of redemption whereby He achieved salvation and true freedom for men, He brought His revelation to completion. For He bore witness to the truth, but He refused to impose the truth by force on those who spoke against it. Not by force of blows does His rule assert its claims. It is established by witnessing to the truth and by hearing the truth, and it extends its dominion by the love whereby Christ, lifted up on the cross, draws all men to Himself." Second Vatican Council, *Dignitatis Humanae*, 11.

the "Mecca over Medina" formula to Muslims today.[16] This is a problematic approach. Indeed, Cragg once told me that he realized that for him to endorse a particular type of Muslim reformism could be the "kiss of death," meaning that such reformism could be discredited by the very fact that it was being commended by a Christian bishop rather than by the scholars of Islam.

I face a dilemma in responding to An-Naʻim on this question of Mecca over Medina. I respect the clarity and courage of his writing. I believe he has raised a fundamental issue and that he is right in stating that Muslims sometimes make vague or historically implausible claims about the compatibility of the Medinan polity and the ideals of contemporary pluralist democracies. But I can also see why the reverse abrogation theory is so unacceptable to the great majority of Muslims. It is, perhaps, as difficult for Muslims to accept this theory as it would be for Christians to accept the prioritization of the Old Testament over the New Testament for their faith and practice today.

We come here to an important question about how Christian scholars of Islam – as well as Christians more generally and, in particular, Christian leaders and commentators – can appropriately position themselves in relation to contemporary debates among Muslims. Of course, Christians and others have a justified interest in debates about the place of non-Muslims in Muslim-majority societies, and Christians may legitimately lend political support to those Muslims whose policies strike them as most likely to lead to a just society. They also do well to take an interest in the intricacies of important intra-Muslim debates. However, even though Christians can legitimately point to the implications for them and other minorities of different interpretations of Islam, they cannot determine what is and is not authentically Islamic. In the end, Muslims have to resolve among themselves how they understand their faith and its application today.

Finally, turning from An-Naʻim's use of Taha's reverse abrogation theory to his different, more pragmatic, arguments in *Islam and the Secular State*, it seems to me that here An-Naʻim sets out an approach that is easier for Christians to endorse and work with. This does not mean that Christians have to take the view that this is "the correct Islamic account" of how Muslims should approach politics. Rather, Christians can simply recognize that while there are a wide range of Muslim approaches to politics, here is an approach with which they find considerable common ground and which provides a promising basis on which to work together. I find An-Naʻim impressive in his account of the

---

16. See Lamb, *Policy of Hope*, 119–22, 168–70. Shabbir Akhtar engages extensively with Cragg on these matters; see, for example, Akhtar, *Final Imperative*, 18–40.

"difficult negotiations" involved for Muslims, Christians, and others as they work out how to share the spaces in which we live alongside each other in God's world. I am moved by the vision that he has crafted out of suffering and long reflection. I respect the clarity and courage of this Muslim scholar who is passionate about his own religious identity but also seeks to make space for the freedom of others. He has set an example to follow.

Bibliography

Akhtar, Shabbir. *The Final Imperative: An Islamic Theology of Liberation*. London: Bellew, 1991.

Anjum, Ovamir. "Who Wants the Caliphate?," Yaqeen Institute for Islamic Research, published 31 October 2019. https://yaqeeninstitute.org/ovamiranjum/who-wants-the-caliphate/.

An-Naʿim, Abdullahi Ahmed. *Islam and the Secular State: Negotiating the Future of Shariʿa*. Cambridge: Harvard University Press, 2008.

———. *Toward an Islamic Reformation: Civil Liberties, Human Rights, and International Law*. Syracuse: Syracuse University Press, 1990.

Cragg, Kenneth. *Am I Not Your Lord? Human Meaning in Divine Question*. London: Melisende, 2002.

Hallaq, Wael B. *The Impossible State: Islam, Politics, and Modernity's Moral Predicament*. New York: Columbia University Press, 2013.

Lamb, Christopher A. *A Policy of Hope: Kenneth Cragg and Islam*. London: Melisende, 2014.

Marshall, David, ed. *Tradition and Modernity: Christian and Muslim Perspectives*. Washington, DC: Georgetown University Press, 2013.

Quast-Neulinger, Michaela. "Believing and Belonging? No Belonging for Believers? A comparative study of Talal Asad's and Abdullahi Ahmed An-Naʿim's discussions of Muslims and their (non-)belonging in the secular liberal state." In *Islam et appartenances*, edited by Michel Younès et al., 167–80. Paris: L'Harmattan, 2020.

Second Vatican Council. *Dignitatis Humanae* (1965). https://www.vatican.va/archive/hist_councils/ii_vatican_council/documents/vat-ii_decl_19651207_dignitatis-humanae_en.html.

Taha, Mahmoud Mohamed. *The Second Message of Islam*. Translated by Abdullahi Ahmed An-Naʿim. Syracuse: Syracuse University Press, 1987.

8

Muslim Minorities in Non-Muslim Lands

A Comparison of the Suwarian Tradition with the Approach of Tariq Ramadan

F. Peter Ford, Jr.

One of the most prominent features of Islam is the way in which religion must be expressed in the social and political spheres of life as well as in private devotional life. This is so often highlighted by Muslims and non-Muslims alike that it hardly needs to be pointed out here. But this public dimension of Islam carries with it certain assumptions that many Muslims have often taken for granted. Throughout their history, most Muslims have normally been able to freely practice their faith in the public arena because they have lived in a society that is both majority Muslim *and* under Muslim rule. Of course, in certain times and places, Muslims have occupied territory in which most of the people were not Muslim. But as long as Muslims exercised political and military hegemony over that area – which, along with other Muslim-majority, Muslim-controlled territory was often designated as *dār al-islām* (the abode of Islam) – the Muslim minority enjoyed full support in expressing their faith unless they belonged to a group that was deemed heretical. And, in most cases, conversion to Islam in those areas eventually resulted in a Muslim-majority population.

The situation in which Muslims reside in territory that is not Muslim-governed – traditionally designated as *dār al-ḥarb* (the abode of war) – has generally been regarded as a kind of aberration. Yet the fact that some Muslims throughout Islamic history have lived in areas not under Muslim rule has forced Muslim scholars to address this reality. This chapter first offers an overview of the diverse approaches that have been proposed regarding Muslim minorities in non-Muslim contexts. It then examines a particularly interesting but often overlooked case from medieval West Africa, whose theological-legal framework is known as the "Suwarian tradition." Next, consideration is given to a contemporary approach to this issue by Tariq Ramadan, a Swiss scholar of Egyptian background. Finally, the chapter notes some parallels between the Suwarian tradition and Ramadan's ideas and concludes with a brief Christian reflection.

The primary argument here is that today's situation of Muslims living in a non-Muslim environment – which is often infused by a secular mindset – is a reality that ought to be affirmed by Muslims as part of the process of globalization and population migration. By taking a proactive approach to the matter, as exemplified in both the Suwarian tradition and Ramadan's thought, Muslim scholars should help make the circumstances of these Muslims both a positive and productive life experience. In this way, such Muslims can also interact respectfully and constructively with their Christian neighbors, who often encounter a similar need to engage directly with their non-Christian context.

Diverse Muslim Views regarding Muslim Minority Contexts

The situation of some Muslims finding themselves living in a non-Muslim context has been a reality throughout Muslim history – even from its very inception, according to Muslim sources such as the earliest *Sīra* (biography of Muhammad) by Ibn Ishaq. Prior to the Hijra (the migration from Mecca to Medina) in 622 CE, Muhammad and the young Muslim community faced a great deal of opposition, and even persecution, in Mecca. This led to an event which is often cited as the first example of a positive Christian-Muslim interaction – namely, the migration to Abyssinia, often called the "First Hijra." Although Muhammad himself remained in Mecca under the protection of his uncle Abu Talib, several dozen Muslims were sent by him in approximately 615 CE to the realm of the Christian king in Axum, where they received temporary hospitality and refuge; eventually, virtually all these Muslims returned to the Hijaz.[1]

Following the Hijra to Medina and the establishment of the community (*umma*) under Muhammad's leadership, the Qur'an presents a different perspective, emphasizing in several passages "the principle that all Muslims are obligated to perform migration" to Medina.[2] Furthermore, Q 4:97–100 – a passage that became especially important to later jurists dealing with the matter – portrays Muslims who had died being criticized by angels for not choosing to migrate when they were "oppressed in the land" where they had lived.[3] Nevertheless, it is recognized in the Qur'an that a number of the faithful had chosen to stay in Mecca rather than emigrate, while converts in more remote areas also remained where they were. Although normally they could not expect any protection from the Medinan community, Muhammad was obligated to assist them if they appealed to him for help because of their situation.[4]

Similarly, the Hadith literature includes material that is not always consistent. Several passages require Muslims to migrate to Muslim-controlled territory and forbid Muslims to dwell among unbelievers. Abu Dawud, for example, conveys these words of Muhammad: "I disavow any Muslim who settles among the *mushrikīn* [polytheists]" and "Whoever mixes with the *mushrikīn* and settles among them is one of them."[5] However, other passages – found in the collections of Abu Dawud, al-Nawa'i, and others – indicate that the obligation to migrate no longer applied following the conquest of Mecca and that it was "better to live under a ruler who is just (though not Muslim) than a Muslim ruler who is unjust."[6]

Subsequent discussion among Muslim jurists and theologians also led to diverse opinions. At first, the issue was deliberated hypothetically, on the assumption that Muslims living under non-Muslim rule would naturally prefer to migrate to Muslim domains.[7] As time passed, scholars needed to address the reality of Muslims residing in lands such as China and India that lay outside Muslim control. Starting in the late eighth century, some

---

1. Guillaume, *Life of Muhammad*, 146–53.
2. Abou El Fadl, "Legal Debates," 130, referring to Q 2:218; 4:89; 4:100; 8:72; 16:41.
3. Abou El Fadl, "Legal Debates," 131; Shavit, "Europe," 372.
4. Q 8:72; Abou El Fadl, "Legal Debates," 130; Nasr, *Study Quran*, 500–501.
5. Shavit, "Europe," 372; see also Abou El Fadl, "Legal Debates," 131.
6. Abou El Fadl, "Legal Debates," 131.
7. Abou El Fadl, "Legal Debates," 133.

Muslim territory fell into non-Muslim hands, and this sometimes involved large numbers of Muslims – for example, Sicily in the eleventh century.[8] The Spanish *Reconquista* of the twelfth to the fifteenth centuries and the Mongol invasion of the thirteenth century intensified this theological and legal debate among Muslim scholars.[9]

The Maliki school of law was the most adamant in forbidding Muslims to dwell in non-Muslim lands even for the purpose of trade. Hanafi and Hanbali jurists generally disapproved of Muslims living under non-Muslim control but allowed for temporary or even permanent situations in which Muslims could live and engage in trade and other activities as long as they could practice their religion freely. The Shafiʿi school tended to be the most open, granting some value to minority Muslim residence in non-Muslim lands because of the hope that converts could be won over through Muslim witness.[10] A key issue in the debate was one's interpretation of "*dār al-islām*" – while many simply presumed that it implied Muslim political and military sovereignty, others suggested that the concept could be extended to cover areas wherever Muslims were in the majority or wherever shariʿa could be practiced.[11] In any case, the dominant view was that all Muslims, wherever they lived, were obligated to observe Islamic law.[12] Muslims who contravened the law while residing in non-Muslim territory could even be prosecuted once they entered an area under Muslim control.[13]

In the modern period, Muslim scholars have begun to take a more pragmatic approach, recognizing the extensive Muslim migration that has taken place in recent decades, especially to non-Muslim Western countries. A number of factors – not least, the economic and political challenges present in their Muslim-majority home countries – has led to such migration. These Muslims establish families, who often remain in their adopted countries for several generations, becoming citizens and contributing to the common good of their new context.[14] In an effort to provide a degree of legitimacy and

---

8. Abou El Fadl, "Legal Debates," 132; Abou El Fadl, "Islamic Law," 145.

9. Abou El Fadl, "Islamic Law," 145; Shavit, "Europe," 372.

10. Shavit, "Europe," 372–73; Abou El Fadl, "Legal Debates," 133–36.

11. Abou El Fadl, "Legal Debates," 142; Abou El Fadl, "Islamic Law," 183–84.

12. The complexities surrounding the question of whether a Muslim should remain under non-Muslim rule or emigrate to Muslim-ruled territory, along with the ultimate obligation of following Islamic law in any case, can be observed in the writings of the Hanbali scholar Ibn Taymiyya; see Ibn Taymiyya, *Muslims under Non-Muslim Rule*, 11–27.

13. Abou El Fadl, "Legal Debates," 146–47.

14. Shavit, "Europe," 373.

religious assistance to these minority Muslim groups, scholars have developed a relatively new branch of Islamic jurisprudence: *fiqh al-aqalliyyāt al-muslima*, meaning "the religious law of Muslim minorities."[15] Many of these arguments invoke as a precedent the First Hijra to Abyssinia. Some scholars – for example, Yusuf al-Qaradawi – see migration almost as a religious duty so as to spread the truth of Islam, noting that many of the emigrants to Abyssinia remained there even after the main Hijra to Medina.[16] Others – for example, those from the Saudi Wahhabi school – view the First Hijra as expedient only because Abyssinia was less evil at that time than Mecca. This group claims that modern Muslims may thus migrate to non-Muslim lands when necessary but must avoid integrating into the religiously inferior way of life in those countries.[17] Still others encourage Muslim integration into the social structure of the non-Muslim context so that they might contribute to its welfare – in much the same way as the Muslims of the First Hijra did for the Abyssinians. Although such migration may eventually result in conversion to Islam, this should not necessarily be its primary motivation.[18] While this diversity of views regarding Muslim minorities living in non-Muslim lands is striking, it is clear that Muslim scholars have taken this issue seriously and that they consider this an important debate in the contemporary world.

The Suwarian Tradition

Although both historically and in present times Muslim scholars have given considerable attention to the question of Muslim migration and residence in non-Muslim territory, a fascinating case that originated in medieval West Africa has been virtually completely overlooked. The "Suwarian tradition," as it is generally called, seems to be a paradigm highlighted exclusively by non-Muslim scholars.

As early as the eleventh century, Muslim merchants from the Sahel region of West Africa were migrating southward to the non-Muslim forest areas along the Atlantic coast, primarily to conduct a trading enterprise in gold.[19] These merchants – along with other Muslim professionals associated with them – became known as the "Juula" (also spelled "Dyula"), a name that referred

---

15. Shavit, 371–72.
16. Shavit, 377–78.
17. Shavit, 380.
18. Shavit, 384.
19. Wilks, "Juula," 93–94; Robinson, *Muslim Societies*, 55.

primarily to their specialized activity as Muslim traders rather than to any specific ethnic identity.[20] Traditional Maliki law, which was – and still remains – the dominant school in the Sahel, forbade such migration and settlement since these areas were considered part of *dār al-ḥarb*. Nevertheless, various Muslim scholars sought to legitimize their business by allowing such trade while also seeking to restrict actual contact between the Muslim merchants and non-believers.[21] In fact, large numbers of these merchants settled in the coastal areas where traditional African religious practices dominated. While remaining true to their faith and practice as Muslims, they took local wives and, in many ways, integrated into the social life of their hosts. In addition, some of the Juula were professional clerics who served as religious leaders and advisers for the mercantile class.[22]

Over time, the Juula developed a theological-legal framework for living as a Muslim minority within their non-Muslim context. This became known as the Suwarian tradition. In addition, a clerical brotherhood that promulgated this approach became known as the Jakhanke.[23] Both groups attributed the source of their guiding principles to an obscure figure known as al-Hajj Salim Suwari (often spelled Suware). Even the century in which Suwari lived is widely disputed. Some scholars place him in the twelfth or thirteenth century, according to the records of the Jakhanke clerics.[24] Others insist that – based on his apparent dependence on the major Qur'an commentary known as *Tafsir al-Jalalayn* that was completed by Jalal al-Din al-Suyuti in 1495 – he must have flourished in the late fifteenth to early sixteenth centuries.[25] In any case, Suwari was known among his many followers as a very pious scholar, who completed the pilgrimage to Mecca many times. While generally following the teachings of traditional scholarship, he also promoted his own more developed

---

20. The Juula (Dyula) have been especially researched by Wilks, "Juula," 93–115, and Launay, *Beyond the Stream*, 78–103. See also the summaries in Robinson, *Muslim Societies*, 55–58; Clarke, *West Africa*, 34, 81–82, 215–18; and Trimingham, *History of Islam*, 31, 143–44, 187–88.

21. Wilks, "Juula," 95–96.

22. Wilks, 94.

23. The Jakhanke – discussed in Clarke, *West Africa*, 34–37, 81 – have been well presented by Sanneh in *Beyond Jihad*, 80–116, and *Crown and the Turban*, 37, 42, 214–15; these writings summarize his earlier book *The Jakhanke Muslim Clerics*, which is devoted to this subject (but largely unavailable today). Sanneh traces his efforts to research this group in his autobiography, *Summoned from the Margin*, 197–205.

24. Sanneh, *Beyond Jihad*, 81; followed by Clarke, *West Africa*, 35, 73 n. 7.

25. Wilks, "Juula," 97; followed by Launay, *Beyond the Stream*, 79, 234 n. 2, and Robinson, *Muslim Societies*, 56, 59.

views. According to Wilks, although Suwari adhered to the Maliki school for most legal opinions, "in matters of Quranic exegesis, [he] followed al-Suyuti, who was a Shafiʿi. He found the latter's relatively liberal attitudes toward non-Muslims congenial."[26] In fact, Wilks suggests that Suwari acquired a copy of *Tafsir al-Jalalayn* on his return from one of his pilgrimages,[27] although Sanneh contests that "this claim has no corroboration in contemporary sources."[28]

Whatever Suwari's time period and connection to *Tafsir al-Jalalayn*, he has had many devoted followers among both the Juula and Jakhanke of West Africa up to the present day, and his tomb in Mali continues to be venerated by his followers.[29] In addition, both groups trace the essence of the Suwarian tradition back to its namesake. Robinson summarizes this approach as follows: "Muslims must nurture their own learning and piety and thereby furnish good examples to the non-Muslims who lived around them. They could accept the jurisdiction of non-Muslim authorities, as long as they had the necessary protection and conditions to practice the faith."[30]

Wilks, based on his own research among present-day leaders of the Juula in West Africa, provides a more detailed outline of the Suwarian tradition, consisting of the following seven points:[31]

1. Unbelief (*kufr*) among the non-Muslims is the result of ignorance (*jahl*), not wickedness; therefore, the condition need not be permanent.

2. Some people should remain in *jāhiliyya* longer than others, according to God's design for the world. (*Al-jāhiliyya* is the formal term used by Muslim historians to refer to the situation of paganism in Arabia prior to the prophethood of Muhammad.)

3. True conversion (to Islam) can only occur in God's time; active proselytism may actually interfere with God's will.

4. Militaristic jihad against unbelievers for the purpose of conversion is unacceptable; this is permissible only for self-defense, when unbelievers threaten the Muslim community.

---

26. Wilks, "Juula," 97.
27. Wilks, 97.
28. Sanneh, *Beyond Jihad*, 81.
29. Wilks, "Juula," 97–98; Sanneh, *Crown and the Turban*, 37; Sanneh, *Summoned from the Margin*, 205.
30. Robinson, *Muslim Societies*, 56.
31. Wilks, "Juula," 98.

5. The authority of non-Muslim rulers can be accepted by Muslims, and they can even support it as long as the Muslims are allowed to follow their way of life according to the sunna (example) of the Prophet.

6. Muslims must present a good example (*qudwa*) to the non-Muslims so that when God's time for conversion comes, emulation (*iqtidā'*) can take place – that is, the non-Muslims will be encouraged to emulate the Muslims.

7. Thus, Muslims must observe the shari'a carefully, through study and practice, so that they can provide a good example.

Wilks concludes that Suwari "thus formulated a praxis of coexistence such as to enable the Juula to operate within lands of unbelief without prejudice to their distinctive Muslim identity, allowing them access to the material resources of this world without foregoing salvation in the next."[32]

Robinson notes how the non-Muslim rulers and people around them respected the Muslims by welcoming them and considering them legitimate members of their society. The non-Muslims would even seek *baraka* (blessing) from the Muslims, especially through their "demand for amulets produced by [Muslim] clerics for their 'pagan' hosts."[33] And a few Muslims were even granted privileged status as advisers to the king.[34] Meanwhile, Suwari's teachings were passed on through the generations from master to student, whereby each new student acquired *ijāza* – a license to teach – and would trace his authority back to Suwari through a recognized *isnād* (chain of transmission).[35] Over the centuries, as both the Juula and the Jakhanke migrated, Suwari's principles spread among various groups throughout much of West Africa.[36]

An especially well-documented example is the Juula community that thrived in the Asante kingdom of Kumasi (in modern southcentral Ghana) during the eighteenth and nineteenth centuries.[37] When the English statesman Joseph Dupuis visited Kumasi in 1820, he found the Muslims there to be "wealthy and influential. . . . They lived close to the palace and thus to the deliberations of the king."[38] On the one hand, they "made an attempt to

---

32. Wilks, 98.
33. Robinson, *Muslim Societies*, 56.
34. Robinson, 57–58.
35. Wilks, "Juula," 98; Sanneh, *Beyond Jihad*, 90.
36. Wilks, "Juula," 98–104; Sanneh, *Beyond Jihad*, 91–111.
37. Robinson, *Muslim Societies*, 124–38; Wilks, "Juula," 104–6; Clarke, *West Africa*, 175–78.
38. Robinson, *Muslim Societies*, 128.

eradicate certain un-Islamic practices for the most part by peaceful persuasion, and even refused to obey the king when they believed it was against their principles."³⁹ On the other hand, they offered "prayers for the well-being of the Asante nation and its non-Muslim king, and even for his ancestors."⁴⁰

The Suwarian tradition thus provides a rich legacy that promotes peaceful coexistence for Muslims living and working in non-Muslim surroundings. Although many of the seven points above focus on Muslim witness that might eventually lead to the conversion of non-Muslims, the emphasis of that witness is on deeds rather than words, and it is implemented in an atmosphere of tolerance and respect. Indeed, aggressive proselytism is forbidden as being not only unproductive but also irreligious (see point 3 above). Overall, this tradition continues to be followed in West Africa today; yet it seems that Muslim scholars elsewhere who seek to promote similar views have not availed themselves of this particular heritage.

The Approach of Tariq Ramadan

Although numerous modern Muslims offer various perspectives regarding Muslim minorities in non-Muslim lands (see the first section above), a contemporary scholar who has dealt extensively with this issue is Tariq Ramadan (b. 1962). Ramadan's approach is especially interesting for our study since many of his ideas and practical suggestions are very similar to what is found in the Suwarian tradition. Although Ramadan was born in Geneva and has retained Swiss citizenship, his Egyptian background highlights the reality of Muslim minorities in the West. It is a well-known fact – and one that is often used against him – that Ramadan's maternal grandfather was Hasan al-Banna, the founder of the Egyptian Muslim Brotherhood. Furthermore, his father was an ardent member of that same group and was expelled from Egypt by Gamal Abdel Nasser. Yet Ramadan studied liberal arts and earned a degree in French literature along with his study of Arabic and Islam. He went on to teach religion and philosophy at Swiss universities, eventually accepting a position at Oxford University.⁴¹

---

39. Clarke, *West Africa*, 177.
40. Wilks, "Juula," 105.
41. Joseph A. Kéchichian, "Ramadan, Tariq Said," Oxford Islamic Studies Online, accessed 22 July 2020, http://www.oxfordislamicstudies.com/print/opr/t236/e0914; Kamrava, *New Voices*, 65–66. See also Ramadan's own biographical comments in the interview of him by McRoy, "European Muslim," 30–34.

Ramadan has drawn from his multinational heritage to address the challenges facing Muslims living in Europe, especially immigrants and their families. He understands the problem of establishing one's identity – whether Muslim or European – and advocates that both identities can be simultaneously affirmed. This approach has led to considerable controversy about Ramadan. On the one hand, traditional Muslims often claim that Ramadan has abandoned Islam – as they did, for instance, when he called for a moratorium against the harsher aspects of Islamic law such as stoning and the death penalty and advocated a greater role for women in the mosque[42] – while reformist Muslims maintain that his approach is only partial and "does not go beyond long-established norms."[43] On the other hand, non-Muslim critics accuse him of duplicity in his calls for reform, asserting that these are little more than a Salafist agenda "under cover of a thin veneer of scholarly respectability."[44] This negative image has been exacerbated by recent charges of rape against Ramadan, who was imprisoned in France for ten months during 2018 and is still awaiting trial; meanwhile, he was recently convicted of rape in Switzerland.[45]

Nevertheless, Ramadan's literary legacy incorporates a powerful call to Muslims living in the West to develop a positive approach to their situation in the midst of the challenges of a secular environment. His primary works deal with two key interconnected themes: (1) the reform of Islam, based on the traditional sources of the Qur'an and Hadith literature, whose principles are appropriately adapted and, indeed, transformed for the modern world;[46] and (2) the legitimate role that Muslims should play within contemporary Western societies.[47]

Ramadan sees two main challenges for Muslims living as minorities in Europe and, by extension, in other Western countries: (1) the lure of secularism,

---

42. Wilson, "Ramadan's Radical Reform," 42–44.

43. Abu Zayd, *Reformation*, 92.

44. As observed by Wilson, "Ramadan's Radical Reform," 44, who especially refers to the book *Brother Tariq* by the journalist Caroline Fourest. See also the critical perspective of Carle, "Tariq Ramadan," 58–69.

45. "Tariq Ramadan Charged in France over Rape Allegations," *BBC News*, 2 February 2018, https://www.bbc.com/news/world-europe-42925424; "Swiss Scholar Tariq Ramadan Released from French Jail," *The Local* (Switzerland), 17 November 2018, https://www.thelocal.ch/20181117/swiss-scholar-tariq-ramadan-released-from-french-jail; Aurelien Breeden, "Renowned Scholar of Islam Is Convicted of Rape in Switzerland," *The New York Times*, 10 September 2024, https://www.nytimes.com/2024/09/10/world/europe/tariq-ramadan-rape-conviction.html. See also Ramadan's personal website, https://tariqramadan.com/english/.

46. Ramadan has especially addressed the issue of Islamic reform in Ramadan, *Radical Reform*. See also Ramadan, *Challenges of Modernity*, 155–98.

47. Kamrava, *New Voices*, 65.

which entices them to assimilate completely into Western society, resulting in a loss of Muslim identity and leaving them without moral values; and (2) the pressure of a "puritanical" Islam, which sees itself as being in complete contrast to Western society and promotes isolation from the public sphere.[48] Since he sees no fundamental conflict between the values of Islam and those that underlie Western civilization, Ramadan strives to enable European Muslims to participate as full members in Western society while simultaneously affirming their Muslim identity.[49] While these themes and concerns are present in some form or another in virtually all his writings, they are especially developed in two of his major works: *To Be a European Muslim* and *Western Muslims and the Future of Islam*.

A central argument in these books has to do with the proper Muslim perspective of non-Muslim society and the Muslim's vocation within that society. Ramadan is clearly dissatisfied with the traditional two-tiered approach of *dār al-islām* and *dār al-ḥarb*. Such concepts, he claims, are not found in the Qur'an or the "Sunna" (that is, the Hadith literature which incorporates Muhammad's sunna); rather, they are the human constructs of later Muslim scholarship dealing with the world as they envisioned it. Furthermore, he notes the situation in classical Islam that was mentioned above – that the criteria for defining each "abode" do not always follow consistent definitions. The classification of a particular region might be based on population, land ownership, government, or laws.[50] Given this lack of clarity, it is possible that "the description of *dar al-islam* [could be] applicable to almost all Western countries" today.[51] Indeed, if the criterion of safety and security is considered, then, according to some Muslim scholars, "Muslims are sometimes safer in the West – regarding the free practise of their Religion – than they are in Islamic countries."[52] The possibility of a third "abode of treaty" (*dār al-'ahd*), as proposed by al-Shafi'i and applied to a nation that has signed an agreement of peace with a Muslim country, does not solve the problem. Used today, such a term would be "more a description of a 'war-free situation' than an adequate definition of an 'area where Muslims live.'"[53]

---

48. Wilson, "Ramadan's Radical Reform," 33; Rippin, *Muslims*, 326.

49. Kamrava, *New Voices*, 65; Rippin, *Muslims*, 326.

50. Ramadan, *European Muslim*, 123–27; Ramadan, *Western Muslims*, 63–66; Ramadan, "Islam and Muslims," 160–61.

51. Ramadan, *Western Muslims*, 66.

52. Ramadan, *European Muslim*, 127.

53. Ramadan, *Western Muslims*, 67. See also Ramadan, *European Muslim*, 127–28.

Instead, Ramadan coins a new term, *dār al-shahāda* – "the abode of testimony"[54] or, as he variously calls it elsewhere, "the area" or "the world" or "the space" of testimony.[55] This of course refers, in part, to the pronouncement of the *shahāda* or the Muslim creed, as required by the first pillar of Islam: *lā ilāha illā allāh, muḥammad rasūl allāh* (which means, "There is no god but God, Muhammad is the messenger of God"). This frequent and sincere pronouncement establishes the Muslim's identity before God, self, and the world. But it also fulfills the qur'anic injunction that Muslims are to "bear witness [to their faith] before humankind" (Q 2:143).[56] Ramadan elaborates on this concept using six points:[57]

1. Reciting the *shahāda* provides the basis for a Muslim's sense of identity as a Muslim – one who accepts and believes God's revelation and is a full member of the *umma*, the community of Muslims worldwide.

2. The *shahāda* also provides the basis on which all the other pillars – prayer, almsgiving, fasting during Ramadan, and the pilgrimage to Mecca – can be performed with integrity.

3. The concept of *shahāda* implies that Muslims should not be prevented from affirming their Muslim identity and should be allowed to perform all the regulations required by their faith.

4. This concept also stipulates that Muslims are people who respect all of God's creation and all other human beings and are people who demonstrate "absolute faithfulness to agreements, contracts, and treaties that have been explicitly or silently entered into."[58]

5. Muslims are called upon to bear witness to their faith, presenting and explaining what Islam is all about. This incorporates the concept of *da'wa* – "invitation" or "mission."

6. Living out *shahāda* includes both verbal witness and witness through good deeds. "To bear the *shahada* means to be engaged in society in every area where a need makes itself felt. . . . It also means being

---

54. Ramadan, *What I Believe*, 51.
55. Ramadan, *Western Muslims*, 77; Ramadan, *European Muslim*, 149.
56. Ramadan, *Western Muslims*, 73. The translation of Q 2:143 is Ramadan's, including the words enclosed in square brackets. See also Ramadan, *European Muslim*, 149–50.
57. Ramadan, *Western Muslims*, 74–75; Ramadan, *European Muslim*, 146–47. See also the summary in Wilson, "Ramadan's Radical Reform," 38.
58. Ramadan, *Western Muslims*, 74.

engaged in the process that might lead to positive reform, whether of institutions or of legal, economic, social, or political systems, with the aim of introducing more justice."⁵⁹

Ramadan builds on these points regarding *dār al-shahāda* in several ways. In the first place, he says that this means that Muslims should not feel alienated in the place where they live but should affirm their country as their own. "Wherever a Muslim, saying [the *shahāda*], is in security and is able to perform his/her fundamental religious duties, he/she is *at home* for the Prophet taught us that the whole world is a mosque."⁶⁰ Furthermore, this concept means being fully involved in one's non-Muslim community and contributing to it as fellow citizens. Muslims should "establish places of real encounter, dialogue, and commitment 'together' in the name of values held in common by virtue of sharing a citizenship lived in an egalitarian fashion."⁶¹

Such participation in this kind of context eliminates any notion of militant jihad. Instead, Ramadan advocates *jihād al-nafs* (the struggle of the soul or self), which manifests itself both spiritually and socially.⁶² This kind of lifestyle is only possible when Muslims emphasize personal faith and piety. "Ramadan's primary concern is for individuals (and communities) to take their faith seriously. It is not enough to slavishly imitate others; intelligent personal choices must be made."⁶³ In sum, says Ramadan, if Muslims "are really with God, then their life must be a *testimony* to a permanent involvement and an infinite self-sacrifice for social justice, the welfare of mankind, the environment, and all forms of solidarity."⁶⁴

There remains, however, a lingering question regarding what expectations a life of *shahāda* might imply, particularly in relation to the fifth point above. Ramadan states that this concept includes the idea of *daʿwa*, which could be

---

59. Ramadan, *Western Muslims*, 74–75.

60. Ramadan, *European Muslim*, 144 (italics Ramadan's). Ramadan does not provide a reference, but he clearly has in mind statements in the Hadith literature such as "The (whole) earth has been made a mosque (or a place of prayer) and a means of purification for me, so wherever a man of my ummah may be when the time for prayer comes, let him pray." Sahih Bukhari, 335, "Holy Quran and Sahih Hadith," 18 July 2010, https://muslimsnation.wordpress.com/2010/07/18/whole-earth-is-mosque/. See also Ramadan, *Western Muslims*, 70–71; Ramadan, "Islam and Muslims," 162–63; and Ramadan, *What I Believe*, 52.

61. Ramadan, *Western Muslims*, 157; see his full discussion on pages 144–71. See also Ramadan, *European Muslim*, 162–79; and Ramadan, *What I Believe*, 35–45.

62. Ramadan discusses the concept of jihad at length in *Challenges of Modernity*, 59–69. See also Ramadan, *Western Muslims*, 113–20; and Ramadan, *What I Believe*, 111, 115.

63. Wilson, "Ramadan's Radical Reform," 35.

64. Ramadan, *European Muslim*, 150 (italics Ramadan's).

understood as proselytism. Here we recall that Yusuf al-Qaradawi, among others, advocates migration to non-Muslim lands as being incumbent on Muslims so as to lead non-Muslims to the faith of Islam. This assertion is based partly on the narrative of the First Hijra to Abyssinia, where many of the Muslims remained even after the Meccan Muslims migrated to Medina. In *To Be a European Muslim*, Ramadan also invokes the First Hijra as an example of Muslims living peacefully in a non-Muslim environment and contributing to its welfare.[65] However, in another book covering the life of Muhammad, in which the First Hijra is recounted at length, Ramadan also claims that the Negus (that is, the Abyssinian king) affirmed the Muslims' belief in the same God and recognized similar aspects of his religion and that, "subsequently, the Negus converted to Islam and remained in continuous contact with the Prophet Muhammad."[66]

In light of this, Wilson raises a legitimate question: "Does *dār al-shahāda* presume eventual conversion to Islam?"[67] There can be no doubt that Ramadan affirms Islam as *the* true revelation of God, seeming to make him essentially a religious exclusivist. However, Ramadan disavows that his approach involves "a disguised form of proselytism.... Converting people ... is the province of God, who alone holds the key to people's hearts."[68] Although the concept of *daʿwa* "is a matter of bearing witness," it should be conducted through an interreligious dialogue that seeks "to engage one another for a more humane, more just world, closer to what God expects of humanity."[69]

Furthermore, Wilson – pointing to Ramadan's more recent work, *The Quest for Meaning* – concludes that, ultimately, Ramadan accepts religious diversity as a fact of life that positively impacts society. Encounters with each other on equal terms need not remove or disregard the honest differences that will remain. But such encounters can and ought to enhance the multireligious community as well as each person within it – including Ramadan himself.[70] In Ramadan's own

---

65. Ramadan, *European Muslim*, 168.

66. Ramadan, *Footsteps*, 62. The *Sira* of Ibn Ishaq gives a brief account of how Muhammad, toward the end of the Medinan period, sent letters to various leaders of neighboring kingdoms inviting them to accept Islam. The later historian Abu Ja'far al-Tabari added significantly to this account, with reports on how each leader responded. According to him, upon reading his letter, the Negus replied, "I have surrendered myself through him [Muḥammad] to the Lord of the worlds.... O apostle of God, ... I bear witness that what you say is true." Guillaume, *Life of Muhammad*, 657–58.

67. Wilson, "Ramadan's Radical Reform," 40.

68. Ramadan, *Western Muslims*, 153.

69. Ramadan, 208. See also Ramadan, *What I Believe*, 87.

70. Wilson, "Ramadan's Radical Reform," 41.

words, "The point is not to *integrate* systems, values and cultures with other systems, values and customs, but to determine – in human terms – spaces of intersection where we can meet on equal terms. The intersection of what we have in common, rather than the integration of difference."[71]

Conclusion and Christian Reflection

In the midst of diverse Muslim opinions regarding the status and role of Muslim minorities living in non-Muslim lands, the parallels between the Suwarian tradition and Tariq Ramadan's concept of *dār al-shahāda* are striking. Although Ramadan, much like other contemporary Muslim reformists, seems unaware of the Suwarian tradition so honored by West African Muslims, it is very likely that he would affirm its tenets as outlined above. Both approaches acknowledge the legitimacy of the minority situations in which, for various reasons, many Muslims find themselves. Furthermore, both recognize that such situations can actually be advantageous for all concerned. Yet both the Suwarian tradition and Ramadan appreciate the challenges inherent in such minority contexts: on the one hand, the temptation to set aside aspects of one's faith or practice, even to the point of assimilating to the non-Muslim environment; on the other hand, the natural reaction of retreating into one's own religious ghetto and isolating oneself from non-Muslim contamination. In order to counter these challenges effectively, both approaches call on Muslims to develop lives of piety and faithfulness to the Islamic heritage as found in the Qur'an and Hadith literature so that they can thrive spiritually in a context that might otherwise inhibit Muslim commitment.

Yet both the Suwarian tradition and Ramadan go further than mere Muslim self-preservation. In both approaches, Muslims in a minority situation are called upon to engage with their non-Muslim community and to participate in its everyday life and culture to the extent that their Islamic identity allows. In renouncing militant jihad while affirming various forms of *jihād al-nafs*, Muslims can contribute positively as fellow citizens to the social and spiritual well-being of the non-Muslim society around them. Furthermore, according to both approaches, minority Muslims have the responsibility to bear witness to their faith by word and deed. Though they may be glad for any conversions to Islam that take place, Muslims need not worry about making converts, leaving that matter to God and the conscience of their non-Muslim neighbors.

---

71. Ramadan, *Quest for Meaning*, 24 (italics Ramadan's).

Instead, they can affirm their multireligious context as something positive in its own right.

Muslim scholars and religious leaders today would do well to promote such values and do all they can to support Muslims who find themselves living in a non-Muslim environment. There is little point in trying to reverse the process of globalization or attempt to prevent Muslim migration to countries where Muslims can earn a much more decent living or join family members who are already there. Appropriate instruction and encouragement by Muslim teachers will help to build up the spiritual resources of these Muslims and enable them to accommodate themselves to their challenging context without straying into either assimilation or isolation. Muslim leaders and laity can work together proactively to enhance not only the spiritual fervor of the Muslim community but also the welfare of the land in which they reside.

Meanwhile, Christians who take *their* faith seriously can easily recognize several aspects of both the Suwarian tradition and Ramadan's *dār al-shahāda* that resonate with their own sense of a responsible Christian expression in a non-Christian environment. Both these approaches seem to approximate the concept of Christians being "in the world but not of it" (see John 17:14–18). Christians ought to be ready to commend their Muslim neighbors who are serious about living out their own faith in a mature and conscientious manner. In so doing, Christians should develop relationships across the religious divide that can foster understanding and trust. This can enable sincere Christians and Muslims to work together for the common good, to bear a mutually respectful witness to their faith, and to jointly address issues of justice and peace within the wider community to which both religions speak. In this way, both communities can exemplify the teachings of their respective scriptures: "Live wisely among those who are not believers, and make the most of every opportunity. Let your conversation be gracious and attractive so that you will have the right response for everyone" (Col 4:5–6 NLT) and "If God had so willed, He would have made you one community, but He wanted to test you through that which He has given you, so race to do good: you will all return to God and He will make clear to you the matters you differed about" (Q 5:48, Abdel Haleem translation).

Bibliography

Abdel Haleem, M. A. S., trans. *The Qurʾan: English Translation and Parallel Arabic Text*. New York: Oxford University Press, 2010.

Abou El Fadl, Khaled. "Islamic Law and Muslim Minorities: The Juristic Discourse on Muslim Minorities from the Second/Eighth to the Eleventh/Seventeenth Centuries." *Islamic Law and Society* 1 (1994): 141–87.

———. "Legal Debates on Muslim Minorities: Between Rejection and Accommodation." *Journal of Religious Ethics* 22 (1994): 127–62.

Abu Zayd, Nasr. *Reformation of Islamic Thought: A Critical Historical Analysis*. Amsterdam: Amsterdam University Press, 2006.

Carle, Robert. "Tariq Ramadan and the Quest for a Moderate Islam." *Society* 48 (2011): 58–69.

Clarke, Peter B. *West Africa and Islam: A Study of Religious Development from the 8th to the 20th Century*. London: Edward Arnold, 1982.

Fourest, Caroline. *Brother Tariq: The Doublespeak of Tariq Ramadan*. Translated by Ioana Wieder and John Atherton. New York: Encounter, 2008.

Guillaume, Alfred, ed. and trans. *The Life of Muhammad: A Translation of Isḥāq's Sīrat Rasūl Allāh*. London: Oxford University Press, 1955.

Ibn Taymiyya. *Muslims under Non-Muslim Rule*. Translated by Yahya Michot. Oxford: Interface Publications, 2006.

Kamrava, Mehran, ed. *The New Voices of Islam: Rethinking Politics and Modernity: A Reader*. Berkeley: University of California Press, 2006.

Launay, Robert. *Beyond the Stream: Islam and Society in a West African Town*. Berkeley: University of California Press, 1992.

McRoy, Anthony. "European Muslim: The Multiple Identity of Tariq Ramadan." *The Christian Century* 124 (21 August 2007): 30–34.

Nasr, Seyyed Hossein, Caner K. Dagli, Maria Massi Dakake, Joseph E. B. Lumbard, and Mohammed Rustom, eds. *The Study Quran: A New Translation and Commentary*. New York: Harper One, 2015.

Ramadan, Tariq. *In the Footsteps of the Prophet: Lessons from the Life of Muhammad*. Oxford: Oxford University Press, 2007.

———. "Islam and Muslims in Europe: A Silent Revolution toward Rediscovery." In *Muslims in the West: From Sojourners to Citizens*, edited by Yvonne Yazbeck Haddad, 158–66. Oxford: Oxford University Press, 2002.

———. *Islam, the West and the Challenges of Modernity*. Translated by Saïd Amghar. Leicester: Islamic Foundation, 2001.

———. *The Quest for Meaning: Developing a Philosophy of Pluralism*. London: Allen Lane, 2010.

———. *Radical Reform: Islamic Ethics and Liberation*. Oxford: Oxford University Press, 2009.

———. *To Be a European Muslim: A Study of Islamic Sources in the European Context*. Leicester: Islamic Foundation, 1999.

———. *Western Muslims and the Future of Islam*. Oxford: Oxford University Press, 2004.

———. *What I Believe*. Oxford: Oxford University Press, 2010.

Rippin, Andrew. *Muslims: Their Religious Beliefs and Practices*. 4th ed. London: Routledge, 2012.

Robinson, David. *Muslim Societies in African History*. Cambridge: Cambridge University Press, 2004.

Sanneh, Lamin. *Beyond Jihad: The Pacifist Tradition in West African Islam*. New York; Oxford: Oxford University Press, 2016.

———. *The Crown and the Turban: Muslims and West African Pluralism*. Boulder: Westview Press, 1997.

———. *The Jakhanke Muslim Clerics: A Religious and Historical Study of Islam in Senegambia*. Lanham: University Press of America, 1989.

———. *Summoned from the Margin: Homecoming of an African*. Grand Rapids; Cambridge: Eerdmans, 2012.

Shavit, Uriya. "Europe, the New Abyssinia: On the Role of the First *Hijra* in the *Fiqh al-Aqalliyyāt al-Muslima* Discourse." *Islam and Christian-Muslim Relations* 29 (2018): 371–91.

Trimingham, J. Spencer. *A History of Islam in West Africa*. Oxford: Oxford University Press, 1962.

Wilks, Ivor. "The Juula and the Expansion of Islam into the Forest." In *The History of Islam in Africa*, edited by Nehemia Levtzion and Randall L. Pouwels, 93–115. Athens: Ohio University Press, 2000.

Wilson, Tom. "Ramadan's Radical Reform." *Islam and Christian-Muslim Relations* 28 (2017): 33–46.

9

"Translatability and Nontranslatability"

Bible, Qur'an, and Land in Northern Nigeria, 1913–1915

Caroline Seed

Introduction

This is a study of the effect of the translation of the Bible in the mission context of a small group of Muslim followers of Isa (Isawa) in Northern Nigeria at the beginning of the twentieth century.[1] It is undertaken in dialogue with Lamin Sanneh's concepts of translatability and nontranslatability as presented in *Translating the Message: The Missionary Impact on Culture*. My study represents twenty years of personal reflection on a small but important part of mission history. Along the way, this has involved the study of the primary and secondary sources and a period of extended residence in the region in which the history took place.[2] The interaction with Sanneh's concepts of translatability and nontranslatability represents a new angle to the research.

This reflection aims to go beyond the biases of autobiography and primary sources to examine what Sanneh calls the "deeper connections and continuities

---

1. A small group of Hausa Muslims, originally from Kano, Northern Nigeria, who follow the Qur'anic prophet Isa and have become known as the Isawa. Isa is the Qur'anic name for Jesus.
2. Seed, *Whose Land?*; Seed "Reception of the Gospel," 258–60.

between mission and the vernacular."³ It asks whether the translation of the Bible into Hausa could have been the catalyst for the reception of the Christian faith among a group of Hausa known as the Isawa. It then considers whether translatability and hospitality were related concepts in the mission theology of the translator, Dr. Water Miller (1872–1952) of the Church Missionary Society (CMS). Next, it asks whether the tragedy of the death of most of the Isawa converts from sleeping sickness (trypanosomiasis) in 1915 was inevitable. It considers this in the light of the interplay between the complex concepts of translatability and hospitality on the one hand and nontranslatability and territoriality on the other, within the broader historical context.

As a mission partner within the Church Mission Society (CMS) – which is the key mission player in this history – I am aware of the dangers of subjectivity in undertaking such a project. Therefore, I present this research as a critical evaluation of mission policy from "within the fold." I do not presume to speak for the descendants of the Isawa or the local church, although they have been consulted where possible. This research is undertaken in the spirit of Andrew Walls's comment in *The Missionary Movement in Christian Mission* that reflection on the mission movement from the West represents a valuable approach to the history of the world church because it offers us the possibility of looking at the mission history "in a better perspective than before."⁴ Yet he notes that even at its onset, early mission history took on a subversive life of its own:

> But it is worth noticing from the story of the missionary movement how often early mission studies – while originating within and never independent of the Western intellectual tradition – frequently revised, expanded, contradicted, and subverted that tradition. This took place because the practitioners were seeking – as they believed, trusted, and prayed – to follow Christ where no one had been before.⁵

This cameo from early mission history shows similar trends. The purpose of this chapter, therefore, is to offer further reflection on the Isawa conversion story in the light of Sanneh's theory of translatability and nontranslatability by relating it to the complexity of concepts of hospitality and territoriality in

---

3. Sanneh, *Translating the Message*, 111.
4. Walls, *Missionary Movement*, xviii.
5. Walls, xix.

Muslim-Christian relations in West Africa. By so doing, it is hoped that this chapter might go some way toward contributing to the "better perspective."

The Sokoto Caliphate, Hospitality, and Territoriality (1804–1915)

It is important to first set the scene by describing the nature of Islam in Northern Nigeria before the period of study to ascertain the precise context in which the history of the Isawa mission developed. It must be noted that the limitations of this chapter mean that it cannot cover in any depth the wealth of published material relating to the history of the Sokoto Caliphate. The material selected serves only to advance the stated research objectives. Historians are divided on their approach to the Sokoto Caliphate, which was established in 1804[6] following what is popularly known as the "Dan Fodio jihad" under the leadership of the Fulani scholar Usman dan Fodio (1754–1817). The central issue for this study lies in concepts of hospitality and territoriality in the prehistory of the caliphate.

The *Kano Chronicle*[7] records that Islam was introduced peacefully in Kano – where the history of the Isawa begins – in the 1340s CE by Sufi scholars from Mali, who set up a learning center there. From the fourteenth to the eighteenth centuries CE, Islam and traditional Hausa practices existed side by side. Lamin Sanneh argues that this was made possible by the capacity of the traditional African religious customs to tolerate and extend hospitality to other religious systems through the principle of "enclavement."[8] This principle allowed the traditional host community to show hospitality to the incoming minority Muslim clerics through limited adaptation but without abandoning their own religious practices. This meant that both Islamic and traditional practices were present during this period. As Sanneh writes, "Traditional Africa sustained the Muslim impact by investing the new religion with its own identity, not by yielding to it."[9]

This settled status under the enclavement principle began to change in the early nineteenth century CE when Usman dan Fodio began to call for

---

6. There is a discrepancy in the secondary sources as to the precise date. 1804 is commonly cited as the beginning of the conquests.

7. A history of Kano written in Hausa. The final compilation dates from circa 1890 CE and combines earlier sources.

8. Sanneh, "Domestication," 3. See also Azumah, *Legacy*, 52.

9. Sanneh, "Domestication," 2.

the purging of the non-Islamic practices in the Hausa states.[10] In contrast to the flexibility of the traditional religious system, Sanneh observes, "The Islamic regime explicitly forbids . . . involvement in African traditional religious customs. It consigns these customs to the sphere of the unclean things. Doctrinally they qualify for *jihad.*" However, he notes that, for practical reasons, Muslims living as small minorities did not have the option of jihad but were tolerated in African societies under the enclavement principle.[11]

Dan Fodio had been born in 1754 CE in a Fulani village called Gobir in Hausaland. The Fulani, who had emigrated from Senegal, had by this time divided into two distinct groups: the nomadic cattle keepers and the town dwellers (known as the *Fulani gida*).[12] Usman dan Fodio belonged to the town dwellers of Gobir. By this time, the Hausa states had become increasingly Muslim, which gave dan Fodio the advantage of studying Islam under a reputed Islamic scholar. After completing his studies, he began preaching against the accommodation of "innovation in religion" through the eradication of "all forms and manifestations that had crept into the fundamental religious duties" of Islam in his hometown of Gobir.[13] His fiery preaching brought him into conflict with the traditional ruler of Gobir, who then attacked him and his followers. Dan Fodio subsequently fled and, in 1804, called for the jihad of the sword.[14] War began, and the ensuing conflict spread through the Hausa states. By 1808, dan Fodio and his followers had subdued the entire region. In 1809, dan Fodio pronounced the Sokoto Caliphate across the Hausa states. In 1817, when dan Fodio died, his son Muhammed Bello was made the first caliph. The Sokoto Caliphate continued to rule the region until their defeat by British forces in 1903.

There is debate on the reasons for the dan Fodio jihad. Scholars cite religious and socioeconomic factors, as well as corruption and taxation.[15] Others, however, give theological reasons based on dan Fodio's teaching on the need for Muslims to follow the Sunna of the Prophet and to perform

---

10. These practices are listed as rites related to the role of traditional priests and syncretistic practices such as the construction of a mosque under a sacred tree in the northern city of Kano. Levtzion, "Islam in Africa," 495.

11. Sanneh, "Domestication," 2–4.

12. A *gida* is the Hausa word for a family compound or home.

13. Basri, *Nigeria and Shari'ah*, 24.

14. Sanneh notes the West African pacifist tradition's preference for the "greater jihad" of moral and spiritual discipline over the "lesser jihad" of armed combat or the jihad of the sword. Sanneh, *Beyond Jihad*, 2, 36, 202.

15. Robinson, *Muslim Societies*, 144; Maishanu, "Jihad," 129.

Hijrah to the *dar al-islam* by waging war against the *dar al-harb*.[16] However, it seems that it was a series of visions of the Prophet Muhammad and another Sufi leader that led dan Fodio to the self-understanding that his role was to herald the coming Mahdi. As Warburg points out, dan Fodio did not claim to be the Mahdi. He called on the Hausa to engage in jihad as a preparation for the coming of the Mahdi.[17] This, then, could have been the primary motivation for the jihad of the sword that brought about the domination of the Sokoto Caliphate in the region.[18]

However, evidence suggests that the delineation of the region into the *dar al-islam* (the Sokoto Caliphate) and the *dar al-harb* (those outside the caliphate) is more nuanced than some commentators would suggest. Sanneh analyzes the debate between Muhammad al-Kanemi (d. 1838) – ruler of Kanem-Bornu – and Uthman dan Fodio (d. 1817) regarding the use of the sword for religious ends. Al-Kanemi objected strongly to dan Fodio's jihad and strenuously opposed him. He argued that there was no point in dan Fodio's forces unleashing constant war between Muslims because there is no age that is free from heresy and sin. He contended that any hard division of the world into the *dar al-harb* and the *dar al-islam* would make a nonsense of the striving of all peoples toward the truth.[19] Further, Sanneh observes that al-Kanemi called for tolerance, claiming that the so-called offenses of the Muslims in his area were not enough for jihad as they did not deny the fundamental truths of the oneness of God or the pillars of faith.[20] Azumah further shows that in the post-jihad period, one of the writings attributed to dan Fodio quotes a fifteenth-century scholar from Timbuktu who maintained that the status of the *dar al-harb* and the *dar al-Islam* in Hausaland depended on the beliefs of the rulers and not of the subjects.[21] Following this rule, it made no sense to engage in the jihad of the sword against fellow Muslims living under Muslim kings. Thus, Sanneh calls for a more nuanced understanding of the Fulani jihadists and their attitude toward territory.[22]

However, Nigerian scholar Yusufu Turaki takes a different position. He proposes that by British colonial times, the Sokoto Caliphate had developed

---

16. Turaki, *Tainted Legacy*, 51; Robinson, "Revolutions," 137.
17. Warburg, " Sufism," 670; Azumah *Legacy*, 98.
18. Azumah, *Legacy*, 98.
19. Sanneh, *Crown and the Turban*, 213.
20. Sanneh, *Beyond Jihad*, 221–222.
21. Azumah, *Legacy*, 77.
22. Sanneh, *Beyond Jihad*, 223.

into a "theocratic empire" that sought to extend its influence over the territory in the Middle Belt of Nigeria as the *dar al-harb*: "The founding fathers of the Sokoto Caliphate regarded the non-Muslim territories of the Middle Belt as Dar-al Harb, the house of war."[23] This was for the purposes of Islamization and slave raids.

In the end, whatever position one takes on perceptions of territory in the Sokoto Caliphate at the end of the nineteenth century, the existence of some kind of theology of Islamic territoriality must be taken into account in the engagement between Christianity and Islam. The engagement was occasioned by the arrival of CMS missionaries and British colonial forces in the region in 1900.

British Colonialism, Hospitality, and Territoriality (1900–1915)

The British occupation of Northern Nigeria should be seen in the broader context of the colonial policy directed from London under the statesman Joseph Chamberlain (1836–1914). In 1886, a charter was awarded to the Royal Niger Company (RNC). Turaki states that this was done with a twofold mandate: (1) to end slavery and (2) to promote legitimate trade as an alternative.[24] Turaki's analysis, however, does not take into account the primary sources available in Lugard's diaries, which make extensive reference to the role of the RNC in quelling unrest and securing land to the north for British economic and political interests and make little reference to the abolition of slavery.[25] As Pearson comments. "Economic pressures were at the heart of Britain's decision to colonize the Niger area, although other factors such as humanitarian desires to put a stop to the slave trade and to spread Christianity played important contributory roles."[26] However, the RNC had only limited success and used aggressive methods that provoked hostility in the northern territories. As a result, in 1898, the British government decided to revoke the RNC Charter to prepare the ground for British colonial rule.

Turaki attributes the British intention to colonize West Africa directly to the abolitionist movement and the desire to bring the slave trade to an end.[27] However, there is no evidence for this in the diaries of Lord Frederick Lugard,

---

23. Turaki, *Tainted Legacy*, 73.
24. Turaki, 162.
25. See Perham and Bull, *Diaries*, 31.
26. Pearson, "Economic Imperialism," 86.
27. Turaki, *Tainted Legacy*, 162.

the man appointed to carry out this task. Rather, the primary issue for him was to keep the French out of the region for economic reasons.[28] Thus, by the turn of the century, the motivation for the colonization of the northern regions of Nigeria was political and territorial, not the ethical motivation suggested by Turaki. When Lugard signed the agreement to create a British protectorate over Northern Nigeria in Lagos on 1 January 1900 and proceeded to march north with his troops, his purpose was the protection of the borders of the British Empire in West Africa against the French. Thus, the motivation of the colonial forces in waging a campaign against the Hausa-Fulani city-states of the Sokoto Caliphate from 1900–1903 was primarily imperialist and concerned with the acquisition of territory for British colonial economic purposes.

By 1900, the Hausa states of the Sokoto Caliphate had already lost their territorial advantage due to political upheaval and infighting. Lugard was able to play on the weaknesses of the emirs in their desire to gain the upper hand over one another. Further, Lugard offered the emirs an informal pledge that the British government would not interfere with Islam and that Muslims would not be compelled to convert to Christianity. Thus, despite concerted resistance in some areas, the Hausa states under Fulani rule were subdued, to a great extent, by diplomacy in 1903, although only after a bloody campaign lasting just over two years. However, when Lugard's small force took over the administration of the region, it soon became clear that they would not have the capacity to administer the whole of Northern Nigeria. To overcome this problem, Lugard devised a system of indirect rule, using the existing Islamic rulers of the Sokoto Caliphate and appointing British Commissioners to report to them. Táíwò quotes Lugard's words from his *Political Memoranda*, "The British role here is to bring to the country all the gains of civilization . . . *with as little interference as possible with Native customs and modes of thought*" [Taiwo's italics].[29] He sees this as a "curious recommendation" in the light of the irony that the "march of civilization" has a change in the customs and worldview of its populations as its central tenet.[30] Nonetheless, in Lugard's thought, it was the duty of the Resident to support the existing rulers and chiefs and to rule through them while educating them in their duties.[31] It appears that he saw no contradiction

---

28. Perham and Bull, *Diaries*, 324–27.
29. Táíwò, Olúfémi. *How Colonialism Pre-empted Modernity in Africa* (Bloomington: Indiana University Press, 2010), 139.
30. Táíwò, *Colonialism*, 139.
31. Táíwò, 141.

between training the Islamic leaders in British administrative processes and a policy of noninterference in Islamic practices.

There was also a striking contradiction in the colonial attitude to land. In his victory speech in 1903, Lugard stated, "The Government will, in future, hold the rights in land which the Fulani took by conquest from the people."[32] This clearly shows the intention to take control of the land. A government survey by Orr in 1911 records that the whole of Northern Nigeria had been declared "public land" – that is, land held administratively by the British, which they had a right to annex on payment of compensation.[33] Yet although the colonial authorities claimed the conquest of the land, they did not exert direct rule over any of the territories during the ensuing decade. As Nigerian historian Z. O. Apata observes, the British colonial government exercised "little or no control" over the Northern Province during this period.[34] Instead, their land policy, together with indirect rule, allowed the Sokoto Caliphate to rebuild its hold on the land as the *dar al-Islam* in the post-1903 political administration. The intricacies of the relationship between the emirs of the Sokoto Caliphate and the British colonial residents have been described by Murray Last in "The 'Colonial Caliphate' of Northern Nigeria."[35] Last maintains that indirect rule was a compromise that suited both sides, "combining the incompatible, Dar al-Islam and British imperialism."[36] This gave the Sokoto Caliphate institutionalized authority over the land, such that it appeared to non-Muslims that the region formed part of the *dar al-islam*.[37]

Integral to the policy of indirect rule – instigated by Lugard and continued by his successors after his departure in 1906 – was an ambivalent attitude toward Christian mission. Eugene Stock – in his *History of the Church Missionary Society* – notes that by 1910, it had become "fashionable to praise Islam and sneer at Christian missions."[38] Covert and overt opposition to Christian evangelism within the region of indirect rule during this period is well-documented, especially regarding the acquisition or donation of land for church and mission purposes.[39] This indicates yet another contradiction in the

---

32. See Orr, *Northern Nigeria*, 296–97.
33. See detailed analysis in Yakubu, *Law of Land Ownership*, 92–94.
34. Apata, "Lugard," 143.
35. Last, "Colonial Caliphate," 67–82.
36. Last, 74.
37. Last, 78.
38. Stock, *History*, 41.
39. Last also notes the strict separation of residential areas for Muslims and non-Muslims, with the early exception of Zaria. Last, *Colonial Caliphate*, 78.

British colonial attitudes toward land in the north, which showed little sign of the imperial territoriality that supposedly motivated the annexure in the first place. Ultimately, it was British colonial self-interest that dictated their attitude toward religious groups, not only in northern Nigeria but throughout their sphere of influence. As Sanneh observes,

> From the first century of its encounter with West Africa, missionary Christianity has encouraged the view that the overtaking of Islam is an overriding consideration. Thus, whatever the real history of relations with Muslims . . . the myth has been perpetuated that Christianity is locked in bitter rivalry with it, with Africa serving as the arena and the prize. Western colonialization merely bolstered this competitive myth and invested it with greater potency.[40]

Therefore, colonial attitudes to land and mission in northern Nigeria served pragmatic political and economic interests.[41]

Church Missionary Society, Hospitality, and Territoriality (1900–1915)

The CMS was founded in 1799 by the Clapham Sect, which included evangelical clergyman and abolitionist William Wilberforce. In 1899, the CMS, as it celebrated its hundredth anniversary, resolved to continue to introduce Christian missions in the non-Christian regions of the world.[42] This included the extension of mission into Northern Nigeria. The historian Ayandele observes that this decision was undergirded by two assumptions:[43] first, a belief in the superiority of the Hausa civilization and its ability to spread the gospel; second, the conviction that the Hausa had been unwillingly colonized by the Fulani jihadists and were only nominally Muslim and, therefore, easy to evangelize.[44] Thus, from the outset, the intentions of the CMS to evangelize the Hausa appeared to have had political and territorial undertones of liberation from Fulani domination.

---

40. Sanneh, *West African Christianity*, 210.

41. Andrew Barnes makes the point that there was no official policy to explain the attitudes of the various colonial authorities to Christian missionaries during the period. Barnes, "Evangelization," 413.

42. Stock, *History*, 11.

43. Ayandele, "Missionary Factor," 504.

44. Ayandele, 504.

The first CMS expedition, under the leadership of Bishop Tugwell and Dr. Walter Miller, left Lagos for Kano in January 1900, at the same time as a British protectorate was pronounced over Northern Nigeria. This coinciding of colonial and mission motivation has led historians to criticize the imperialist intentions of the CMS.[45] It seems that a similar conclusion was reached by the emir of Kano, who imprisoned the group on charges of being agents of the colonial forces. Miller records that they were only released when he threatened the emir with military reprisals. Thus, from the outset, Christian mission in Northern Nigeria was, in the eyes of the leaders in the Sokoto Caliphate, linked with aggressive British territorial expansion. This territorial perception of Christian mission would later play a part in the history of the evangelization of the Isawa under CMS missionary Walter Miller.

Walter Richard Samuel Miller (1872–1952) heard the call to mission as a medical student and later joined the CMS. From the outset, he was interested in the Hausa people of Northern Nigeria and, in 1899, went to Tripoli to learn Hausa from pilgrims gathered there. In a letter to the CMS, written from Tripoli, he maintains that the Hausa were eager for the British to come and liberate them from the Fulani oppressors who had colonized the region.[46] Ayandele comments that CMS missionaries expected the Fulani to "acquiesce in British occupation in the vein of the prophecy which Usman dan Fodio was alleged to have made . . . that the Fulani regime would not last more than a century." It is also evident from the primary sources that the CMS had been convinced, by Mahdist prophecies circulating in the wider region, that expectations of the coming Mahdi would be realized when their missionaries brought the gospel message.[47] The time for mission to Northern Nigeria was, therefore, ripe and, in Miller's eyes, the advance of the British troops to lay claim to the territory made it even more so.

Although the mission party had been turned back from Kano, they had received a warmer welcome in the Hausa state of Zaria due to the infighting within the Sokoto Caliphate. The emir was hoping for assistance from the British forces to settle quarrels with his neighbors. Miller returned to Zaria in 1902 and lived with the British forces during the military campaign. During this time, he acted as interpreter for Lugard and played a diplomatic role,

---

45. Ayandele maintains that the CMS believed that the military subjugation of the Fulani was the only way to evangelize northern Nigeria. He calls the five missionaries "knights-errant of British imperialism." Ayandele, 509.

46. CMS G3/A3/08 Miller to Baylis 11/5/1899 in Ayandele, 509.

47. See Ayandele, 510. For further discussion on Mahdism in the region, see Lovejoy and Hogendorn, "Revolutionary Mahdism," 217–44.

establishing cordial relations with the Hausa emirs on behalf of the British government. In 1903, Lugard offered Miller a political residency in Zaria, but he turned it down in favor of mission work. Lugard then persuaded the emir of Zaria to offer Miller a compound in the walled city to set up a pharmacy and a school. Miller accepted the offer willingly, unaware that the land was considered "haram" and shunned by the local people as the place of jinn and a burial ground for dogs. In later reflections on the emir's donation of land for Christian mission, Miller comments, "Our Emir . . . did not think we should be in the compound long. If he could have induced the jinn and spirits to do what he was much too polite to do himself, I think he would have been glad."[48] What Miller had interpreted as a gift of hospitality by the emir in 1903 appeared to him in 1936, in hindsight, as a deliberate attempt on the part of the emir to use jinn and evil spirits to prevent successful Christian mission in Zaria. The question that needs to be asked is this: What happened to change Miller's mind about the emir's apparent hospitality? This question can only be answered by following the history of Miller and early mission in Zaria.

Initially, Miller made little headway. His pharmacy was not well received, and he had negligible success with his medical mission. Instead, he turned his attention to setting up a school. Although he had enjoyed a good relationship with Lugard, once Lugard left for Lagos in 1906, Miller's subsequent mission work was restricted by the British authorities, because they feared offending the Muslim rulers. Andrew Barnes observes that the colonial administrators tried to determine not only where the missionaries could evangelize but even the content of their messages.[49] In *The Crown and the Turban*, Sanneh comments that indirect rule promoted the territorial interests of Islam.[50] Thus, while the Islamic rulers were able to strengthen their position through indirect rule, the missionaries were weakened by the opposition of their own government.

Frustrated, Miller turned his attention to the translation of the Bible into Hausa. If he could not succeed in his medical mission, his grasp of the Hausa language meant that he could successfully translate the Bible and set up a school to teach a few of the wealthier Muslim boys in Zaria. CMS historian Eugene Stock writes, "Dr. Miller gave much time to Bible translation in the Hausa language, whose 'wonderful beauty and wealth' charmed him."[51] By being forced to spend his time working in Hausa, Miller built up an expertise

---

48. Miller, *Reflections*, 87.
49. Barnes, "Evangelization," 413.
50. Sanneh, *Crown and the Turban*, 205.
51. Stock, *History*, 71.

in the language, which no doubt aided the accessibility of the translation.⁵² However, this work was done quietly and out of the eyes of the Islamic and colonial authorities. As Sanneh observes, as Miller worked in the school and on his translations, most of the time he was relegated to "work in fringe communities."⁵³ Forced to restrict his work to teaching and translating the Bible, the scene was now set for Miller's first significant mission encounter with a fringe group – the Isawa.

The Isawa, Bible Translation, and Land (1913–1915)

Originating from Kano during the mid-nineteenth century CE, the Isawa were a small group of Muslim followers of Isa who had been expelled from Kano after the execution of their leader, Mallam Ibrahim. According to Miller, Ibrahim had obtained an Arabic copy of the New Testament in Cairo, and this had convinced him that Isa – and not Prophet Muhammad – was the prophet that he should follow.⁵⁴ The origins of Isawa beliefs can, therefore, be traced to the translatability of the Bible, albeit not into the vernacular at this stage. When he returned to Kano, Ibrahim rejected, among other things, the primacy of Prophet Muhammad. This perceived challenge to the emir's leadership led to a death sentence for Ibrahim. Before his execution, Ibrahim gathered his small group of followers and instructed them to flee and then wait for a White man who would come and tell them more about the Prophet Isa.

In 1913, Miller was overseeing a game of hockey at his school in Zaria when he was approached by a group of Muslim teachers (*mallams*). According to historian Ian Linden, these teachers introduced themselves as "the children of the Israelites" and said that they knew that Prophet Isa was the Messiah. They explained that they had come to Miller because their leader had instructed them to find the White man who would explain more about him. Miller stopped the game of hockey and invited them inside. He then read part of his Hausa translation of the Gospel of John with them, explaining from John 1 how Isa was the *logos* of God. Linden comments, "The dense theology and mysticism of this Gospel seems to have struck a chord in the visiting mallams."⁵⁵ Certainly, the reading of the Gospel of John in the vernacular seemed to have made an immediate impression on them because they accepted the message

---

52. Although, by the end of the twentieth century, the translation needed revision.
53. Sanneh, *Translating the Message*, 118.
54. The dating of the execution is unclear.
55. Linden, *Between Two Religions*, 84.

and, within a few days, called their families to join them in Zaria for further teaching and discipling.[56]

However, it is doubtful that the reason for their acceptance lay in the "dense theology and mysticism" of John's gospel, as proposed by Linden. In previous research – employing comparison with the similar use of a translation of John's gospel among a monotheist group in China – I have suggested that reasons for the Isawa reception of John's gospel lie in the evangelistic nature of the Gospel of John, as well as in a combination of factors such as messianism, monotheism, and self-identity with the "children of Israel."[57] The Isawa had already absorbed the essence of the gospel of Jesus Christ through Ibrahim's teaching and were waiting for the fulfillment of the prophecy about the White man who would bring them the rest of the story. When Miller read the Gospel of John to them, they recognized Jesus Christ, the "Word" of God (John 1:1), the "true light" who had come into the world (John 1:9). Reading the gospel with Miller in the vernacular would only have served to highlight the hospitality of the Christian message: "But to all who did receive him, who believed in his name, he gave the right to become children of God" (John 1:12 ESV). The translatability of the gospel and the hospitality of the message, therefore, intersected in the communal reading of John with the Isawa in Hausa.

Miller's immediate assumption was that the converts should be given land on which to settle as a Christian community. In this, Miller showed that his understanding of the hospitality of the gospel had territorial overtones to it. In 1913, Miller appealed for land to the then governor-general of a unified Nigeria – his old friend, Sir Frederick Lugard. However, as we have already noted, the colonial policy of indirect rule meant a reluctance to requisition public land. Rather than annex land for the CMS, Lugard turned to the emir of Zaria and asked him to donate land on which to build a village for this group of Muslims who had converted to the Christian faith. The emir responded by donating a tract of land with a river, suitable for agriculture, close to Zaria at a village called Gimi. Miller viewed this as a hospitable gesture and spoke warmly about the "experiment" in his correspondence with the CMS.[58] In later reflections, however, he was more negative about what he had at first interpreted as a hospitable act on the part of the emir.

Upon the invitation of Rev. W. A. Thompson from the West Indies to be their resident missionary, Miller moved the group of converts to Gimi

---

56. Stock, *History*, 73.
57. Seed, "Reception of the Gospel," 258.
58. Stock, *History*, 73.

and set about establishing a self-sustaining community there. For Miller, this was an experiment in discipleship, which historian Shobana Shankar sees as "exceptional" in the history of mission in Northern Nigeria.[59] The first year appeared to go well. Sugar plantations were established, and the fledgling church at Gimi studied the Bible and the Qur'an together as part of the discipleship process. However, during the second year, members of the community began to fall ill and die. Miller was slow to diagnose the illness as sleeping sickness (trypanosomiasis). By 1915, most of the village had succumbed to the disease, and the few who survived had fled to other regions. The Isawa "experiment" was, therefore, soon over.

In his autobiography, written several decades after the event, Miller shows a less than congenial attitude toward the emir's act of "hospitality" in donating the land than he had evidenced at the time of his grateful acceptance in 1913. He opines that the emir must have considered the request for land for converts from Islam as "gall and wormwood" and complains that "we discovered only too late that in giving us the village of Gimi, he had chosen a place of sad repute."[60] These words are reminiscent of his earlier interpretation of the motives for the donation of land in Zaria in 1903. However, concerning Gimi, he admits, "We were told . . . that this village had been inhabited and deserted several times previously, and always because of the strange disease which the people, ignorant of medicine, had attributed to evil spirits."[61] It appears that Miller was ready to accept land which had a reputation for disease because he had confidence in his own medical knowledge, as opposed to what he saw as the ignorant superstition of the people. It is possible that Miller had knowingly accepted the land from the emir and then failed to manage the medical situation. It would be incorrect, therefore, to accuse the emir of intrigue against the Christian converts even though Miller later suggests that the emir's motives were less than sincere. What can be determined, however, is the way the Muslims interpreted the death of the converts. Miller writes, "It was natural, though hard to bear, that Moslems [sic] should reproach them for their apostasy."[62]

It is difficult to discern exactly what happened or to attribute blame to either the emir or to Miller. Certainly, there was a history of fatal illness in the area, which Miller and the emir both knew about. Did the emir intentionally

---

59. Shankar, *Who Shall Enter Paradise?*, 149.
60. Miller, *Autobiography*, 52.
61. Miller, 54.
62. Miller, *Reflections*, 117.

donate bad land to punish the converts for their apostasy, or did he donate the land in good faith believing that Miller would be able to use his medical skills to overcome the problems? Similarly, did Miller accept the land from the emir in good faith, ignoring the history of illness, or did he do so knowingly, convinced of his own ability to diagnose and medicate against the illness? Either way, it seems that both parties were aware of the health risks associated with the village. It is difficult to discern the true motivations. Autobiographical sources are inevitably biased. This problem relates to Sanneh's comments about the dangers of "missionary self-documentation and epistolary success" in historical mission research.[63] Objectivity through triangulation with third-party source materials is not possible in this microhistory. What can be known, however, is that Miller, with the benefit of hindsight, interpreted the emir's hospitality as covert inhospitality toward converts.

This short history – which is essentially a failed Christian experiment in hospitality for converts from Islam within the territory of the *dar al-Islam* – can now be examined within Sanneh's framework of the translatability and nontranslatability of the sacred scriptures of Christianity and Islam. This will enable us to consider the complex relationships between translatability and hospitality, and nontranslatability and territoriality, as they played out in the Isawa conversion history.

Translatability and Hospitality, Nontranslatability and Territoriality?

In chapter 7 of *Translating the Message*, Sanneh lays out a theory of translatability in Islam and Christianity. He acknowledges their common missionary ambitions but notes "strikingly different" attitudes to translatability.[64] The Islamic paradigm assumes the nontranslatability of the Qur'an due to the "revered status" of sacred Arabic.[65] This leads Islam to a mode of mission that Sanneh describes earlier in the book as "diffusion."[66] The diffusion model is present in Islam, where Arabic culture carries the message and conversion means assimilation. This initially seems to suggest a fixed attitude toward territoriality. For the Christian faith, however, the model is one of translation, and the ability to translate is the lifeblood of the transmission of the message. This initially seems to suggest a settled attitude toward hospitality. However,

---

63. Sanneh, *Translating the Message*, 111.
64. Sanneh, *Translating the Message*, 211.
65. Sanneh, 224.
66. Sanneh, 29.

in reality, the interplay between the concepts is more complex than it first appears to be.

The opposing concepts of translatability and nontranslatability can now be evaluated as they played out in the Isawa microhistory. The Isawa had first been introduced to the portrayal of Jesus Christ in the gospels by Mallam Ibrahim after he read an Arabic translation of the New Testament. The Isawa had retained the Arabic Qur'an throughout the period after Ibrahim's execution, while they were waiting for the prophesied messenger to come. During this time, they were still ostensibly Muslim followers of the Prophet Isa as portrayed in the Qur'an. It was only when Miller read the Hausa translation of the Gospel of John with them that they responded with full commitment to the portrayal of the Lord Jesus Christ in the Christian gospel. This suggests at least an anecdotal link between the translatability of the gospel and concepts of the hospitality of the Christian faith within the history of the Isawa conversion.

The question we need to ask is whether translatability has a leaning toward hospitality and nontranslatability has a leaning toward territoriality. This is not a simple question to answer. In terms of the relationship between translatability and hospitality, the act of translating the Bible into the vernacular languages of the receptor cultures implies that it is the message and not the form of the language that is the subject of transmission. Translating the Bible into other languages means bringing the message of faith in Jesus Christ in the language of the people to whom it is addressed. This, it might be argued, implies an act of hospitality. The gospel takes root in the receptor culture, and the recipients are invited to participate, by faith, in Christ as the gift of the grace of God. As written in the prologue to the Gospel of John, "For from his fullness we have all received grace upon grace. For the law was given through Moses; grace and truth came through Jesus Christ" (John 1:16–17 ESV). Christ receives those who come to him by faith and gives them "the right to become the children of God" (1:12). This is not a territorial hospitality but an invitation to become citizens of the kingdom of God.

However, if we make this link between translatability and hospitality, we must also ask the opposite question: Is there also a relationship between translatability and territoriality? This is where the complexity of the situation comes to the fore. In the mission microhistory of the Isawa, we have noted an observable relationship between British colonial territorial expansionism and the arrival of the first CMS missionaries. We have also noted that Miller expected to receive land for the mission from the hands of the emir and that he conveyed his request for land through his friend Sir Frederick Lugard and the British colonial government. The expectation that land that was under the control of the Islamic rulers under indirect rule should be ceded to Miller for the disciplining of converts points to the assumption that Christian mission in Muslim areas has a right to obtain land in the *dar al-islam*. It can be noted, therefore, that for Miller and the CMS, translatability, hospitality, and expectations of land were inextricably linked.

In terms of the relationship between nontranslatability and territoriality, this history has observed the concept of the territoriality of the *dar al-islam* within the Sokoto Caliphate, following the dan Fodio jihad. It has also observed the strengthening of the Muslim hold on territory in Northern Nigeria under the principle of indirect rule and the opposition by the colonial government to Christian mission, leading to a reluctance to annex land for mission purposes. This led Lugard to ask the emir for land for the Isawa. However, in the microhistory of the Isawa, we have noted a possible ambiguity in the motives of the emirs toward the donation of land for Christian mission. Miller interpreted both the donation of "haram land" in Zaria in 1903 and the donation of the "bad land" in Gimi in 1913 as indirect acts of persecution against the converts, who were considered as apostates. For him, as he looked back in retrospect, the emirs were covertly inhospitable. Yet this evaluation fails to take into account the previously noted principle of enclavement at work in traditional cultures, which allows for external groups to reside within and receive hospitality. Indeed, in 1929, the emir gave the missionaries a square mile of land outside Zaria on which to build a mission station and church, a donation that has lasted until the present time.[67] As Azumah argues, the dynamics of the fundamental African concepts of religion have to be taken into account, particularly the principle of enclavement.[68] This enables us to ask the further question as to whether there was a relationship between the nontranslatability of Arabic Islam and hospitality. In Miller's evaluation of the situation, the answer was negative. However, Walls's comments about revising, reviewing, and subverting historical analyses come into play here. Historical evidence simply cannot determine the motivation behind the "tragedy" at Gimi. The emir's actions were either covertly hostile to the donation of land or ostensibly hospitable under the traditional cultural principle of enclavement.

This would indicate, therefore, that there is no simple line to be drawn between translatability and hospitality or nontranslatability and territoriality in the Isawa history. There are, however, general trends – such as the translation of the Gospel of John into Hausa and the impact this had on the Isawa in

---

67. Wusasa is situated three kilometers from Zaria city.
68. Azumah, *Legacy*, 52.

their conversion and acceptance of Jesus Christ as portrayed in the Bible. This points to a relationship between translatability and the hospitality of the gospel message. We can also see the general link between concepts of the nontranslatability of the Arabic Qur'an and the nonaccommodation of other religious practices within the territory of the *dar al-islam* – in this case, the Sokoto Caliphate of Northern Nigeria. However, both parallels need to be carefully nuanced in the evaluation of this history. Translatability and hospitality were intertwined with concepts of mission as territorial advancement in terms of the procurement of land by donation for Christian mission. The gospel was translated and offered hospitality to the converts, but Miller and the CMS assumed the need for territory in the form of land for a mission station. This brings about a confluence of translatability, hospitality, and territoriality. Similarly, Islamic concepts of nontranslatability appeared to function through the overarching concepts of the territoriality of the *dar al-islam* but were immersed in the underlying principles of hospitality and enclavement of the traditional cultures. This brings about a confluence of nontranslatability, territoriality, and hospitality. It appears that Sanneh's concepts of translatability and nontranslatabilty are valid in terms of attitudes toward the scriptures of Christianity and Islam, but concepts of hospitality and territoriality were more complex in the case of the mission history of the Isawa.

Conclusion

The purpose of this chapter was to examine the Isawa mission history at Gimi (1913–1915) with fresh eyes to gain a "better perspective" on the failure of the "experiment." We have suggested that further reasons can be adduced by applying Sanneh's concepts of translatability and nontranslatability to the history of the Isawa. Sanneh concludes *Translating the Message* with the observation that "Christianity and Islam are perfect mirrors . . . of each other."[69] For Sanneh, this is evidenced in the opposing themes of translatability and nontranslatability. From the mission history of the Isawa, we have added to Sanneh's categories the more nuanced themes of hospitality and territoriality.

Our task was to consider the connections between translatability and hospitality, nontranslatability and territoriality, to introduce a new perspective to the evaluation. First, we asked whether the translation of the Gospel of John acted as a catalyst for the conversion of the Isawa. Although we have not been able to answer that question definitively, we have shown that there

---

69. Sanneh, *Translating the Message*, 234.

is a high probability that translation, coupled with other factors, led to their acceptance of the Christian faith. Second, we asked whether translatability and hospitality were assumed in the mission theology of Walter Miller, and we have shown that not only were they assumed but that Miller also maintained a conception of the territoriality of Christian mission, which brought into play not only translatability and hospitality but also territoriality. This was further complicated by the colonial government's opposition to Christian mission in the region. Third, we showed that the concept of the *dar al-islam*, as understood by the Sokoto Caliphate, was further strengthened by the British policy of indirect rule after 1903. This territoriality was related to Sanneh's concept of the nontranslatability of the Qur'an and Arabic culture. However, we also noted that Miller did not immediately interpret the land donations in 1903 and 1913 as acts of covert hostility. Instead, his change in attitude developed in hindsight. This led to the possibility of considering the donation of "bad" land at Gimi as an act of hospitality under the enclavement principle of the traditional culture, with the assumption that Miller's medical expertise could overcome the known health risks. If this were the case, then nontranslatability and territoriality could also be inextricably linked with traditional concepts of hospitality.

The history of the Isawa conversion (1913–1915) serves to underscore the complexity of the attempt to interpret mission history. It is worth repeating the late Andrew Walls's comment, which was cited at the beginning of this chapter:

> But it is worth noticing from the story of the missionary movement how often early mission studies – while originating within and never independent of the Western intellectual tradition – frequently revised, expanded, contradicted, and subverted that tradition. This took place because the practitioners were seeking – as they believed, trusted, and prayed – to follow Christ where no one had been before.[70]

The microhistory of the Isawa has already shown that it defies simple explanation. The conversion of the Isawa was a first in mission history. Miller was attempting "to follow Christ where no one had been before." It is possible that, as a pioneer, he failed to understand the motives of the emirs precisely because Western interpretation of hospitality and territoriality had failed to perceive the traditional principle of enclavement that was at play in the donation of land. However, history cannot avoid the uncomfortable fact

---

70. Walls, *Missionary Movement*, xix.

that the land at Gimi was known to be inhospitable for human habitation and that the emir donated it to the Isawa. Neither can it avoid the fact that Miller knowingly accepted the donation. Therefore, the history of the Isawa experiment at Gimi awaits further revision and expansion.

Bibliography

Apata, Z. O. "Lugard and the Creation of Provincial Administration in Northern Nigeria, 1900–1918." *African Study Monographs* 11, no. 3 (1990): 143–52.

Ayandele, E. A. "The Missionary Factor in Northern Nigeria 1870–1918." *Journal of the Historical Society of Nigeria* 3 (1966): 503–22.

Azumah, John Alembillah. *The Legacy of Arab-Islam in Africa: The Quest for Interreligious Dialogue*. Oxford, Oneworld, 2014.

Barnes, Andrew E. "'Evangelization Where It Is Not Wanted': Colonial Administrators and Missionaries in Northern Nigeria during the First Third of the Twentieth Century." *Journal of Religion in Africa* 25, no. 4 (1995): 412–41.

Basri, Ghazali. *Nigeria and Shari'ah: Aspirations and Apprehensions*. Leicester: Islamic Foundation, 1994.

Esposito, John L., ed. *The Oxford History of Islam*. Oxford: Oxford University Press, 2000.

Last, Murray. "The 'Colonial Caliphate' of Northern Nigeria." In *Le Temps des Marabouts: Itinéraires et stratégies islamiques en afrique occidentale française v. 1880–1960*, edited by David Robinson and Jean-Louis Triaud. Paris: Karthala (2012): 67–82.

Levtzion, Nehemia. "Islam in Africa to 1800: merchants, chiefs and saints." In *The Oxford History of Islam*, edited by John Esposito. Oxford: Oxford University Press, 2000.

Linden, Ian. *Between Two Religions of the Book: The Children of the Israelites (1846–1920)*. University of Birmingham, Harold Turner Collection, 1982.

Lovejoy, Paul E., and John S. Hogendorn. "Revolutionary Mahdism and Resistance to Colonial Rule in the Sokoto Caliphate, 1905–1906." *Journal of African History* 31 (1990): 217–44.

Lugard, Frederick. *The Dual Mandate in British Tropical Africa*. Abingdon: Cass, 1922.

Maishanu, Hamza Muhammad, and Isa Muhammad Maishanu. "The Jihad and the Formation of the Sokoto Caliphate." *Islamic Studies* 38, no. 1 (1999): 119–31.

Miller, Walter. *Reflections of a Pioneer*. London: Church Missionary Society, 1936.

———. *Walter Miller, 1872–1952: An Autobiography*. Zaria: Gaskiya Coorporation, 1953.

Orr, C. W. J. *The Making of Northern Nigeria*. London: Darf, 1987.

Pearson, Scott R. "The Economic Imperialism of the Royal Niger Company." *Food Research Institute Studies* 10 (1971): 1387–2016.

Perham, Margery, and Mary Bull, eds. *The Diaries of Lord Lugard*. 4 vols. Evanston: Northwestern University Press, 1963.
Robinson, David. *Muslim Societies in African History*. Cambridge: Cambridge University Press, 2004.
———. "Revolutions in the Western Sudan." In *The History of Islam in Africa*, edited by Nehemia Levtzion and Randall L. Pouwels, 131–52. Athens: Ohio University Press, 2000.
Sanneh, Lamin. *Beyond Jihad: The Pacifist Tradition in West African Islam*. Oxford: Oxford University Press, 2016.
———. *The Crown and the Turban: Muslims and West African Pluralism*. Boulder: Westview, 1997.
———. "The Domestication of Islam and Christianity in African Societies: A Methodological Exploration." *Journal of Religion in Africa* 11, no. 1 (1980): 1–12.
———. *Translating the Message: The Missionary Impact on Culture*. Maryknoll: Orbis Books, 1992.
———. *West African Christianity: The Religious Impact*. London: Hurst, 1981.
Seed, Caroline G. "Reception of the Gospel of John among the Isawa of Northern Nigeria and the Qiang of Western China, 1913–1935." *International Bulletin of Mission Research* 44, no. 3 (2019): 257–66.
———. "Whose Land? Islam, Colonial Rule, and the Church Missionary Society in Northern Nigeria, 1900–1930." MA thesis, University of Birmingham, 2001.
Shankar, Shobana. *Who Shall Enter Paradise? Christian Origins in Muslim Northern Nigeria*. Athens: Ohio University Press, 2014.
Stock, Eugene. *History of the Church Missionary Society*. 4 vols. London: CMS, 1916.
Táíwò, Olúfẹ́mi. *How Colonialism Preempted Modernity in Africa*. Bloomington: Indiana University Press, 2010.
Turaki, Yusufu. *Tainted Legacy: Islam, Colonialism, and Slavery in Northern Nigeria*. McLean: Isaac Publishing, 2010.
Walls, Andrew. *The Missionary Movement in Christian History: Studies in the Transmission of Faith*. New York: Orbis Books, 1996.
Warburg, Gabriel R. "From Sufism to Fundamentalism: The Mahdiyya and the Wahhabiyya." *Middle Eastern Studies* 45, no. 4 (2009): 661–72.
Yakubu, Musa Gella. "The Law of Land Ownership and Succession in the Northern States of Nigeria: An Exposition and Critical Analysis of the Existing Laws of the Hausa-Fulani Community." University of Birmingham, PhD thesis, 1980.

10

"The Kingdom of God Is Like a Mustard Seed"

Reconsidering the Nature of the Kingdom in a Post-Christendom World

Martin Accad

Since 313 CE, Christianity has continued to expand, largely through political influence and often conspicuously supported by military power.[1] So much so that it has become customary to speak of "Christian culture" or of "Judeo-Christian culture" as though it were some sort of homogenous reality. As a result, many writers over the past three decades have described global conflicts as a clash between the Judeo-Christian and Muslim cultures or civilizations.[2] The boundaries of these so-called cultures often rise so high that the central notion of hospitality, so present in the teaching of Jesus, has become blurred through the reactionist and self-protective instincts of Christendom societies.[3] The original inclusive invitation of Jesus into his kingdom becomes diluted when the gospel is expressed through fearful and exclusivist religious boundaries.

---

1. Michael W. Stroope, in his recent book – *Transcending Mission: The Eclipse of a Modern Tradition* – documents how the military and missionary enterprises went hand-in-hand during much of Christian history – since 313 CE, through the period of the Crusades, and into the colonial period. See in particular chapters 5 and 6.

2. See Lewis, *Cultures in Conflict* and Huntington, *Clash of Civilizations*.

3. I offered a critique of Christendom in light of the original message of Jesus in a recent article. See Accad, "Sacred Misinterpretation," 173–78.

In the present chapter, I will revisit the "mustard seed" metaphor of the kingdom through a hermeneutic of hospitality. I will argue that the increasingly dissolving lines of a so-called Christian culture in our post-Christendom world is a blessing to be celebrated rather than a phenomenon to be feared or grieved. We will look at the implications of this reading for interreligious relations in multifaith societies and consider what lessons can be learned from the realities of Lebanon and how these apply to an increasingly level field of globalized realities resulting from conflicts and human migration.

The Mustard Seed and the Yeast (Matthew 13)

> He told them another parable:
> "The kingdom of heaven is like a mustard seed,
> *which a man took* and **planted** in his **field**.
> Though it is the <u>smallest</u> of all **seeds**,
> yet when it *grows*, it is the <u>largest</u> of **garden plants**
> and <u>becomes</u> a **tree**,
> <u>so that</u> the birds come and <u>perch</u> in its **branches**."
> He told them still another parable:
> "The kingdom of heaven is like **yeast**
> *that a woman took* and *mixed* [hid, encrypted] into about
> <u>sixty pounds</u> [30 kg] of **flour**
> until it *worked* <u>all</u> through the **dough**" (Matt 13:31–33 NIV; emphasis mine)

The Elements in the Parables

In this passage from Matthew, Jesus used two metaphors – one agrarian, with which first-century men could identify; the other a culinary metaphor, with which first-century women could identify. Jesus frequently adopted this practice of addressing different groups in his audience when he told parables. In Luke 15, he emphasized God's compassion for the lost, first addressing men, through his parable of the shepherd who goes after the lost sheep (15:1–7), then addressing women, through a story of a homemaker who lost a coin (15:8–10), and, finally addressing middle class families through his story of the two lost sons (15:11–31). His disciples also reproduced this pattern when they organized their gospels. In the Gospel of John, for example, John tells of Jesus's night encounter with Nicodemus, a Jewish male religious leader, in chapter 3, followed by Jesus's midday encounter with a Samaritan woman of questionable lifestyle in chapter 4. Both encounters extend the kingdom beyond the realm of institutional religion through a critique of religious boundaries, represented by descendance from Abraham ("Flesh gives birth to flesh, but the Spirit gives birth to spirit" [John 3:6]), and affiliation to Jacob ("Are you greater than our father Jacob . . .? Everyone who drinks this water will be thirsty again" [John 4:12–13]).

In the Matthew 13 passage, both metaphors emphasize how something small can become something big. The smallest known seed of the day becomes a tree with many branches, and the small amount of yeast works its way into the flour, transforming it into a large amount of dough – thirty kilograms. Furthermore, what the double parable communicates to us is that both the mustard seed and the yeast have hidden and unexpected powers. The seed is taken and *hidden* in the earth, while the yeast is taken and *hidden* and *encrypted* (Gr. ἐνέκρυψεν) in the flour. Both elements are revolutionary and subversive; they hold in them the power to surprise.

It is interesting that Jesus uses yeast as a positive metaphor in this parable since yeast is typically used negatively elsewhere in the Bible. In Exodus 12, on the night when the angel of the Lord passed through Egypt and struck down every firstborn, both people and animals, the Israelites were ordered to eat the bread of the Passover without yeast because they had to eat in haste, with their cloak tucked into their belt, their sandals on their feet, and their staff in their hand (12:11). The Israelites had to commemorate that night permanently to remember their deliverance from slavery, and this ritual became an important part of the first month of the year for them. During that month, every year, the Israelites now had to eat bread without yeast – the "bread of affliction." "And anyone, whether foreigner or native-born, who eats anything with yeast in it must be cut off from the community of Israel" (Exod 12:19 NIV). Later, the Israelites were instructed that all bread offered to the Lord had to be burned along with their sacrifices, which was also to be without yeast (see, for instance, Leviticus 8:2, 26, and many other passages of the Old Testament).

In the New Testament, every reference to yeast – apart from this one in Matthew 13 – symbolizes something negative. Jesus warned his disciples against the "yeast of the Pharisees and Sadducees," which represents their teaching (Matt 16:6, 11–12 NIV) and against the "yeast . . . of Herod" (Mark 8:15 NIV). Luke explains that the yeast represents the Pharisees' hypocrisy (Luke 12:1). Paul, writing to the church at Corinth, uses the metaphor to symbolize the infesting power of sin and boasting and instructs the church to "get rid of the old yeast" in order to become "a new unleavened batch" because "Christ, our Passover lamb, has been sacrificed." For the old bread is "leavened with malice and wickedness," whereas the new unleavened bread is characterized by "sincerity and truth" (1 Cor 5:6–8 NIV). In Galatians, Paul describes false teaching as "a little yeast [that] works through the whole batch of dough" (Gal 5:9 NIV).

This idea of the subversive role of yeast is perhaps still to be assumed in the yeast metaphor of the parable in Matthew 13. Here, yeast carries positive connotations about the irresistible power of the gospel to transform its environment. Although the Canon Law of the Roman Catholic Church maintains the use of unleavened bread for communion, Eastern Churches came to prohibit its use because of its association with the old covenant. Bread with yeast was now to be used as a symbol of the new covenant.[4]

The fact that both elements – the mustard seed and the yeast – are small and initially seem insignificant was important for the early church to remember when they retold the parables of Jesus because, in the first century, they, too, were still very small in number. Remembering this is also important for Christians in the Middle East and North Africa today because, over time, we too have returned to a state of numerical insignificance. We are at a stage of our existence when many of us feel that we no longer have a place in our present societies and no hope for the future. Many of us feel persecuted, violated, and oppressed, and many are willing to face the hardships of emigration to the West for the sake of giving our children a more promising future.

The Actor

The actor in both metaphors represents God. In the seed metaphor, the actor is a man, a farmer; in the yeast metaphor, the actor is a woman, a baker. God "takes" the mustard seed and the yeast (ὃν λαβὼν and ἣν λαβοῦσα) – it is the same Greek verb in both – and shoves or hides it in the field or in the flour. Children of the kingdom have been "inserted" and "planted," like subversive elements, in the world. They are hidden there for a time with a specific intent. When they begin to take effect, they will completely transform their environment.

Jesus used many agrarian metaphors that are recorded by Matthew in this section of his gospel. In the preceding chapter, Jesus declared himself Lord of the law, Lord of the temple, and Lord of the Sabbath. He came head-to-head with the Jewish teachers of the law, for whom these core components of

---

4. See Ware, *Orthodox Church*, 66.

postexilic Judaism had become a means of control by which they held their people in bondage through a rigid interpretation of religion. Jesus would reclaim religion out of their hands and restore the law to its original intent. He rebuked the Pharisees by citing Hosea 6:6 to them: "If you had known what these words mean, 'I desire mercy, not sacrifice,' you would not have condemned the innocent. For the Son of Man is Lord of the Sabbath" (Matt 12:7–8 NIV). He then healed a man with a shriveled hand in their synagogue on a Sabbath day, which prompted the Pharisees to begin plotting his murder (12:9–14). When Jesus then healed a man who was blind and mute because of demon possession, the Pharisees accused him of deriving his power from "Beelzebul, the prince of demons" (12:24). A few verses later, Jesus began using agrarian language to address harsh criticism against the Pharisees:

> Make a tree good and its fruit will be good, or make a tree bad and its fruit will be bad, for a tree is recognized by its fruit. You brood of vipers, how can you who are evil say anything good? For the mouth speaks what the heart is full of. A good man brings good things out of the good stored up in him, and an evil man brings evil things out of the evil stored up in him. But I tell you that everyone will have to give account on the day of judgment for every empty word they have spoken. For by your words you will be acquitted, and by your words you will be condemned. (Matt 12:33–36 NIV)

The lessons that his audience, both religious leaders and Jewish people, were to derive from this rebuke are quite clear. The Jewish religious leaders had been entrusted with the law, the temple, and the Sabbath to serve God's people, but they had turned these into tools of control and oppression. Their bad fruit revealed the evil content and nature of their hearts. From then on, the divine farmer would set out to reveal a different sort of fruit from a new type of seed. This is the context within which Matthew places Jesus's agrarian metaphors of chapter 13.

The Process

The metaphors from the agricultural world that Jesus uses in Matthew 13 express, very simply, the process of transformation that God has begun. Two parables precede the ones that we are focusing on in this paper: the parable of the sower, with its explanation (13:1–23), and the parable of the weeds (13:24–30). In the first, we see that the good news of God's kingdom, though it was destined for good soil, was in some cases allowed to fall on defective soil. Some seed falls along the path, never gets to take root, and is snatched by birds – a symbol of the evil one. Other seed falls among rocks, only spreading shallow roots, and quickly withers in the heat of the day, which represents trouble and persecution. Some seed falls among thorns and, though it is able to take root, is eventually choked by the worries of life and the deceitfulness of wealth. The bulk of the seed, however, falls on good soil. Jesus explained that this good soil represents the one who hears the good news and understands it. The crop gathered from this batch yields "a hundred, sixty or thirty times what was sown" (13:23 NIV).

In the parable of the weeds, the work of the farmer is sabotaged by an enemy, who plants weed among the good seed. The farmer orders his servants to let both kinds of seed grow; at the time of the harvest, the weed is collected and fed to the fire, while the good crop is gathered into the barns. Many in Jesus's audience would have immediately understood the implications of this parable. God had allowed, for a time, the twisted Pharisaic interpretation of the law to survive; but now that the Son of Man had come, he was inaugurating the true interpretation of the law and the false teaching would not be allowed to survive. The oppressive and controlling interpretation of the law would be lifted, and the liberating good news of God's kingdom was at hand and manifest in Jesus. At those words, the Jewish teachers would only have become more resolute about getting rid of Jesus.

From verse 31 onward, Jesus began revealing the new process of the kingdom. In the midst of the rigid religious forms of his day, God had planted a new kind of seed, a mustard seed. Like a woman expert in her baking realm, God had hidden the subversive element of yeast into the flour. In both metaphors, growth occurs slowly; and is progressive but inevitable. The seed is planted in a field (13:31), grows into a garden plant (13:32a), and then becomes a tree with generous branches (13:32b). Similarly, the yeast is literally hidden or "encrypted" into the flour (13:33a), where it then transforms a large amount of dough. Now, the world holds its breath. The teachers of the people could hardly believe what Jesus was implying. The people who were beginning to breathe a new air of freedom would have been bubbling with anticipation.

The Outcome or the Result

In both metaphors, the work of the farmer and the baker result in elements that, in Eastern culture, are symbols of hospitality. The tree is a shelter that hosts many, and the dough feeds a neighborhood or an extended family. The hospitality offered is nondiscriminatory. God's message, which had hitherto been monopolized by one people and controlled by a religious elite, has now transformed into a large tree whose branches extend shade and protection to host a multitude of birds. It has transformed into a large quantity of leavened bread anticipating a multitude of guests for a feast and fellowship.

Both outcomes are generous invitations to enter into communal living. The tree offers hospitality to "the birds of the air" (Matt 13:32 ESV) so that they would find shelter in its many branches. The large amount of dough – about thirty kilograms – would be baked into bread to feed family, friends, and travelers. Both the tree and the bread invite into fellowship all those who recognize that they are in need of shelter and food. In effect, a small seed that transforms into a large tree and a little bit of flour that expands into a large amount of dough may also symbolize the invasiveness of space, territoriality, control, or even violence. But given the harsh critique Jesus had leveled against the controlling religious leaders in the previous section (Matt 13:24–30), these two parables more naturally read as a challenge to the Pharisees.

If the weeds of the preceding section had been allowed to exercise their influence for a time, the children of the kingdom are now invited to exercise their irresistible power. But this power is not violent or oppressive. It is the power of invitation, warm hospitality, welcome, and the kindness of fellowship. The children of the kingdom become an unapologetic blessing to all those who respond to their presence and invitation into the kingdom of God.

But chapter 13 has yet another lesson hidden in its verses. The welcoming act of hospitality invites a response. The generous tree stands there with its sheltering branches. The warm bread awaits its hungry guests. But the guests still need to respond positively to the invitation. The parable of the king's wedding banquet (Matt 22:1–14) comes to mind. In that story, the wedding guests respond harshly or not at all, and they are replaced by people off the street corners – anyone that the king's servants could find. In Luke's version of the parable, the master commands his servants to "go out quickly into the streets and alleys of the town and bring in the poor, the crippled, the blind and the lame" (Luke 14:21 NIV).

At the end of Matthew 13, we are told that Jesus returned to his hometown. Matthew tells us that the people of the town, although amazed by Jesus's teaching, responded mockingly: "'Where did this man get this wisdom and these miraculous powers?' they asked. 'Isn't this the carpenter's son? Isn't his mother's name Mary, and aren't his brothers James, Joseph, Simon and Judas? Aren't all his sisters with us? Where then did this man get all these things?' And they took offense at him" (Matt 13:54–57 NIV).

Jesus responded, "A prophet is not without honor except in his own town and in his own home," and we are told that "he did not do many miracles there because of their lack of faith" (13:57–58). The sheltering branches are there. The warm bread awaits. But generous hospitality – extravagant though it may be – still invites a response. Only those who respond joyfully to the blessing on offer will join the children of the kingdom.

Lessons for Us

Jesus's parables hold many lessons for us. They teach us how to behave and how not to behave. They exemplify for us the extravagance of divine hospitality. And they invite us to live a life that extends blessing to all those around. God has already planted us in the world. We may be small and feel insignificant, but God has a plan for us. We will no longer feel insignificant once we begin to yield the harvest for which we were called. We are not to remain hidden and shy. Our subversiveness must lead to blessing for all those around us.

As Arab Christians living in Muslim-majority societies, we are not to feel like outsiders, with no past and no future, within our contexts. This is a message that needs to be heard in this day and age, where Christianity has been all but wiped out in Iraq, shrunk considerably in Syria and Palestine, and continues to bleed through emigration in Lebanon, Jordan, Egypt, and other places. But neither are we to blend into society as though we were one plant among many or simply a handful of yeast vanishing meaninglessly into a sack of flour.

We are to practice hospitality intentionally and be a special blessing in our societies. We are to be *countercultural* where culture ignores the weak and hungry, *hospitable* where people are poor and marginalized, *peacemakers* where there is violence, *reconcilers* where there is conflict. This is our calling, which derives from our very nature as children of God's kingdom.

Implications for the Global Church

The parables of the mustard seed and the yeast also offer an important challenge to the global church. Today, many in the Western church grieve the loss of Christendom. They speak of a "Christian culture" that is being violated and overtaken by migrants and refugees, particularly those from other faiths. But the metaphors of the mustard seed and yeast challenge several of these assumptions. They challenge the false impression that large is good and small is bad, and they challenge the very idea that there is such a thing as a "Christian culture."

A mustard seed, if it is kept among other seeds, is of little value; and yeast, if set aside in isolation and not mixed into the flour, is powerless. The message of Jesus never sits comfortably within human culture. It is always countercultural and constantly challenges our cultural habits and traditions as well as our attitudes toward the marginalized and the outcasts. As soon as the gospel begins to shape a new culture anywhere, it must inspire prophetic subversion that overturns our sense of comfort in this newly established culture. Such is the nature of the gospel and of the kingdom of God. Rather than grieve the loss of a so-called Judeo-Christian culture, the global church is to celebrate its return to the pristine state of salt and light in which its Lord first birthed it.

The Practice of Hospitality through Peacebuilding

As followers of Jesus, we are constantly called to discern how the gospel of Christ's kingdom informs our relational engagement with our surrounding culture, whether our own constituents in evangelical churches, our Christian Orthodox and Catholic neighbors, or the dominant culture of our Muslim neighbors. The nature of our witness is to span from vibrant oral proclamation to faithfully committed theological dialogue, compassionate relief and humanitarian engagement, and comprehensive faith-based and politically engaged peacebuilding activism.

In Lebanon, I was involved for five years in peacebuilding initiatives that embraced principles of hospitality as a primary relational vehicle. Our *Khebz w Meleh* (in Arabic, "Bread and Salt") initiative equipped young Muslims and Christians between the ages fourteen and seventeen with guidelines for dialogue that became tools for respectful conversations about faith.[5] Our "Friendship Network of Church and Mosque Goers" formed networks of faith leaders in various parts of Lebanon and, through them, brought together nuclei of twenty-five to thirty Christian and Muslim men and women of all ages to reflect on their experiences of friendship with those of the other faith.[6] Through our "Forum for Current Affairs," we worked with a core group of

---

5. See "Khebz w Meleh," Arab Baptist Theological Seminary, last accessed 5 March 2024, https://abtslebanon.org/institute-of-middle-east-studies/peacebuilding/khebz-w-meleh/.

6. See Tim Brys, Martin Accad, and Brent Hamoud, "Christians and Muslims Praying Together: Compromise or a Sign of Hope?," Arab Baptist Theological Seminary, 14 September 2020, https://abtslebanon.org/2020/09/14/christians-and-muslims-praying-together-compromise-or-a-sign-of-hope/; and "A Gesture of Love: An Interfaith Peacebuilding Project," Arab Baptist Theological Seminary, https://abtslebanon.org/portfolio-item/a-gesture-of-love-an-interfaith-peacebuilding-project/, last accessed 5 March 2024.

leaders from our evangelical churches, using contextually appropriate methods and values to explore avenues of conflict resolution and reconciliation within our churches, and these eventually spilled out beyond our ecclesiastical walls.[7] A final initiative consisted in the visitation of leading Lebanese political actors to engage them in explorative conversations regarding peace and reconciliation across political and sectarian lines.

In all these initiatives, food and fellowship were central. We sat in the shade of the "mustard tree" and shared in the warm "leavened bread" of the kingdom as we sought together new avenues that would contribute to the common good of our multifaith society. Christ and common faith values were at the heart of our conversations. In those social networks and gatherings, there was no clash of cultures and no clash of civilizations. There was no cultural or religious chauvinism and no attempt at domination. Those circles of friendship were cultivated in an atmosphere of humility and mutual respect. We came as guests of God and dwelled in his rich divine hospitality. As children of God's kingdom, inaugurated by Christ, those of us who are disciples of Jesus must seek to be salt and light (Matt 5:13–16), shining truth and adding taste to a society where, historically, religions have often been a source of darkness and bitterness. We "let [our] light shine before others, that they may see [our] good deeds and glorify [our] Father in heaven" (5:16). We must seek to be a blessing by restoring faith to its rightful place in society, sidelining the religious travesty of sectarianism by pushing it to the margins.

Throughout the twentieth century, the Middle East and North Africa (MENA) region was dominated by experimentations of religious and secular extremism, oscillating between the two like a pendulum. This has led to abusive regimes, sometimes dominated by nationalist dictators and other times by religious extremism and anarchy. Both have been oppressive to their citizens and lethal to social peace. In this twenty-first century, it has become incumbent upon people of faith to lead the world along new pathways to peace. Centers of innovation – such as the Institute of Middle East Studies in Lebanon and The Sanneh Institute in Ghana – have a divine mandate to lead the way, in both thinking and practice, into these new pathways that will establish the right balance between territoriality and hospitality, religious distinctives and full citizenship, and diversity in equality. May we be beacons of hope that offer new models to the world for how life can be lived joyfully in the beauty of diversity.

---

7. See "Forum for Current Affairs: Reconciliation within the Church," Arab Baptist Theological Seminary, 10 March 2020, https://abtslebanon.org/institute-of-middle-east-studies/peacebuilding/forum-for-current-affairs/, last accessed 5 March 2024.

Bibliography

Accad, Martin. "Sacred Misinterpretation across the Christian-Muslim Divide." *International Journal of Frontier Missiology* 36, no. 4 (October–December 2019): 173–78.

Huntington, Samuel P. *The Clash of Civilizations and the Remaking of World Order.* New York: Touchstone, 1997.

Lewis, Bernard. *Cultures in Conflict: Christians, Muslims, and Jews in the Age of Discovery.* New York: Oxford University Press, 1995.

Stroope, Michael W. *Transcending Mission: The Eclipse of a Modern Tradition.* Downers Grove: InterVarsity Press, 2017.

Ware, Timothy. *The Orthodox Church.* London: Penguin, 1964.

11

Separation without Marginalization

Church, Mosque, and State in the Political Theology of Lamin Sanneh

Joshua Ralston

One of the greatest challenges to positive interfaith relations in West Africa is the persistent question of the relationship between religion and the state. Clamors for government-endorsed shari'a as a faithful Islamic alternative to ardent secularism and the Christian backlash that often ensues has created a volatile and competitive interfaith situation. Politics in postcolonial African states becomes the new prize for the competition between these two missionary religions.[1] Nowhere is this more apparent than in Nigeria, "the greatest Islamo-Christian nation in the world."[2] Shortly after national elections in 1999, twelve northern states formally adopted full shari'a, ostensibly diminishing all non-Muslim residents to the legal status of "dhimmi," even though constitution of Nigeria upholds equality under the law. Unsurprisingly, increased tension and

---

1. It is important to note that while Nigeria and Sudan are examples of the competitive political component of religious encounter, Africa also offers a number of examples of positive political pluralism in countries with both Christian and Muslims majorities – for instance, Senegal and Gambia on the predominately Muslim side and Ghana on the predominately Christian side.

2. A statement attributed to Archbishop Teissier of Algiers. See Onaiyekan, "Being Church," 48.

suspicion between religious and ethnic communities has flared, as exemplified by the outbreaks of violence in Kano and Aba in 2001.[3]

While the formal codification of shari'a in Nigeria has elicited a great deal of attention in the West, popular and academic opinion has focused almost solely on the Islamic breach of the sacred separation of religion and politics. The solution to what ails Nigeria appears clear: reject religious politics in the name of political secularism, national identity, and a multireligious state. However, the journey from state-enforced shari'a to political secularism is not nearly as easy as it appears from the orientalizing eyes of the West. Philip Ostien astutely notes, "One has the distinct impression that even mentioning the word 'secularism' is taboo in Nigeria."[4] Christians, Traditionalists, and Muslims often perceive secularism as a form of neocolonialism that continues to impose the so-called moral superiority of the West upon Africans. Furthermore, secularism is construed as marginalizing religion and artificially severing the holistic and integrated worldviews theoretically present in most African societies. Denny Weaver sums up the negative approach to secularism by saying that "it would be a serious mistake for the African church to embrace secularism" and that "secularism is not an option of Islam."[5]

Hence, to advocate for a secular state in Nigeria, diverse religious rationales must be marshaled and alternative political modes of secularism presented. More specifically, shari'a cannot simply be dismissed; it must be part of the solution. For a religiously diverse Nigerian state to thrive, it must travel through the mire of colonialism, the continued failure of leaders in Abuja or Lagos, the claims of Muslims for religious freedom, and regional and ethnic divides that are constantly inflamed by being overlaid with religious rhetoric. Neither Western secularism nor theocracy offer adequate solutions to the challenge of post-colonial politics in Nigeria.

This chapter presents a theo-legal philosophy rooted in important religious arguments through engagement with the thought of Lamin Sanneh and Abdullahi Ahmed an-Na'im. By coupling these two thinkers together, I present two models of religion and the state that neither privatize religion – thereby excluding it from politics – nor co-opts religion for purposes of political power. Together, Sanneh and an-Na'im present a multireligious perspective

---

3. For a study on the history of religious violence in Nigeria in the past two decades, see Falola, *Religious Violence*.

4. Kogelmann, "The 'Shari'a Factor' in Nigeria's 2003 Election," 267.

5. Cited in, McCain, "Which Road?," 14.

with strong religious justification for a nonestablished state.⁶ In addition to the analysis of Sanneh and an-Naʿim, the paper also offers a threefold theological and interfaith proposal.

First, I aim to educate non-Muslims about the diversity, history, and richness of Islamic jurisprudence. Continuing to equate the whole of shariʿa with just sensationalized criminal punishment or patriarchy hinders intellectual engagement with the diversity of Islamic public theology. Second, I seek to find common political ground for a religiously neutral state through recourse to the particularity of each religious tradition. I argue that a major strength of both Sanneh's and an-Naʿim's proposals is that they base their arguments for the separation of religion and state on religious reasons and for the benefit of religious practice. Following them, I propose that interfaith relations would benefit from a shift away from a critique of shariʿa per se to supporting Islamic scholars who seek to recapture the deeper memory of shariʿa as a source for moral formation that resists state enforcement.⁷ Shariʿa is central to Islam; therefore, it will continue to have a future. The question is, what type of future will shariʿa have in a pluralist world?

Lamin Sanneh: Separation without Marginalization

Lamin Sanneh wisely begins not with the problem of a state-centric approach but with the problem of shariʿa. Sanneh contends that in order to understand Islamic calls for shariʿa, one must understand Nigeria's postindependence state and its failings. Beginning with shariʿa enshrinement ignores the history of colonialism and the sociopolitical histories in many postcolonial African states from the 1970s to the late 1990s. Sanneh points out that state absolutism is a particular danger in Africa since the nation-state and its philosophical underpinnings are a recent arrival: "Without the benefit of the long development of the Western secular state tradition and the fruitful role of religion in preparing the soil and demarcating the boundaries, the new societies of Africa were exposed to the distortions and excess of secular dogmatism."⁸ Western nation-states, with Enlightenment presumptions of religious and state separation, were haphazardly imposed during the colonial period. This

---

6. Since the major focus of the paper is to present a framework for religious involvement in politics that does not lead to enshrinement, the Nigerian situation is only implicitly present as part of the background to the paper.

7. This chapter presents an alternative to the polemics so prevalent in both Muslim and Christian discussion of politics, particularly in Nigeria.

8. Sanneh, *Crown and the Turban*, 180.

act drew together diverse ethnic and religious groups, accustomed to their own integrated religious, social, and political systems. Political secularism was demanded without rejoinder.

Sanneh thus maintains that ideological secularism has helped produce the "enduring crisis of the state in Africa"[9] by justifying the overextension of the state into all spheres of human existence. In this situation, the state creates the illusion that politics offers a universal salve to whatever ails. "Only now magistrates have upstaged mullahs and commissar cardinals . . . religious metaphysics has been replaced with political metaphysics, with political messianism the creed in which people place their trust."[10] The original idea of separation of church and state gives way to the elevation of the state over religion, and, thus, the sovereign state actually becomes the true and absolute authority over and against religion. "Those who have followed Machiavelli and Bodin in arming the sovereignty of the state in full panoply have also dissolved the separation of the church and state by awarding authority to the state in religious matters."[11]

Secular politics, then, are not free from the problems of theocracy or religious sectarianism insofar as the state claims universal moral authority and relevance, thereby marginalizing and privatizing the religious contribution to human well-being. Ostien aptly notes, "Nigeria's real problems have nothing to do with religion. Religious controversy is just a diversion, which the Christians no less than the Muslims are guilty of exploiting whenever they think it will serve their own interests."[12] A simplistic accusation against shari'a alone fails to recognize the shortcomings of the state and the multiple factors at work in state failure. In particular, state absolutism heightens the problems by ignoring religious and traditional insights on morality, politics, and social well-being, not to mention transethnic connectivity. Sanneh's postindependence genealogy reveals that the original idea of separation of church and state has actually created the myth of an omnicompetent state. "The state as it presses its case to be the ultimate arbiter of human destiny contradicts its nature, to an effective, if limited, instrument of justice and equity."[13]

In critiquing ideological secularism, Sanneh shares broad sympathy with Islamic critiques of contemporary Western liberal democracy. It is in response

---

9. Sanneh, "Religious Sources," 70.
10. Sanneh, *Piety and Power*, 91.
11. Sanneh, 89.
12. Ostien, "Opportunity Missed," 221.
13. Sanneh, *Piety and Power*, 91.

to the failings of the state in Nigeria and the perception that secularism is a Western and Christian practice that some Muslims have sought to establish and codify shari'a through state apparatus. But Sanneh is as quick to acknowledge the dangers of theocracy as he is to recognize the problems of ideological secularism. "Muslim critics are correct that rights without God are meaningless, but mistaken to suggest that a religious state would do better."[14]

What is interesting about Sanneh's critique is that it is primarily focused on the danger of enshrinement for genuine religious practice, not for state stability. While many other scholars have focused on the cost of shari'a for the nation, few have focused as incisively on the cost of state-enforced religion for religion's own well-being. By arguing against religious establishment for the sake of religion with religious arguments, Sanneh advances his position in a persuasive manner. In a situation where religious and ethnic identities compete, or are stronger than national identity, appeal to religious logic is vital.

Sanneh contends that the attempt by religion, whether Islam or Christianity, to enshrine itself in the legal and political apparatus of the state undermines religious principles. State enforcement of shari'a runs contrary to "Islam's position on faith as *tasdiq*, sincerity, and obedience as moral commitment."[15] By forcing faith in a multireligious environment like Nigeria, Muslims run the risk of compromising the more important Islamic insight regarding the true character of upright faith – confession and submission to God and the revelation of the Qu'ran by the Prophet. The inherent attraction and intrinsic worth of religious faith does not need state enforcement for its survival. To assume so is to lower religion's persuasive and transcendent power to the level of mere human rhetoric, thereby putting God on the level of a human peddler. To refuse political enshrinement is to demand more for Islam, not less.

Furthermore, Sanneh notes how religion will become visibly compromised through political control. "Muslim confidence should be tempered by the realities of the world, because even in places where *qadi* courts have operated, the Islamic code has not been free of its share of corruption and exploitation."[16] Religious claims to holiness, economic reform, true justice, and transparency are necessarily soiled by the complexity of political practice, particularly as politicians use religion for their own political gain. Sanusi Lamido Sanusi incisively observes that calls for state-enforced religion in Nigeria tend to result

---

14. Sanneh, 138.
15. Sanneh, "Sacred Truth," 45.
16. Sanneh, *Piety and Power*, 128.

from an "ongoing struggle among various factions of the political elite for ascendancy."[17]

However, political calls for state religion inevitably result in a compromise of religious principles. For example, take the implementation of shari'a in a federal nation like Nigeria, where Islamic-run states receive funding from a nation that openly practices *riba*. Moreover, Islamic law will not solve the "existing failures of mismanagement, public incompetence, judicial corruption, social injustice, the absence of safety and security, falling standards of living, and widespread loss of morale"[18] rampant in Nigeria but, instead, will open up Islam to the discontent directed at the "corrupt" and "incompetent" government. Political establishment necessarily results in religious compromise since it looks to the "government to overcome the handicaps of government."[19]

Sanneh also mines historical examples within Islam in order to argue against state enforcement. There is a "large body of material in both Christian and Muslim traditions to support a public role for religion without requiring theocratic rule."[20] Sanneh points to the writings of Ibn Khaldun and the existence of the Jakhanke clerical class as examples of internal Islamic unease with political religion. He also notes Muhammad al-Kanemi's argument against Uthman dan Fodio's jihad: "the sword is too rough and ready a weapon to use in settling religious questions, especially questions between Muslims themselves."[21] Islam is not abiding by Western values when it refuses political enshrinement; rather, it is acting on its own best insights and for its own self-interest. "Muslim religious thought, understood first by its own prescriptive rules and then additionally by its modern-day Westernized tendencies, has enough of a voluntarist impetus in it to fit in with democratic liberalism in which religion is de-theocratized without being disenfranchised."[22] Religion, whether Islam, Christianity, or Traditional, recognizes that salvation is not through the state alone. By attempting to establish shari'a via the state, Islam ironically affirms this state-centric soteriology. "Politics as religion redeems no more than religions as politics."[23]

---

17. Sanusi, "Politics and Shari'a," 184.
18. Sanneh, "Sacred Truth," 50.
19. Sanneh, 43.
20. Sanneh, *Piety and Power*, 125.
21. Sanneh, 122.
22. Sanneh, 3.
23. Sanneh, 93.

According to Sanneh, the problems created – whether theocracy or ideological secularism – are essentially identical. In absolutizing themselves, both eliminate the other, seek state-centric solutions, ignore diversity, and force obedience, thereby eliminating human freedom and dialogue. In the process, genuine politics and religion cease to serve their proper function. "They complement each other when church and state are separated, but each corrupts – and is in turn corrupted – when the other co-opts it."[24]

In contrast to either ardent secularism or theocracy, Sanneh proposes a separation of religion and politics that recognizes "the religious sphere as nonidentical, though connected, with the political sphere."[25] The proper legal and political structure is a religiously neutral state that allows for the participation of religion in politics and moral development but does not enshrine any one religion through the law. This model would free the state from its pretensions and allow it to function as a limited but competent authority in human society. Additionally, religion is free to recapture its focus on "personal salvation grounded in freedom as a response to God"[26] and its role in training moral human beings and offering prophetic witness to the state. "Such considerations need not deny the connection of ethics and politics, of church and society, of principle and precedent, or of faith and public order . . . the buffer zone between church and state, between piety and power."[27] Under Sanneh's model, then, religion and civil society will continue to interact, but the state will consistently remain religiously neutral.

Sanneh's reading of the relationship between religion and politics in Africa is one of the more persuasive accounts presently available, insofar as it neither overestimates nor undervalues the role of religion in state instability while also seeking to provide theological reasons for functional separation. In contrast to Toyin Falola – who interprets the problems of Nigeria to be, in large, part due to religious involvement in politics and its propaganda of exclusivity – Sanneh is able to show how the religious situation is inflamed by a failing state. Considering Nigeria's struggle for transparency and its long history of government corruption and military dictatorships, Sanneh's ability to locate the religious problem within the social and ethnic situation is a much more viable interpretation of the causes and possible solutions to this complex situation.

---

24. Sanneh, 139.
25. Sanneh, 99.
26. Sanneh, "Sacred Truth," 55.
27. Sanneh, *Piety and Power*, 129.

Additionally, Sanneh's work benefits from seeking to argue against theocracy in religious terms. The important book by Simeon Illesanmi on religious pluralism and Nigerian politics, for all its benefits in "encouraging just relationships between the state and the different religious bodies,"[28] never provides internal religious reasons for mediating truth-claims or Muslims attempts for political superiority. The desired goal of religious mutation is never explicitly religious but is, instead, couched in terms such as social stability, political well-being, and the common good. Sanneh recognizes the shortcomings of this approach insofar as it subsumes religious identity in national and political structures. In contrast, his work seeks to show the theological and religious benefits to Islam of remaining politically "neutral" and not being co-opted by political expediency.

However, for all Sanneh's strengths in critiquing both ideological secularism and theocracy – particularly regarding the historical quagmire that is religious involvement in the state – the question remains: Is separation without marginalization tenable for Muslims? One of Sanneh's great insights is to recognize the importance of arguing for separation based on internal religious justification. But does his conclusion of a religiously neutral state emerge as a merely Western model, supported by Christian conceptions of the world? Ali Ahmad voices a common concern that so-called neutrality is actually "biased against *Shari'a*,"[29] and as Is-Haq Oloyede argues, "No genuine dialogue is going on between Islam and the West on the *Shari'a*. What the West wants is the capitulation of Islamic culture, ethics and laws to its own norms and values."[30] Has Sanneh succeeded in presenting a tenable way of engaging with Islam on the question of shari'a?

I contend that while Sanneh has advanced the conversation considerably, his insights must be pressed forward through more substantial engagement with the actual history and methods of shari'a. The historic fragility of establishing or legitimizing religion through political authority, particularly as this practice leads to a compromise of religious integrity, is made abundantly clear by Sanneh. However, it is doubtful that Sanneh's historic study and pragmatic arguments for functional separation will be persuasive in countering the theological and normative claims of Islamic scholars and lawyers. Normative truth claims, especially when rooted in revelation, are rarely defeated by examples from the complexity of history and practice.

---

28. Illesanmi, *Religious Pluralism*, 253.
29. Ahmad, "Future of *Shari'ah*," 369.
30. Oloyede, "Intercultural Dialogue," 301.

In particular, I wonder if Sanneh understood the actual complexity in the history and practice of shari'a. He continually equates shari'a with state enforcement and is thus unable to find a place for it within his model. However, Ali Ahmad, a former professor at Bayero University in Kano, explains the complexity of the question of the role of shari'a in Islam:

> Islam is a total package; and a community cannot be Muslim by choosing between the three aspects of Islam: a monotheistic faith, practical rituals (prayer, fasting, charity etc.), and law or *Shari'ah* (marriage, inheritance, contract, crime etc.). By accepting the Islamic faith, one is obliged to submit and let all the three categories apply to his entire life. Salvation, according to Islam, depends on the three jointly.[31]

Therefore, the argument cannot be about whether or not Muslims should have shari'a, but, rather, what variety of shari'a is appropriate for a pluralist nation. If, as Sanneh claims, genuine pluralism and religious diversity that does not reduce or eliminate the particularity of each faith is the goal, attention must shift from the broad question of shari'a or no shari'a to more substantial questions of what shari'a actually is. If shari'a must be equivalent with an Islamic state that enforces itself upon non-Muslims, then, in a pluralist world, a clash between Islam and modern human rights is inevitable. However, shari'a is actually far more diverse and mutable than Sanneh recognizes.

Must shari'a relegate non-Muslims to "dhimmi" status? Are women necessarily inferior to men under Islamic law? Is the state the proper guardian of Islamic legal practice? Can shari'a incorporate the notion of the nation-state or human rights? Can the gates of *itjihad* be reopened? These are a few of the many questions being asked by some Islamic scholars seeking to maintain Islam's traditional connection to politics without seeking state enshrinement. To find some answers to these questions, we must turn away from Sanneh and toward the history of Islamic jurisprudence and a contemporary Islamic proposal that resonantes with Sanneh's own final position on separation without marginalization but does so from an explicitly Islamic perspective with marked engagement with the nature of both shari'a and the state.

---

31. Ahmad, "Living with Conflict."

Interlude: A Very Brief Detour into Islamic Jurisprudential History

Sanneh employs historical examples from West Africa to critique shari'a in Nigeria, but he does not turn to the history of shari'a itself. If he had, he would have found that shari'a's own history might have been useful for the development of his position. A brief journey into the complicated theo-legal history of shari'a reveals that it "was not codified, nor has it ever been – unlike Roman church law."[32] It is not surprising, then, that the *fiqh* – or legal reasoning – of various Muslims has differed throughout Islamic history and that the interpretation of shari'a has developed into four major Sunni schools. In contrast to Western images of a monolithic shari'a that moves directly from divine revelation to state enforcement, the diversity of *itjihad* and the schools of law refuse easy state appropriation. In fact, the development of the schools of law occurred during the same period of Abbasid rule. Furthermore, none of the founders of the schools of law – such as Shafi'I or Malik – or jurisprudential minds – like Ibn Rushd or al-Ghazali – accepted political or even legal office.

In other words, the diversity of Islamic law developed under and within one empire, which neither favored nor enforced one interpretation of shari'a universally. It was not until the late nineteenth century, when the Ottoman Empire enforced shari'a, that Islamic law become equated with state law. However, the choice to enforce shari'a as the law of the state diminished the variety of opinions and interpretations present within Islamic law, thereby jeopardizing its diversity and contextual nature. Prior to codification by the state, judges were able to draw from and appropriate the range of legal opinions from throughout the schools, exercising discernment and judgment for each individual case.

Shari'a, then, is actually better understood as a way of thinking, interpreting, and relating to the law – particularly as it relates to divine revelation – rather than as the legal codification of a particular state. How might the current political situation in Nigeria, Sudan, or elsewhere change if Muslim in power recognize this aspect of shari'a's critical history with the government? I contend that one way for these important questions to be answered is for Christians, African Traditionalists, Africanists, and secularists in Nigeria and the world at large to shift their critiques away from shari'a per se and toward a critique of shari'a as modern state law. Critiquing shari'a is often interpreted as a critique of Islam; however, the critique need not be framed as a challenge to shari'a but, rather, to its domestication by the state and its enforcement upon non-Muslims. Highlighting the importance and diversity of shari'a, even as it

---

32. Kung, *Islam*, 261.

is critiqued in contemporary state practice, may help overcome Islamic fears of neocolonialism.[33]

Yet if shari'a is both a theological and politico-legal practice, it is difficult to conceive how it might remain pertinent to modern-day Muslims and still be free from complete state enforcement. In our state-centric world, where laws are established by the state, how a system of law can exist without state enforcement is an open question. The call for Islamic states and government-enforced shari'a by Islamists simply recognizes the reality of modern nation-states. As Noah Feldman astutely notes, "The constitutional proposals of Islamism . . . are products of twentieth-century ideology."[34] Given the constraints of the modern nation-state, the only apparent solution is for shari'a to be enforced. However, the application of classical shari'a to contemporary problems without attending to the legacy of modernity, human rights, and colonialism has already been shown to be fraught with compromise and difficulty. It is no wonder that Wael B. Hallaq claims that the contemporary situation has created a crisis of "Islamic legal identity."[35] He bluntly contends that "*shari'a* is no longer a tenable reality"[36] since it has been "so flagrantly manipulated that it lost its organic connection with traditional law and society."[37] Hallaq's worries are accurate, yet continued calls for Islamic states makes ignoring shari'a tantamount to burying one's head in the ground.

If shari'a is to contribute to the flourishing of justice and human rights in pluralist nations, what is needed are Muslim jurists proposing interpretations of shari'a that are rooted in jurisprudential history and the revelatory sources of Islam as well as postcolonial and modern realities. Showing people that they can faithfully practice their religion, even in civil society and the political realm, depends on showing them that faithful adherence to shari'a, whatever its particular form, does not depend on the state. Do such proposals exist?

Abdullahi an-Na'im: Why Muslims Need a Secular State

Abdullahi Ahmed an-Na'im presents a provocative and controversial proposal for reinterpreting shari'a in light of the challenges of religious pluralism, human rights, and the contemporary nation-state. In his controversial book,

---

33. For a longer argument, see Ralston, *Law and the Rule of God*, chapter 6.
34. Feldman, *Fall and Rise*, 106.
35. Hallaq, "Can the Shari'a?," 22.
36. Hallaq, 22.
37. Hallaq, 25.

Islam and the Secular State, an-Na'im claims that state enforcement of shari'a compromises the best insights of Islam and serves to undermine shari'a. He contends that the true practice of shari'a – as individual or corporate voluntary religious belief – depends upon a secular state that is religiously neutral and does not "claim or pretend to enforce *Shari'a*."[38] An-Na'im is quick to maintain that separation of shari'a and the state does not mean that religion is privatized or that Islam's traditional connection with politics is sundered. Religious motivation and commitments, particularly those shaped by shari'a, will continue to be brought to bear on politics and civil society. However, he argues that religious motivations need not, and indeed should not, be enforced via the state but, instead, be debated and presented publicly through a process of "civic reason." If laws are to be enacted by the state, they must be persuasive even to those who do not share one's religious beliefs. An-Na'im avers, "Securing institutional separation of Islam and the state is necessary for affirming and encouraging the interaction between Islam and politics."[39] An-Na'im, then, presents a model of mosque and state that, like Sanneh's proposal, seeks to neither enshrine nor privatize religion. The state will be secular but society need not be since politics, religion, and civil society will continue to exist in a dynamic interplay.

At first glance, an-Na'im's proposal may appear as nothing more than the capitulation of Islamic values and models to Western liberal ones. A separation between religion and the state that does not allow shari'a to be fully practiced through legal enforcement runs contrary to the dominant late twentieth- and twenty-first-century Islamic paradigms. According to Islamists, for an-Na'im to argue for a religiously neutral state must entail surrendering the central importance of Islam's role in public life. They contend that arguments for religiously neutral states simply cannot be faithfully Islamic but represent a compromise with modernity and Western liberalism.

An-Na'im protests such monolithic readings of Islamic history, maintaining that his proposal for a secular state is "from an Islamic perspective for Muslims."[40] He calls on the deeper memory of Islamic history, arguing that "adaptation to these realities is in fact more consistent with historical Islamic traditions than are the totalitarian post-colonial claims of an Islamic State."[41] An-Na'im seeks to illustrate that the free practice of faith, and not

---

38. An-Na'im, *Islam and the Secular State*, 1.
39. An-Na'im, 275.
40. An-Na'im, 64.
41. An-Na'im, 9.

political expediency, demands a secular state that does not enforce shari'a. He wisely observes, "The condition of secularism is likely to be seen as merely expedient and temporary by religious adherents unless they are able to find secularism consistent with (or preferably, implied or stipulated by) their religious doctrine."[42] An-Na'im's project, then, is to show precisely why Islam and a secular state are friends, not foes.

In order to understand how an-Na'im can maintain that a religiously neutral state is necessary for the practice of Islam, one must attend closely to his definitions of Islam, shari'a, and the history of Islam's relationship to the state. An-Na'im begins by noting that Islam's center rotates around the "living and proactive confession of faith in an infinitely singular omnipotent, and omnipresent God."[43] Islam is the personal confession of God's oneness and the recognition of God's revelation through the prophet Muhammad of the Qu'ran and, derivatively, the Sunna. Shari'a is not *tawhid* but a vital tool in guiding Muslims in their obligations before God, one another, and society.

Furthermore, shari'a is not a fixed or monolithic divine law but, rather, the interpretation of divine revelation by flawed, historical, and mutable human beings. This means that humans, with both their insights and myopia, have been influential in the establishment of shari'a and *fiqh*. To approach shari'a is to encounter "the layered filters of the experiences and interpretations of preceding generations."[44] There is no pure shari'a, at least on this side of the grave, that has not been soiled by human history. For an-Na'im, this complex historical reality is not a negative aspect of shari'a but, rather, part of its dynamic possibility. What has been accepted as proper interpretation of shari'a developed through scriptural reflection, legal reasoning, and consensus of the community. As we have already seen, the interpretative aspect of shari'a, coupled with various contingencies of time and place, led to a multiplicity of schools adept at relating to new situations. Therefore, if the interpretations by, and needs of, human beings have been instrumental in the codification, interpretation, application, and alteration of shari'a, then the implication is that Muslims today are free to encounter their tradition with the same contextual dynamism of the past.[45]

---

42. An-Na'im, 42.
43. An-Na'im, 10.
44. An-Na'im, 11.
45. An-Na'im presents his model for reform in *Toward an Islamic Reformation*. He offers a hermeneutical model drawn from Ustadh Mahmoud Mohamed Taha that prioritzes the universal peaceful message of the Meccan period over the concrete proposal meant for the particular community of Medina. Furthermore, an-Na'im engages with Quran, Sunna, *qiyas*, and *ijma*

The complexity of shari'a's human history, coupled with Islam's central claim of submission to the will of God, places radical demands on each individual. Falling back on the schools of law does not eliminate personal accountability and responsibility before God. As Marshall G. S. Hodgson notes, "No man, no institution, no human structure of any sort could legitimately be vested with any responsibility which could relieve the individual Muslim of his direct and all-embracing responsibility before God."[46] Shari'a is a guide or gateway into right practice; it does not create either orthodoxy or orthopraxy before God. An-Na'im is on good Islamic grounds, then, when he claims, "The fact that knowing and upholding shari'a is the permanent and inescapable responsibility of every Muslim means that no human being or institution should control this process."[47] Even the particularity of the schools of interpretation does not override the need to exercise personal responsibility and judgment. The "founding scholars of *Shari'a*" recognized this, and they "objected to the adoption of their views by the state and did not claim exhaustive authority."[48] Adherence to shari'a is an act of personal free submission and adherence based on religious motivations.[49]

If the fundamental nature of Islam and shari'a is based on submission through personal free assent, then the nature of the modern state is at odds with the voluntary aspects of Islamic faith. An-Na'im notes that the state's power is not based on either moral assent or voluntary submission but on coercive power. Political authority draws on acquired power, not superior religious piety or knowledge. To enforce Islam – or even a particular brand of Islam or interpretation of shari'a through the state – is to compromise Islam's own commitment to noncoercive faith and foreclose the dynamic possibilities latent in shari'a. The legal apparatus of the state is not geared toward viewing law as a diverse religious hermeneutic and practice. Since the state must enact uniform and particular laws, it will only selectively apply shari'a. An-Na'im illustrates how this was the case in the Ottoman Empire, where state implementation of shari'a was necessarily "specific and limited" and only "codified some Hanafi

---

in the hopes of reopening the gates of *itjihad* in order to relate shari'a with international law, women's rights, and criminal law.

46. Hodgson, *Classical Age*, 320.
47. An-Na'im, *Islam and the Secular State*, 14.
48. An-Na'im, 285.
49. This is not to ignore the communal aspect of Islam and the importance of consensus in the recognition of shari'a. In fact, an-Na'im gives pride of place to the importance of consensus in his understanding of shari'a's creation and reformation.

principles."⁵⁰ Shari'a is not enacted by the state; state laws are. These laws may be rooted in some aspect of shari'a, but the authority of the law always resides in the state's power.

Demands to return to a classical period of Islam through state-enforced shari'a today are a siren call, and one that leads toward state implementation over and against the religious independence present in much of Islam's own history. Since enforcing shari'a by the state will necessarily be selective, this will contradict the diversity, vitality, and elasticity of classical shari'a schools. Furthermore, state enforcement leads to a "growing rigidity, over determination, and trivialization of *Shari'a* among Muslims."⁵¹

To resist the siren's wail, an-Na'im presents an alternative historical genealogy of Islam, government, and law that begins with Abu Bakr and stretches up to the collapse of the classical Islamic period. He argues that this alternative reading "is more consistent with Islamic history than is the so-called Islamic state model."⁵² An-Na'im proposes that the very notion of an Islamic state is a chimera, both historically and practically. "It is not simply a matter of improving upon a bad experience in any country, there or elsewhere, but an objective that can never be realized anywhere."⁵³ The state, by its very nature, cannot be Islamic since the nature of religious and governmental authority are irreconcilable. To enforce shari'a through the state is not to enforce the laws of God but, rather, the particular interpretation of the ruling elite. Muslim jurists of the past have recognized this truth; it remains for Muslims of today who seek state-enforced shari'a to be convinced. The law intersected with the power of the government in Islamic history, but it cannot be contained or fully grasped by it.

An-Na'im thinks that if freed from the totalizing demands of the state, it might be possible for shari'a to be reformed, thereby recovering the vibrancy, elasticity, and creativity that were prevalent in its classical history. Although this will undoubtedly look different than the form of shari'a practiced in the Abassid period, adaptation is a faithful act, not a compromise. An-Na'im is one among many Muslims calling for reform on issues of human rights, religious freedom, women's rights, and constitutionalism. However, as long as old-style Islamic states remain the orthodoxy, these conversations will not flourish. Once so-called shari'a ceases to be the public law of a particular state,

---

50. An-Na'im, *Islam and the Secular State*, 16.
51. An-Na'im, 283.
52. An-Na'im, 45.
53. An-Na'im, 2.

it can act as a moral force developed in creative dialogue with tradition, the community, and the present realities of Muslim lives. This freedom from state control and prescription will open up the possibility for reinterpretation and reform within shari'a. In this way, "*Shari'a* should be known and experienced as a source of liberation and self-realization, not a heavy burden of oppressive restriction and harsh punishment."[54]

An-Na'im recognizes that a major obstacle for Muslims assenting to both his proposal for a secular state and his reading of Islamic history is the challenge of secularism and the history of colonialism. As we have previously noted, to call for a secular state appears to marginalize faith commitments and ignore Islam's traditional connection with politics. An-Na'im demurs from this suggestion: "It is not possible, nor desirable in my view, for people of any society to keep their religious beliefs, commitments, and concerns out of their political choices and decisions."[55] Religious and moral motivations cannot be legislated out of the hearts and minds of citizens and will necessarily influence human decision-making. A strict separation of religion and politics or civil society is artificial and will eventually enthrone a normative system, whether theocratic or ideologically secular.

Therefore, an-Na'im proposes a threefold distinction between the state, the political arena, and religion. The state will be secular, but politics will interact with religion. He claims that his model of "institutional separation" of state and religion "encourages continued connectedness"[56] between religion and politics. He maintains, "*Shari'a* principles can and should be a source of public policy and legislations."[57] Religious involvement in politics, though, cannot be based on appeals to divine will since this forecloses the possibility of change, enthrones one interpretation of shari'a over another, and denies the rights of others.

Recognizing the fluidity between religion, politics, and civil society, an-Na'im proposes that religious motivations be brought to the public square through the process of civic reason. "The concept of civic reason refers to the combination of civic reasons and civic reasoning, whereby any citizen can publicly express view about matters of public concern."[58] Civic reason does not exclude religions motivations from also entering into public discourse but asks

---

54. An-Na'im, 290.
55. An-Na'im, 275.
56. An-Na'im, 275.
57. An-Na'im, 29.
58. An-Na'im, 93.

that they be shown to be persuasive and beneficial to the whole of society. In the realm of civic reason, religions are asked not to appeal to divine authority but to "support their proposals in ways that are open to public and inclusive debate."[59] Under this model, shariʻa is neither marginalized and privatized nor enthroned and prescribed. Instead, Islam in all its diversity is brought into the ongoing dynamic process of public debate and civic exchange.

Whether we like it or not, religious beliefs, morals, and commitments will continue to interact and influence every society. The appeal to a secular state is a way to safeguard both the state and religion. While shariʻa will certainly be influential in society and politics, particularly in Muslim-dominant areas, it should be kept free from the control of the state. An-Naʻim recognizes the tenuous nature of such a delicate separation. Religion, politics, and the state will consistently seek to overpower one another, especially when appeals to religion prove useful for gaining political power. Constant vigilance and mediation is necessary for each society to negotiate the relationship between religion, state, and politics. This process cannot be prescribed upon any one society or territorial state but must be continually balanced in connection to the unique issues facing each nation. His proposal, then, is not a universal political model or solution but a framework presented by religious arguments for mediating between the state, politics, and religion.

An-Naʻim's work advances our study of Sanneh's position in two key ways. First, an-Naʻim offers explicitly Islamic arguments with historical precedents for why Muslims would benefit religiously from a secular state. Doing so would open up the possibility for creative reform and debate within Islam about the nature and future of shariʻa and invite practical consideration about how Islam, religion, and the state can interact in each unique environment from Ghana to Sudan, from Nigeria to Tanzania. Second, his model of separation of religion and state – but not of religion and politics – is better able to recognize the fluid frontier between what we in the West have grown too accustomed to simply calling religion and politics.

Sanneh and an-Naʻim recognize that the challenge of shariʻa offers the opportunity both to the state and to religion to reconsider their foundation, role, and telos. Both point us toward the importance of reconsidering normative claims about the role of religion in politics and the nature of the state, as well as the need for religions to provide their own individual reasons for engaging with the state and civil society without enshrinement. Reconsidering these questions might allow religion to enliven and enrich Nigeria through moral training,

---

59. An-Naʻim, 95.

interfaith cooperation, and prophetic critique. Let us remember that one of the most stable and far-reaching strands of civil society in Nigeria is religion and that, therefore, religions have much to offer in the quest for a stable, just, and well-rounded political society that includes, but does not enshrine, religion.

Bibliography

Ahmad, Ali. "Commentary: The Future of Shari'ah." In *Comparative Perspectives on Shari'ah in Nigeria*, edited by Phillip Ostien, Jamila M. Nasir, and Franz Kogelmann, 358–72. Ibadan: Spectrum Books, 2005.

———. "Living with Conflict: Shari'ah and One Nigeria." Address at Emory University, 7 November 2002.

An-Na'im, Abdullahi Ahmed. *Islam and the Secular State: Negotiating the Future of Shari'a*. Cambridge: Harvard University Press, 2008.

———. *Toward an Islamic Reformation: Civil Liberties, Human Rights, and International Law*. Syracuse: Syracuse University Press, 1990.

Falola, Toyin. *Religious Violence in Nigeria: The Crisis of Religious Politics and Secular Ideologies*. Rochester: Rochester University Press, 1998.

Feldman, Noah. *The Fall and Rise of the Islamic State*. Princeton: Princeton University Press, 2008.

Hallaq, Wael B. "Can the Shari'a be Restored?" In *Islamic Law and the Challenges of Modernity*, edited by Yvonne Yazbeck Haddad and Barbara Freyer Stowasser, 21–53. Walnut Creek: AltaMira, 2004.

Hodgson, Marshall G. S. *The Classical Age of Islam*. Vol. 1 of *The Venture of Islam*. Chicago: University of Chicago Press, 1977.

Illesanmi, Simeon O. *Religious Pluralism and the Nigerian State*. Athens: Ohio University Press, 1997.

Kogelmann, Franz. "The 'Shari'a Factor' in Nigeria's 2003 Elections. In *Muslim-Christian Encounters in Africa*, edited by Benjamin F. Soares, 256–74. Leiden: Brill, 2006.

Kung, Hans. *Islam: Past, Present, and Future*. Oxford: Oneworld, 2007.

McCain, Danny. "Which Road Leads Beyond the Shari'ah Controversy?" In *Comparative Perspectives on Shari'ah in Nigeria*, edited by Phillip Ostien, Jamila M. Nasir, and Franz Kogelmann, 7–26. Ibadan: Spectrum Books, 2005.

Oloyede, Is-Haq. "Commentary: The Intercultural Dialogue on Shari'ah in Nigeria." In *Comparative Perspectives on Shari'ah in Nigeria*, edited by Phillip Ostien, Jamila M. Nasir, and Franz Kogelmann, 301– . Ibadan: Spectrum Books, 2004.

Onaiyekan, John. "Being Church in an Islamo-Christian Nation." In *Towards the African Synod*, edited by Giuseppe Alberigo and Alphonse Ngindu Mushete, 44–52. London: SCM Press, 1992.

Ostien, Philip. "An Opportunity Missed by Nigerian Christians: The 1976–78 Sharia Debate Revisited." In *Muslim-Christian Encounters in Africa*, edited by Benjamin F. Soares, 221–55. Leiden: Brill, 2006.

Ralston, Joshua. *Law and the Rule of God*. Cambridge: Cambridge University Press, 2020.

Sanneh, Lamin. *The Crown and the Turban: Muslims and West African Pluralism*. Boulder: Westview, 1997.

———. *Piety and Power: Muslims and Christians in West Africa*. Maryknoll: Orbis Books, 1996.

———. "Religious Sources of Political Renewal: Some Reflections with Reference to Africa." In *Christianity in Africa in the 1990s*, edited by Christopher Fyfe and Andrew Walls, 68–77. Edinburgh: Centre of African Studies, 1996.

———. "Sacred Truth and Secular Agency: Separate Immunity or Double Jeopardy? Shari'ah, Nigeria, and Interfaith Prospects." *Studies in World Christianity* 8, no. 1 (January 2002): 31–62.

Sanusi, Sanusi Lamido. "Politics and Sharia in Northern Nigeria." In *Islam and Muslim Politics in Africa*, edited by Benjamin F. Soares and Rene Otayek, 177–88. New York: Palgrave Macmillian, 2007.

Historical and African Perspectives

12

Territoriality, Xenophilia, and Xenophobia

Religious Change in the West African Sahel and Savannah

Patrick Ryan

Introduction

A Marxist undergraduate and I – friends despite very different commitments – walked together to an earth shrine in northeastern Ghana. The time was the late 1970s. Drought had ravaged the West African Sahel and the Savannah for years. The military government in Ghana at the time did nothing but lie about the extent of the problem. We walked through dusty fields toward a group of angular rocks and a towering tree whose roots extended like bony fingers across the hard, dry soil. In the shade of the tree at midmorning sat the two sons of the earth shrine's custodian, tired from weeding a nearby field. We talked with them about farming, about rain, and about politics.

Drought, famine, misrule – the Marxist student and I were obsessed with similar thoughts. We were not the first, nor will we be the last, to bring such problems to an earth shrine. Earth shrines provide territorial[1] centers for

---

1. Territoriality means the land or earth as a sacred theme in any people's world vision – the way they mentally and even physically arrange their geographical settings: what they farm or do not farm, where they hunt or fish or do not hunt or fish, and whom they consider their

farmland throughout the West African Sahel and Savannah. The earth governs the life of farmers; through the earth shrine custodian, it mediates their land disputes and, sometimes, even their lineage controversies. The earth punishes the greedy, withholding the rain and retaining dead seed in its womb. The earth rewards the just, allowing the rain to fall and fructify the thirsty soil. The earth practices xenophilia – it welcomes the stranger, as long as that stranger does not violate its sacred territoriality. The earth also practices xenophobia, rejecting the stranger who comes to ravage.[2]

The Cults of the Earth in West Africa

Among the people who lived on the Sahel-Savannah frontier were the Soninke – one of the three principal populations speaking Mande languages – who played important roles in the history of West Africa. Most medieval scholars who work in Arabic agree that the Soninke formed the core population of the ancient kingdom called Ghana. Ancient Ghana probably corresponds to the state called Wagadu in Soninke oral tradition. Renowned in the late first millennium CE as a source of gold in the North African world, the kingdom of Ghana was later absorbed into what were once the Mali and Songhay empires.[3] A kingdom known for its xenophilia, Ghana welcomed strangers coming from North Africa. Abu 'Ubayd 'Abd Allah al-Bakri – the eleventh-century Andalusian geographer – narrates how Tunka Manin, ruler of Ghana in the 1060s CE, relied on Muslim ministers in his court, probably Berbers, whom he exempted from the local custom that obligated courtiers to greet the king by pouring dust on their heads. "As for the Muslims, they greet him only by clapping their hands."[4]

Desiccation and conflict with Berber nomads moving southward in search of pasturelands seem to account for the dispersion of the Soninke today. Under various names – Wakore, Wangara, Serahuli, Marka, Jakhanke, Dyula, Yarse –

---

neighbors and whom they consider strangers. In territorial rulerships, a single individual may take on royal prerogatives; in other societies, rule may be exercised more collaboratively by clan heads.

2. Xenophilia and xenophobia – the latter, alas, better known than the former in modern times – are terms denoting the ways in which human beings deal with the stranger (in Greek, *xenos*), either the unknown other or the barely known other. If we welcome the stranger, we are xenophiles; if we fear the stranger, we are xenophobes. Sometimes, we are a little of both. Paradoxically, the Greek word *xenos* can mean both "friend" and "enemy."

3. Levtzion, *Ancient Ghana*, 45. For a new synthesis of the history of Ancient Ghana and Mali, see Gomez, *African Dominion*.

4. Quoted in Hopkins, *Corpus*, 80.

the Soninke can be found in cultural enclaves spread throughout the West African Savannah at the corner which is the meeting place of Mauritania, Senegal, and Mali on the west and the middle-Volta basin (Burkina Faso and the northern areas of Côte d'Ivoire and Ghana) on the east.[5] The western Soninke preserve their own language, but the more sparsely distributed people of Soninke descent in the east have adopted the languages of their neighbors. The Soninke diaspora is markedly Islamized. Only the Soninke who continue to farm in western Mali preserve their pre-Islamic sacred traditions. One element in those traditions reflects a basic cleavage in their social structure – between the descendants of the original inhabitants of the area and those who migrated into the area; with the latter group deriving the right to farm from the former.[6]

Numerous oral traditions confirm this pattern. At some point in the past, possibly after the Soninke diaspora from ancient Ghana or Wagadu in the twelfth or thirteenth century CE, the powers and the responsibilities of autochthones and immigrants were divided by the former: "I give you warfare; but I keep the land."[7] Both groups practiced agriculture, but the immigrants did so at the sufferance of the autochthones. The territorial rulership[8] that has developed out of the immigrants' warrior status may be the choice portion today, but this was not necessarily true of either the original occupants of the area and their descendants or the immigrants who settled among them. A local ruler among the contemporary western Soninke is called a *debegumme* (master of the village) – an immigrant farmer turned warrior and, afterward, a politician.[9] An older form of nobility belongs to the original dwellers, those autochthonous clans who produce the *nyinyagumme* (master of the earth).[10]

The Mossi (Moore) of Burkina Faso and some of their cultural cousins in the Mole-Dagbani language family living in the northern third of Ghana today share with the Soninke a similar tradition of social cleavage between the territorial rulers who trace their descent from immigrants and the

---

5. Pollet and Winter, *La Société*, 33.

6. Pollet and Winter, 44–52.

7. Pollet and Winter, 56.

8. In territorial rulerships, a single individual may take on royal prerogatives. In other societies, rule may be exercised more collaboratively by clan heads.

9. Pollet and Winter, *La Société*, 313.

10. To the present day, the eldest member of a *nyinyagumme* clan still maintains the right to rent farmland to any newcomer in the area. But the largely secular meaning of his landlordship today has developed as the result of centuries of Soninke Islamization. In an earlier period, it was the *nyinyagumme* (master of the earth) alone who could pacify the troublesome forces that prevent the farmer from clearing away the bush and cultivating the soil.

autochthonous guardians of the earth. The Mossi, as well as the Dagomba and the Tallensi, claim that their ancestors came from Gambaga – in what is now the Mamprusi traditional area in northeastern Ghana – and nearby parts of Togo.[11] The development of a ruling class, especially in the case of the Mossi, has also entailed the elaboration of a perspective on the mystery of existence that lays considerable emphasis on celestial symbols and, in particular, on Naba Wende (Wennam), the Absolutely Transcendent One imaged as the royal sun.[12]

The solar or heavenly orientation of the Mossi ruling class who descended from immigrants – the *nabissi* (children of the ruler) – plays a far less important role in their religious practice than the earthward orientation of the commoner descendants of the autochthonous population – the *tengbissi* (children of the earth). The sun and the sky, like the ruling class, keep their distance from the ordinary farmer. Both sunlight and rain, gifts from heaven, are necessary for the farmer's agricultural pursuits, but the farmer supplicates for such benefactions through the mediation of the earth. "The King-Sun drinks no *dolo*," the Mossi say as they pour a libation of millet beer, "but his wife, the Earth, does drink it."[13]

If the more developed ruling class of the Mossi has led to a certain political emphasis on celestial rites and symbols of the transcendent, the less developed territorial rulership of the Tallensi in northeastern Ghana has preserved for the earth shrine (*tongban*) and the master of the earth (*tendaana*) an absolute primacy in ritual terms. In economic and political terms, the Tallensi *tendaana* controls the distribution of farmland and arbitrates disputes about property rights that may arise between two or more contiguous lineages. In Tallensi myths of origin, the first *tendaana* emerged from the earth, but the territorial rulership derives from a Mamprusi immigrant named Mosuor. However, authority is mainly exercised in Tallensi society not by the territorial rulers but by elders within the structure of the patrilineal descent group. The local ruler's authority – *naam* in Tallensi – extends mainly to secular concerns. The rulers themselves seek the mediation of the masters of the earth when interlineage disputes arise or when some violation of the earth's interdictions takes place.

---

11. Rattray, *Tribes*, xi–xii.

12. The sun's counterpart on earth, the paramount chief of the Mossi (the Mogho Naba), customarily enacts a dawn ritual in which he exits from his palace in Ouagadougou by the eastern gate of the courtyard, dressed in red, just as the sun is rising. As the morning progresses, he exchanges this red tunic for a white one, symbolic of the brightness of day. On Fridays, he mimes an attempted dawn departure on horseback from the royal compound from which his courtiers ritually dissuade him, supposedly representing the commoner beneficiaries of the Mogo Naba's radiant rule. See Delobsom, *L'Empire*.

13. Badini, "La representation," 25.

The masters of the earth mediate in what has been called, at various times, a stateless or acephalous society, more accurately described as a segmentary-lineage society. In such a society, everyone is ruled in their descent group or lineage, but some lineages align in social segments (combinations of lineages) against a perceived common enemy. There is no territorial ruler unless colonial or postcolonial governments have invented them.[14] The tensions between ethnic groups in contemporary South Sudan illustrate the most problematic aspects of such a social setting.

The Tallensi ruler has one ritual function – the control of rainfall, for which, in a curious reversal of their normal relationships, the *tendaana* must seek permission for his ceremonial action.[15] Not unlike the development of the solar theology of the Mossi with the ascendancy of the ruling class, such a claim to ritual power is meant to enhance the authority of the one making the claim. In the colonial and postcolonial eras, such claims have often been exaggerated by territorial rulers who are anxious to exalt themselves in the eyes of outside political authorities, either colonial or nationalist. The more usual ritual subordination of the ruler to the *tendaana* in Tallensi society manifests itself most dramatically in the installation (or "enskinment") of the traditional ruler in Tongo, a ritual that can only be performed with the cooperation of the *Gbizug-tendaana* – the senior master of the earth.[16] It is only the xenophilia of the master of the earth that makes possible territorial rule.

Whereas Tallensi society exemplifies an intricate dialectic of territorial ruler and *tendaana*, among the Dagaaba of northwestern Ghana and adjacent areas of Burkina Faso, the rulership represents a very modern innovation, introduced by the British colonial government in the early twentieth century. For the Dagaaba, the earth shrine (*tengaan*) and its custodian (*tengaansob*) mediate interlineage disputes, especially when the source of conflict in this agricultural society involves farmland.[17] One additional taboo attests not only to the Dagaaba lack of territorial rulership but also to a certain rejection of its symbols. The horse, imagistically associated with immigrants and their ruling descendants throughout much of the West African Savannah,[18] may not enter the precincts of certain Dagaaba earth shrines. When such a shrine in Kaleo

---

14. Fortes, "Political System," 248–55.
15. Fortes, 254.
16. Fortes, 254–55.
17. Goody, *Social Organisation*, 35.
18. Goody, *Technology*, 57–72.

was violated by a horse in 1976, the Wa Naa – ruler of the small Wala state located in the midst of the Dagaaba area – was obliged to expiate the crime.[19]

In the Dagaaba area, there exist separate shrines where the gift of rain may be implored, especially at a time of drought, but the inhabitants of various minor earth shrine "parishes" often seek out a major earth shrine (*tengaankpee*) when it is thought that drought had resulted from unexpiated crimes against the earth.[20] The dualities of agricultural life in the West African Savannah – the sky and earth, rainy season and dry season, farm and bush – do not exhaust the religious imagination of the peoples who have lived in this zone for many generations. Along with many other Savannah populations – whose indigenous religious traditions have received little scholarly investigation or whose traditional ways have been wholly or partially obscured with the coming of Islam – the Dagaaba and the Tallensi understand the closeness and distance of the absolutely transcendent. It is as close as the local earth shrine and as distant as the vault of the sky.

Earth Shrines and Muslim Rulers: Territorialities in Conflict

In religious terms, the cultus surrounding the rulership and its heaven-sent emblems also seems to have been a secondary development added onto, and sometimes obscuring, the more elemental cultus at the earth shrine. The earth shrine, however, has proven more xenophile than xenophobic toward territorial rulers as long as the rulers recognize the limits of their power. With the development of territorial rulership, God comes to be imaged as an exalted ruler, dealing with mortals not so much through or at the earth shrine but, rather, through other subordinate powers, sometimes called gods. Bureaucracy multiplies.

Islam has generally flourished in those sedentary West African societies where territorial rulership had already developed. It has hardly flourished at all where so-called stateless or acephalous or segmentary-lineage political traditions prevail. How did Islam first enter into a traditional rulership in the West African Sahel and Savannah? One of the earliest accounts we have would seem to indicate that Islam was first perceived, at least in ancient Mali, as a new and more effective way for the traditional ruler (or earth shrine custodian) to exercise his ritual control of rain. Al-Bakri, already quoted above, narrates how

---

19. I was visiting in that area of Ghana when this happened.
20. Goody, *Social Organisation*, 32.

a ruler in Malal, somewhere in Mali, found a religious solution for drought no later than the early eleventh century.

Living in the ruler's court at that time was a Muslim guest. Nowhere in al-Bakri's text is it said that this Muslim was a merchant; and in fact, the opposite might be implied. The Muslim guest is described as a devout reciter of the Qur'an and a student of the Prophet's Sunna. Was the ruler's guest a xenophile holy man, who had taken the post of Muslim-in-residence at the court of an equally xenophile territorial ruler? After the ruler had sacrificed nearly all his cattle to obtain rain, he turned in desperation to his Muslim guest. The guest, however, asked the king to become a Muslim before they both engaged in what may be the Muslim ritual prayer for rain, the *salat-al-istisqa'*:

> [The Muslim] then asked [the ruler] to wait until the eve of Friday, at which time he told him to undergo a total ablution. The Muslim then clothed [the ruler] with a cotton robe that [the Muslim] had with him. Then the two of them went out to a hillock of earth. The Muslim stood to perform the worship with the ruler on his right, executing it after him. The two of them worshipped for as much of the night as God allowed. The Muslim led the prayer of petition and the ruler answered "Amen." Hardly had dawn broken when God brought rain down on them.[21]

It is important to note where al-Bakri locates the site of prayer: "a hillock of earth" (*rabwatin min al-'ard*). Muslim worship would normally be performed on a flat surface, not a hillock. Why does al-Bakri specify the composition of a hillock of earth? Can it be that this hillock is an earth shrine on a slight rise in the Malian savannah?

The *Kano Chronicle* (*Ta'rikh Kanu*), a dynastic record compiled and revised over many centuries, records a first encounter – probably in the fourteenth century – between the indigenous people of Kano and immigrant Muslims coming from the Mali diaspora, the Wangarawa (Hausa plural of Wangara).[22] The xenophile territorial ruler (*sarki*), whose nickname was Yaji (meaning "pepper"), welcomed the Wangara to Kano. With his permission, they built their first mosque underneath a sacred tree in the city's center, directly challenging the traditional earth cultus. Enemies of the newly arrived Muslims

---

21. Cited in de Slane, *Description de l'Afrique*, 389 (French). This is my translation from the Arabic; for another translation, see Hopkins, *Corpus*, 82.
22. al-Hajj, "Seventeenth Century Chronicle," 28–32.

befouled the open mosque with human excrement. Since a Kano militia proved unable to prevent this desecration, the immigrant Muslims took to prayer:

> They . . . gathered on a Tuesday in the mosque from the time of the evening worship until sunrise, cursing the pagans, and going back to their homes in mid-morning. God responded to their appeal and blinded [the pagans'] leader on that day, and later blinded everyone who did such a thing, together with their womenfolk.[23]

What is going on in this narrative? In the stories of previous generations recounted in the *Kano Chronicle*, much is made of the religious significance for the indigenous people of Kano of a sacred tree at the center of the city. In many cultures round the world, the earth as a numinous force is venerated at the base of certain trees.[24] The social anthropologist Robin Horton has noted that the "earth-spirit, considered as a principal spiritual guardian of the community . . . is an age-old feature of religious life in West Africa, and one invoked to account for and support age-old socio-political structures." Horton goes on to note the precise political significance of this earth symbolism:

> It seems to have been inspired by the recurrent observation that particular communities had, during the course of their histories, become enlarged through the gradual and peaceful influx of groups unrelated in lineage and clan terms to their original founders, and by the further observation that such communities, despite their resulting heterogeneity, had preserved high degrees of cohesion. This recurring situation was neatly accounted for in terms of the idea that, whilst the continued adhesion of individual lineage groups was due to their several sets of ancestral forces, the continued cohesion of the community as a whole was due to an earth-spirit under whose aegis these forces worked.[25]

The *Kano Chronicle* suggests that even before Muslims came to Kano in any substantial numbers or influence, tensions were rising between the territorial rulers and the guardians of the earth shrine at the tree. In Hausa oral tradition, the legendary Bayajida – sometimes said to be the grandfather of Bagauda,

---

23. This translation, with slight emendations, was made from the Arabic manuscript of the *Kano Chronicles* (MS O/AR10/2) originally owned by Sir Richmond Palmer, now in the National Archives, Kaduna. The late Professor John O. Hunwick of Northwestern University, once a colleague at the University of Ghana, made this translation available to me.

24. See van der Leeuw, *Religion in Essence*, 56–57.

25. Horton, *Patterns*, 356.

founder of Kano – began his career in Daura by marrying the female ruler there after conquering the snake named *sarki* that had inhabited and restricted access to Daura's only well.[26] This story, meant to explain (among other things) the origin of the title *sarki*, represents the beginning of a challenge to the earth shrine and its mediation between various clans by a new phenomenon, the territorial ruler – the supreme mediator of interclan relations in a particular area. The earth shrine seems to have developed, as Horton suggests, in response to the challenge of multiple clan lineages settling in a common territory. New immigration or the imperatives deriving from population increase in a particular territory may have led to a change in government from earth-shrine mediation of local clans to governance by a territorial ruler different from the local custodians of earth shrines.

In light of the above, I suggest that the *Kano Chronicle* account of the building of the first mosque under the sacred tree represents a further stage in the developing relationship between the territorial rulers and the earth shrine and its guardians. The Islamization of Yaji – or, if he and some of his predecessors were at least nominal Muslims, his more intense Islamization – was concretized by his surrounding himself with immigrant Muslims, the Wangara.[27] We may, then, take the *Kano Chronicle* account of Yaji and the advent of the Wangara as a symbol of the definitive implantation of Islam in Kano, strengthening the *sarki* in his battle with the earth shrine.

The alliance of Islam with the territorial rulership against the earth shrine eventually led to a corruption of Islam by the territorial rulers. The *Kano Chronicle* narrates how the Qur'an, wrapped in skins, had been transformed into *dirki*, an object of sacrificial veneration. In the late eighteenth and early nineteenth century, Muhammad al-Wali – the last Hausa ruler in Kano – depleted his resources by sacrificing to *dirki* in a time of drought. A new stage was about to develop in the history of sacred governance in Kano – the replacement of the last Hausa *sarki* in Kano by a Fulbe (Peulh, Fula, Fulani) emir bearing the reformist Islamic standard of Uthman dan Fodio.

Islam, having filtered into the West African Savannah through the courts of its territorial rulers, eventually saturated several major cultural areas. The Sokoto jihad of the early nineteenth century broke out throughout the Hausa

---

26. See "Legend of Daura," Johnston, 111–13.

27. Mervyn Hiskett has suggested that the *Kano Chronicle* narrative may telescope several waves of both Mande-originated and Sarakole-originated migration into the Kano area from the territory of the Songhay Empire from the fourteenth through the fifteenth centuries CE. Hiskett, *Development of Islam*, 45–46. On the influence of the Sarakole clerical caste called Jakhanke, see Sanneh, *Jakhanke Muslim Clerics*, 79–88.

territorial rulerships of what is today the northern third of Nigeria. Later jihads, often led by sophisticated Muslim scholars of Fulbe origin, upset the established political order in a broad range of territorial rulerships stretching from Senegal on the west to northern Cameroon on the east. The Fulbe spread throughout this zone, who were originally nomadic cattle herders, brought with them wherever they went the *torodbe* – a Muslim clerical class of considerable erudition. Divorced from the agricultural rites of sedentary populations like the Hausa, all of the Fulbe were inclined to look down upon the compromised Islamic practice of populations who had never completely abandoned the cultus at the earth shrine.

If territorial rulership paved the way for the first development of Islam in the West African Savannah, the worst enemy of traditional rulers in the era of reform has been the xenophobic militant Muslim cleric. The Sokoto jihad commenced with Uthman dan Fodio and his disciples emigrating from the realm of the Hausa ruler of Gobir in 1804. In their judgment, it was no longer possible for true Muslims to pledge their fealty to a ruler whose authority rested on non-Islamic foundations. Uthman dan Fodio consciously modeled the emigration (hijra) of his community from Gobir on the emigration of Prophet Muhammad from hostile Mecca to receptive Medina in 622 CE. Religious xenophobia replaced religious xenophilia in the quest for territorial rule.

Showers of Blessing in the Savannah

Although there were individual converts to Christianity along the Atlantic coast of West Africa before the nineteenth century, the real foundation of Christianity in what is now the Republic of Ghana dates from 1828. In that year, the Basel Mission – Reformed Church agents from Europe – inaugurated the work of evangelization around Accra, now the capital of Ghana. The Basel Mission had strongly identified itself with abolitionism, as had the Church Missionary Society in Britain. Roman Catholic missionary work – which also identified with abolitionism by the second half of the nineteenth century – commenced evangelizing activity in earnest near the old Portuguese trading post of Elmina in 1880 precisely because Portuguese Catholics seeking gold and slaves had first landed there in the late fifteenth century. Some meager remnants of that Portuguese Catholicism remained. The long connection of the Portuguese, the Dutch, and the British with the slave trade had caused justified xenophobia toward Christianity among local people in West Africa for several centuries.[28] Similar xenophobia toward agents of Islam has persisted since the slave raids of Samori[29] and Babatu in what is now northern Ghana in the late nineteenth century.

In view of the relatively recent date for effective evangelization along the Atlantic coast of West Africa, it is not surprising that missionary effort further inland had hardly commenced before the first decades of the twentieth century. Members of the Catholic evangelizing congregation – known as the Missionaries of Africa ("White Fathers")[30] – gradually filtered down into French West Africa from their original base in Algeria in the late nineteenth century. Anticlerical laws enacted in France in 1905, thought at first to threaten French missionary work in the African colonies of France, proved to have no such effect. But the possibility of such laws reaching French colonies prompted the Missionaries of Africa in West Africa to venture further south into the British-colonized Northern Territories of the Gold Coast, where they established a mission outpost at Navrongo in 1906, several years before other Christian churches began to evangelize in that area. Having experienced the xenophilia of the Kassena and other populations of what is now Ghana's Upper East Region, in 1929, three Missionaries of Africa were sent from Navrongo to what is now the Upper West Region of Ghana, an area where no Christian missionary had yet worked.

The first Missionaries of Africa to reach Dagaaba territory, in what is now the Upper West Region of Ghana, were Father Remigius McCoy (an Irish-Canadian), Father Arthur Paquet (a French-Canadian), and Brother Basilide Koot (a native of the Netherlands). Father McCoy had first come from Canada to Navrongo in 1925 and had learned the local Kassem language. It is important to note that some Navrongo Catholic laypeople also accompanied

---

28. The Portuguese, despite their involvement in the slave trade, did have some success in evangelizing local people in and around Elmina in the sixteenth century, as did Philip Quaque, the Anglican chaplain at Cape Coast Castle, in the eighteenth century. For one Elmina example, see the account by Pieter de Marees, a Dutch observer in the year 1602, who lived in Moree, about fifteen kilometers east of Elmina. He had met a local Elmina Catholic who struck the Dutch observer as fairly well instructed in Christianity, even though Calvinist predestinarianism made de Marees opine that "God has not seen fit to call them into our Christian faith." See de Marees, *Gold Kingdom*, 74. On Philip Quaque and the earliest Anglicans in Ghana, see Bansa, "Quaque, Philip," *Encyclopaedia of African Biography*, 170–73.

29. For a brief introduction to Samori Ture, see Triaud, "Samori Ture," *Encyclopaedia of Islam* 8:1048b–49b.

30. Founded in North Africa in 1868 by Charles Martial Allemand Lavigerie, the French Archbishop of Algiers and Carthage, the Missionaries of Africa came to be known as the "White Fathers" because of their white *gandoura* and *burnous*, which distinguished them from the French diocesan clergy in North Africa, who wore black clerical dress.

the first Missionaries of Africa to Dagaaba territory. One of these Navrongo laypeople, Ludger, spoke More – the Mossi language – and could also make himself understood in Dagaare before any of the expatriate missionaries had learned the language. Ludger's work as the first evangelist in that language should be underlined.[31]

The beginnings in Jirapa proved none too easy. The site allocated to the Catholic missionaries by Ganaa – the first person to bear the title of Jirapa Naa (ruler of Jirapa) – was a bush area thought by the local people to be inhabited by spirits (*kontome*). It was the only site that Ganaa, the territorial ruler, could obtain from Taabe and Moyanga, the custodians of the two earth shrines in Jirapa. Since colonial administrators never stayed very long in northwestern Ghana, the people of Jirapa did not expect the missionaries to remain very long either, and they were surprised when they did. When the missionaries demonstrated that they were also able to offer basic medical services in Jirapa and the neighboring villages, the Dagaaba started to perceive these White men as healers of bodily ills as well as advocates for heavenly concerns. These missionaries were different, however, from the other advocates for heavenly concerns, such as the Muslims from Wa, who were usually called *Mwinpuorobo* (worshipers of *Naamwin*). The first difference the Dagaaba noticed was tangential to the missionaries' purpose but made a definite impression: these new *Mwinpuorobo* drank *pito*, which is fermented millet beer.[32]

During the first two and a half years of the Catholic mission in Jirapa, a fair amount of local people approached the missionaries for catechetical instruction. A simple catechism in the Dagaare language had been printed in Algeria and made available in 1931. The Missionaries of Africa usually insisted on a three-year catechumenate: in the first year, the catechumens were given a medal of the Virgin Mary to wear and were thus called *medailles*; in the second year, they were given a rosary and were called *chapeletes*; upon completion of the third year, those who had prepared adequately became *baptises*. Eleven adults and one boy of about fourteen years were baptized at the midnight mass of Christmas Eve in 1932. That boy, Peter Poreku Dery, eventually became the first of the Dagaaba to be ordained a priest (1951) and then a bishop (1960). Later, he became the Archbishop of Tamale (in the current Northern Region of Ghana). During his retirement, Dery was elevated to the College of Cardinals (2006). He died in 2008, at the age of about ninety.

---

31. McCoy, *Great Things Happen*, 43.
32. McCoy, 45–46.

Drought prompted elders from the village of Daffiama, about twenty kilometers away from Jirapa, to approach the Missionaries of Africa for their prayerful intervention. Although the first rains back in the late 1920s and the early 1930s usually began in April, in the spring of 1932, the rains had still not commenced by early June. After much discussion, Father McCoy persuaded the Daffiama elders to join him in prayer to *Naamwin*, the one God of heaven and earth. As he led them in prayer in the small house chapel of the missionaries, McCoy periodically asked the Daffiama elders significant questions: (1) Were they willing to forsake the veneration of lesser spirits?; (2) Were they willing to allow their fellow villagers who wished to worship with the Christians to do so?; and (3) Were they willing to let their daughters marry whomever they wanted to marry? McCoy recognized the growing reluctance of the Daffiama elders to accept all these conditions, especially the third, but accept they did. McCoy kept them kneeling with him on the bare mud floor for more than an hour, repeating with them the *Our Father* and the *Hail Mary* in Dagaare over and over again, along with a special prayer of petition for rain. Stiff from kneeling, the Daffiama elders left the chapel, some of them heeding the priest's admonition that they must wait on God's will, others more skeptical of such pieties. McCoy returned to the chapel alone and begged God for rain. Father McCoy narrates what happened next.

> It was ten o'clock [a.m.] by the time we left the chapel . . . When the swiftest walkers reached Daffiama four hours later, they were met by soaking rain. Their immediate reaction was one of jubilation and the urge to retrace their steps to Jirapa to give thanks. But the rain was falling so heavily, they finally decided to wait until the next morning. Had they carried through their original impulse, they would have been surprised to see that as soon as they left the boundaries of the village, all was as dry as before.[33]

Rains normally began by late April, in that area, and the skeptic might see nothing unusual in their delayed advent in early June 1932. Rain in the savannah is often irregular, and the pattern of precipitation on any occasion is hard to predict. Something like that apparently happened at Daffiama shortly after Father McCoy's prayer in Jirapa with the Daffiama elders. Old men and women of that area, whom I met in the 1970s, swore that rain fell on the fields of those who heeded Father McCoy's advice to await God's good favor but not on the fields of those who had said Father McCoy's prayer was nonsense.

---

33. McCoy, 116.

In the weeks and months after that first "rain event," the Catholic mission at Jirapa was overwhelmed by petitioners from other Dagaaba villages, all of them seeking similar prayerful intervention for rain.[34]

Thus began the dramatic history of the Catholic Church among the Dagaaba. Today, nearly nine decades later, the Catholic Church in the Wa diocese is probably the most Africanized in Ghana in liturgy, catechesis, and spiritual life. It differs dramatically from other dioceses in Anglophone West Africa, where some clergy and laity still hanker for the return of Latin masses. The impetus for such Africanization has come, at least partially, from missionaries with an understanding of the local culture. The early and vigorous church leadership provided by Peter Poreku Dery, one of the first converts, was a major factor contributing to the growth and development of the Catholic Church in northwestern Ghana. In 1960, at his episcopal ordination by Pope John XXIII, when Dery was asked by the Pope what he needed for his diocese, he asked for a vernacular sung liturgy. Pope John heartily agreed with the new bishop. Without consulting with Vatican underlings, Dery and his collaborators commenced the project of elaborating a completely vernacular liturgy; and they were more than prepared for the official introduction of the vernacular throughout the Catholic Church in 1964.

Throughout his life, Dery was also known as a dowser – one who can divine for water with a stick. Many people who were anxious to sink a well – including expatriate missionaries – would often ask Dery to help them find a suitable place to dig. Neither should we forget Father McCoy. It was his luck or his grace – whatever you will – to offer the Dagaaba an alternative to traditional control over rain precisely at a point when an alternative was desperately needed. Like the nameless Muslim guest of that ruler in medieval Mali, Father McCoy, a man of prayer, was *there* at the right time.

Conclusion

New phases in the history of the West African Sahel and Savannah opened up as a result of natural crises such as drought or political crises such as slave-raiding. First, the earth shrine and its custodian originally controlled rain and agricultural fertility and sometimes mediated interlineage disputes as well. Second, when territorial rulerships developed, they sometimes proved xenophobic toward the masters of the earth, and sometimes xenophile. Third, territorial rulers whose control of rain or agriculture was threatened or whose

---

34. McCoy, 247–48.

dominance of ethnically varied territories was challenged sometimes turned to Islam in such critical moments. Medieval Mali and Songhay reached their respective zeniths precisely when their leaders transcended purely local religious symbols and based their plans for imperial dominion on the more universal symbols provided by the Islamic tradition. Fourth, however, it is important to note that so-called stateless or acephalous or segmentary-lineage societies like the Dagaaba, when confronted with an environmental or political crisis, have not converted to Islam but to Christianity – and in large numbers. Does this also help to explain the massive conversion to Christianity, starting in the early twentieth century, of another segmentary-lineage society – the Igbos of southeastern Nigeria – for whom the earth has great religious significance? Both the Dagaaba – from northern Muslim raiders (Samori and Babatu) – and the Igbos – from both northern and southern raiders – suffered the depredations of slave-raiding well into the late nineteenth century.

The orphan or stranger who is to be joined on a permanent basis to an earth "parish" among the Dagaaba must be introduced to the shrine by participating in a sacramental eating of its clay as well as by drinking from the allied local stream. These rites of xenophilia suggest that all the orphan or stranger religious traditions that have migrated into West Africa in the last millennium or so have had to taste the soil of the earth shrine and drink the water of the local stream. The Malian sage Amadou Hampâté Ba (ca. 1900–1991) once said that "Islam has no more color than water and that is what explains its success. It takes on the colors of the soils and the stones."[35] Yes and no. In its later developments in West Africa, originally xenophile Islam has sometimes turned xenophobic, as the history of Muslim reform movements from the Sokoto jihad to Boko Haram suggests. Likewise, while a xenophile Christianity has sometimes settled peacefully into West African settings, sometimes it has not; the xenophobia of some of the recently developed neo-charismatic churches to what they define as idolatry has been dramatic. Xenophilia, rather than xenophobia, remains the ideal. Let me end with some words of scriptural encouragement: "Let mutual love continue. Do not neglect to show hospitality to strangers, for by doing that some have entertained angels without knowing it" (Heb 13:1–2 NRSV).

Bibliography

Badini, Amadé. *La representation de la vie et de la mort chez les Mose traditionnels de Haute-Volta*. Dissertation for the Doctorat du troisieme cycle, Universite de Lille III, Paris, 1978.

---

35. Quoted in Monteil, *L'Islam noir*, 48.

Delobsom, A. A. Dim. *L'Empire du Mogho Naba*. Paris: Domat-Montchrestien, 1932.
Fortes, Meyer. "The Political System of the Tallensi of the Gold Coast." In *African Political Systems*, edited by Meyer Fortes and E. E. Evans-Pritchard, 238–71. London: Oxford University Press, 1940.
Gibb, Hamilton Alexander Rosskeen, ed. *Encyclopaedia of Islam*. 2nd ed. Leiden: Brill, 1995.
Gomez, Michael. *African Dominion*. Princeton: Princeton University Press, 2018.
Goody, Jack. *The Social Organisation of the LoWiili*. 2nd ed. London: Oxford University Press, 1967.
———. *Tradition, Technology, and the State in Africa*. London: Oxford University Press for the International African Institute, 1971.
Hajj, Muhammad al-. "A Seventeenth Century Chronicle on the Origins and Missionary Activities of the Wangarawa." *Kano Studies* 1, no. 4 (1968): 7–42.
Hiskett, Mervyn. *The Development of Islam in West Africa*. London; New York: Longman, 1984.
Hopkins, J. F. P., trans. *Corpus of Early Arabic Sources for West African History*. Edited by Nehemia Levtzion and J. F. P. Hopkins. Fontes Historiae Africanae Series Arabica IV. Cambridge: Cambridge University Press, 1981.
Horton, Robin. *Patterns of Thought in Africa and the West*. Cambridge: Cambridge University Press, 1993.
Johnston, H. A. S. "The Legend of Daura." In *A Selection of Hausa Stories*, edited and translated by H. A. S. Johnston, 111–13. Oxford: Clarendon Press, 1966.
Leeuw, G. van der. *Religion in Essence and Manifestation*. Translated by J. E. Turner. New York; Evanston: Harper & Row, 1963.
Levtzion, Nehemia. *Ancient Ghana and Mali*. London: Methuen, 1973.
Marees, Pieter de. *Description and Historical Account of the Gold Kingdom of Guinea (1602)*. Translated and edited by Albert van Dantzig and Adam Jones. Union Académique Internationale: Fontes Historiae Africanae. Series Varia V. Oxford: Oxford University Press, 1987.
McCoy, Remigius F. *Great Things Happen: A Personal Memoir*. Montreal: Society of Missionaries of Africa, 1988.
Monteil, Vincent. *L'Islam noir*. Paris: Éditions du Seuil, 1971.
Ofosu-Appiah, L. H., ed. *The Encyclopaedia of Africana: Dictionary of African Biography: Ethiopia to Ghana*. Accra: Africa Press, 1977.
Pollet, Eric, and Grace Winter. *La Société Soninke*. Brussels: Éditions de l'Institut de Sociologie, 1971.
Rattray, R. S. *Tribes of the Ashanti Hinterland*. Oxford: Clarendon, 1932.
Sanneh, Lamin. *The Jakhanke Muslim Clerics: A Religious and Historical Study of Islam in Senegambia*. Lanham: University Press of America, 1989.
Slane, Mac Guckin de., trans. and ed. *Description de l'Afrique septentrionale*. 2nd ed. Paris: Geuthner, 1913.

13

Beyond Exclusivism

Exploring, Engaging, and Expanding Interreligious Hospitality in Yorubaland

Akintunde E. Akinade

Introduction

The Sanneh Institute in Ghana honors Lamin Sanneh, a brilliant, courageous, and creative scholar, whose spirit hovers over the conceptualization and articulation of the topic of my paper.

Sanneh, an indomitable *nwalimu* (teacher) spent his academic career grappling with paradigms for interreligious engagement and hospitality. His fertile mind called for cross-cultural perspectives in theological discourse. Andrew Walls, in his insightful foreward to *A New Day: Essays on World Christianity in Honor of Lamin Sanneh*, invokes the name of Ibn Battuta, the famous Moroccan traveler, in his effort to articulate Sanneh's academic journey and penchant for cross-cultural conversations. At twenty-one years of age, Ibn Battuta set out to explore the Middle East and Iran, traveled through Russia, and visited India, China, Sri Lanka, and West African grasslands. His journeys took thirty years to complete. He traveled seventy-five thousand miles and visited forty-four different countries.[1] Lamin Ousman Sanneh's travels started in Gambia and outstripped Ibn Battuta in the number of countries he visited. Sanneh's cultural sensitivity was deeper than that of the fourteenth-century

---

1. See Walls, "Tribute to Lamin Sanneh," ix.

explorer and scholar. The Sanneh Institute is a bold salute to this intrepid African scholar. Sanneh's intellectual mind had no place for smallness. The quenchless light of his intellectual imagination propelled us to new heights in interreligious engagements. His legacy looms large on any serious scholarly project on Africa's triple religious heritage.

My effort aims to move the conversations in interfaith engagement beyond mere tolerance to the absolute recognition of the other's faith in God as one's own or to what Laurie Patton described as "pragmatic pluralism." According to Patton, "in the twenty-first century, there are no more distant strangers. There are only proximate ones."[2] The geo-religious reality in the twenty-first century compels scholars to contemplate new and creative models in interreligious dialogue. According to Lesslie Newbigin,

> it has become a commonplace to say that we live in a pluralist society – not merely a society which is in fact plural in the variety of cultures, religions and lifestyles which it embraces, but pluralist in the sense that this plurality is celebrated as a thing to be approved and cherished.[3]

Here, the British theologian makes a crucial distinction between pluralism as a fact of life and pluralism as an ideology. This is about the need to make a distinction between the belief that pluralism is to be encouraged and desired as opposed to considering pluralism as imperialistic and divisive.

For all intents and purposes, Yorubaland provides creative paradigms and templates for contemplating interreligious discourse. Since the nineteenth century, Christians, Muslims, and practitioners of indigenous religions have engendered new insights into engaging diversity. This paper offers snippets into the complex religious terrain in Yorubaland and also provides some critical insights into what I describe as "interreligious leveraging" in Yorubaland. On the issue of trajectory, it is imperative to connect interreligious paradigms in Yorubaland to issues relating to ethics, solidarity, and human wholeness. My paper grapples with the inevitable connection between religion and transformation. The "interfaith industry" continues to engender creative paradigms in religious tolerance, hospitality, and peacemaking. These themes are important in world Christianity, ethics, and theology today. This paper grapples with the meaning and parameters of interreligious hospitality and "dialogue of life" among the Yoruba people of southwestern Nigeria. I will

---

2. Patton, "Pragmatic Pluralism," 23.
3. Quoted in McGrath, *Christian Theology*, 448.

further examine how the two issues of justice and societal transformation can contribute to expanding the discourse on "dialogue of life" in Yorubaland. The paper straddles the intersection between territoriality and border crossing.

Religion and the Making of the Yoruba

It has been unanimously agreed that there was Islam and there were Muslims in Yorubaland when Christianity was introduced among the Yorubas in the 1840s. A Yoruba adage states that *Aiye laba'fa, aiye laba Imale, osan gangan ni igbagbo wole de.* This means that "there was *Ifa*, and there was *Imale* [Islam] in Yorubaland from the ancient time but Christianity came in the afternoon." Islam came to Yorubaland, probably from Mali, a long time ago. Some scholars argue that that is why it is known as *Imale* – that is, the religion of the people of Mali. Other researchers argue that Islam reached Yorubaland through the Fulani from Sokoto. It came first to Ilorin in Kwara State, and from there it spread to the Oyo Empire and then to other parts of Yorubaland. It should also be noted that the Muslims in Yorubaland were the only literate people before the arrival of Christian missionaries to Abeokuta. Thus, Muslim scholars and teachers were employed by local kings as secretaries and advisers in the palace.

From a Yoruba's perspective, believing in God or in any religion was an innate quality of human beings. Also, Yorubaland being a free society, everyone had freedom to believe in whatever they wanted as long as this served the need of such individuals. Hence, being a Muslim, a Christian, or a follower of African indigenous religions was an acceptable norm. No one frowned upon anyone else for believing in any religion.

In the marketplace of Yoruba religion, there has been both interdependence and mutual influence between Christianity and Islam. The spirit of Yoruba liberalism contributes to a deep sense of interreligious hospitality among the Yorubas. In terms of interreligious relations, before the advent of Christianity in Yorubaland, Islam enjoyed three centuries of cultural prestige among the Yorubas, especially in the northwestern and central regions. Just as Europeans often adopted Arabic terms in medicine, science, and astronomy, the Yoruba Christians often adopted Arabic terms in religious expression. The Yoruba terms for a Christian priest (*alufa*), a saint (*woli*), prayer (*adura*), and heathen (*keferi*) are derived from the Arabic. Yoruba missionaries adopted Islamic modes of thought to conceptualize and present Christian messages to their converts. Both Bishop Ajayi Crowther and Bishop James Johnson understood the importance of engaging Muslims in different contexts in Yorubaland, as evidenced in the fact that both clergymen exemplified the values of conscious contextualization.

In Yorubaland, Christians and Muslims live side by side, celebrate their differences, and do not see doctrinal differences as constituting a veritable barrier to interfaith encounters and relations. The result is not a lazy pluralism, where the particularity of each religion is obliterated for the sake of "getting along." I submit that one of the significant points of departure in interfaith encounter on the level of civil society among the Yoruba people is the acceptance of the presence and legitimacy of other religions as symbolic mediations of the sacred encounter. This understanding of other religions is not derived from an evaluation of them as abstract systems or structures. Rather, it is based on an unequivocal appreciation of the experience of the people who practice them and of the activity of God in their lives as portrayed in their ethical and spiritual commitments. In the words of Wande Abimbola:

> The African point of view is one in which there is respect for all the religious traditions of humankind. While we hold steadfastly to our beliefs, we respect the right of others to practice their own religions in their own ways, provided they do not infringe on the rights of others.[4]

The Primacy of the Ancestral Home

Interreligious experience in Yorubaland has been greatly influenced by the valorization of ancestral identification and legitimacy. The identification and identity of Ile-Ife as the ancestral home of all Yoruba people continues to contribute to the high level of interreligious hospitality in Yorubaland. Laitin, in his *Hegemony and Culture: Politics and Religious Change among the Yoruba*, proposed a theory of culture that would replace William Geertz's social systems theory and Abner Cohen's rational choice theory. He believed that both theories cannot satisfactorily explain why religious change among the Yoruba – which produced Muslim and Christian subcultures with different socioeconomic statutes and different ways of viewing politics – failed to replace the ancestral city of origin with religion as the determining factor in the political affiliation and preferences of the Yorubas.

Modifying Antonio Gramsci's theory, Laitin developed a hegemonic theory of culture that argues that it is not the subsystems that interact with

---

4. Abimbola, "Attitude of Yoruba Religion," 145.

other subsystems to determine choice and preferences. Rather, one specific subculture becomes hegemonic, ensuring that its values and preferences are seen as obvious, commonsensical, and unquestioned, while choices involving other interests are made secondary and more variable.[5] In the case of the Yoruba people, Laitin sees ethnicity or loyalty to the ancestral city of origin as the hegemonic subculture that overrides other criteria of choice. This perspective provides the formidable foundation for the non-politicization of religious cleavage among the Yorubas. Beyond the narrative concerning the "clash of civilizations," Yorubaland offers a paradigm that moves beyond the narrative concerning the "clash of civilizations" and in which violent competitive impulses are mediated by nonnegotiable cultural mandates and standards. In the context of Yorubaland, religion is perceived not only as beliefs but as practical ideologies and philosophies in daily life.

Appropriating the Dialogue of Life

One viable resource for appropriating the contextual model in interreligious relations in Yorubaland is an understanding of the dialogue of life that is part and parcel of the daily encounter of Christians and Muslims in many parts of Nigeria. Western theories of dialogue tend to be text-centered and doctrinally centered. The dialogue of life, on the other hand, takes into consideration other issues that are not considered in this theoretical approach to interreligious relations.

One of the most remarkable contributions of the Yoruba context to interfaith ventures is the dialogue of life. The Yoruba have made significant strides in this area. It is my contention that the advances in this area are no less significant than abstract academic discourse on dialogue. The Yoruba people, with their enduring legacy of interreligious connections across religious lines, provide the best case study for understanding a contextual approach to Christian-Muslim relations. Within the Yoruba context, Islam and Christianity have adapted to the continuing influence of traditional Yoruba religion. In addition, one of the distinctive characteristics of Christian-Muslim relations in Africa is that it is intimately part of family and communal life. In the dialogue of life, one relates to the Other (cultural and religious) with respect and attention in all of their Otherness. In spite of difference, one recognizes one's basic community with the Other at the human and even the religious level. One discovers one's own true identity in the relationship with the Other,

---

5. See Laitin, "Hegemony," 272.

and one is truly enriched by such interpersonal contacts and connections. The dialogue of life underscores essential issues and conditions that are imperative for developing a theology of hospitality. This is a theology that is based on the love of God and one's neighbor.

On 13 October 2007, the Royal Aal al-Bayt Institute for Islamic Thought in Amman, Jordan, invited Christian leaders from all over the globe for interreligious dialogue with Muslims based on two important scriptural themes: to love God and to love one's neighbor. Entitled "A Common Word between Us and You," the message represents the agreement of 138 Muslim scholars and religious leaders to engage in dialogue with people from other religious traditions. This important call beckons Christians and Muslims to cherish the religious encounter and dialogue in the ordinary course of life – in the street, in the marketplace, in schools, and in everyday encounters. In a world where religion, with all its multiple manifestations, has become an increasingly powerful and divisive force, the gains within the context of dialogue of life provide hope for the future within the context of Nigeria. I also affirm that a theology of religions that is consistent and meaningful to the human experience can only be pursued by taking seriously some of the useful paradigms that have emerged in the everyday stories and experiences of Christians and Muslims. Christian-Muslim engagement and dialogue must be deeply rooted in the concrete experiences of people. Since these experiences take multiple forms, scholars must seek to interrogate the various issues that constitute the context in which Christians and Muslims find themselves. Although this is not an organized form of dialogue, it has the potential to facilitate community understanding and community building. The nonnegotiable aspect of being a Christian or a Muslim in Yorubaland is the common life they share together. They are inevitably drawn into the same struggles, concerns, and agitations. The dialogue of life valorizes what is already present or occurring within a Nigerian context. It is neither a prefabricated nor contrived form of dialogue. Rather, it is a daily engagement and encounter with people's existential realities. It wrestles with the fundamental factors and circumstances that make people human.

The Yoruba worldview is sated with injunctions that affirm the considerations for the well-being of others. The concept of *ajobi* (consanguinity) and *ajogbe* (co-residentship) emphasize that people live together both as blood relations and non-blood relations.[6] The overall imperative is for the need for interdependence and tolerance in social, religious, and political behavior. We have to be intentional about discerning the appropriate responses to this

---

6. For a full exposition of this perspective, see Akiwowo, *Ajobi and Ajogbe*.

phenomenon. Chinua Achebe describes this situation as the "crossroads in our culture." This is the way Achebe, a guru of English and Igbo metaphor, describes this intriguing phenomenon:

> To be at the crossroads is very important because something is always happening there. When we are thinking of crossroads in our culture, that is where the spirits cross and the people cross, so you can meet the spirits there. It can be dangerous but also very rewarding if you wrestle there and succeed. But if you run away from the crossroads because it is perilous, well, you'll survive but you'll never know.[7]

He continues,

> Diversity is very important because that is what the crossroads is about – the meeting of opposites . . . For me when I see an artist proposing a simplification which eliminates diversity, I can't understand it, because if you eliminate diversity the basis of your aspiration is gone. An artist is not a dogmatic person who is seeking the way, the truth and the life. There must be many ways, many truths and many lives.[8]

This description has tremendous implications for the interreligious encounter. It is an encounter that signifies some of the experiences of the crossroad. Although sated with many potential pitfalls, this encounter is replete with rewarding possibilities. It is a risky phenomenon that must be embraced with courage.

In Praise of Hospitality

The theme of hospitality continues to be an important factor in interreligious relations, especially in Christian-Muslim relations in Africa. In Yorubaland, *itoju alejo* – hospitality to a guest – promotes the ethos of empathy to a stranger and the willingness to transcend parochial sensibilities and self-limiting agendas.[9] Hospitality offers the elixir for communal regeneration and wholeness. In its unadulterated form and manifestation, it is the antidote

---

7. Chinua Achebe, "The Crossroads in Our Cultures," *Sunday Times*, 12 November 1989, 18.
8. Achebe, 18.
9. For an excellent analysis of Yoruba moral values from the vantage point of an avid *onisegun* (traditional healer), see Hallen, *The Good, The Bad, and the Beautiful*.

to unfettered anarchy and chaos. Within the "community of practice"[10] – to borrow a phrase from Akinwumi Ogundiran – the lures of hospitality can engender the capacity to transcend narrow religiocultural provincialism and embark on a new journey that is defined by empathy and tolerance. Hospitality to the neighbor offers a beacon of hope in a world torn apart by violence, hatred, and apathy. It reminds us that the human spirit is endowed with the power to ruminate about hope and transformation even in the darkest times.

Hospitality to the Other is firmly entrenched in Yoruba culture. The *Ifa* literary corpus celebrates the imperative of treating strangers with kindness and respect. In fact, this indigenous divination system recognizes the divinity in the other. Wande Abimbola writes about the positive attitude of Yoruba religion toward non-Yoruba religion. According to him, "In the African primal traditions there is a continuing witness against violence, brute force and intolerance of each other's belief . . . our traditional belief system still remains the harbinger of the deepest truths that have become available to our society."[11] I hasten to say that cultural insights such as the *Ifa* literary corpus can shape theological reflection and engagement in Africa. In his address at the 1992 Biennial Meeting of American Theological Schools (ATS), the late Kosuke Koyama lamented that "no group looks down on its own religious and cultural heritage more than Asian (and perhaps African) Christian theologians."[12] A sound contextual theology in Africa cannot dismiss the positive cultural perceptions in different contexts and settings in Africa. The discourse on interreligious relations in Africa can definitely benefit from the copious cultural insights that are unique to Africa.

Yoruba folklore and proverbs are sated with indigenous insights concerning the virtues of hospitality to strangers and visitors. Therefore, it is imperative to articulate hospitality in interreligious engagement as a veritable verb rather than an innocuous noun. It must be celebrated as a praxis that is carried out and practiced within civil society and in the context of interreligious relations. This perspective has tremendous implications for Christian-Muslim relations in Africa, a context with a long tradition and ethos concerning hospitality to neighbors, guests, and strangers. Through its resolve to introduce practical and pragmatic approaches to resolving conflicts, Yoruba people have contributed invaluable insights to the lexicon of conflict resolution and peacebuilding. The Yoruba traditional worldview is imbued with maxims and anecdotes

---

10. Ogundiran, *Yoruba*, 128.
11. Abimbola, "Attitude of Yoruba Religion," 145.
12. Koyama, "Theological Education," 97.

concerning peaceful resolution of conflicts. Some of these insights include *ija o dola* (conflicts do not yield concrete benefits), *alaafia lo ju* (peace reigns supreme), and *alaafia to ayo* (peace is analogous to joyfulness).

In the Judeo-Christian tradition, the value of hospitality is deeply rooted in the story of Abraham, who graciously hosted three strangers in his home. Abraham, a quintessential symbol of submission, obedience, and piety hosted these unexpected guests with unalloyed hospitality and grace. Under the shade of the oak trees at Mamre, he received these unexpected strangers with warmth and shared his food and friendship with them. In this rural and rustic setting in Palestine, Abraham did not treat these visitors with contempt or disdain; rather, he invited them to have communion and fellowship with him. This story remains a symbol of divine communion in Orthodox Christian spirituality. The Orthodox icon of "Abraham's Hospitality" offers a solemn plea and invitation to allow space for the stranger at the table of interreligious engagement.

Liberation, Religious Plurality, and the Social Order

The concepts of liberation and social order are intimately connected to well-being and wholeness. In all its various dimensions, the quest for liberation deals with the whole being. The social, political, economic, and cultural aspects of liberation are linked together by the desire to experience life as it is meant to be. Any factor that diminishes authentic living contributes to human bondage and oppression. The ethical implications of this concept cannot be overemphasized. This ethical dimension safeguards the well-being of the individual and the community. The overall well-being of the two is enhanced by an unequivocal commitment to peace and tolerance. The concept of *alaafia* (holistic well-being) among the Yoruba people of southwestern Nigeria is helpful for understanding the overall ramifications of human responsibility vis-à-vis personal and communal well-being. This is a word that is freely used among the Yorubas and Hausas to emphasize the pervasive power of holistic well-being. The word *alaafia* is related to the Arabic word *afiyah* and conveys the importance of physical and mental well-being. It is a commitment to seeking the welfare of the Other. It entails the search for an abundant life and meaningful existence. Properly understood, the discourse on *alaafia* emphasizes both human and communal wholeness. One can submit that *alaafia* is both a question and an answer. As an ethical policy, it indicates a show of concern for the wholeness and well-being of other people, irrespective of their religious identity and, by extension, the community to which they belong. In terms of an answer, it is a bold assurance of wholeness for both the investigator and the respondent. It may also be interpreted as an opportunity for the investigator to contribute positively to the wholeness of the community by concrete social and civic acts.[13] In Yoruba traditional religion, it is one of the cardinal prayer requests which are: *ire owo*, *ire omo*, and *ire alaafia*, which means blessings in three areas: financial prosperity, many children, and abundant wholeness. In contemporary Yorubaland and Hausaland, *alaafia* is used as a form of greeting across religious lines. A bold departure from the phrase *suum cuique* (meaning "to each his own"), the concept of *alaafia* safeguards communal balance and progress. This concept stands in contrast to, for example, the Socratic approach to justice that emphasizes individual probity, thereby providing the foundation for distributive justice – but does not account for a deeper sense of commitment that is needed for social equilibrium and well-being.

The concept of *alaafia* provides a more comprehensive framework for dealing with both personal and communal well-being. It also reinforces social cohesion and balance. Individuals are compelled not to intentionally destabilize the rhythm and flow of the society. The whims and caprices of individuals do not constitute a hindrance to achieving harmony in society. Although individuality is not totally abrogated, it is valued in relation to an individual's responsibility to the community. People are free to assert their individuality but not at the detriment of the family or the wider society. Young people are encouraged to follow the norms and expectations of the society. The result, to use Francis Deng's lucid analysis, "is a purposeful, proud, psychologically gratified, and socially integrated youth delighting in the pleasures of today yet aspiring to the utilitarian promises of a later age. In satisfaction, they conform to the essential norms of the system: the dictates of the elders."[14] The positive insights associated with *alaafia* resonate with *shalom* and *salaam*.

The rich intercultural boundaries that the term *alaafia* encompasses underscore the extent to which different communities and religious traditions grapple with the issue of holistic well-being. This cardinal principle also provides an indigenous perspective on peace, development, and reconciliation. Why is it important to be concerned about the well-being of others? Basically, Yoruba people believe that human well-being is mutually reinforcing. The notions of "I am because you are" and "a person is a person through other people"

---

13. I am very grateful to Professor Yomi Durotoye, Wake Forest University, for this insight.

14. Deng, *Dinka of the Sudan*, 24. The quality of *alaafia* – which is analogous to the concept of *dheeng* among the Dinka people of Sudan – represents qualities such as generosity, kindness, compassion, and good manners. The opposite of such positive virtues is *yuur*, which means selfishness, ugly manners, and wanton disregard for others. See Ray, *African Religions*, 94.

still directs the people's sensitivity and sensibilities toward one another. This disposition is analogous to the feeling of *Ubuntu*. According to Desmond Tutu,

> A person with *Ubuntu* is open and available to others, affirming of others, does not feel threatened that others are able and good, based from a proper self-assurance that comes from knowing that he or she belongs in a greater whole and is diminished when others are humiliated or diminished, when others are tortured or oppressed.[15]

This presents an ideal construct for self and society. There may be instances when the sense of personal and social equilibrium may be destabilized, but there is still a vision for moral responsibility toward the group. Mbiti states that the individual is still conscious of self in terms of "I am because we are, and since we are, I am"[16] – and this concept still undergirds people's allegiances and relations with one another.

Conclusion

The robust capacity for tolerance, hospitality, and peace is deeply engrained in Yoruba culture. Naturally, these values have had tremendous implications on interreligious relations in Yorubaland. Pragmatic sensibilities have informed and conditioned interpersonal engagements. The congenial disposition of traditional Yoruba religiocultural milieu continues to foster peaceful coexistence among Christians and Muslims in Yorubaland. This inclusive community continues to thrive without repudiating particularity.

The Christian tradition is endowed with the enduring insights that promote solidarity with the oppressed and the marginalized in society. Apart from affirming and endorsing nonnegotiable interreligious mandates, it is also imperative for African Christians to promote narratives and praxis that can engender societal transformation. This pathway accentuates the values of affirmation and collaboration as the guiding light on the tortuous path of interreligious engagement and understanding. In pursuing what Kenneth Cracknell has described as "good and generous faith,"[17] Christians have to reaffirm what is noble in their tradition and then seek the various ways through which these values can be further expanded through interfaith projects and

---

15. Tutu, *No Future*, 31.
16. Mbiti, *African Religions*, 282.
17. See Cracknell, *Good and Generous Faith*.

solidarity. If charity begins at home, it definitely does not end at home. This is a vision that is truly relevant to the African context.

Bibliography

Abimbola, Wande. "The Attitude of Yoruba Religion toward Non-Yoruba Religion." In *Attitudes of Religions and Ideologies toward the Outsider*, edited by Leonard Swidler and Paul Mojzes, 145. Lewiston: Edwin Mellen, 1990.

Akiwowo, Akinsola. "Ajobi and Ajogbe: Variations on the Theme of Sociation." Inaugural Lecture Series 46. Ile-Ife: University of Ife Press, 1983.

Cracknell, Kenneth. *In Good and Generous Faith: Christian Responses to Religious Pluralism*. Cleveland: Pilgrim Press, 2006.

Deng, Francis Mading. *The Dinka of the Sudan*. New York: Holt, Rinehart & Winston, 1972.

Hallen, Barry. *The Good, The Bad, and the Beautiful: Discourse about Values in Yoruba Culture*. Bloomington: Indiana University Press, 2000.

Koyama, Kosuke. "Theological Education: Its Unities and Diversities." *Theological Education Supplement* 1 (1993): 97.

Laitin, David D. "Hegemony and Culture: Politics and Religious Change among the Yoruba." *Journal of Religion in Africa* 18, no. 3 (1988): 272–83.

Mbiti, John S. *African Religions and Philosophy*. New York: Doubleday, 1970.

McGrath, Alister E. *Christian Theology: An Introduction*. Oxford: Wiley-Blackwell, 1994.

Ogundiran, Akinwumi. *The Yoruba: A New History*. Bloomington: Indiana University Press, 2020.

Patton, Laurie L. "Toward a Pragmatic Pluralism." *Emory Magazine*, Autumn 2013: 23.

Ray, Benjamin C. *African Religions: Symbol, Ritual, and Community*. Upper Saddle River: Prentice Hall, 2000.

Tutu, Desmond. *No Future without Forgiveness*. New York: Doubleday, 1999.

Walls, Andrew F. "A Tribute to Lamin Sanneh." Foreword to *A New Day: Essays in World Christianity in Honor of Lamin Sanneh*, edited by Akintunde E. Akinade, ix. New York: Peter Lang, 2010.

14

African Christianity and the Religious Question

Pentecostalism and Indigenous Religions

Elias Bongmba

Introduction

To continue a critical conversation on religious pluralism, in this chapter, I discuss the place of African indigenous religions at a time when Christianity in Africa is experiencing significant growth. To continue a critical conversation on religious pluralism, in this chapter, I discuss the place of African indigenous religions at a time when Christianity in Africa is experiencing significant growth. I will begin with a brief review of Lamin Sanneh's classic text, *West African Christianity: The Religious Impact*, and I will discuss what Sanneh referred to as "the religious impact" on the growth of Christianity, assuming that this includes indigenous African religions. I will then discuss aspects of Christian practice today that have returned to what some think is a precolonial denigration of indigenous religions in some churches in Africa. Finally, in the last section of the essay, I will discuss the prospects for religious pluralism in Africa by examining African ideas about hospitality, with a view to developing an outline for adapting such ideas to foster respect for different religions.[1]

---

1. I am thankful to Matthew J. Krabill for reading this chapter and giving me excellent feedback. I also thank the copy editor for great questions that clarified some of my ideas.

Early Encounters in Houston

The celebrated growth of Christianity in Africa today has been welcomed and will continue to be welcome news. When I moved to Houston in 1995, I was delighted to see in the city so many religious traditions with a connection to Africa. There was a mosque frequented by Africans; and there were several churches initiated by Africans, most of whom had Pentecostal leaning and some who were clearly connected to the Redeemed Christian Church of God. Some of these congregations were started by immigrants who had moved to the US and wanted to have a place "to feel at home."[2] The Eternal Sacred Order of the Cherubim and Seraphim also had two churches. I was a board member of an Orisha institute that was started by several Nigerians, but this was not successful because the organization could not replicate the popular Nigerian worship style in the African churches in Houston. In addition to Pentecostals, African Catholic and Presbyterian churches were also increasingly visible.

During those early years, it became clear to me that African Christianity, in Houston, and as I would later learn, even at home, had turned a corner. Among the African Christians attending African churches in the city, there was what Francis Machingura describes as a superiority complex, which was clearly manifested by some Zimbabwean Pentecostal churches and leaders.[3] The first demonstration of this shocking superiority was the attitude of Pentecostals toward African Traditional Religion (ATR). During a particular wedding ceremony I observed the officiating Pentecostal pastor perform a simple ritual to cleanse the new couple from "ancestral curses and religion" so that they would "receive their blessings and prosperity." In a discussion with a few people shortly after the service, I expressed my surprise at what seemed to be a rejection or disregard for African traditions and the church's role in carrying it out. They responded that all traditional religion is a curse that prevents Africans from receiving blessings. The bride and groom were both Pentecostal pastors, and the groom led a church in the United Kingdom (UK). It turned out this was the groom's second wife and that he was still happily married in the UK. Some joked that his new wife was his wife away from home.

The second criticism of ATR occurred at a funeral service in Houston. Several well-known members of the Cameroonian community were returning from Dallas when their SUV had an accident. One of the women was ejected through the back window and killed by a passing truck. At her funeral service,

---

2. F. B. Welbourn and B. A. Ogot, *Place to Feel at Home: A Study of Two Independent Churches in Western Kenya*. London: Oxford University Press, 1966.

3. Machingura, "Glossolalia," 91.

the presiding pastor, who had started several churches in the northeast, criticized ancestral traditions, saying that they were "holding people back from their riches." He also suggested that immigrants who were still living in apartments after being in the US for more than ten years were being "held back" from enjoying God's blessing. Although he did not specifically mention sin, when I asked several church members what he had meant, they told me that he wanted people to know that so-called traditional religion was "holding Africans back." I would later learn that someone from this pastor's church was charged with Medicare fraud.

These two incidents reflect a growing tradition in Africa. The best example of this belief at the highest level occurred when former Zambian president Frederick Chiluba, a leading Pentecostal Christian, waited more than three months after his election as president of Zambia before occupying the State House so that his charismatic friends could cleanse it. Isabel Phiri notes that they went from room to room, "with the intention of chasing out evil spirits associated with Eastern religion" because of rumors that Kenneth Kaunda, Zambia's former president, had brought a sea horse into the State House at night.[4]

Having made these introductory comments, I now revisit the question of the relationship between Christianity and indigenous religions as it is being framed by Pentecostals today. In 1995, I accepted an appointment to teach African indigenous religions at Rice University. I had just completed my degree in the philosophy of religion track at the University of Denver and Iliff School of Theology. In my undergraduate training at Sioux Falls College, my professor, Randy Maddox, had introduced me to Lamin Sanneh's book *West African Christianity: The Religious Impact*. As an undergraduate student, I appreciated that book very much because, compact as it is, it is written in a comprehensive and lucid style that is unique to Sanneh.

I thought at the time, and still do, that the chapter "Christianity, Islam and African Traditional Religion" was its most significant contribution because Sanneh did not treat ATR as *praeparatio evangelica* but, instead, as independent historic religions in their own right. Sanneh argues:

> A process of internal change was thus initiated in which African Christians sought a distinctive way of life through mediation of the Spirit, a process that enhanced the importance of traditional religions for the deepening of Christian spirituality. The

---

4. Phiri, "President Frederick Chiluba," 101.

charismatic churches, therefore combined the two fundamental elements of Christianity and African culture in a way that advertises their Christian intentions without undervaluing their African credentials. Biblical material was submitted to the regenerative capacity of African perception, and the result would be Africa's unique contribution to the story of Christianity.[5]

In an earlier essay published in 1980, Sanneh begins by simply stating that a critical question for the student of religion in Africa was the "continuing vitality of indigenous religions and their status in Muslim and Christian Africa."[6] Sanneh's text is loaded with tough questions that must be part of the conversation today. For instance, he cautions that it would be a mistake to continue down an "anti-Christian path" that argues that Islam is more tolerant of indigenous religions than Christianity. Thus, the idea that both Christianity and Islam simply "carved up" the continent to exert spheres of influence is not correct. The task of scholars is to engage in a critical analysis of the ways the two religions engaged African religiosity. Furthermore, the idea promoted by some scholars that Islam was to be scrutinized since "the Islamic regime explicitly forbids, quite apart from refusing to recognize, involvement in African traditional religious customs" is not correct.[7] Thus, indigenous religious and cultural practices were part of things considered unclean. Muslims were granted accommodation through what Sanneh describes as "the widespread African principle of enclavement . . . What clearly emerges from this situation is that traditional African [religion] sustained the Muslim impact by investing the new religion with its own identity, not by yielding to it."[8]

Sanneh further argues that Africa, and not Arabia, had become the context of religious life. An African order provided patronage for Islam – and, one could argue, for Christianity – to grow. Also, the vital nature of traditional religion functioned as a mitigating force to the exclusive spiritual regime of Islam. Finally, the principle of *enclavement* allowed the traditional host community to impinge on Muslim *zongos* enough to enable Islam to appear prominent without any diminution of existing religious structures. This demonstrates that, to a certain extent, Islam was also critical, if not dismissive, of ATR. Cheikh Babou notes that the spread of Islam cannot be seen as an anti-indigenous religious activity.

---

5. Sanneh, *West African Christianity*, 180.
6. Sanneh, "Domestication," 1.
7. Sanneh, 2–3.
8. Sanneh, 2–3.

What is unique about Islam is that it was spread in the longue durée by indigenous Africans who were able to work paths of accommodation with ATRs that allowed the emergence of local Islamic cultures through a discursive process. This was mostly a bottom-up process, because Islam did not enjoy political hegemony in Africa south of the Sahara.[9]

In light of the argument that is made here regarding the disdain and disregard of indigenous religions by Pentecostal leaders, it is important to underscore the fact that Sanneh thought Africans had a preponderance to absorb new religious ideas. Africans were capable of this because their religions did not have an "exclusive controversial attitude to religious options."[10] This openness to other religions is often viewed as syncretistic. The debates surrounding syncretism, which deepened during the last quarter of the twentieth century, are well-known. The anti-syncretic discourse was championed by the evangelical tradition, especially by Byang Kato and Tokunboh Adeyemo, both graduates of Dallas Theological Seminary and now of blessed memory.[11]

Africans accepted the missionary religions like Christianity and Islam and both religions grew and the result was the emergence of an interreligious context – which Sanneh describes as "lively."[12] He defines the term indigenization as a dynamic relationship and process in which the new religions offered "mental and spiritual cross-roads wherein old religious loyalties acquire a kerygmatic significance then African religions may assume a new role as bearers of hope."[13] He argues that both Christianity and Islam redefined their creeds in conversation with their contexts. Here, Sanneh is referring to the many ways in which the teachings of the new religions bore some resemblance to local religious thought – including beliefs about suffering, the second coming, and the end of the world – as well as the arts, literature, music, local political leadership, and educational institutions.[14]

Sanneh queries whether adherents of indigenous religions could be regarded as Abraham's children. His response indicates that this was not the

---

9. Cheikh Babou, personal communication to the author, 13 March 2023. I am grateful to Cheikh Babou for this clarification and his careful reading of the essay.

10. Sanneh, 2.

11. See Kato, *Theological Pitfalls*; Kato, *Theological Perspectives*; and Adeyemo, *Is Africa Cursed?*

12. See Sanneh, 7.

13. Sanneh, "Domestication," 8.

14. I am indebted to the editor and copy editor for this language.

case: "Given the central importance of sacred images and carvings at religious shrines in Africa, it is clear that shrine worshippers and their sacred images could not be said to have an affinity with the qur'anic Abraham."[15] However, probing further, Sanneh wonders whether the teachings, rituals, and beliefs of both religions had not previously been articulated in embryonic form in ATR. One could say that the answer is yes. Sanneh argues that Africans demonstrated a spirit of adaptation evidenced in the failure of both Islam and Christianty to erase local religions. He further notes that the future of Islam and Christianity depended on how each developed a favorable view of indigenous culture:

> On the face of the available evidence, Christianity is at least as capable of this transformation as Islam, with the striking difference that Islam emphasizes African agency while it remains profoundly opposed to African religions while Christianity encourages a rediscovery of indigenous cultural roots even if historically it may have achieved this by a provocative concentration power in expatriate missionary hands.[16]

Sanneh concludes his essay with a call for, and appreciation of, indigenous religions. He states, "The mother parish church may be ostensibly successful in launching a Mother's Union which is enthusiastically supported, but what existing rubric can it discover that the Union is merely an extension of the flourishing women's secret societies?"[17] Spirit possession, scriptural heritage, and oral culture require careful thought. Sanneh argues that "a recognition of the inclusive, tenacious nature of Africa's ancient heritage should enable us to recover a vast and significant field, while helping us to relinquish relics of antiquated feuds."[18]

By way of brief summary, Sanneh's preliminary conclusion in the essay is that Islam was opposed to traditional African religious ideas even though it lived with it. Christianity, on the other hand, promoted a reform tradition that revitalized African traditions and religions. He argues that "Christianity seeks to take shelter in the flowering of local culture and tradition which in the independent African churches assumes eruptive force but which nevertheless exists even in the historic churches under the agency of African recipients."[19]

---

15. Sanneh, 9.
16. Sanneh, 10.
17. Sanneh, 12.
18. Sanneh, 12.
19. Sanneh, 10.

From a Delicate Balance to Demonization

I have devoted a great deal of time in this essay to address an important issue in the development of Islam and Christianity in Africa – namely, that indigenous religions and culture provided, if you like, a safe haven for missionary religions to grow. African religious ideas and belief systems, and their devotees, were their hosts. The importance of local traditions and religious beliefs as being instrumental in the growth of Christianity became clearer when African leaders began to take responsibility for their own faith. The churches they started incorporated elements of African culture into the celebration of their Christian faith, such as: ancient wisdom and teachings, ancestral traditions and beliefs, extensive rituals that anchored beliefs in power and politics, the economy, community, and expectations of future communion with departed ancestors. Laurenti Magesa's work, for example, speaks of ATR's capacity to provide wholesome perspectives about a life that is lived in relationship with others and to participation in the divine project that maintains and sustains all forms of it.[20]

Yet one must admit that there is a delicate balance between a recognition of local and indigenous religions as important for human thriving and the Pentecostal revival that is sweeping through the continent. Writing about developments in African Christianity, Birgit Meyer eloquently argues that African Christianity in the late twentieth century shifted from stressing Africanness and independency to emphasizing Pentecostal charismatic Christianity.[21] It is difficult to pinpoint what exactly transpired or to what to attribute the Pentecostal and charismatic distaste for African religions and ancestral cultures. But the change from peaceful coexistence to hostility is evident.

In any case, the question here is not whether one has the religious freedom to be critical of another religious tradition but, rather, why that disagreement should be expressed with denigration and denial. Africans from different cultures, classes, and communities are fascinated with Pentecostalism. Even politicians who are responsible for the mismanagement of the continent have joined the Pentecostal train; and this despite the fact of rumors, in many parts, that they simultaneously consult and depend on ritual experts for charms in

---

20. See Magesa, *African Religions: the Moral Traditions of Abundant Life* (Maryknoll: Orbis Books, 1997).

21. See Meyer essay "Christianity in Africa: From African Independent to Pentecostal-Charismatic Churches." In Elias Kifon Bongmba, *The Wiley-Blackwell Companion to African Religions* (Malden: Wiley-Blackwell, 2010), 153.

order to hold on to their political appointments. In public, however, these same politicians flock to Pentecostal churches and emphatically proclaim Pentecostal views on prosperity, wealth, and healing.

For example, Matthew Kérékou, former president of Benin, confessed his sins to Isidore de Souza, the Catholic Archbishop of Cotonou, and asked for forgiveness.[22] Patrick Claffey, who has studied the situation in Benin, argued that Kérékou was inspired by Pentecostal ideas and claimed that he had abandoned the promotion of *vodun* and Marxism.[23] Kérékou reportedly told the country that he wanted a liberation of "an entire people being held hostage by the forces of money, the powers of the night, a family and a clan of privileged [individuals] who despise the supreme law and prefer obscure interests with which they have clearly associated themselves."[24] Kérékou won the presidential election and deployed Christian symbols at his inauguration, telling his compatriots that he had been given a prophetic word that would transform Benin's economy.[25]

While not every Pentecostal denigrates African religions, the rhetoric against Pentecostals in Africa is frightening. Pentecostal leaders today would do great service to the faith if they would work with African leaders who are interested in revitalizing their traditions since doing so would strengthen the religious and moral foundations of many African communities.

Pentecostalism and African Religions: A Critique

The position taken by Pentecostals today must be contested on several grounds. First, African religions were not merely a preparation for Christianity but independent religions with complete worldviews that needed no updating. Their strength and force were never in doubt among Africans themselves, as is particularly evident in the early work of theologians and Christian religious leaders who boldly studied and taught indigenous religions. The early publications on African traditional religions are well known for the fact that the leading scholars espoused the notion that indigenous religions offered a rich way of life and are traditions that are as complex as any other.[26] The

---

22. Claffey, "Kérékou," 98–101; see also Claffey, *Christian Churches*, 114 ff.

23. Strandsbjerg, "Kérékou," 401.

24. Cited in Strandsbjerg, "Kérékou," 402; for original source, see "Programme politique du candidat Mathieu Kérékou," *La Nation*, 23 February 1996.

25. Strandsbjerg, "Kérékou," 408.

26. These texts include, for example, Evans-Pritchard, *Nuer Religion* (Oxford: Clarendon Press, 1956); and Idowu, *Olódùmarè: God in Yoruba Belief*.

scholarship of John Mbiti and Bolaji Idowu immortalized African religions, which propelled these traditions to universities, where they were taught all over the world.[27]

Second, some have remarked that the Pentecostal emphasis on miracles and healing has attracted great attention in Africa due to the collapse of the healthcare system in the face of HIV/AIDS and the Ebola virus. But the reality is that Pentecostalism does not have a monopoly on healing. Writing about the religious fever that both preceded and anticipated Pentecostalism, namely, the African Initiated Churches (AIC), Ogbu Kalu argues, "The emphasis of African Independent Churches on healing, and their worldview of mystical causality in etiology and diagnosis are retained in the healing and deliverance sectors of African Pentecostal ministries."[28] The flamboyant displays by Pentecostal pastors is consistent with the way ritual healings worked in the past, particularly the roles played by ritual specialists like the *ngangas* who, in some African communities, served as spiritual leaders and healers.

Third, some Pentecostal pastors and members preach against and promote negative views of indigenous religions because they consider them "ungodly." These leaders despise indigenous religious practices on the grounds that their rituals are satanic practices. However, African scholars and theologians such as Joseph Danquah, Jomo Kenyatta, John Mbiti, and Bolaji Idowu have published groundbreaking studies of African indigenous religions and religious life.[29] Their studies of African rituals point to the way in which these rituals function to organize personal and communal life. Malidoma Patrice Somé writes persuasively about the significance of rituals as a source of knowledge and as a core aspect of African religious life.[30] Other studies of ritual practice in Africa have developed a close connection with the notion of transitional praxis, whereby religious belief, cultural thoughts, and ideas provide spiritual and ethical knowledge to members of the community.

The point here is that Africans were neither pagans nor ungodly as early Europeans had assumed when they embarked on the missionization and destruction of local African religions. African religion and culture have provided enormous material for ritual analyses, which makes Pentecostal

---

27. See Mbiti, *African Religions*; Idowu, *African Traditional Religion*.
28. Kalu, *African Christianity*, 340.
29. See Danquah, *Akan Doctrine*; Jomo Kenyatta, *Facing Mount Kenya*; Mbiti, *African Traditional Religions*; Mbiti, *Concepts of God*; Idowu, *Olódùmarè: God in Yoruba Belief* (New York: Wazobia, 1994).
30. See Somé, *Water and the Spirit*.

attacks not only offensive but, at best, ignorant of the basic structure and practice of the faith. The many interpretations of African rituals – which some Pentecostal leaders decry as occultism and paganism – are what Jean Comaroff refers to as a "historical practice."[31] What was and continues to be compelling in Comaroff's study is the idea that rituals, as a historical practice, offer continuity but are also a mode of resistance to cultural, political, economic, religious, and linguistic domination.[32] If one attends a Pentecostal service in Africa today, one cannot miss the prevalence of linguistic domination since Pentecostal pastors seem to prefer preaching in English or French. One wonders if God prefers European languages!

Fourth, negative Pentecostal attitudes toward traditional religion are based on two historically interconnected ideas – namely, missionary proclamation and the concept of revelation. The task of the missionary was not only to introduce Christianity to Africans but to do so by denouncing existing religions as idolatrous. African religious iconography was despised; even when missionaries collected these as art, they were described as "fetish art."

While a new and full history of fetishism is necessary to explain what researchers thought were its fallacy, we already know quite a bit from William Pietz, whose sixteenth-century study mapped out the use of the term.[33] What is surprising to Africanists and other scholars today is that a term that is so vacuous and considered a denigration of spirituality is still widely used by African clergy.

Part of the issue stemmed from the missionaries' presentation of the holy scriptures. The missionaries came preaching a new religion that was contained in a "magical book" of God. According to missionary teaching, this book contained revelations from God about the beginning of life and the destiny set by God for everyone on earth. Since non-Christian religions that did not have a biblical mythos were not considered true religions, this approach was a tacit condemnation of African indigenous religions. This was despite the fact that every religious tradition is derived from a large body of myths that are as compelling – or one might say, as unreasonable – as the Christian mythos. Although the missionaries sought to kill the African mythological corpus,

---

31. Comaroff, *Body of Power*, 194.

32. See Bongmba, "Witchcraft, Ritual and Gender," 253–72.

33. See Pietz, "Fetish," 5–17. See also Rattray, *Religion and Art*, 9; I am indebted to Pietz for this citation. See Pietz, 6.

they were unsuccessful. African mythic accounts remain because they present as compelling and magical a view of the cosmos as those of other religions.[34]

Faith leaders should appropriate what Cameroonian theologian Fabien Eboussi Boulaga calls a critique and recapture of Christianity.[35] Boulaga's scholarship represents one of the most critical works concerning the African resistance to negative missionary praxis. Boulaga refers to missionary discourse as "the language of refutation" that was intended to bring shame. This perspective promotes the idea that "pagan beliefs are an outgrowth of unbridled silliness . . . The veneration of idols is pure foolishness."[36] Boulaga also calls missionary discourse "the language of demonstration" whereby Christian truths were presented using the language of orthodoxy and the language of conformity. He further notes that missionary proclamation was intended "to create a syntax of derision."[37] That syntax of derision and despoliation has returned with a vengeance. One might argue that Boulaga anticipated the tenacity of a religious discourse that was grounded in absolute difference, where what is "Other" would be despised and rejected.

While one cannot reject the tradition of revelation, the question that must be asked today is why it should be reserved exclusively for religions other than African indigenous religions. It is disingenuous for African Pentecostals to respect the sacred texts of other religions while ignoring the sacred teachings of indigenous African religions, which include teachings that have been transmitted orally. While it is important to appreciate the role of textual traditions, African religiosity reminds us that religion and revelation may not always be captured in written texts, given that rituals offer practitioners many opportunities to encounter divine beings. Moreover, an uncompromising attachment to texts as the sole mode of divine revelation has produced many conflicts around the world.[38]

Pentecostal practices have also pushed the boundaries of "breaking with the past" to new dimensions. From early on, many Protestant churches practiced

---

34. See two well-known accounts of mythology in Africa; Soyinka, *Myth, Literature and the African World* (New York: Cambridge University Press, 1976); Isidore Okpewho, *Myth in Africa* (New York: Cambridge University Press, 1983).

35. Boulaga, *Christianity without Fetishes*.

36. Boulaga, 35.

37. Boulaga, 35.

38. See, for example, John Campbell and Asch Harwood, "Boko Haram's Deadly Impact," Council on Foreign Relations, 20 August 2018, https://www.cfr.org/article/boko-harams-deadly-impact.

enculturation in relation to church life. For example, the Limbum language[39] was already the church vernacular by the 1950s. Nearly all congregational songs were composed in the Wimbum area and sung in Limbum. In the 1960s, the Baptist pastor at Ntumbaw formed an English choir to introduce variety and provide church members the opportunity to sing English hymns. We used the hymn book *Sankey's Sacred Songs and Solos*, compiled by Ira D. Sankey.[40] African Pentecostal churches have introduced a new style of songs, composed primarily in English or French, which is contributing to the dominance of European languages. In fact, many Pentecostal preachers today preach in English, even in local villages where most people share the same indigenous language.

Fifth, the positions taken by Pentecostal pastors today have not only rejected local religions but closed the door to religious pluralism. From a historical perspective, Vatican II took an important step in clearly articulating a new and measured appreciation of indigenous religions beyond merely seeing indigenous religions as *praeparatio evangelica*. *Nostra aetate* notes that

> the church, therefore, exhorts her sons, that through dialogue and collaboration with the followers of other religions, carried out with prudence and love and in witness to the Christian faith and life, they recognize, preserve and promote the good things, spiritual and moral, as well as the socio-cultural values found among these men.[41]

The window opened by Vatican II coheres with the existing theological outlook of African scholars. As recently as 2009, Cardinal Jean-Louis Tauran noted that

> African traditional religion still exercises a strong influence over Africans, who are naturally religious . . . In order to respond to the question, what new things does the evangelist have to say to Africans, it is indispensable to understand and appreciate the religious roots of the people of the content since, according to African wisdom, "it is in pushing its roots into nourishing earth that the tree grows."[42]

---

39. The language of the Wimbum people of Donga Mantung, a division in the Northwest Region of Cameroon.

40. Sankey, *Sacred Songs and Solos*.

41. Paul VI, *Nostra Aetate* (1965), 2.

42. Sourou, "African Traditional Religion," 144.

Later, the Pontifical Council for Interreligious Dialogue, under the leadership of Cardinal Arinze – whom many consider conservative – would make a strong point that Christian churches should promote an understanding of indigenous African religions. The council noted that if more messengers of the gospel understood African religions (or for that matter other world religions) "the more suitable would be the presentation of Christianity traditional to Africans. . . . In this way the church will be more and more at home in Africa, and Africans will be more and more at home in the church."[43] The impact of these positions was felt in many places, and the reforms initiated by Vatican II launched a vigorous theological debate on inculturation which strengthened church life.

Finally, the denigration of African religions raises important questions regarding ecumenism. How do we understand ecumenism today as a practice that promotes tolerance and respect for each faith tradition? Can followers of indigenous religions be given a seat at the ecumenical table that moves beyond the polite courtesy one sees during national celebrations? I do not want to be misunderstood here because these public gestures of inclusion are important; but, at a substantive level, what good is this kind of inclusion in a context where so many Pentecostal pastors claim that these are "devilish" religions that are keeping Africa hostage?

While so-called mainline denominations now recognize African Initiated Churches (AIC) these churches were not always embraced. In the early days, as their leaders worked to plant AICs and grow them, they faced criticism from some missionaries. Some African leaders and scholars viewed their efforts mainly as attempts to escape colonial oppression,[44] while others portrayed this as a revival of "nativism."[45] Based on an understanding of nativism as "any conscious organized attempt on the part of a society's members to revive or perpetuate selected aspects of its culture,"[46] this latter group viewed AICs as an emerging form of religion that conflicted with the Christianity introduced by the missionaries. The latter perspective interpreted an emerging form of Christianity, which conflicted with that introduced by missionaries, based on the following definition of nativism: "any conscious organized attempt on

---

43. Pontifical Council for Interreligious Dialogue, "Pastoral attention to African Religions" (letter to the Episcopal Conferences of Africa and Madagascar"), Rome, 25 March 1988, Online document with no page number.
44. See, for example, Sindima, *Critical Theories*, 406.
45. See Linton, "Nativistic Movements," 230–40.
46. Linton, 230.

the part of a society's members to revive or perpetuate selected aspects of its culture." Therefore, while early theologians and social scientists celebrated the nascent AICs, there was always a sense that something was lacking because these new churches overemphasized indigenous beliefs. At the same time, these attitudes did not prevent the emerging sense that African indigenous religions had something to offer the wider body of Christ.[47]

The path that many Pentecostal leaders in Africa have adopted seems like a replay of a long-standing prejudice against African indigenous religions. Will Pentecostals be allowed to chart their own course? While there is no doubt that they have the right to do what they want, it is important to pose some questions. Given their emphasis on the presence and power of the Holy Spirit, how are these churches serving the communities in which they live? In light of the distinctions they draw between their own faith and that of other Christians, what does their attitude communicate about a welcoming spirit? Does the abuse and insults directed at indigenous religious practitioners reflect the gospel and the love of Christ, which they purportedly preach?

Conclusion

These reflections, which have been structured around the research and scholarship of Lamin Sanneh, are an invitation for us to reconsider how different religions treat each other. I have claimed that the Pentecostal attitude toward indigenous religions fails to answer the current appeal for religious pluralism and religious tolerance in Africa. These ideas call on faith communities to develop and promote hospitality to one another even when they do not share the same theological views. What is at stake here is not the degree to which one may detest the beliefs of another's faith community but, rather, how Pentecostals might show hospitality to other faiths, especially African indigenous religions. This is just the beginning of an educational process and a long conversation that we must have with one another.

Bibliography

Adeyemo, Tokunboh. *Is Africa Cursed?* Nairobi: WordAlive, 1997.

---

47. Religious pluralism that embraces Christianity and other religions has been studied for most of the twentieth century. See, for example, Knitter, *One Earth*; D'Costa, *Theology and Religious Pluralism*; Panikkar, *Intra-religious Dialogue*.

Bongmba, Elias Kifon. "Witchcraft, Ritual and Gender." In *Religion, Social Religions*, edited by William B. Parsons, 253–72. Farmington Hills: Gale CENGAGE Learning, 2016.

Boulaga, Fabien Ebbousi. *Christianity without Fetishes: An African Critique and Recapture of Christianity*. Translated by Robert R. Barr. Maryknoll: Orbis Books, 1981.

Claffey, Patrick. *Christian Churches in Dahomey-Benin: A Study of Their Socio-Political Role*. Leiden: Brill, 2007.

———. "Kérékou the Chameleon, Master of Myth." In *Staging Politics: Power and Performance in Asia and Africa*, edited by Julia C. Strauss and Donald B. Cruise, 98–101. London: I. B. Tauris, 2007.

Comaroff, Jean. *Body of Power, Spirit of Resistance: The Culture and History of a South African People*. Chicago: University of Chicago Press, 1985.

Danquah, Joseph B. *The Akan Doctrine of God: A Fragment of Gold Coast Ethics and Religion*. London: Lutterworth, 1944.

D'Costa, G. *Theology and Religious Pluralism: The Challenge of Other Religions*. London: Blackwell, 1986.

Evans-Pritchard, E. E. *Nuer Religion*. Oxford: Clarendon, 1956.

Idowu, E. Bolaji. *African Traditional Religion: A Definition*. Maryknoll: Orbis Books, 1973.

———. *Olódùmarè: God in Yoruba Belief*. London: Longman, 1962.

Kalu, Ogbu U. *African Christianity: An African Story*. Trenton: Africa World Press, 2007.

Kato, Byang. *Biblical Christianity in Africa: A Collection of Papers and Addresses*. Achimota: Africa Christian Press, 1985.

———. *Theological Pitfalls in Africa*. Kisumu: Evangel, 1975.

Kenyatta, Jomo. *Facing Mount Kenya*. New York: Vintage Books, 1965.

Knitter, Paul F. *One Earth Many Religions: Multifaith Dialogue and Global Responsibility*. Maryknoll: Orbis Books, 1995.

Linton, Ralph. "Nativistic Movements." *The American Anthropologist* 45, no. 2 (April–June 1943): 230–40.

Machingura, Francis. "'All of them were filled with the Holy Spirit and began to speak in other tongues' (Acts 2:4): Glossolalia as a Defining Characteristic of Zimbabwean Pentecostalism." In *Aspects of Pentecostal Christianity in Zimbabwe*, edited by Lovemore Togarasei, 91–109. Cham: Springer, 2018.

Magesa, Laurenti. *African Religions: The Moral Traditions of Abundant Life*. Maryknoll: Orbis Books, 1997.

Mbiti, John S. *African Religions and Philosophy*. Nairobi: East African Publishing House, 1969.

———. *Concepts of God in Africa*. London: SPCK, 1969.

Meyer, Birgit. "African Christianity in Africa: From African Independent to Pentecostal-Charismatic Churches." In *The Wiley-Blackwell Companion to African Religions*, edited by Elias Kifon Bongmba, 153–70. Malden: Wiley-Blackwell, 2012.

Okpewho, Isidore. *Myth in Africa: A Study of Its Aesthetic and Cultural Relevance.* Cambridge: Cambridge University Press, 1983.

Panikkar, Ramon. *The Intra-religious Dialogue.* New York: Paulist, 1999.

Paul VI. *Nostra Aetate: Declaration on the Relation of the Church to Non-Christian Religions* (1965). https://www.vatican.va/archive/hist_councils/ii_vatican_council/documents/vat-ii_decl_19651028_nostra-aetate_en.html.

Phiri, Isabel Apawo. "President Frederick Chiluba and Zambia: Evangelicals and Democracy in a 'Christian Nation.'" In *Evangelical Christianity and Democracy in Africa*, edited by Terence O. Ranger, 95–130. New York: Oxford University Press, 2008.

Pietz, William. "The Problem of the Fetish." *Anthropology and Aesthetics* 9 (Spring 1985): 5–17.

Pontifical Council for Interreligious Dialogue. "Pastoral attention to African Religions." Letter to the Episcopal Conferences of Africa and Madagascar, Rome, 25 March 1988. Online document with no page number.

"Programme politique du candidat Mathieu Kérékou," *La Nation*, 23 February 1996.

Rattray, R. S. *Religion and Art in Ashanti.* Oxford: Clarendon, 1927.

Sankey, Ira D. *Sacred Songs and Solos.* London: Morgan & Scott, n.d.

Sanneh, Lamin. "The Domestication of Islam and Christianity in African Societies: A Methodological Exploration." *Journal of Religion in Africa* 11, no. 1 (1980): 1–12.

———. *West African Christianity: The Religious Impact.* Maryknoll: Orbis Books, 1983.

Sindima, Harvey J. *Classical Theories in African Religion.* Trenton: Africa World Press, 2018.

Somé, Malidoma Patrice. *Of Water and the Spirit: Ritual, Magic and Initiation in the Life of an African Shaman.* New York: Penguin Books, 1995.

Sourou, Jean-Baptiste. "African Traditional Religion and the Catholic Church in Light of the Synods of Africa: 1994 and 2009." *African Human Rights Law Journal* 14 (2014): 142–49.

Soyinka, Wole. *Myth, Literature and the African World.* Cambridge: Cambridge University Press, 1976.

Strandsbjerg, Camilla. "Kérékou, God and the Ancestors: Religion and the Conception of Political Power in Benin." In *African Affairs* 99, no. 396 (2000): 395–414.

Welbourn, F. B., and B. A. Ogot. *A Place to Feel at Home: A Study of Two Independent Churches in Western Kenya.* London: Oxford University Press, 1966.

15

Pulaaku: The Fulani Notion of Land and Hospitality

Haruna Yussif Mogtari

Introduction

The people who originally called themselves *Fulbe* or *Pullo* (singular) – in their mother tongue Fulfulde – are referred to by many West Africans as Fulani. The worldview of Fulani herdsmen is an important area of academic study that needs serious attention, particularly in Ghana and other West African states. The term *pulaaku*, which means Fulani custom or way of life (conduct) is the key to understanding the heart of Fulani society. Findings from *pulaaku* studies have proven to be indispensable in engaging the larger Fulani group on issues of farmer-herder conflicts. It is within the scope of this significant Fulani custom that this chapter will examine the concepts of territoriality or land[1] and hospitality, using the Bible as the hermeneutical tool. Essentially, this chapter seeks to identify and examine aspects of *pulaaku* that have affinities with territoriality and hospitality, especially with regard to the Bible's understanding of land.

Most studies on the Fulani in Ghana have concentrated on the perennial farmer-herder conflicts in order to understand the root causes and nature of the violence. It is these clashes that first caused the media to bring the Fulani to the limelight toward the end of the twentieth century. The manner in which the media has reported these conflicts has contributed to the general

---

1. Note that I will be using the terms "land" and "territory" interchangeably.

negative perception of the Fulani within Ghana.[2] However, a careful look at their past and current situation shows that Fulani tradition plays a key role in how the Fulani relate with their environment as well as with people they consider as foreign.

Unfortunately, even though the problem between herdsmen and crop farmers has been a threat to the general peace and security of the nation for decades, the subject of the Fulani in theological and missiological studies has yet to garner significant interest. Due to many years of biased media reporting against the Fulani regarding their pastoral practices and their cultivator counterparts, a negative perception has been generated within the Ghanaian populace. Therefore, it is important that research related to this group be open, independent, and objective, which is what this essay attempts to do in honor of the Fulani of Ghana, who have served faithfully in different sectors of the economy.

This essay will first discuss the paradox of Fulani life in Ghana, illustrating their sufferings and challenges as a marginalized minority group. This will then lead to a broad study of the Fulani custom of *pulaaku* as an essential characteristic and determining factor concerning their views on land and hospitality.

Study Area and Method

This study was conducted in many of the significant Fulani communities in Ghana, including Nalerigu, Buipe, Tamale, Saboba, Walewale, Wa, Techiman, Ashiyie Fulani, Sakogu, Karaga, Gushiegu, Bawku, Tumu, Han, Kumasi, Agogo, Cape Coast, Takoradi and Sakpalua. However, 85 percent of the informants involved live in northern Ghana, the region that is host to nearly 50 percent of the Fulani population. The research methods used include focus group discussions, interviews, participant observation, and media reports from both electronic and print sources. Secondary sources from experts in the field of study were also used. The research group included samples of Fulani inhabitants, indigenous Ghanaians, missionaries who work with the Fulani, state officials, chiefs, and local leaders. While its main interpretative tool is Christian scripture, the study embraces an open posture of dialogue with other religious views, particularly those of Islam and African Traditional Religion.

---

2. Mogtari, "Fulani Herdsmen Traditions," 178.

The Paradox of Fulani Life

The paradox of the Fulani life can be traced to the numerous speculative theories that arose in the early twentieth century about their origin, many of which had racial inferences. In 1910, a considerable number of writers were preoccupied with the physical appearance of the Fulani. For instance, A. J. N. Tremearne describes the Fulani as being of "many shades, from the black or yellow . . . to the dull white"[3] and concludes that the Fulani were from Semitic origins. A decade later, H. R. Palmer supported this idea that the Fulani were a hybrid of Arab and Jewish stock.[4] During the same period, Harry Johnson publicized a similar view that argued that the Fulani were of Arab ancestry, thus affirming the Fulani traditional view about their own origins. M. D. W. Jeffreys agrees with M. Delafosse[5] that the Fulani were of Judeo-Syrian origin.[6] Even the present generation of Fulani in Ghana and the subregion claim kinship with the biblical patriarch Abraham, a notion that may be a result of Islam's historical influences. The findings of Joseph Greenberg and Derrick J. Stenning give more credence to West Africa as their origin and heritage, which explains why the Fulani can be found throughout the subregion.[7]

The story of Fulani life in Ghana can be described in the words of Charles Darwin as the "survival of the fittest," particularly when examining farmer-herder conflicts. The implications of these herder-host conflicts – described by Kaderi Noagah Bukari and Nicholaus Schareika as ethnic-based victimization – are wide-ranging and pervasive stereotypes, prejudices, and discrimination within certain Ghanaian societies.[8] In Ghanaian society, the general perception is that the Fulani are herdsmen suspected of "highway robberies." This term, which is meant to communicate deviance and criminality, has gained widespread popularity. In addition to being viewed as the cause of farmer-herder conflicts, the Fulani herdsmen are also labeled uncivilized, primitive, dirty, and cattle-rustlers.[9]

The stigma of being a Fulani was the main reason many refused to enroll their children in school, accounting for the high rates of illiteracy within their society. State policies by various governments promulgating the expulsion

---

3. Tremearne, "Origin of the Filani," 715.
4. Palmer and Johnston, "Fulas," 121, 128.
5. Mukoshy, "Ful'be and Their Language," vi–xvii.
6. Jeffreys, "Speculative Origins," 47–54.
7. Mogtari, "Mission to Fulbe," 19–20.
8. Bukari and Schareika, "Stereotypes," 1.
9. Bukari and Schareika, 4–5.

of herdsmen from many spaces have further worsened Fulani victimization, marginalization, and stigmatization. The basis of Fulani suffering stems from the fundamental Ghanaian prejudice that the Fulani are not citizens and, therefore, have no rights whatsoever.

Nevertheless, in an article entitled "Fulani in Ghana: Emerging Mission Possibilities and Approaches," I shared contrary views regarding some groups of Fulani in Ghana. These thoughts are worth reiterating here:

> One truth stands out, the majority of the cattle that are cared for by many Fulani households are for Ghanaian farmers, the privileged, and the ruling class. However, poor Fulani families become the object of attacks and castigation. Many Fulani who are not even herdsmen become victims of ethnic victimization in the hands of the media, the state, and local people. Still, the hard truth that Ghanaians must face is that there are significant numbers of the Fulani in Ghana who are citizens. The Citizenship Act, 2000 (Acts 591), section 1–7 of Ghana's Constitution, affirm descendants of early Fulani migrants (before and after 1957) who either by birth or naturalization and registration have since made Ghana their home.[10]

The idea that the same people who care for these animals would turn around and attack them is quite puzzling. The testimony of a government official confirms the fact that Fulani herdsmen care for cattle belonging to chiefs and landowners in their traditional areas as part of fees paid to them in exchange for settlements on their estates. The authorities who lose out in the tough competition to host the Fulani turn the community against them by criticising them for destroying people's farms.[11]

Similarly, in northern Ghana, the Fulani and their cattle-owner employers create contractual agreements and obligations that enable the former to take care of the cattle belonging to the latter.[12] This means that the problem of cattle and crop farming is a mutual one that must be resolved by all the stakeholders. As part of the steps taken to significantly reduce security threats, the Fulani in Buipe of the Central Gonja district have asked the government to formulate much-needed policies to regulate the activities of herdsmen and farmers.

---

10. Mogtari, "Fulani in Ghana," 257–63.
11. See Tonah, "Migration," 165.
12. Mogtari, "Mission to Fulbe," 57–58.

According to these Fulani, the nation needs the services of both farmers and herdsmen.[13]

Undeniably, the Fulani are ardent and highly skilled pastoralists who have remained loyal to their ethnic profession and support Ghana with a consistent supply of beef, an important source of protein. The fact remains that many second- and third-generation Fulani descendants are citizens of Ghana as set out in the constitution. Thus, it is a misconception to think that all Fulani in Ghana are alien herdsmen, a term commonly used to mean uncivilized and primitive. Their rights – including the permission to freely participate in the sociopolitical activities of the country – must be upheld and respected.

In 2020, the Republic of Ghana conducted an exercise to register all its citizens and residents, and issue them with a national identity card. In certain places in the Ashanti region, Fulani citizens were prevented from receiving this identity card. Similarly, during the 7 December 2020 poll, many Fulani would-be voters felt threatened and intimidated. Ironically, at the Adentan constituency in the Greater Accra Region, Mohammed Adamu Ramadan, a Fulani by descent, won a parliamentary seat for the National Democratic Congress (NDC), defeating the incumbent MP, Yaw Buaben Asamoa, of the New Patriotic Party (NPP). Interestingly, Fulani have always been part of the nation-building agenda of Ghana. Earlier, Fulani were drafted into the Gold Coast Regiment and the Police Service.[14] Epitaphs of some Fulani ex-soldiers can be found at the Osu Military Cemetery.[15] Fulani in Ghana are not just herdsmen but include a wide range of businesspeople, traders, scholars, commercial drivers, teachers, health professionals, and politicians.

In contrast to places such as Agogo and Kwahu in the Ashanti Region, where herder-host conflict has been a fundamental problem, it is noteworthy that in other places – including parts of northern Ghana as well as Accra – certain Fulani groups generally live in peace with their neighbors. For instance, some Fulani families living in Wa, Nalerigu, Tumu, Sakpalua, Bawku, Saboba, Techiman, and Accra invite their neighbors to their children's naming ceremonies and weddings. Many factors account for these cordial relations, including their shared Islamic faith, the value of hospitality toward people of other ethnic backgrounds, and the hard work for peace between the *suduu*

---

13. Focus Group Discussion, Buipe, 1 August 2015.
14. Issah Norga, interview by author, 19 July 2015.
15. Mogtari, "Mission to Fulbe," 166.

baaba[16] and local chiefs. Unfortunately, these peaceful relations do not garner media attention because they do not perpetuate the stereotypes of violent clashes that have captured the imagination of many Ghanaians. However, Bukari and Schareika have promoted narratives of neighborliness between Fulani and ethnic groups in the north, pointing out that

> not in all cases [that] . . . Fulani [are] stereotypically and prejudicially discriminated. Fulani have been *cultural neighbours* to the Dagomba, Mamprusi, Gonja and Builsa ethnic groups in northern Ghana and have engaged in very productive cooperative relations with them. Cooperation and strong social networks between them and these communities are built in many ways such as exchange of goods and services, entrustment of cattle to them, friendship, visitation, trade, communal labour, social solidarity and even marriage with some Ghanaians. The wife of the vice-presidential candidate of the New Patriotic Party (who himself comes from the chiefly Mamprusi ethnic group) is of Fulani extraction. And there have been many inter-marriage between members of indigenous Ghanaian ethnic groups and Fulani. Also, Ghanaian veterinary services are made available to Fulani herdsmen across the country.[17]

It is worth mentioning that the then vice presidential candidate of the NPP, Mahamudu Bawumia, has been sworn in as vice president of the Republic of Ghana for a second term, making his wife Samira Bawumia, who is of a Fulani background, the second lady. Samira undoubtedly played a key role in the NPP's general election success over the past eight years. The couple also serve as a model of interethnic marriage, which demonstrates a kind of peaceful coexistence.

An Overview of *Pulaaku*

Central to this essay is *pulaaku* – the Fulani worldview and cultural practice. Among Fulani, *pulaaku* can be explained and expressed in different parts or segments, where each one is important for understanding the whole. *Pulaaku* is commonly used to connote Fulani society and/or essentially an embodiment of

---

16. That is the sociopolitical group drawn from the larger Fulani community entrusted with the responsibility of leading the group and acting as its mouthpiece when dealing with indigenous authorities.

17. Bukari and Schareika, "Stereotypes," 6.

the expected conduct of a *Pullo* that expresses the values and aspirations of their culture. These cherished ideals include but are not limited to the following: gentleness, respect, humility, "patience and fortitude (*munyal*), wisdom (*hakkillo*), and modesty and reserve (*semteende*)."[18] These qualities are held in high esteem by all Fulani and enforced by the *maudo suudu baaba* (elders of society). Those who flout the rules of conduct are chastised or ostracized. For all Fulani living in Ghana, an important element of *pulaaku* is the Fulfulde language, which parents are expected to teach their children as part of passing on unique Fulani practices and behaviors. Peter Braimah, a *maudo suudu* in Saboba, adds that *bodaaji* (taboos) and *mbodaaji* (prohibitions) within the Fulani community are part of *pulaaku*.[19] These specify how one has to dress, sit, eat, and feel shy in front of people (that is, fear of shameful things). Some Fulani in Buipe note that their occupation of caring for cattle is an intrinsic aspect of this custom.[20]

For centuries, Islam has found a home among a great number of Fulani in West Africa, an important fact that cannot be ignored. The Fulani were among the first people in sub-Saharan Africa to embrace Islam in the ninth century, and they became agents for the spread of the faith. During the nineteenth century, they staged the jihad campaigns throughout West Africa that established the Fulani Empire in that era.[21] Ryo Ogawa intimates that when the Fulani become devout Muslims, they also become disloyal to their ethnic tradition of *pulaaku* as they identified themselves with the global *umma*.[22] Catherine Ver Eecke, however, suggests that in some other Fulani jurisdictions, *pulaaku* appears identical to Islam despite the seeming divergences between the two.[23]

Fulani Notions of Territoriality and Hospitality as Reflected in the Bible

At this point, it is important to have a working definition of territory from a biblical perspective. Territory connotes land under someone's jurisdiction. Benjamin Abotchie Ntreh's article "The Bible and Caring for the Land" is an

---

18. Smith, "Burkina Faso," 180. The translation of Fulfulde words into English language limits their broader meaning. Thus, Semteende can also mean shyness. When a person is shy, he or she is also showing respect and this makes him or her become reserved.
19. Peter Braimah, interview by author, Saboba, 25 July 2015.
20. Focus Group Discussion, Buipe, 1 August 2015.
21. Mukoshy, "Fulbe and their Language," x–xi.
22. Ogawa, "Ethnic Identity," 119.
23. Ver Eecke, "Pulaaku," 312–13.

appropriate backdrop for this section due to his African perspectives and insights. Ntreh draws from Genesis 1:1, noting that the word *'eres* in Hebrew is interpreted as "earth" or "land." He agrees with Walter Brueggemann that land is always closely connected to the history and experiences of the Israelites in the territories where they once settled. Ntreh also shows linkages between Ga and Hebrew worldviews regarding land, noting that land comprises of the "earth, the sky (air) and the sea (water bodies)."[24]

The images of land that emerge from the pastoral worldview of the Fulani are linked to cattle, water, and pasture. In Genesis 1:26–30, cattle, water (or water resources), and vegetation are considered part of the land. Among Fulani, the land becomes valuable only when it has the capacity to support the grazing of their cattle, which must also include sufficient water. The Fulani's survival is directly dependent on cattle – which in turn are reliant on the rich resources of the land – and their staple meal is *kosam* (milk), which they drink from childhood and throughout their adult life. Milk is the second major economic commodity from which they produce the popular delicacy *waagashi*, as well as body lotion and medicine for treating fractured bones. They sell the milk products and occasionally trade a cow in exchange for money in order to buy essential commodities for the household. On a daily basis, the Fulani's primary task is to drive their cattle to water sources and pasturelands to graze so that they can produce enough milk to sustain the family. The fertility of the cattle is also dependent on the vegetation of the land.

Reflecting on Genesis 1:28, which says ". . . be fruitful and increase in number; fill the earth and subdue it. Rule over the fish of the sea and the birds of the air and over every living creature that move on the ground" show that Fulani tradition of caring for cattle has fulfilled scripture. The Fulani have maintained their long-held ethnic tradition of care for the land and cattle through natural methods that have no adverse effect on the ecosystem. These practices align with Ntreh's assertion that "our care for the land is intrinsically related to our care for the other living creature."[25] Furthermore, the Fulani discourage the cutting down of trees and bush burning[26] because their herdsmen are conscious of the implication of environmental degradation. "Egypt is the Nile and the Nile is Egypt" is a familiar saying that depicts the invaluable contribution of the Nile River to the development of ancient Egyptian civilization. Similarly, the Fulani past should not be interpreted as primitive in a negative sense but,

---

24. Ntreh, "Bible and Caring," 4–5.
25. Ntreh, 7.
26. Mogtari, "Fulani Herdsmen Traditions," 182–83.

rather, as something positive since their identity is wedded to cattle, the land, and the very flourishing of the earth.

Fulani Notions of Territoriality and Hospitality as Practiced in History

The ancestral home of the Fulani in the Senegambia and the western part of present-day Mali have been impacted by various unpredictable environmental factors.[27] Since many of these areas lie in desert regions, the ecosystems could not sustain their cattle because of the lack of foliage and water. This became the major catalyst for Fulani migration toward other parts of the continent, where the needed land resources for their cattle could be found. The first pastoral Fulani migration is unknown, but Delafosse hints that they emigrated from the kingdom of Tekrur, Senegal, during the eleventh century CE.[28]

Over time, migration has become a fundamental feature of the Fulani's ethnic identity. In fact, a popular Fulani saying affirms their transhumance, a distinctive cultural attribute that is communicated in the phrase "the Fulani are like sand" – a suggestion that they are unable to gather at any one particular geographical location for a long period of time but move easily. The saying is demonstrated in the fact that the Fulani have become one of the single largest ethnic groups throughout the subregion. Most now live outside their original homeland and can be found in several countries including Burkina Faso, Benin, Ivory Coast, Niger, Cameroon, Nigeria, Togo, and Ghana.

It would be a mistake to assume that the Fulani have no sense of land ownership or territorial tenure simply because they are a nomadic group who are constantly on the move, seeking new pasturing lands. However, the traditional pastoral practices of Fulani throughout generations have proved that they know no territorial boundaries. Their cross-country and cross-cultural movements are often determined by changes in the vegetation and not by a laissez-passer[29] in the subregion. There are a few historic exceptions where the Fulani settled, permanently or partially, establishing two great territorial states. These settlers became the pioneers of the ancient West African states of Sokoto in northern Nigeria and Masina in northern Mali. These states forced

---

27. Mukoshy, "Fulbe and heir Language," x.

28. Maurice Delafosse, Haut-Senegal-Niger (Soudan Francais), ed. Clozel. Iere series, tomes 1–3. Paris: Larose; cited in Stenning, *Savannah Nomads*, 21.

29. A document that permits the holder to travel freely into another country.

many pastoral Fulani to settle permanently and take up farming, while those who remained herdsmen continued migrating with their livestock.[30]

The first recorded case of the arrival of Fulani in Ghana was not until 1911. Since then, they have increased exponentially, dominating the area of animal husbandry in the agricultural sector and spreading to all sixteen regions of Ghana. In the 1930s, the Fulani herdsmen were entrusted with the management of the Native Administrative Farms and government-owned livestock farms, and this was probably the beginning of their permanent and semi-settled life in Ghana.[31] Most who have settled are now of the second and third generations of those who consider themselves Ghanaians. They own estates or have built permanent home structures. Many of them, although still herdsmen, are engaged in different sectors of the economy. In some local communities, a section of the land has been leased to the Fulani for the grazing of their cattle, as is the case in Karaga, Daffiama-Busie, Tamale, Buipe, Wa, Bawku, and Ashiyie Fulani. Over time, these settlements have become exclusive Fulani areas.

Another group of Fulani – often described as "alien herdsmen" – periodically move into Ghana to graze their cattle. Some come with nothing and, therefore, take advantage of the cattle market and also find jobs as hired herdsmen. Unfortunately, some Fulani cross the border with their cattle and destroy farm crops, all the while hiding in the bush. Some media houses have reported that these alien herdsmen use weapons to protect their cattle and grazing lands against threats from indigenous farmers. The other group are those who enter the community through the approved immigration channels and obtain permission through contractual agreement from local authorities to settle on their land. Some of these towns have become popularly known in the country due to the influx of Fulani herdsmen and their clash with native farmers.

It is important to understand that the Fulani acknowledge the source of creation and life as *Joomiraado*, the Supreme Being. The land and its resources – the earth, pasture, herds, and rivers – come from him, and the Fulani affirm that everything living and nonliving is accountable to him. Even in the spiritual realm, the Fulani are conscious – to some extent – of territorial spirits. They seek protection and provision from their *maama* (ancestors).[32] These views resonate with the wider African worldviews that the "custodianship of the

---

30. de Bruijn and van Dijk, "Changing Population Mobility," 291.
31. Tonah, *Fulani in Ghana*, 28–29.
32. Mogtari, "Mission to Fulbe," 112, 136.

ecosystems . . . lies in the hands of transcendent beings." Human beings are only recognized as trustees and caretakers of the environment.[33]

Abraham Akrong and John Azumah articulate the notion that African worldviews draw attention to a great many resources that can serve as bridges to promote interdependent relationships within African contexts. One such key resource is kinship, which serves as a unifier irrespective of people's religious affiliations.[34] This idea resonates profoundly with the Fulani concept of *pulaaku*, which was explained earlier.

As previously mentioned, the Fulani are not in a state of constant tension with their neighbors. In fact, the Fulani usually live in harmony and tranquility with their hosts. This manner of coexisting with their neighbors is not simply a survival strategy aimed at acceptance in neighboring communities but is authentically a part of their worldview. The three key Fulfulde words that capture the essence of hospitality, peace, and gentleness are *tommottaaku*, *jam*, and *heesindaade*, respectively. These are described as part *pulaaku*, the character of a true *Pullo*. Failure to exemplify these values signifies that one has deviated from the way of *pulaaku*.[35]

The Fulani believe that observing these values affects one's mannerisms, behavior, and right responses to issues as expected in society. Moreover, parents – and especially the *jom wuro* (household head) – are expected to instill shyness in their children. Failure to do so brings shame on the family. Here, shyness goes beyond the literal understanding of timidity and also means *semteende*[36] (respect for others) and *leeyinkinaare* (humility). These cultural aspirations in Fulani society are inherent ingredients of hospitality.

Thus, on many occasions, Fulani residents in the northern part of Ghana live hospitably with their indigenous neighbors and, thereby, enjoy the opportunity to share the social amenities and utilities of the community. One cannot disregard the Fulani youths – some of whom are products of various primary, junior, and senior secondary schools in these districts – who have been impacted by this kindness. The Nalerigu Baptist Medical Centre deserves special mention because it has served an immeasurable number of Fulani since its establishment.

---

33. Asamoah-Gyadu, "Earth Is the Lord's," xii.
34. Akrong and Azumah, "Hermeneutical and Theological Resources," 75–76.
35. Hussein, interview by author, Nalerigu, 1 August 2015.
36. The translation of Fulfulde words into English language limits their broader meaning. Thus, Semteende can also mean shyness. When a person is shy, he or she is also showing respect and this makes him or her become reserved.

The Fulani readily admit that modeling *pulaaku*, especially hospitality, should not be exclusive to their own community but should also affect their neighbors. Some have confessed that when their cattle destroy the crops of farmers, they negotiate proper compensation so as not to jeopardize their relationship with their host. This admission of neighborliness allays the fear raised among many that "the strong sense of kinship and its tenacious bonds in African societies may make us . . . just as exclusivist and unwelcoming to the outsider or stranger."[37] Akrong and Azumah reiterate that in "African societies the sense of kinship is accompanied by an ingrained sense of hospitality to the stranger,"[38] which is described by Lamin Sanneh as "the African principle of 'enclavement,' which accords protection and guarantees to the stranger and non-kin groups."[39]

Conclusion

The crux of this essay was an examination of the Fulani notion of territoriality or land and hospitality. It explored Fulani life in Ghana and highlighted the paradox of the Fulani being victims of bigotry and discrimination, while they have also contributed in meaningful ways to Ghana's developmental agenda. Furthermore, the essay explained the underlying Fulani worldview of *pulaaku* – that underpins the notions of territoriality and hospitality – and showed that the biblical concept of land in Genesis 1:26–30 correlates, to some degree, with the Fulani concept of land that is wedded to and integrated with the cattle, pasture, and water. For the Fulani, land is deemed valuable if it has the capacity to provide their cattle with natural resources such as pasture and water sources for grazing, as well as to supply the basic necessities for survival and maintenance of the home.

This essay has also established that because of their migratory nature, the pastoral Fulani's worldview of land has no regard for territorial borders of any kind. They constantly move from place to place in an unofficial manner in order to find pasture and water for grazing their cattle. This idea of free movement hinges on the belief that the land and all resources connected to it originated from God, who has given it freely to humankind. However, the historical record shows that some Fulani in Nigeria and Mali established permanent Islamic territories such as Sokoto and Masina, altering their long-held nomadic past

---

37. Akrong and Azumah, "Hermeneutical and Theological Resources," 81.
38. Akrong and Azumah, 81.
39. Sanneh, "Domestication," 6.

and compelling many into settled lifestyles. Similarly, in Ghana, many second- and third-generation Fulani migrants have broken away from their past and embraced a stable life in the quest for better economic opportunities, which includes owning their own estates.

Finally, the notion of hospitality among ethnic Fulani is described as *tommottaku*, an intrinsic component of *pulaaku*. The concept of *tommottaaku* is reinforced by *semteende* (shy, reserve or respect for others), *leeyinkinaare* (humility), *jam* (peace), and *heesindaade* (gentleness). It was also noted that the Fulani idea of hospitality is deeply rooted in their tradition, which is closely linked to the general perception that Africans, by nature, are hospitable. For the Fulani, to personify hospitality means to be inclusive of people irrespective of their ethnicity. In this way, the Fulani have generally lived hospitably with their neighbors, which has led to their having a positive impact on the societies in which they reside.

Bibliography

Akrong, Abraham A., and John Azumah. "Hermeneutical and Theological Resources in African Traditional Religions for Christian-Muslim Relations in Africa." In *The African Christian and Islam*, edited by John Azumah and Lamin Sanneh, 75–83. Carlisle: Langham Academic, 2013.

Asamoah-Gyadu, J. Kwabena. "'The Earth Is the Lord's': Mainstreaming Ecological Issues in African Theology." Foreword to *Essays on the Land, Ecotheology, and Traditions in Africa*, edited by Benjamin Abotchie Ntreh, Mark S. Aidoo, and Daniel Nii Aboagye Aryeh, xi–2. Eugene: Wipf & Stock, 2019.

Bruijn, Mirjam de, and Han van Dijk. "Changing Population Mobility in West Africa: Fulbe Pastoralists in Central and South Mali." *African Affairs* 102 (2003): 285–307.

Bukari, Kaderi Noagah, and Nicholaus Schareika. "Stereotypes, Prejudices and Exclusion of Fulani Pastoralists in Ghana." *Pastoralism* 5 (2015): 1–12. DOI 10.1186/s13570-015-0043-8.

Jeffreys, M. D. W. "Speculative Origins of the Fulani Language." *Africa: Journal of the International African Institute* 17 (1947): 47–54.

Mogtari, Haruna Y. "Fulani Herdsmen Traditions and Care for the Land." In *Essays on the Land, Ecotheology, and Traditions in Africa*, edited by Benjamin Abotchie Ntreh, Mark S. Aidoo, and Daniel Nii Aboagye Aryeh, 178–91. Eugene: Wipf & Stock, 2019.

———. "Fulani in Ghana: Emerging Mission Possibilities and Approaches." *E-Journal of Religious and Theological Studies* (ERATS) 6, no. 5 (August 2020): 257–63.

———. "Mission to Fulbe: An Examination of the Affinities between the Worldview of Fulbe Migrants in Ghana and the Christian Faith." Unpublished MTh diss., Akrofi-Christaller Institute of Theology, Mission and Culture, Akropong-Akuapem, 2016.

Mukoshy, I. A., ed. "Some Aspect on Ful'be and Their Language." In *A Fulfulde English Dictionary*, edited by I. A. Mukoshy, vi–xvii. Kaduna: Nigerian Educational Research, 1991.

Ntreh, Benjamin Abotchie. "The Bible and Caring for the Land." In *Essays on the Land, Ecotheology, and Traditions in Africa*, edited by Benjamin Abotchie Ntreh, Mark S. Aidoo, and Daniel Nii Aboagye Aryeh, 3–14. Eugene: Wipf & Stock, 2019.

Ogawa, Ryo. "Ethnic Identity and Social Interaction: A Reflection on Fulbe Identity." *Senri Ethnological Studies* 35 (1993): 119–37.

Palmer, H. R., and H. H. Johnston. "'The Fulas' and Their Language." *Journal of the Royal African Society* 22, no. 86 (1923): 121–30.

Sanneh, Lamin. "The Domestication of Islam and Christianity in African Societies: A Methodological Exploration." *Journal of Religion in Africa* 11, no. 1 (1980): 1–12.

Smith, Richard W., ed. "Burkina Faso Fulfulde-English/English-Fulfulde Dictionary." 2nd ed. Burkina Faso: Tenkodogo-Ouagadougou, 2007.

Stenning, Derrick J. *Savannah Nomads; A Study of the Wodaabe Pastoral Fulani of Western Bornu Province Northern Region, Nigeria*. Munster; Hamburg: LIT Verlag, 1994.

Tonah, Steve. *Fulani in Ghana: Migration History, Integration, and Resistance*. Accra: University of Ghana Press, 2005.

———. "Migration and Farmer-Herder Conflicts in Ghana's Volta Basin." *Canadian Journal of African Studies* 40 (2006): 152–78.

Tremearne, A. J. N. "Notes on the Origin of the Filani." *Journal of the Royal Society of Arts* 58 (1910): 715–25.

Ver Eecke, Catherine. "Pulaaku: Adamawa Fulbe Identity and Its Transformations." PhD diss., University of Pennsylvania, 1988.

Contextual Perspectives

16

The Pacifist Hijab

Typologies of Religious Co-existence Amongst Muslim and Christian women in Madina Zongo

Kauthar Khamis

Introduction

Over the years, Ghana has been described as a relatively peaceful country, where people from different religious frontiers coexist at different levels. However, for a decade now, hijab use has generated tensions in some public spaces, leading to discrimination and marginalization of female Muslims. The Muslim community has reacted to this development, with some seeking an interpretation of the 1992 constitution that allows Ghanaians to profess the religion of their choice and also manifest it in any public environment. Inspired by Lamin Sanneh's research into pacifist practices of Muslim clerics in the history of Islam in West Africa (2016), this essay examines the binary framing of the hijab not only as a matter that is contested in public spaces but also as a manifestation of "pacifism" in the Madina Zongo space.

My own trajectory of hijab use dates back to 2001 when I enrolled in a newly established Islamic school, the Ghana-Lebanon Islamic Secondary School (GLISS). The hijab – a long skirt with a long-sleeved shirt – was part of my school uniform and mandatory for both Muslim and Christian students. Most Ghanaian Muslims admired the hijab, and many parents enrolled their children at GLISS. However, around the school, in the busy streets of Kwame

Nkrumah Circle,[1] other people were far from positive about the hijab. *Trotro* (commercial) drivers and their *mates* (conductors), whom I identified as non-Muslims, called us names such as Al-Qaeeda, *Al-Shabaab*, and *Osama bin Laden's people*. Sometimes, the *trotro mates* asked whether we had bombs in our schoolbags. It was obvious that they linked our hijab practices to the activities of jihadists across the globe. In this paper, I use the Madina Zongo space as an entry point for an analysis of the different typologies of religious coexistence that have been produced as a result of donning the hijab. The formal public space is characterized by boundaries and territories that the hijab is not supposed to cross. In contrast, in the Madina Zongo space, the pacifist characteristics of the hijab lead to remarkable religious borrowings and cross-religious appropriation.

The theoretical basis of this paper is Sanneh's proposition of pacifism, which he employs to describe the passive growth of Islam across West Africa and the complex interrelationship between West African Muslim clerics and their host communities during the seventh century. Sanneh states that the role of the clerics "in maintaining mosques, providing services for disciples and clients seeking professional religious services and generally overseeing observances of the religious calendar" played an instrumental role in "promoting a quietist, tolerant form of Islam," contrary to the popular narrative that Islam was spread through the jihad of the sword.[2] He adds that conversion to Islam was influenced by scholarship, tolerance, and peaceful accommodation rather than by violence.

Similarly, the association of the hijab with the everyday life of women in Madina Zongo has given it a pacifist characteristic to the extent that women from different religious boundaries borrow the hijab for social and religious reasons. However, contrary to the pacifist tradition as claimed by Sanneh, the hijab, as it interacts with the Madina Zongo space, does not appear to be aimed at conversion; rather, it produces a variety of forms of religious coexistence. This essay originates from a six-year ethnographic research study in Madina Zongo. The methodology I employed included in-depth interviews, focus group discussions, participant observation, and content analysis of the document issued in relation to the hijab discourse in Ghana.

In this essay, I highlight the modalities of religious coexistence in the formal public space and day-to-day encounters in the Madina Zongo space. Where hijab use creates tensions and territorial issues in public spaces, it

---

1. One of the commercial areas in the city of Accra.
2. Sanneh, *Beyond Jihad*, x.

creates divergent types of relationships in the Zongo. As far as the larger Ghanaian community is concerned, the hijab evokes memories of poverty, illiteracy, oppression, and Islamic radicalism in public spaces. However, the associations it evokes in the Zongo space are different; there, the hijab relates to issues of piety, spirituality, decency, and fashion. In the following discussion, I present narratives of religious coexistence in these two distinctive and shared territories: public space and the Madina Zongo space.

Religious Plurality and Secularism in Ghana's Public Institutions

Ghana is a religiously pluralistic country, with adherents from different religious inclinations such as African indigenous religions, Christianity, Islam, Hinduism, Rastafarianism, Bahai, and Eckankar, among others. Since the democratization of Ghana's social, political, economic, and religious landscape, the 1992 constitution has continued to play an important role in ensuring peaceful relationships among individuals from diverse backgrounds. The constitution describes Ghana as a secular country, where freedom of religion is the right of every individual and no particular religion is accorded the status of a state religion.[3] However, Meyer argues that this ideal exists only at the formal level because "Ghanaian society and politics are heavily inflected with religion..."[4] Religion and politics continue to intersect, and all past and present presidents have continued to mix religion with politics in an attempt to gain political power.[5] For example, after losing elections for the second consecutive time, the current president of Ghana, Nana Akufu-Addo, resorted to the slogan "the battle is the Lord's."[6]

Within the framework of mixing religion with politics, Christianity appears to occupy a dominant position in Ghana's social and public space. The activities of British missionaries during the pre-independence era have left footprints in most sectors of the country, especially in the south. Realizing the potential danger of the hegemonic position of Christianity to Ghana's democratic dispensation, the Education Act was promulgated in 1961. As a result, mission schools – which were formerly controlled by British missionaries – became an

---

3. See Meyer, "Religious and Secular," 91–92; Quashigah, "Religion and the Secular State," 304.
4. Meyer, 107.
5. Asamoah-Gyadu, "God Bless Our Homeland," 165–66.
6. This is taken from a Bible verse: "This is what the LORD says to you: 'Do not be afraid or discouraged because of this vast army. For the battle is not yours, but God's'" (2 Chr 20:15 NIV).

integral part of the state machinery, controlled by the Ministry of Education through the Ghana Education Service. This act made it possible for state actors to take charge of developing policies for the administration of pre-tertiary education, including the training and appointment of staff, building and renovating schools, and a curriculum with a multireligious approach.[7] However, heads of mission-owned schools are appointed by their respective religious groups, who continue to insist on adhering to the teachings and practices of their faith in the management of these schools. In some private[8] and public[9] mission schools, as well as in public schools,[10] Muslim students are not allowed to perform their daily prayers, fast during the month of Ramadan, or wear the hijab.[11] Rather, it is mandatory that they participate in Christian worship services within the school premises. Muslims have described this practice as a violation of their constitutional rights, and they continue to put pressure on state actors to ensure that their rights as a minority group are respected.

Reacting to this situation, politicians continuously make attempts to take a neutral position and play the religious card by providing both Muslims and Christians in Ghana with equal opportunities in the highest political offices. For instance, the two major political parties[12] have made conscious efforts to ensure that there is a religious balance of Christian and Muslim representation in the office of the president and the vice president. For more than a decade, the current political party in power has continued to ensure that their vice presidential candidates are Muslims in order to appeal to their Muslim voters.[13] Meanwhile, this initiative by politicians has resulted in tension between the state, Muslims, and Christians in the Ghanaian community. Quite recently, some Christian groups, including pastors, have expressed anxiety over the

---

7. See Sarbah, "Religious 'Rights,'" 213.

8. Schools built by Christian practitioners that have not been handed over to the government.

9. Schools built by Christian practitioners that have been handed over to the government.

10. Schools built by the state.

11. In 2008, a Muslim student met his untimely death when he fell from the fourth floor of a school building in an attempt to avoid a mandatory Christian morning devotion. Again, in 2015, there were complaints from some Muslim students across the country that some public school authorities were compelling them to attend Christian worship programs in school.

12. New Patriotic Party (NPP) and National Democratic Congress (NDC).

13. The party has also moved a step forward to elect its current vice presidential candidate, a Muslim as the flag bearer who will contest for presidency in the 2024 general election. See https://www.theafricareport.com/327052/ghana-bawumia-makes-history-as-npps-first-muslim-flag-bearer/

attention politicians continue to give to the Muslim public.¹⁴ They fear that a Muslim will soon become president of the nation and turn Ghana into a Muslim state. While this initiative by Ghanaian politicians affords Muslims the opportunity to practice their religion and to insist on their identity in the public space, Christians feel challenged and have become stricter in their insistence on their identities in places they manage so that they do not risk losing their dominant position in the country.¹⁵

Thus, the Christian community and the state are sharply divided on the idea of promoting religious diversity in the school environment. While the government continues to make efforts to promote religious coexistence in its public spaces, the Christian community aims to manage its institutions according to its teachings and principles.¹⁶ Meanwhile, the government insists that the public space – including schools and hospitals – is part of the microcosm of the society where individuals of different religious groups have the right to express their religious beliefs.

The Politics of the Hijab in Ghana's Public Space: A Chronology

The generic meaning of the term "hijab" is a veiling practice used by Muslim women to cover their heads, necks, and bodies. The hijab found its way into Ghana due to the activities of Muslim women's organizations, the aftermath of the 9/11 attacks, and transnational connections between Ghana and North Africans, as well as between Ghana and Middle Eastern Arabs. Yunus Dumbe argues that the postindependence diplomatic relations between Ghana and the Arab world exposed Ghanaians to the lifestyles of the Arabs, including their dress practices.¹⁷ Similarly, Fatimatu Sulemana and Kauthar Khamis illustrate how the activities of Ghanaian Muslim women, which contributed to the formation of Muslim women's associations, also played an instrumental role in popularising the hijab in Ghana.¹⁸ These women, through proselytization

---

14. Through funding Muslims' annual pilgrimage to Mecca, making donations during Muslim religious celebrations, and the inclusion of Islamic Religious Studies as an examinable subject at secondary level.

15. Darko, "To wear or not to wear," 494. Darko discusses how Muslim nurses are prohibited from wearing the hijab at the Pentecost hospital in Madina. Also, a Muslim student at the Wesley Girls' High School was not allowed to observe the Ramadan fast, see https://www.myjoyonline.com/intolerance-at-wesley-girls-must-stop-headmistress-must-be-called-to-order-tamale-central-mp/.

16. See Bolaji, "Secularism," 77–85; Sarbah, "Religious Rights," 216–17.

17. See Dumbe, "Transnational Contacts," 112.

18. See Sulemanu, "Leadership," 165; Khamis, "Hijab and Niqab," 19.

and sharing of personal experiences, popularized the hijab among Muslims in Ghana. In recent times, trading activities of Ghanaian women in the Middle East and in Northern Nigeria have also contributed to promoting the hijab and widening its market and acceptability in Ghana. Currently, northern Nigeria – due to proximity and cultural similarities to Ghanaian Muslims, some hijabs in Ghana are imported from Northern Nigeria.

This expansion of the hijab economy in Ghana has made the hijab more fashionable, and most female Muslims continue to don the hijab in different public spaces – including schools, hospitals, banks, and other public institutions. However, this increasing visibility of the hijab has generated tensions between some Muslims and non-Muslims in public spaces. For instance, in 2013, the Ghana Muslim Students' Association sued the West African Examinations Council (WAEC) for disallowing some female Muslim students to write their final exams dressed in their hijabs.[19] In July 2013, the court ruled that WAEC should "not prevent any candidate from writing their papers solely because of their dress code which may be attributable to their religious beliefs or otherwise."[20] In a similar incident in 2015, a group of Muslims demonstrated against what they described as a profound discrimination against their fundamental human rights after a Muslim nurse was sacked from her post for wearing the hijab in one of the government hospitals in Accra. In 2019, a student named Ola Shade was prevented from doing her mathematics exams because she refused to take off her hijab. Another group of Muslim nursing students reported that they were denied entry to the premises of the Midwifery Council in Accra because of their hijabs. While some of them complied and removed their hijabs, one nursing student refused and was denied a posting.[21] In addition to these examples, Muyad Social Services (MSS), an Islamic organization, petitioned the Social Security and National Insurance Trust over complaints from a national service personnel that she was denied the opportunity to commence her compulsory national service because she had insisted on donning her hijab.[22]

---

19. "The *hijab* judgement," Ghana Muslim Students' Association, Fatima Uthman, Adelaide Dodoo Versus the West African Examination Council, 28 June 2013.

20. A statement issued by the court in Ghana.

21. See Bilkis Nuhu Kokroko, "#Hijabisanidentity: The Fight Continues," *Daily Mail GH*, 18 October 2019, https://www.dailymailgh.com/hijabisanidentity-the-fight-continues/.

22. See Adnan Adams Mohammed, "Muslim Group Threatens Court Action against SSNIT over Anti-hijab Posture," *GhanaWeb*, 17 September 2019, https://www.ghanaweb.com/GhanaHomePage/NewsArchive/Muslim-group-threatens-court-action-against-SSNIT-over-anti-hijab-posture-781579.

These incidents culminated in the popular #*hijabisanidentity* campaign in October 2019. This campaign sought to fight for the rights of female Muslims in Ghana to don the hijab in public spaces. Their engagements with both social and mainstream media, security personnel, politicians, and various Islamic organizations gave the campaign wider publicity. The impact of this kind of politicization of the hijab discourse in Ghana cannot be overestimated as it continues to heighten tensions between the state and Christian and Muslim communities. The politicization of the hijab was first initiated in 2015 by former President John Dramani Mahama and his minister for communication, Dr. Omane Boamah, who stated that it was unlawful to discriminate against Muslims in public institutions and called on the heads of such institutions to desist from doing so.[23] Again, in 2019, at a press briefing in Accra, the Minister for Inner Cities and Zongo Development, Dr. Mustapha Abdul-Hamid, was very blunt about the need to respect the constitutional rights of Muslim women to manifest their Islamic identity through the hijab. Even though he spoke on behalf of the president, some Ghanaian Muslims have challenged the current president to publicly declare his position on the hijab just as the former president did. Some Muslims have attributed the transfer of Dr. Hamid from a ministerial position to that of the Chief Executive Officer of the National Petroleum Authority to his vocal stance on the hijab issue.

Meanwhile, Hajia Samira Bawumia, Ghana's second lady, has remained silent on the hijab issue. She is a Muslim whose beauty practices are scrutinized in public spaces as she rarely dons the hijab except during political campaigns and religious programs. Her behavior has been interpreted by some Muslims as a complete disregard for the discrimination against Muslims on the basis of their hijab. Also, the Muslim caucus in parliament and the National Chief Imam's spokesperson have cautioned against the consequences of marginalizing minority groups, adding that doing so is likely to threaten the peace in the country. The security implication of the hijab discourse was heightened when the Muslim leadership in Ghana criticized the Ghana Catholic Bishops' Conference (GCBC), the Christian Council of Ghana (CCG), the Ghana Education Service (GES), and the Ghana National Association of Graduate Teachers (GNAT) about their entrenched positions related to Christian religious practices in secondary schools, maintaining that these could threaten

---

23. See Umaru Sanda Amadu, "Ghana Muslims Hail President's Stand on Hijab," *Anadolu Agency*, 3 February 2015, https://www.aa.com.tr/en/world/ghana-muslims-hail-presidents-stand-on-hijab/70608.

peaceful coexistence in the country.²⁴ According to the GCBC, CCG, GES, and GNAT, these Christian religious activities in schools should be seen in the light of ensuring "conformity and uniformity"²⁵ among students and not as an attempt to marginalize and discriminate against a religious group.

Hijab Protest²⁶

To a large extent, the constitutional declaration of Ghana as a secular state and attempts by state actors to promote religious coexistence and tolerance and

---

24. See Bolaji, "Secularism," 88.
25. See Sarbah, "Religious Rights," 222.
26. Picture taken by Abdul-Lahie Abdul-Rahim Naa, used with permission.

to control the hegemony of a particular religious group in the public sphere exists only in theory but does not operate in practice. The politicization of the hijab contributes to persistent tensions between Muslims and Christians in the public space. The secular idea that no religion is privileged above the other affords Muslims the constitutional right to express their religious identity in public spaces. On the other hand, the preexisting colonial infrastructure continues to give Christian religious practitioners a hegemonic position in public space, as is the case in Kenya.[27]

The "Pacifist" Hijab in Madina Zongo

Despite the contestations around the hijab in Ghana's public sphere, Madina Zongo seems to present a different scenario. There, the pacifist characteristics of the hijab in the Zongo are accommodated, appropriated, or tolerated. In this section, I will show how the coexistence of Muslims and Christians is lived out in Madina Zongo through the hijab. First, I will briefly describe Madina Zongo; and then I will examine everyday encounters between Muslims and Christians, using the hijab as an entry point.

Founded in the late 1950s, Madina Zongo is a pluralistic community within the La Nkwantanang Madina Municipality in the southeastern part of Accra. In Hausa, zongo suggests a "camping place of a carrier," "lodging place of travelers," or "strangers' quarters."[28] Zongo is often used to name a section of a community occupied by Muslim traders and migrants. Madina Zongo hosts people of diverse religious backgrounds, with Muslims as the dominant religious group, followed by Christians. For several decades, Christians, Muslims and practitioners of African Indigenous Religion have gone to great lengths to coexist and maintain peaceful relationships in this space.[29]

The relationship between Christians and Muslims in zongo is enhanced through mutual imitation of each other's religious practices and clothing styles, including the hijab. Within the Zongo, the hijab reveals ideas about piety, fashion, character, spirituality, and status. It is considered a mark of piety and decency, used for the performance of Islamic religious rituals such as the Muslim's five daily prayers. For some Muslims, it offers spiritual protection

---

27. See Meinema, "Regulating Religious Coexistence," 19.

28. See Schildkrout, *People of the Zongo,* 67; Pellow, "What Housing Does," 217.

29. Meyer and Ntewusu, "Modalities of Co-existence in Madina, Ghana," 486. Alhassan Adum-Atta, "Politics of Purity, Disgust and Contamination," 3–4; Fosu-Ankrah, *Kla,* 488; Khamis, "Beautiful and Precarious," 497.

against evil jinns who are attracted to female hair. The hijab also serves as a fashion accessory that is used by Muslim women of different backgrounds for various occasions. It is also used as a criterion for judging a female Muslim's moral behavior in the Zongo. For instance, the description of a female Muslim in Hausa as *mai saa hijab* (meaning "one who dons the hijab") implies that she is morally upright and stands a better chance of becoming a responsible wife and mother.

In the busy streets of the Madina Zongo, there are diverse pedestrians from different parts of the community – for example, students, public and private workers, market women, *trotro*[30] drivers and their *mates*, and taxi drivers. The most visible images during the early hours of every working day are the dress practices of female Muslim students who attend public and Christian schools in Madina and its adjoining communities. I observed that these students mix their Islamic dress practices with their school uniforms. Several of them use hijabs, abayas,[31] and sometimes niqabs[32] while in their school uniforms but remove these Muslim garments at the school entrance and put them on again afterward. In interviews with some of these students, they explained that they were uncomfortable with wearing their uniforms – the school uniforms are designed in a sleeveless formfitting dress extending to knee level, or a short-sleeved shirt with a formfitting skirt that covers up to the knees – in public because these clothes expose parts of their bodies.

In a similar case, the narratives of some female Muslims who work as nurses in both public and mission hospitals in Madina illustrate their daily struggles to navigate the boundaries of Islamic religious dress practices with their professional dress codes. One of the respondents, who works as a nurse at the Madina Polyclinic, explained that even though the hijab is not part of the nursing uniform, the female Muslim nurses in the polyclinic have managed to incorporate it into their uniform. She cited herself as an example, explaining that she had extended the length of her uniform from knee level to about two inches below the knees and also used the hijab to cover her head. However, this practice puts an additional pressure on these nurses not to flout any other clinic rules. As she put it, "Once you find a supervisor who tolerates the hijab, you are always careful not to put yourself in trouble by flouting other rules."

Another respondent, who works in a Christian mission hospital in Madina, said that she was given to understand during her interview that the hospital

---

30. Public transport operators.
31. A loose overgarment used by Muslim women in the Arab world.
32. A face veil.

would not accept her hijab since it is a mission hospital. She agreed with this position, uncovered her head, and then found the disposable hairnet used by medical practitioners to be a perfect replacement for the hijab. Thus, she would usually replace her hijab with the disposable hairnet once she entered the hospital premises.

The above illustrations show that even though hijab use is a constitutional right in any institution, whether public or private, the views and practices of majority and minority religious groups continue to be in conflict, especially in light of the fact that Christians insist on their identity in public institutions such as hospitals. However, through creative improvisation, Muslim nurses have been able to appropriate a medical tool such as the disposable hairnet and use it in place of the hijab.

This negotiation of the boundaries of religious dress practices and professional dress codes sometimes generates tensions between Christians and Muslims. For instance, in 2020, thirty-five female Muslim candidates of the Anisa Senior High School in Madina and the Mercy Islamic Senior High School in Accra – where the hijab is part of the school's uniform – were prevented from writing their West African Senior Secondary Certificate Exams (WASSCE) in their hijabs at an examination center located in Madina. The reason cited was that during the previous year, a female Muslim was caught hiding written material in her hijab for the purpose of cheating during exams. The supervisor in charge of the examination insisted that all examinees had to remove their hijabs to prevent a reoccurrence of such an incident. The management of the Anisa School and some executives of the Ghana Muslim Students' Association (GMSA), using a previous court injunction involving a case between GMSA and WAEC, managed to convince this supervisor to retract. Muslims argued that if the hijab enabled students to engage in malpractice at examinations, then all candidates should go into the examination hall naked, the hijab is part of the school's uniform. They further suggested that all candidates be subjected to body searches before being allowed into the examination hall, adding that whoever flouts examination regulations should be made to face the appropriate sanctions.[33]

In addition, in the compounds and streets where Muslim and Christian women encounter one another in close proximity, some Christians have copied the hijab used by Muslim women. These Christian women refer to their own lost tradition of donning the veil and explain that pictures of Mary always

---

33. Interviews with Muhsin Islam (patron of GMSA at Annisa Senior High School) and Mr. Idriss Amin (teacher at Annisa Senior High School) on 24 February 2021.

show her wearing a veil. The habits of the Catholic nuns were also used as a reference point for the adoption of the hijab by some Christian women in Madina Zongo. At the Our Lady of Apostles Catholic Church in the Madina Libya quarters, the leader of the women's fellowship explained that modernity has contributed to abandoning the tradition of head covering among female congregants. She explained that it is now the preserve of Catholic nuns and members of the Women's Fellowship, adding, however, that "any time a woman is expected to perform an activity in the church which requires that she mounts the podium, she does so with her head covered."[34]

Another respondent, who worships at True Faith Ministry, Agbogba, explained that all the female congregants in her church use the head covering, which she compared to the hijab. She also cited the example of the Church of Pentecost (COP), where the head covering was the trademark of the church until a communique was issued recently, abolishing this practice. She called the actions of the COP unfortunate since the veil plays an important role in the religious life of every Christian woman. This respondent further explained that angels who serve as intercessors would, without any delay, deliver a woman's prayer to God if she is veiled. For her, veiling signified submission, humility, and connection with the creator.

Furthermore, some Christian respondents who have lived in Madina Zongo for decades mentioned that the hijab has become an integral part of their daily life even though they continue to practice Christianity. Three respondents – an Ewe and two Ada women – pointed to the spiritual significance of pregnant women donning the hijab. Among ethnic groups such as the Ewe-Dome, pregnant women are considered fragile, exposed, and vulnerable to evil spirits, especially at night.[35] These spirits are likely to harm them and their unborn babies. Even though the government has introduced measures to improve maternal healthcare through education and the provision of affordable healthcare, these women take personal initiatives such as using the hijab to ensure their own safety and that of their unborn babies. They believe that the big hijab – which covers the body from head to toe – protects them from evil spirits and blinds the eyes of evil people, preventing them from seeing pregnant women especially at night.

---

34. Interviewed 11 June 2021.
35. See Ganusah, *Christ Meets the Ewe-Dome*, 62–63.

Conclusion

This essay has examined the binary framing of hijab practices in Ghana's secular space and the Madina Zongo space as a marker of tension and pacifism. It expounds the modalities of religious coexistence in both shared spaces using secularity in Ghana and Sanneh's concept of "pacifism." Unlike the Muslim clerics of West Africa, who decided to keep "the political class at arm's length"[36] by ensuring that state actors do not meddle in the affairs of religion, the secular framework and its role in regulating religious diversity in Ghana needs to be further interrogated. For instance, the constitutional rights and freedom to worship and manifest one's religion may also imply that religious groups who establish and operate public facilities have the right to insist on certain teachings and practices, as is the case with GLISS and the mission hospital in Madina.

However, the hegemony of Christianity, the insistence of the Muslim minority on their constitutional right to wear the hijab, and the politicization of the hijab discourse continue to heighten tensions between Muslims and Christians at the national level, which some people believe has significant security implications. This is evident in the uncompromising attitude of some Christians toward the hijab because of its association with Islamic jihadist groups. On the other hand, in Madina Zongo, the association of the hijab with faith, fashion, and spirituality provides an opportunity to discern how religious coexistence is lived out at the everyday level. Taking all this into account, this essay argues that hijab use in Madina Zongo space can be seen as ingenious, accommodative, hospitable, tolerant, and peaceful.

Bibliography

Alhassan Adum-Atta, Rashida. "The Politics of Purity, Disgust, and Contamination: Communal Identity of Trotter (Pig) Sellers in Madina Zongo (Accra)." *Religions* 11, no. 8 (2020): 421.

Asamoah-Gyadu, J. Kwabena. "God Bless Our Homeland Ghana: Religion and Politics in a Post-Colonial African State." In *Trajectories of Religion in Africa: Essays in Honour of John S. Pobee*, edited by Cephas N. Omenyo and Eric B. Anum, 165–81. Amsterdam; New York: Editions Rodopi, 2014.

Azumah, John. "Beyond Jihad: The Pacifist Tradition in West African Islam." *International Bulletin of Mission Research* 41, no. 4 (2017): 363–69.

---

36. Azumah, "Beyond Jihad," 366.

Bolaji, M. "Secularism and State Neutrality: The 2015 Muslim Protest of Discrimination in the Public Schools in Ghana." *Journal of Religion in Africa* 48, nos. 1–2 (2018): 65–104.

Darko, Martin Luther. "'To Wear or Not to Wear' Contesting Hijab at the Pentecost Hospital in Madina." *Material Religion* 18:4 (2022): 494–95, DOI: 10.1080/17432200.2022.2111113.

Dumbe, Yunus. "Transnational Contacts and Muslim Religious Orientation in Ghana." PhD diss., University of Ghana, 2009.

Fosu-Ankrah, Joseph Fiifi. "*kla*: A Tutelary Deity at the Jamaica Marketplace in Madina, Accra." *Material Religion* 18 no. 4 (2022): 488–91, DOI: 10.1080/17432200.2022.2111102.

Ganusah, Rebecca Yawa. *Christ Meets the Ewe-Dome of Ghana*. Ghana: Legon Theological Studies, 2008.

Khamis, Kauthar. "Hijab and Niqab: A Cross-Religious COVID-19 Safety Measure in Madina Zongo." *Entangled Religions* 12, no. 3 (2022).

———. "Beautiful and Precarious Female Dummies in Madina." *Material Religion* 18, no. 4 (2022): 496–97. DOI: 10.1080/17432200.2022.2111114.

Meinema, Erik. "Regulating Religious Coexistence: The Intricacies of 'Interfaith' Cooperation in Coastal Kenya." PhD diss., Utrecht University, 2021.

Meyer, Birgit. "Religious and Secular, 'Spiritual' and 'Physical' in Ghana." In *What Matters? Ethnographies of Value in a Not So Secular Age*, edited by Courtney Bender and Ann Taves, 86–118. New York: Columbia University Press, 2012.

Meyer, Birgit, and Samuel Aniegye Ntewusu. "Modalities of Co-existence in Madina, Ghana." *Material Religion* 18, no. 4 (2022): 486–87.

Pellow, Deborah. "What Housing Does: Changes in an Accra Community." *Architecture & Behavior* 4 (1988): 213–28.

Quashigah, Kofi. "Religion and the Republican State in Africa: The Need for a Distanced Relationship." *African Human Rights Law Journal* 14, no. 1 (2014): 78–92.

Sanneh, Lamin. *Beyond Jihad: The Pacifist Tradition in West African Islam*. New York; Oxford: Oxford University Press, 2016.

Sarbah, Cosmas Ebo. "Religious 'Rights' in the State Regulated Mission Schools in Ghana." In *Religion and Sustainable Development: Ghanaian Perspectives*, edited by George Ossom-Batsa et al., 213. Rome: Urbaniana University Press, 2018.

Schildkrout, Enid. *People of the Zongo: The Transformation of Ethnic Identities in Ghana*. Cambridge: Cambridge University Press, 1978.

Sulemanu, Fatimatu. "Leadership in the Ghanaian Muslim Community: The Role of FOMWAG." Masters diss., University of Ghana, 2006.

17

Reimposing *Dār Al-Salām* and the Kingdom of God in the Indonesian Context

A Detour from Geopolitical Territorialization to Religioethical Conversation

Ferry Y. Mamahit

Introduction

Several factors have triggered world religious conflicts. Aside from scriptural and doctrinal issues, one crucial factor is territory or territorialization. Simply put, the question often boils down to this: Who is in control of a particular place? Given a religious framing, the critical question at hand is what specific religion dominates a specific area. In Islam, the bipolar concept of *dār al-islām* versus *dār al-ḥarb* – based on literal, geopolitical, doctrinal, and legal foundations – divides the world into two irreconcilable dichotomic poles: *the abode of peace* and *the abode of war*. Historically, Christianity has demonstrated the same geopolitical territorialization, especially during Western Christendom (200–1000 CE) and, later, European colonialism (1700–1940 CE). During these eras, particularly the latter, Christian rulers divided the world into regions consisting of the conquered and the unconquered. Unfortunately, this dichotomic concept and power-dominating motif has caused conflicts and separated territories, frustrated identities, and disintegrated communities.

Thus, these realities pose challenges to peaceful interreligious relationships in both global and local contexts.

Against this backdrop, this essay argues that the terms *dār al-islām* and its counterpart, *dār al-ḥarb*, have no scriptural basis and, thus, are neither normative nor relevant. They occur in neither the Qur'an nor the Sunna. Instead, this binary emerged within the progressive development of international affairs and relations between Muslims and non-Muslims. The Christian counterpart of this binary territorial concept is also similar, it emerges outside of specific religious scriptures. Consequently, such a notion is difficult to accept and apply, even among larger Muslim and Christian groups. The argument in this essay is based on the qur'anic idea of *dār al-salām* (Q 6:127; 10:25). This writing conceives, constructs, and promotes the religioethical idea of civilization or the making of a just and peaceful society. Such an idea is also compatible with and corresponds to the biblical idea of God's kingdom in the Christian tradition, particularly its religious-ethical values of justice and peace. Both Islam and Christianity should make these religious-ethical values a platform for constructing Muslim-Christian relationships marked by mutuality. Such efforts might appear subversive, turning geopolitical territorialization into a religioethical conversation. This shiftw ould no doubt enhance just and peaceful Muslim-Christian relations in the future.

The Territorial Binary in Islam and Christianity: A Brief Discussion

In Islam, the idea of a territorial binary occurs in a pair of terms: *dār al-islām* and *dār al-ḥarb*. The meanings of these terms remain debatable today. The complexity of the subject stems from different perspectives regarding Islam as a whole.[1] Anti-Islam populists and Orientalists perceived it in Manichaean terms: a dualism between Islam and non-Islam where there is "a constant state of war"[2] between the two forces until one wins and dominates the other. Within this frame, Islam is diametrically opposed to the rest of the world. Sarah Albrecht, however, cautions against such a caricature and suggests a critical reevaluation of this dichotomy based on its historical development.[3] She notes a protracted internal debate among traditional and modern Muslim *maḏhabs* (that is, schools) on the legal aspects of territoriality that relate to sovereignty

---

1. See Albrecht, *Dār al-Islām Revisited*, 36.
2. Lewis, *Political Language*, 73; see also Nagel, *Das islamische Recht*, 102.
3. Albrecht, *Dār al-Islām Revisited*, 21–22.

over lands, wars, peace, international law, and international relations. Albrecht's suggestion is constructive as it avoids an oversimplification of the problem.

It is essential to discuss how different interpretations of the terms *dār al-islām* (territory of Islam), *dār al-ḥarb* (territory of war), and *dār al-kufr* (territory of unbelief) – as well as their implementation – came about within Islamic tradition. These terms do not occur in either the Qur'an or the Sunna. They originated and evolved during the early stages of Islam in its religious, social, legal, and political contexts. There is a common contextual consensus (*ijtihad*) among the foremost premodern Islamic jurists (the *fuqahā'* from *maḏhabs* like Hanafi, Shafii, Malike, and Hanbali) that views *dār al-islām* as the territory where Muslims can live in security and freedom. This term mainly deals with the political and legal systems, the provision of security, and the ability to practice Islamic law and rites as applied by Muslims in their inherited and conquered lands. It also includes rules applied to the subdued and unconverted non-Muslims – the protected dhimmi – who are under the authority of an imam, pay jizya (tax), and acknowledge Muslim authority.[4] However, *dār al-islām* implementation is slightly different from one jurist to another. For example, while the Hanafi, Maliki, and Hanbali jurists emphasize the application of the Islamic rule as necessary, the Shafii jurists do not assume that law to be compulsory.[5]

In any case, the term *dār al-ḥarb* or *dār al-kufr* refers to any place outside the "Islamic" territory. Muslim scholars have developed the idea of Islamic and non-Islamic territories for centuries. Premodern Islamic jurists made adjustments concerning this division because of changing political contexts. Since the Reconquista and Mongol expansion, which affected the decline of the Abyssinian and Ottoman Islamic empires, Muslims initiated an option other than the dichotomic poles of *dār al-'ahd* (territory of the treaty) and *dār al-ṣulḥ* (territory of truce),[6] which represented new "gray" territories.

Jurists further disagreed on how to relate this new territory with the previous dichotomic ones. Albrecht suggests three different categories representing their views:[7] first, as part of *dār al-islām*, as the majority of Shafii and Hanafi jurists placed it; second, as part of *dār al-ḥarb*, as some Hanbalis retained it; and, third, as another new category independent of the two (*dār al-islām* and *dār al-harb*) held by the majority of Hanbalis and some Hanafis

---

4. Emon, "Religious Minorities," 330, 338.
5. Albrecht, *Dār al-Islām Revisited*, 48–63.
6. See Verskin, *Islamic Law*, 83.
7. Albrecht, *Dār al-Islām Revisited*, 50–58.

and Shafiis, notably al-Mawardi and al-Shaybani. Thus, the first view makes *dār al-ʿahd* or *dār al-ṣulḥ* a new territory, forming the following tripartite territorial paradigm: Islam-war-treaty.

In the modern period, Muslim scholars have had to face new realities. The geopolitical, social, and demographic factors were changing through the colonization of Muslim lands, the formation of modern states, the unique system of international relations, and the migration of millions of Muslims to Western Europe. This context led scholars to question the relevance of all territorial paradigms previously employed in the premodern period, particularly the identification and definition of these "new" formations of Islamic and non-Islamic territories. Modern scholars have proposed several territorial binary models: first, all Islamic countries that implement shariʿa are a part of *dār al-islām*; second, the colonized lands remain part of *dār al-islām*, where Muslims can perform jihad (Q 2:216; 9:5), legitimize the spreading of Islam, and encourage mass migrations (hijra); third, the predominantly Islamic countries with non-Islamic governments are part of *dār al-ḥarb*; and fourthly, non-Islamic countries, including Western nations, with Muslim populations, whose legal systems align with both Islamic and international law, and are validated by international treaties, are considered part of *dār al-ʿahd*.[8] These various modern views demonstrate the diminishing importance of the madhab (school of jurisprudence) as a determining factor in conceptualizing the territorial binary. These new realities changed Islamic discourses on the normativity of territoriality.

Surprisingly, these changes have also left some Muslims or Islamic groups such as Hizb ut-Tahrir activists, the IS (Islamic State), and al-Qaeda propagandists questioning an idealistic state's relevance based on *dār al-islām*. They aim to bring back Islam's golden era through victorious battles, refabricating the territorial dichotomy, and promoting hostility against their enemies.[9] According to these groups, it is the establishment of *dār al-islām* in the form of a caliphate that supplants the borders of existing nation-states.

---

8. Albrecht, 87.

9. Such narratives have been developed to justify the wars against and victories over the enemies of Islam – that is, non-Muslims or even Muslims who do not support them, as was sometimes the case during the early Islamic conquests. According to John Esposito, "Muslim extremists and terrorist groups, past and present, like Al Qaeda, ISIS and Boko Haram, have used Q 9:5 to justify unconditional warfare against all unbelievers, non-Muslims, as well as Muslims who do not accept their militant beliefs. Both conveniently overlook or reinterpret the end of Q 9:5 which clearly states that, while Muhammad's followers had permission to fight to defend themselves, they were to stop if the enemy stopped its aggression . . . (9:5)." Esposito, "Islam and Political Violence," 1070.

Differing from the diversity, adaptability, and flexibility of the territorial notions of Islamic legal discourses in the past, these groups cling to a binary rigidity. They regard all non-Muslim countries as part of *dār al-kufr*. Therefore, they view these places as part of *dār al-ḥarb* and, hence, subjected to jihad and *daʿwa*. Further, they consider any Muslim-majority country that does not apply the Islamic legal system as an "un-Islamic territory" that must, therefore, be reestablished as *dār al-islām* under the rule of a caliphate. A more moderate view is espoused by Ibn Taymiyya, who regards such a country as a "third domain" (*qism thālith*) or "composite territory" (*dār murakkaba*).

Regardless, the binary perspective and its variants proposed by the these classical Muslim scholars seem irrelevant today. It is opposed to, for instance, the global order, particularly the contemporary international system of the nation-state. Most Muslim countries neither uphold nor implement such a dichotomy. Instead, they believe that Muslims are not currently in a state of perpetual war against non-Muslims. As members of the United Nations (UN), they have accepted the UN charter to respect and agree that other nations (including non-Muslim ones) are part of the international diplomatic community. The purpose of adhering to these principles may serve as a divine call to be fulfilled in every true and righteous Muslim (see Q 2:177). Such a qur'anic demand is more compelling and relevant nowadays than the classical jurists' binary ideas in the past. Therefore, this modern development demonstrates the improbability that the caliphatic *dār al-islām* can coexist with the international system of nation-states.

The territorial binary has also existed throughout the history of Christianity. However, it took place within the context of Christian religiopolitical developments rather than in its ideological-political polemics, as is the case in Islam. Its occurrence predates the beginning of the Islamic era (ca. 610 CE) and goes back to Christianity's acquired status as the Roman Empire's official religion in the third century.[10] Following its initial stage as a religious movement during the first three centuries – namely, from Pentecost (Acts 2:38) to the Apostolic Age (ca. 30–312 CE) – Christianity became a powerful political force. Following the great schism between the Western Roman and Eastern Orthodox churches (ca. 754 CE), such a pattern of control over territory remained prominent on both sides. The Byzantine Empire then encountered the Sassanids from Persia, making an emergent and expanding Islam its other geopolitical competitor. Thus, the history of the post-Apostolic Age illustrates

---

10. Under the Roman emperor Theodosius I or Theodosius the Great (379–395 CE). See Brown, *Rise of Western Christendom*, 76–78.

forms of Christianity that have struggled with (geo)politicization, marked by domination and territorial control.[11]

One can trace the origin of this binary to Emperor Constantine's conversion from paganism to Christianity. His conversion occurred following a dream in which he saw a cross-shaped trophy with the message "By this conquer!" (Lat. *Hoc signo victor eris* or Gk. τούτῳ νίκα).[12] Constantine then saw Christ appear, which inspired him to adopt the Christian faith's sacred signs – the cross and the Greek letters chi and rho – which he believed would bring victory to his army. Successful military campaigns and spiritual guidance from Lactantius in the West, Eusebius in the East, and several Christian bishops seemingly confirmed that Constantine was God's special servant.[13] In *Divine Institutes*, Lactantius writes that the emperor would play his role by divine appointment and providence as the restorer of justice, the protector of the human race, the restorer of the holy religion, and the performer of works of righteousness.[14] Lactantius's statement implies that God had chosen and entrusted the emperor with a mission to bring order and peace to protect the Catholic Church within and through the Roman Empire and to propagate the Christian faith throughout the world.

Since then, the idea of Christendom or a Christian kingdom emerged and developed in the form of Christian imperial theocracy. Christendom's domination continued through disputes and tensions over territories between Roman Catholic and Protestant religiopolitical powers. The principle of *eius regio, cuius religio* (whose land, his religion), established by the Peace of Westphalia in 1648, promulgated the idea that the religion of the ruler should be the religion of the ruled.[15] Long before this treaty, Catholic religiopolitical powers had already embraced the principle that "unoccupied lands (*terra nullius*) become the possession of whosoever first occupies them, in the sense of putting them to some productive use."[16] This idea is evident in the Bulls of Donation (1493), where Pope Alexander VI divided overseas territories (the entire *orbis terrarum*) into two discrete spheres of jurisdiction, split between Spain and Portugal's Catholic monarchs. Thus, during this period, there was

---

11. See also Jefferson, *Christianity's Impact*, 4–13.

12. See Barnes, *Constantine*, 74–80.

13. Constantine claimed the title *famulus Dei*. See also Odahl, *Constantine*, 137–41; Bardill, *Constantine*, 271–75, 280–84, 290–99; and Pottenger, "Servant of God," 31–45.

14. *Divine Institutes* VII. 26. 11–17. See Bowen and Garnsey, *Lactantius*, and Schaff, *Fathers*.

15. See Harrington and Smith, "Confessionalization," 77–101. See also Lehning, *European Colonialism*, 16–58.

16. Pagden, "Christian Tradition," 110.

a reconfiguration of the political and geographical relationships between territory, sovereignty, and religious identity.

The Implications of a Territorial Binary in the Contemporary Indonesian Context

The territorial binary is relevant to the Indonesian context. Before the nation's independence in 1945, some leaders discussed whether to become a nation-state or a religious state. A few Muslim political and intellectual figures initially proposed a draft of the first article of Pancasila[17] stating, "Belief in One God with the obligation of Muslim adherents to carry out the Islamic *sharīʿa*."[18] However, some of their nationalist counterparts rejected the proposal. They argued that Indonesia is a pluralistic nation and that a separation based on religious identity would be exclusive, thus harming the unity of its people. Although a few were not in agreement, the majority finally rejected the original draft and revised it to "Belief in One God." Such a legal consensus became the basis for identifying Indonesia as a (religious) nation-state and not an (Islamic) religious state.[19]

Unfortunately, after independence, the nation encountered opposition from those who could not accept this political reality. As a result, Islamic militant movements emerged and have persisted throughout the history of the nation. The first and most prominent among these was the Darul Islam (DI) movement led by Kartosoewirjo. In 1949, inspired by the zeal of his great Muslim anti-colonial predecessors and mentors, Kartosoewirjo proclaimed the Indonesian Islamic state "Darul Islam." He also formed Tentara Islam Indonesia or TII (Tentara Islam Indonesia, or Indonesian Islamic Armed Force) as its defense force.[20] This movement spread from West Java to Central Java through Amir Fatah; then to Aceh through Teungku Daud Beureueh; to South Kalimantan, led by Ibnu Hadjar; and, finally, to South Sulawesi under the leadership of Kahar Muzakkar. Operations by the Indonesian military successfully halted all movements of the DI/TII. Then, the Komando Jihad (Jihad Command) movement emerged during the 1970s, some of whom were

---

17. *Pancasila* is a composite word, made up of two Sanskrit words – *panca* (five) and *sila* (basis, foundation, or principle). So, the literal meaning of *pancasila* is "the five bases" or "the five foundations" or "the five principles" of the nation. See Ismail, "Religion, State, and Ideology," 19–58.

18. Muslimin, "Islamic Law," 15–26.

19. Muslimin, 15–26.

20. See Formichi, *Making of the Nation*, 6.

former DI/TII members.[21] More recently, various religious groups such as the Hizbut Tahrir, Ikhwan al-Muslimin, Lil Alamin Jihad, Jama'ah Islam, Majelis Mujahidin Indonesia, and others have emerged in the region.[22] They all share a territorial idealism and vision predicated on establishing Indonesia as an Islamic state based on the caliphatic model of *dār al-islām*.

The territorial binary also exists in so-called Christian regions in Indonesia. The intense Christian missionary activities in some parts of the country have resulted in people's conversions to Christianity. These areas have become so-called Christian territories. Unfortunately, escalated tensions and frequent conflicts between Muslims and Christians have triggered hatred and fear among Christian communities. One may see banners or posters "tanah Injil" ("the land of the Gospel") and the construction of gigantic statues of the Christian cross and Jesus Christ, which signify a particular region's territoriality and religious identity. These symbolic pronouncements are counterproductive because they communicate that these territories are under Christian control. Furthermore, the Christian majority uses these religious symbols for political purposes – to marginalize, discriminate against, or even oppress minorities. This weakens peaceful ties between the majority and minority religious groups, a dynamic that Christians should be aware of.

The territorial binary has negatively impacted the socioreligious sphere, particularly the relationship between Islam and other religions – mainly Christianity. Religious tensions and conflicts, including bloody ones, have occurred. The Setara Institute for Democracy and Peace, which monitors religious freedom, reported 216 cases of violent attacks on religious minorities in 2010, 244 cases in 2011, and 264 cases in 2012.[23] Meanwhile, the Wahid Foundation reported similar religious freedom violations in Indonesia, verifying that there were 313 cases with 204 incidents of religious intolerance in 2016, 265 cases with 213 intolerant religious incidents in 2017, and 276 cases with 192 intolerant religious incidents in 2018.[24] Unfortunately, these reports also exposed cases where Indonesian government officials, including some military personnel, facilitated harassment and intimidation of minorities by the radical and militant religious groups.

---

21. See Mubarak, "Dari NII ke ISIS," 80–81.

22. See Ritaudin, "Dār al-ḥarb," 287–304.

23. See "Atas Nama Agama: Pelanggaran terhadap Minoritas Agama di Indonesia" (In Religion's Name: Abuses against Religious Minorities in Indonesia), *Human Rights Watch*, 28 February 2013, https://www.hrw.org/id/report/2013/02/28/256410.

24. See Mubarak, "Presentasi Laporan," 5.

A Shift: Reimposing *Dār Al-Salām* and the Kingdom of God

This essay explores a more scriptural and constructive understanding of the concept of territory in Islam and the positive implications for peaceful interreligious relations. It proposes a concept of territory in the Islamic context through the reimposition of the term *dār al-salām* instead of the dichotomic *dār al-islām/dār al-ḥarb*. There are several reasons for this. First, while the term *dār al-salām* occurs in the Qur'an (Q 6:127; 10:25), neither *dār al-Islam* nor *dār al-ḥarb* appear at all.[25] The Qur'an use of *dār al-islām* implies that the most authoritative Islamic source for theological truth, morals, and conduct endorses it. Second, the term is less polemical since it does not contain geopolitical connotations. Third, the theological concept of *dār al-salām* is compatible and correlative with the idea of God's kingdom in Christianity. Although appealing to a scriptural basis may seem to oversimplify the geopolitical complexity, doing so would be more widely authoritative and, thus, acceptable to both communities.

As previously mentioned, the term *dār al-salām* occurs in two places in the Qur'an – namely, Surah al-An'am (Q 6:127) and Surah Yunus (Q 10:25). The word *salām* in *dār al-salām* – which has its root in *s-l-m* – has several meanings: peace, safety, tranquility, completeness, freedom from obstacles, or submission.[26] This shows that both *islām* (total surrender or [act of] surrendering, submitting) and *salām* (peace, safety, security) have the same etymological roots.[27] Ibn 'Arafa interprets both terms as the absence of hostility or, ideally, the state of commonality without war.[28] According to Ibn Manzur, both words share a theological connection since God gave *al-islām* to humanity to spread *al-salām*.[29] Further, in the Arabic world, the word *salām* or *al-salām* is theologically understood as having divine attributes or characteristics.[30] As a follower of God, a Muslim should reflect this divine character in daily life. Therefore, the term *salām* – since it shows a Muslim's intimate relationship with God as well as with others – implies spiritual, moral, and ethical values.

The use of the term *salām* in the qur'anic *dār al-salām* also has significance. Surah al-An'am 6:127 states, "For them shall be the abode of peace (*dār al-*

---

25. See Amoretti, "Some Observations," 74. See also Villano, "The Qur'anic Foundations," 126.
26. Badawi and Haleem, *Arabic-English Dictionary*, 450.
27. Badawi and Haleem, 452.
28. As quoted by Safri, "Reinterpretasi," 31.
29. See Ibn Manzur, *Lisan al 'Arab*, 268–70.
30. See Safri, "Reinterpretasi," 32.

salām) near their Lord, and He will be their friend because of what they used to do."³¹ This translation is a bit vague about how the locus of "the abode of peace" is identified, particularly when one connects it with the phrase "near their Lord." In a Malay translation, the phrase "the abode of God" is translated and interpreted as *Syurga Darusallam* (the paradise of the abode of peace) with a parenthetical note, "the home of safety and prosperity."³² It suggests that this place is the eschatological heaven. The term also appears in Surah Yunus 10:25: "God invites to the abode of peace, and He guides whomever He wishes to a straight path."³³ Again, this English translation is unclear about the identification of the actual place. It is also different from the Malay translation, which provides an additional bold parenthetical note at the beginning of the verse: "This is the end of worldly life." This interpretive note refers to the time when God will invite people to enter the heaven of *dār al-salām* (the home of safety and prosperity).³⁴ The occurrences of the qur'anic *dār al-salām* point to an eschatological vision within a heavenly locus. It implies that the abode of peace is an ideal future place prepared for those who have an intimate relationship with God.

Such an eschatological vision of *dār al-salām* is significant in dealing with territoriality. Since the texts mention words synonymous with "friends of Allah" (the Muslims), "actions or conduct of the Muslims," and "a straight path" (Islam), one may refer to these as the spiritual, ethical, and moral values and conduct every Muslim should have before entering paradise, the abode of peace. As a result, this vision should be a guiding factor or a moral compass for human conduct and action in this world. Aref Ali Nayed, who views *dār al-islām* and *dār al-salām* as synonymous, suggests that the qur'anic texts that speak of *dar* be interpreted theologically as primarily denoting paradise (otherworld).³⁵ He further argues that the idea of *dār al-salām* focuses more on the inner state of being in every Muslim. The heart of a true Muslim is already an abode of peace, and such abode, as Nayed argues, is "the essential seed(s) from which worldly peaceful environments grow, and through which the eternal abode is prepared for."³⁶ This view proposes that Muslims need to move beyond a legal-geopolitical discourse to a more ethical or spiritual one.

---

31. Reynolds, *Qur'an and the Bible*, 241.
32. Brown, *Kitab Suci Al-Qur'an*, 99.
33. Reynolds, *Qur'an and the Bible*, 331.
34. Brown, *Kitab Suci Al-Qur'an*, 99.
35. As inferred by Albrecht in *Dār al-Islām Revisited*, 305–9.
36. Quoted by Albrecht, *Dār al-Islām Revisited*, 307.

In modern Indonesian Islamic contexts, some Muslim scholars have reacted against the binary territorial concept because it has caused horizontal conflicts in society. One such scholar, Nurcholis Madjid, proposes that the term *dār al-islām* can still be used as long as it is given its correct meaning – namely "the citied-society where Muslims live coexistent with non-Muslim, as fellow citizens, in a shared territory."[37] This should be a place for human flourishing, especially in establishing civilization in a modern and plural Indonesian context. In short, the idea of an abode of peace (*dār al-salām* or even *dār al-islām*) should refer to a place where a civilized and shared society is established. The Qur'an as a whole supports this truth – as seen intertextually in several parts of it[38] – and, therefore, should be applied wherever Muslims live.

Stereotypically negative images of Islam have caused the largest Muslim organization in Indonesia, the Nahdlatul Ulama (NU), to rethink its identity. This group has responded by proposing and promoting a moderate and elegant brand of Islam, emphasizing its central doctrine as *rahmatan lil-'alamin* (a mercy to all creation; see also Q 21:107),[39] which Siswoyo Munandar argues is an inclusive form of Indonesian Islam with the following positive and constructive characteristics:[40] *tawassuth* (moderation), *i'tidal* (straight), *tasamuh* (toleration), and *tawazun* (balanced). Based on these values, the NU organization has developed a culture that accepts, understands, and honors diversity, especially concerning nonfundamental principles (see also *khilafiyah furu'iyyah* or the dispute over the nonessentials). According to Muhammad Machasin, the concept of *rahmatan lil-'alamin* is the only suitable way for Indonesian Muslims to encounter and navigate plurality issues.[41] In fact, there is a consensus among moderate Indonesian Muslims that there must be a greater concern to establish a civilized and shared Islamic society than to establish an Islamic state. The latter may lead them into "the path of Allah" (a straight path), which is closely related to a shared society that builds up humanity, justice, peace, and welfare for all human beings.

---

37. Madjid, *Khazanah*, 52; see also Madjid, *Islam Doktrin*, 225; Azra, *Wajah Baru*, 74; and Wahid, *Islam Kosmopolitan*, 7.

38. For example: "There is no compulsion in religion" (Q 2:256); "So let there be a body among you who may call to the good, enjoin what is esteemed and forbid what is odious. They are those who will be successful" (Q 3:104); and "Of all the communities raised among men you are the best, enjoining the good, forbidding the wrong, and believing in God" (Q 3:110).

39. See Muzadi, *Mengenal Nahdlatul Ulama*, 1.

40. See Rasyid, "Islam Rahmatan," 87–102.

41. Machasin, *Islam Dinamis*, 219–20.

The notion of *dār al-salām* also corresponds to the Christian concept of the kingdom of God. However, the term kingdom symbolizes the spiritual reign of God in Christ. The term kingdom of God (Gk. ἡ βασιλεία τοῦ θεοῦ, *hē basileia tou theou*) is central in Jesus's teaching as recorded in the Synoptic Gospels. Interestingly, the possessive form (either genitive or subjective) "of God" determines the concept of "reign." Thus, it is the reign that is theocentric.[42] Since this kingdom has a God-determined character, Christians, as representative agents of the kingdom, should manifest God's dynamic character in their lives. In the Sermon on the Mount (Matthew 5–7), these divine characteristics are described as holy, just, truthful, love, peaceful, transcendent, cosmic, and eschatological.[43] The suggestion here is that the gospel idea of the kingdom is quite different from the political kingdom embodied by Christendom. Indeed, the kingdom of God is not a physical or political Christian kingdom and has no implications for territoriality.

Reimposing the kingdom of God is an attempt to integrate the heavenly and earthly abodes of peace. This view of the kingdom of God is present in the Lord's Prayer: "Your kingdom come, your will be done, on earth as it is in heaven" (Matt 6:10 NIV). Both *dār al-salām* and the kingdom of God might be new paradigms for rethinking territoriality since they have the potential to promote a shared understanding of a religious-ethical idea of civilization and the making of a just and peaceful society. To put this into practice, Indonesian Muslims and Christians need time and space whereby communities can connect and converse with one another. In borrowing this Islamic cardinal principle, both Islam and Christianity should be a means for showing mercy to all human beings. This vision of *telos* (end destiny) is crucial for improving interreligious relations in the Indonesian context. The late Lamin Sanneh once asserted that for the salvation of humanity, each religion should be regulated as a controlled substance because "human destiny is more than a matter of political calculation."[44] Sanneh's insights invite us to shift from a geopolitical territorial discourse to a religious-ethical conversation.

Concluding Reflection

The paradigm discussed in this essay raises further questions: What will this new shared territorial paradigm look like in the future? What might be its

---

42. See du Toit, "Kingdom of God," 548.
43. du Toit, 545–63.
44. Sanneh, *Beyond Jihad*, 258.

impact on the enhancement of peaceful interreligious relations? How can Muslims and Christians implement this new paradigm in their daily lives? These questions are challenging, and they are not easy to answer. The issue of territoriality is quite complex because it is closely related to other factors such as religious tradition, authority, identity, and interpretation. While these questions defy simple explanations, the discussions in this chapter hopefully provide an alternative route for Muslim-Christian relations – a shift away from geopolitical territorialization to religious-ethical conversations. The Sanneh Institute, Ghana, can be a place that will reflect Lamin Sanneh's passion for providing space for a *dār* (an abode) where religious-ethical conversations and interactions can take place.

Bibliography

Albrecht, Sarah. *Dār al-Islām Revisited: Territoriality in Contemporary Islamic Legal Discourse on Muslims in the West*. Leiden; Boston: Brill, 2018.

Amoretti, Biancamaria S. "Some Observations on *dār al-ḥarb/dār al-islām* in the Imami Context." In *Dār al-islām/dār al-ḥarb: Territories, Peoples, Identities*, edited by Giovanna Calasso and Giuliano Lancioni, 74–89. Leiden; Boston: Brill, 2017.

Azra, Azyumardi. *Wajah Baru Islam di Indonesia* (The New Face of Islam in Indonesia). Yogyakarta: UII Press, 2004.

Badawi, Elsaid M., and Muhammad Abdel Haleem. *Arabic-English Dictionary of Qur'anic Usage*. Leiden; Boston: Brill, 2008.

Bardill, Jonathan. *Constantine, Divine Emperor of the Christian Golden Age*. Cambridge: Cambridge University Press, 2012.

Barnes, Timothy D. *Constantine: Dynasty, Religion and Power in the Later Roman Empire*. Chichester: Wiley-Blackwell, 2014.

Brown, Peter. *The Rise of Western Christendom: Triumph and Diversity, AD 200–1000*. Chicester: Wiley-Blackwell, 2013.

Brown, William B., ed. *Kitab Suci Al-Qur'an: Bahasa Melayu Translation of the Meanings*. https://www.muslim-library.com/dl/books/ms2392.pdf (accessed June 1, 2020).

Emon, Anver M. "Religious Minorities and Islamic Law: Accommodation and the Limits of Tolerance." In *Islamic Law and International Human Rights Law*, edited by Anver M. Emon, Mark Ellis, and Benjamin Glahn, 323–43. Oxford: Oxford University Press, 2012.

Esposito, John S. "Islam and Political Violence." *Religions* 6 (2015): 1067–81.

Formichi, Chiara. *Islam and the Making of the Nation: Kartosuwiryo and Political Islam in Twentieth-Century Indonesia*. Leiden: KITLV Press, 2012.

Harrington, Joel F., and Helmut W. Smith. "Confessionalization, Community, and State Building in Germany, 1558–1870." *Journal of Modern History* 69 (1997): 77–101.

Ibn Manzur, *Lisan al-'Arab*. Beirut: Dar Sader, 1979.

Ismail, Faisal. "Religion, State, and Ideology in Indonesia: A Historical Account of the Acceptance of Pancasila as the Basis of the Indonesian State." *Indonesian Journal of Interdisciplinary Islamic Studies* 1 (2018): 19–58.

Jefferson, Kurt W. *Christianity's Impact on World Politics: Not by Might, Nor by Power*. New York: Peter Lang, 2002.

Lactantius. *Divine Institutes*. Translated by Anthony Bowen and Peter Garnsey. Liverpool: Liverpool University Press, 2003.

Lehning, James R. *European Colonialism since 1700*. New York: Cambridge University Press, 2013.

Lewis, Bernard. *The Political Language of Islam*. Chicago: University of Chicago Press, 1988.

Machasin, Muhammad. *Islam Dinamis, Islam Harmonis: Lokalitas, Pluralisme, Terorisme* (Dynamic Islam, Harmonious Islam: Locality, Pluralism, Terrorism). Yogyakarta: LKiS, 2011.

Madjid, Nurcholish. *Islam Doktrin dan Peradaban: Sebuah Telaah Kritis tentang Masalah Keimanan, Kemanusiaan, dan Kemodernan* (The Islamic Doctrine and Civilization: A Critical Analysis on the Problem of Faith, Humanity, and Modernity). Jakarta: Yayasan Wakaf Paramadina, 1992.

———. *Khazanah Intelektual Islam* (Islamic Intellectual Treasures). Jakarta: Bulan Bintang, 1985.

Mubarak, Husni, ed. "Presentasi Laporan Kemerdekaan Beragama/Berkeyakinan Wahid Foundation 2018" (Presentation of 2018 Wahid Foundation Report on Religious/Faith Freedom). https://wahidfoundation.org/index.php/publication/detail/Presentasi-Laporan-Kemerdekaan-BeragamaBerkeyakinan-Wahid-Foundation-2018.

Mubarak, M. Zaki. "Dari NII ke ISIS: Transformasi Ideologi dan Gerakan dalam Islam Radikal di Indonesia Kontemporer" (From Indonesia Islamic State to ISIS: An Ideological Transformation and Movements in Contemporary Indonesian Radical Islam). *Episteme* 10 (2015): 77–98.

Muslimin, J. M. "Islamic Law in the Pancasila State." *AHKAM* 12 (2012): 15–26.

Muzadi, Abdul M. *Mengenal Nahdlatul Ulama* (Acquainted with the Nahdlatul Ulama). Surabaya: Khalista, 2006.

Nagel, Tilman. *Das islamische Recht: Eine Einführung*. Westhofen: WVA-Verlag, 2001.

Odahl, Charles M. *Constantine and the Christian Empire*. London; New York: Routledge, 2012.

Pagden, Anthony. "The Christian Tradition." In *States, Nations, and Borders: The Ethics of Making Boundaries*, edited by Margaret Moore and Allen Buchanan, 103–26. Cambridge: Cambridge University Press, 2003.

Pottenger, Andrew J. "The 'Servant of God': Divine Favour and Instrumentality under Constantine, 318–325." *Studies in Church History* 54 (2018): 31–45.

Rasyid, Muhammad M. "Islam Rahmatan lil-'ālāmin Perspektif K. H. Hasyim Muzadi" (The Rahmatan lil-'ālāmin Islam in K. H. Hasyim Muzadi's Perspective). *Episteme* 11, no. 1 (2016): 93–116.

Reynolds, Gabriel S. *The Qur'an and the Bible: Text and Commentary*. New Haven; London: Yale University Press, 2018.

Ritaudin, M. Sidi. "Dār al-ḥarb dan Dār al-Islām: Dwipolar Politik Islam" (Dār al-ḥarb and Dār al-Islām: The Two Poles of the Politics of Islam). *Kalam* 9 (2015): 287–304.

Safri, Arif Nuh. "Reinterpretasi Makna Al-Islām dalam Al-Qur'an: Menuju Keagamaan yang Etis dan Dialogis" (Reinterpretation of the Meaning of Al-Islām in the Qur'an: Toward an Ethical and Dialogical Religiosity). *ESENSIA Jurnal Ilmu-Ilmu Ushuluddin* 17 (2016): 29–38.

Sanneh, Lamin. *Beyond Jihad: The Pacifist Tradition in West African Islam*. New York: Oxford: Oxford University Press, 2016.

Schaff, Philip, ed. *Fathers of the Third and Fourth Centuries: Lactantius, Venantius, Asterius, Victorinus, Dionysius, Apostolic Teaching and Constitutions, Homily, and Liturgies*. Vol. 7 of *Ante-Nicene Fathers*. Grand Rapids: Christian Classics Ethereal Library, 2004.

Toit, A. B. du. "The Kingdom of God in the Gospel of Matthew." *Verbum et Ecclesia* 21, no. 3 (2000): 545–63.

Verskin, Alan. *Islamic Law and the Crisis of the Reconquista: The Debate on the Status of Muslim Communities in Christendom*. Leiden; Boston: Brill, 2015.

Villano, Raoul. "The Qur'anic Foundations of the *dār al-islām/dār al- ḥarb* Dichotomy: An Unusual Hypothesis." In *Dār al-islām/dār al-ḥarb: Territories, Peoples, Identities*, edited by Giovanna Calasso and Giuliano Lancioni, 125–46. Leiden; Boston: Brill, 2017.

Wahid, Abdurrahman. *Islam Kosmopolitan: Nilai-nilai Indonesia dan Transformasi Kebudayaan* (Cosmopolitan Islam: Indonesian Values and Cultural Transformation). Jakarta: Wahid Institute, 2007.

18

The Akan Cognate Bonds, Indigenous Hospitality, and Christian-Muslim Relations in Ghana

Cosmas E. Sarbah

Introduction

Any attempt to study Christian-Muslim relations among the Akan people of Ghana would be incomplete without a critical look at the dynamics of the indigenous socioreligious worldview. The Akan people constitute an ethnic and social group that claim a large portion of Ghana, from the coast to the middle belt, as their land or territory. The Akan groups include Asante, Akim, Akwapim, Brong, Kwahu, Assin, Wasa, Fante, Agona, Nzima and Ahanta, Afema, Sehwi, and Chakosi.[1] Apart from their claim to common territory, the Akan people are organized along the lineage system according to blood relationship (however putative), which often brings cognates of Christians and Muslims together at the personal level. The dynamics of cognate relations are critical for the understanding and appreciation of Christian-Muslim encounters among the Akan people in particular and Ghanaians in general. The Akan people have developed seven lineages that are subgroups of the various clans – referred to locally as *ebusua* – whose membership is largely based on blood relations. The lineage is, thus, a kinship group of close relatives,

---

1. Manoukian, *Akan*, 9–10.

which extends to the third or fourth generation of descendants. The kinship group (the lineage) is also bound by customary practices that help sustain it.

Most members of Akan lineage groups have embraced Christianity or Islam. The process of conversion to Christianity and Islam has been gradual, spanning a period of over two hundred years. Conversions to Christianity started from the sixteenth to the twenty-first centuries with the arrival of European missionaries and have continued until the present time.[2] Major conversions of the Akan people to Islam started in 1985 at Ekumfi Ekrawfo in the Central Region when Benjamin Sam and Mahdi Appah founded a form of Islam that eventually became the Ahmadiyya Muslim Movement.[3] Over time, some Akan people have joined other doctrinal groups such as the Maliki-Tijaniyyah, Hanbali-Ahlus-Sunnah, Ja'fari-Shi'ah and the Istiqamah. It is important to note that Akan kin systems, particularly lineage membership, often plays a crucial role in the formation and organization of religious denominations or sects (Christian or Muslim). In particular, denominations, churches, and mosques are often founded by, or organized based on, kinship or lineage relations. As a result, lineages are often identified based on their associations with Christianity or Islam or both.

In spite of the great influence Christianity and Islam have had over time in terms of conversions, Akan social organizations based on lineage and customary practices continue to be strong. Thus, attempts by Christian and Muslim bodies to redefine and reorganize Akan society from lineage and family-based to religion-based systems have been largely unsuccessful.[4] The old indigenous foundations of society could not be supplanted by new ones, whether political or religious.

As a result, it is common to come across Christians and Muslims of the same lineage who are cognates and so claim common ancestry and territory as Akan people. As cognates, Christians and Muslims are also obligated by indigenous customs and traditions to offer each other support in times of need. In this chapter, I will demonstrate that the cognate bonds of Christians and Muslims among the Akan people are often so strong that they help promote Christian-Muslim encounters and protect them against "foreigners" or non-cognates, who may even be members of their religious bodies.

The research methodologies I used for this essay included both fieldwork and archival research, combining anthropological and historical approaches.

---

2. Eshun, "Speaking for Ourselves," 56.
3. Fisher, "Muslim-Western Education," 288–89.
4. Nukunya, *Tradition and Change*, 11.

Data was collected during ethnographic fieldwork in Ghana in 2009–2010, and continued from 2020–2021 in selected towns in the Central Region. Questionnaires were responded to in the following areas: (1) Christian-Majority urban areas: Agona Swedru (40 respondents) and Oguaa Abura (40); (2) Muslim-majority enclaves of urban areas: Kotokoraba Zongo (40), Agona Nyakrom (40); (3) Christian-majority rural areas: Gomoa Assin (40), Ekumfi Essarkyir (40); and (4) Muslim-majority rural areas: Gomoa Kokofu (40), Ekumfi Ekrawfo (40). Archival research was conducted in libraries and at the Public Records and Archives Administration Department (PRAAD) in Accra and Cape Coast. Based on this research, I argue that kinship-lineage dynamics play an essential role in the understanding and appreciation of Christian-Muslim encounters among the Akan people of Ghana.

Kinship and Change in Contemporary Ghanaian Society

The kinship-lineage system and its relevance to modern life have received considerable attention over a number of decades in sociocultural studies by prominent Ghanaian scholars and social commentators. Professor K. A. Busia, a renowned sociologist and a former prime minister of Ghana has noted that the kinship ideals of the Akan people are "hardly congruous with life in a large, heterogeneous, competitive society" such as modern Ghana.[5] Others, such as G. K. Nukunya – Emeritus Professor of Sociology, University of Ghana – while agreeing with the idea of the diminishing significance of kinship, disagree with Busia's contention that kinship structure is incompatible with modern urban life and even with the foreign religious traditions of Christianity and Islam.

Despite changes in Ghanaian life, Nukunya argues that the kinship institutions have "not completely disappeared."[6] He contends that Ghanaians, even as Christian and Muslims and urban dwellers, continue to support the lineages in many ways such as offering contributions to their village coffers. Nukunya concludes that the kinship institutions remain formidable and relevant in the new forms they have taken. Thus, after many years, Nukunya has confirmed the observation of the British social scientist and historian J. S. Trimingham that the change brought about by Islam – as well as Christianity and even modernity in tropical Africa – should "not be exaggerated, the old bases of community remain paramount and the ideal of the unity of believers

---

5. Busia, *Challenge of Africa*, 34.
6. Busia, 12.

a superimposed linkage."⁷ To further strengthen the position of the continuous relevance of kinship connectivity, Max Assimeng – Professor of Sociology at the University of Ghana – opines that though urbanization and modernization bring people without blood connectivity together in voluntary associations, the eventual interaction is "ephemeral, temporary, and without much emotional investment."⁸ In this way, Assimeng admits to the permanence and resilience of indigenous social structures such as kinship in contemporary African societies. Even as Christians and Muslims, the Akan still hold dear the structure of kinship relations and its attendant ideals. Despite Western education and modernity, the Akan continue to believe that they are indebted to or obligated to support their fellow kins. Thus, J. B. Danquah's assertion regarding the unbreakable tie that exists among family members still holds true after so many years.⁹ Furthermore, lineage connectivity is often cited as the reason the rather puritanical policy of the early Protestant missionaries, which led to the creation of *salems* or *oburoni-kurom* (white man's town) – to bring Christian converts together to practice their faith away from their "heathen" relatives – did not materialize in the Akan stations.¹⁰

'Tūba' and 'Alien' Muslims

Muslims in Akanland are often categorized into two main groups. First, there are the "tuba" Muslims, who are, largely, native Akan converts to Islam. Second, there are "alien" Muslims, who are, largely, migrants to Akanland. "Tuba" is a Hausa term which literally means "convert." It is usually employed in a derogatory sense to indicate that natives of southern ethnic groups or even lineages cannot be true Muslims. It is used to cast doubt on Muslims of Fante, Asante, Akyem, or Ewe ethnicity in terms of their acceptance of the Islamic religion. Therefore, it is not surprising that a significant number of the "tuba" Muslims are members of the Ahmadiyya Muslim Movement.

Serious Islamic missionary activity among the Fante people was initiated by two local Fante men in 1885. Benjamin Sam and Mahdi Appah are associated with the establishment of Islam in Fanteland, also known as Fante *kramo* (Fante Islam).¹¹ Sam, a Wesleyan (Methodist) catechist at Ekumfi Ekrawfo near

---

7. Trimingham, *Influence of Islam*, 85.
8. Assimeng, *Religion and Social Change*, 65.
9. Danquah, *Gold Coast*, 194.
10. See Mobley, *Ghanaian's Image*, 68.
11. Debrunner and Fisher, "Early Fante Islam II," 14.

Mankessim, adopted Islam and soon thereafter used his catechetical experience to form a sizable Muslim community of about five hundred people who later scattered throughout Fanteland.[12]

As a moderate "tuba" Muslim and imam, Sam did not abhor traditional customary practices, allowing Muslims to adhere to their lineage relations and duties. His brand of Islam contained many elements of both Christianity and indigenous culture.[13] The "tuba" Muslims have also established a national association, an indication of their reluctance to be under the leadership of the "alien" Muslims.[14] Most "tuba" Muslims typically live in mainland towns and villages with their other cognate, non-Muslim relatives. The term "alien" is used to refer to Muslims who are not considered native or indigenous inhabitants of Akanland. These "alien" Muslims are Ghanaians, descendants of ethnic groups who emigrated primarily into northern Ghana many years ago and eventually settled in the southern territories of Ghana. They include the Hausa, the Kotokoli, the Fulani, and the Tuareg groups arrived in Ghana from countries such as Mali, Niger, Burkina Faso, and beyond.

Muslim migrants can be categorized into three groups. The first group consists of the descendants of Muslim immigrants of mainly Wangara, Kotokoli, Hausa, Yoruba, and Fulani ethnic groups who moved into the Gold Coast (present-day Ghana) during the colonial period for purposes of trade. Some of these Muslims also engaged in farming, particularly, in the plantations of the Western Region as well as gold-mining, including the small-scale mining often referred to, in local parlance, as *galamsey*.[15] The second group is made up of the descendants of migrant Muslims who entered Akan territory following the abolition of the slave trade. Two of these groups were brought from Brazil to the *zongos* of Elmina, Kumasi, and Cape Coast. A third contingent moved from Mali, Niger, and Burkina Faso to Akan territory to engage in trade.[16] Such Muslim migrants keep in constant touch with their communities back home and retain their unique cultural practices such as those related to eating, dressing, and the speaking. Thus, one can observe among the *zongos* a marked difference in cultural practices based on lineage and clan ties, which often

---

12. Fisher, "Muslim-Western Education," 290–91.
13. Debrunner, *History of Christianity*, 241.
14. Samwini, *Muslim Resurgence*, 191–208.
15. Buah, *History of Ghana*, 73–74.
16. This includes activities such as rearing of cattle, begging, selling cassettes, DVDs, and cloths, Kayaye (head vending), and also small-scale fuel stations.

creates problems with regard to the management and leadership not only of the *zongos* but also of the mosques.

The "alien" Muslims largely inhabit the *zongo* quarters – a Hausa term that means "temporary settlement." Initially, the term *zongo* was used to describe the areas or fringes of towns where traders would stop to rest and undertake their trading activities.[17] These *zongo* settlements are founded in many modern West African countries and are still viewed as places inhabited by "strangers" and, therefore, identified with Muslims since Islam is the religion of the majority of the dwellers.[18]

The Muslim migrants constitute the "alien" Muslim category even though, as we have seen, most not only belong to different lineage groups based on ethnicity but have also lived in Ghana for a long time and are, therefore, citizens. It must be noted that both "alien" and "tuba" labels are social constructs, which indicate the underlying issues of relationship and acceptability. The "alien" tag is a social contract of the native inhabitants with reference to outsiders – namely, people who do not belong to their clan or lineage. The "tuba" tag is also used by "alien" Muslims for those who do not belong to their lineage. Above all, these terms indicate and reinforce the importance of lineage, kinship, and the attachment to customary practices.

Christian and Muslim Relations among Cognates

The family unit among the Akan is the extended family, which is the lineage. The Akan are divided into seven clans. Each lineage belongs to one of these seven clans: *Nsona, Anona, Twidan, Aboradze, Ntwaa, Kona* and *Adwenadze*.[19] Relationships between Christians and Muslims of the same lineage are largely based on cultural prescriptions and not religious tenets. It is the lineage that defines the boundary of relationship. Among the Akan, inhabitants of any town or village are classified into cognates and non-cognates. Cognates are members of the same lineage. Non-cognates are considered visitors or outsiders. Thus, within the Akan, Christians and Muslims often belong to the same lineage or family. Native Christians and "tuba" Muslims of the same lineage get along quite well and have inherited or created shared social spaces. These positive relations can be attributed largely to their common lineage ties based on common ancestry and shared values surrounding hospitality.

---

17. See Schildkrout, *People of the Zongo*.
18. See Casentini, "Migration Networks," 452.
19. Hagan, "Fanti Kinship," 59.

The notion of common ancestry enables members of the lineage to perceive themselves as blood relatives. For example, a lineage formed along these lines becomes an organized, formalized, corporate group, owning property that must be managed for the optimum benefit of all its members.[20]

The lineage (cognate) territoriality, comparable with any religious community, accommodates Christians and Muslims alike.[21] It is a corporate body that claims ownership of property, the most important of which is the land it occupies. It has a spiritual leader (*ebusua panyin*), who holds the family property in trust for its members. Like all religious communities, the lineage has a sacred space (the shrine) in which the ancestral stool is kept and which is reserved for members alone. The shrine is a symbol of unity, highly comparable to the *ka'aba* for Muslims, the Temple of Jerusalem for Jews, or the St. Peter's Basilica in Rome for Catholics. As the leader of the lineage and the living representative of the ancestral stool, the *ebusua panyin* ensures that the unity of the entire membership is upheld. The lineage members even identify themselves with a particular totem – typically an animal – that serves as the emblem on the lineage staff and which binds the membership further together. The ancestral stool occasionally receives adoration and libation to secure protection and blessings for the entire membership.

Unlike Christian and Muslim religious communities – whose membership is based on faith and, therefore, is also comprised of different lineage groups of the same ethnicity – the lineage community is founded primarily on common ancestry through the maternal line and comprises both Muslims and Christians. Whereas the Christian and Muslim communities together comprise people who hold the common belief in Jesus as the Son of God and Muhammad as the final Prophet of Allah respectively, the lineage is able, in a unique manner, to hold together adherents of both Christianity and Islam as cognates into a complex, spiritual whole. This whole entity takes up a socioreligious space in which Christians and Muslims can coexist in mutual helpfulness.

Cognates, Disagreements, and Disunity

Typical of human organizations, the lineage system is also marked by disagreements and disunity among members. Nukunya observes that the segmentation found in the lineage is not according to religious differences but is "relative to their genealogical positions" and that "the closer they are

---

20. Arthur, *Cloth as Metaphor*, 82; Jennings, *Leading Virtue*, 64.
21. Assimeng, *Religion and Social Change*, 63.

on the chart, the closer and more intimate the relationship."[22] Consequently, it must not be assumed that Christian-Muslim tension and acrimony do not take place among cognates. Various reasons account for such enmity and strife, including attempts to settle personal and family scores or inhospitality toward the other due to exclusivist interpretations of doctrine.

Religiously extremist attitudes, which in most cases seek to demonize other religious adherents, are almost always neutralized by the strong and unyielding power of lineage affiliations. The lineage spiritual tie has also been a unique model for minimizing, if not completely eliminating, interreligious animosity, violence, and conflicts. People united by descent groups, however putative, are more likely to stand together and resist any force – religious or otherwise – that might attempt to disintegrate and tear them apart. It is a prime duty of the *ebusua panyin* (family head), whose religious affiliation has nothing to do with his duty, to instill discipline and ensure that peace and harmony prevail.[23] He sees to it that enmity, strife, quarrels, and dissension among cognates either do not occur at all or are minimized and resolved completely.

Cognates, Hospitality, and Christian-Muslim Relations

In order to maintain the territoriality earmarked for its members, the lineage upholds values of hospitality expressed in reciprocal obligations to members in accordance with their prescribed status. Akan indigenous hospitality is the important basis for the brotherhood or sisterhood between members of the same family group and those of the same lineage. Akan hospitality is an extension of kindness, which is extended freely to the other person without expecting anything in return. It is, thus, the willingness to give, to help, to assist, to love, and to carry one another's burdens without profit or reward as the driving force.

Ghanaian historian F. K. Buah underscores some benefits of lineage affiliations to its members with regard to mutual helpfulness and cooperation, stating that wherever the Akan finds himself, he "is received as a member of the local *abusua* or the extended family, enjoying all privileges and rights, and sharing in the customary obligations with his 'brothers' and 'sisters' there. He also looks to the protection and embraces the rights and duties of his paternal *ntoro* in the area."[24]

---

22. Nukunya, *Tradition and Change*, 16.
23. Arthur, *Cloth as Metaphor*, 82; Jennings, *Leading Virtue*, 83.
24. Buah, *History of Ghana*, 8.

Thus, the lineage space, apart from giving its Christian and Muslim members a claim to common ancestral property such as land, also offers mutual assistance in relation to education, health, and funeral expenses.[25] Funerals are one of the occasions during which the unity, solidarity, and generosity of the lineage receive public expression. For example, adult Christians and Muslims share funeral expenses to lessen the burden on the bereaved cognates. This public display of *ebusua* or lineage hospitality, unity, and solidarity is depicted by the *adinkra* symbol *ebusua dɔ fun* (the family loves the corpse).[26]

In line with this demonstration of cooperation, Rev. Yedu Bannerman – a former Methodist minister and a director of the Methodist Museum of Ghanaian Indigenous Life at Ampia-Ajumako in the Central Region – acknowledges, in his memoirs, the contribution of his mother's uncle to his education:

> As the practice was among Akan matrilineal ethnic groups . . . it was not a child's biological father who usually educated him. Rather, matrilineal uncles or brothers were responsible for their niece or nephew's education . . . My mother's uncle readily agreed to bear his school expenses. Without any delay I was provided with a pair of khaki shorts and shirt, a piece of a blackened wooden slate and chalk, plus six shillings for a half-year school fees.[27]

Later, in an interview in June 2008, Bannerman admitted that his mother's uncle was a Muslim. The uncle footed his bills and supported his pursuits in theological formation. In a similar vein, John A. Azumah of The Sanneh Institute recounts his priestly ordination service at which his uncle, a devout Muslim, generously provided a ram to be slaughtered for the ceremony, at which relatives from both religions were present.[28] Lamin Sanneh of Yale Divinity School acknowledges this unique family and lineage bond in African contexts and the opportunity it offers for reciprocal helpfulness, irrespective of religious connectivity: "African family is saying something to the West about inter-religious encounters based on the virtues of hospitality which might help to relate Christians and Muslims to each other in society at large."[29]

---

25. Jennings, *Leading Virtue*, 64.
26. Arthur, *Cloth as Metaphor*, 35.
27. Bannerman, *Born to Be a Pioneer*, 10.
28. Azumah, "Ahmadiyya Concept of Jihad," 69.
29. Sanneh, "Christian Experience," 65.

Cognates, Non-Cognates, and Christian-Muslim Relations

The argument throughout this paper has been that lineage and kinship, not religion, are what differentiate one community from another among the Akan people. It is in view of this that Azumah notes that indigenous societies of the Northern territories of Ghana viewed Muslim groups as lineages or clans, with their own culture and customary practices distinct from any religious group.[30] In general, the Akan, kinship or lineage contributed significantly to either the acceptance or rejection of the Islamic religion. For example, the Dyula Muslims were initially unsuccessful in converting the Akan people because they were deemed to be outsiders who belonged to kinship groups other than their own.

The positive and accommodating attitudes of the Dyula Muslims proved to be unsuccessful in the Asante and Bono states. For this reason, Trimingham's three-stage process of gradual assimilation of Islamic traditions into northern Ghanaian communities is hardly applicable to the southern states of Bono and Asante. This does not mean that Muslim influence was not initially felt in Asante at all. Besides serving in the royal courts, the Dyula Muslims "were allowed to preach and teach Islam"[31] and introduce a new Islamic way of life into Asante culture. They even tried to change some of the un-Islamic rituals, evidenced in the fact that Muslim prayers were solicited to supplement indigenous Asante and Bono prayers.[32] There was extensive use of Muslim amulets, including instances where local chiefs referred people to Muslims for healing, divination, and charms.[33]

Several reasons are given to explain the diminishing Muslim influence in Asante over time. According to Mervyn Hiskett, the Asante people were afraid of growing Muslim power in the north, which threatened Asante dominance and social systems.[34] According to W. Hutton, Muslim influence diminished because of the desertion of Baba during the war of 1818 against Gyaman and Kong.[35] Ivor Wilks, however, argues that this diminishing influence was due to three geographical factors: (1) the humid climate and forest vegetation of the south, which prevented invading people from moving southward; (2) the poor communication and the dispersion of population in the southern Sudan, which also made contact difficult; and (3) the incidents of yellow fever, malaria, and

---

30. Azumah, "Ahmadiyya Concept of Jihad," 57.
31. Clarke, *West Africa*, 107.
32. Clarke, 107.
33. Levtzion, *Muslims and Chiefs*, 186.
34. Hiskett, *Development of Islam*, 135.
35. Hutton, *Voyage to Africa*, 323.

sleeping sickness, as well as famine and tsetse-fly zones, that rendered many regions of the south impenetrable.[36]

Even though economic, political, and geographical reasons have been proposed to explain the worsening Dyula Muslim influence in the southern states, it is also fair to say that the people of Bono and Asante simply did not seem to like Islam and its new culture.[37] We could say that the Asante people saw the Muslims as belonging to completely different social groups. Though the Asante and Bono people derived enormous benefits from the Dyula Muslims, they were not ready to trade their beliefs, customs, and time-tested lineage systems for Islam. It appears that Asante received what pleased it of Islam but on its own terms and without surrendering its cultural identity and familial relations for a universal Islamic community. Islam, however, was not completely weeded out of Asante since the Muslims who stayed were integrated into Asante society without being compelled to surrender their faith. Finally, Islam was completely eliminated with the destoolment of Asantehene Osei Kwame (1777–1801), in whose reign the Muslim influence commenced, and who is reported to have been "a believer at heart." The next Asantehene, Osei Bonsu (1801–1824), began his reign as an enemy of Islam, executing several Muslims – most probably to win back the support of the people.[38] Currently, the situation of Islam in Asanteland and even Bonoland has changed for the better, and this has contributed greatly to improved Christian-Muslim encounters there.

In the other southern communities, especially in the coastal regions, the native people first came into contact with non-cognate or "alien" Muslims following the abolition of the slave trade. The first batch of freed Muslim slaves arrived in 1836 from Brazil and were settled in James Fort and Ussher Fort in Accra, Elmina, Cape Coast, and Keta Zongos. The second group arrived in July 1872, when three hundred Hausa Muslim troops were brought to Ghana.[39] Muslim immigrants of Wangara, Kotokoli, Hausa, and Yoruba origin could also be found in the *zongos*.[40]

Upon arrival, these Muslims set up their quarters in the urban trading and mining towns and villages of Tarkwa, Prestea, and Takoradi. Unlike their counterparts in the northern parts of the country, these Muslims kept to their

---

36. Wilks, "Position of Muslims," 19.
37. See Buaben, "Islamic Law of Inheritance," 2–3; Ward, "Gold Coast History," 28–44.
38. Levtzion, *Muslims and Chiefs*, 187.
39. Debrunner, *History of Christianity*, 240–41.
40. Buah, *History of Ghana*, 73–74.

quarters and did not become involved in the local politics and socioreligious affairs of the chiefs and their people.[41] In fact, they actually made little impact in terms of Islamizing the local people. Hans W. Debrunner suggests that this lack of involvement or engagement could perhaps be due to the fact that the coastal people despised these Muslims – who were largely Hausa and Dyula – because they were unimpressed by their lack of formal English education and their inability to speak any of the local dialects.[42] It must be noted that the indigenous cognate ties played a role in the inability of the Muslim migrants to integrate into the communities. The Akan people saw in these migrant outsiders people of different social communities who would not mingle with them. The resultant mistrust and tension that characterized the interactions of the two groups have persisted to date, challenging intrareligious and interreligious relations.

Concluding Thoughts

The Akan lineage members are encouraged not only to show hospitality to each other but also to outsiders or complete strangers. This is because it is an important customary practice among the Akan to offer hospitality to outsiders, strangers, or non-cognates. An outsider is any person who is not a member of the lineage or family. Hospitality as perceived and practiced by Akan is open-handed, instinctive, and natural. In accordance with their hospitality practices, the Akan elders and chiefs offered the priceless gift of land to Muslim migrants for their settlements (*zongos*) and farming.[43] In most African communities, it is believed that unexpected guests are the embodiment of ancestors; hence, they are given the food and drink of the ancestors. The Akan will drop at least the first morsel of food or drink on the ground for the ancestors. They also commune with the ancestors through such impromptu service to guests, thus maintaining a relationship with their ancestors through the practice of hospitality.

Akan hospitality is to be rendered in moderation, avoiding excesses and exercising prudence. This idea of moderation in hospitality is expressed by the Akan proverb: "too much generosity depletes the goats of the visited." This explains the reason being a visitor is not a permanent state. A visitor who wants to settle is often incorporated into the family or lineage. Another proverb that cautions against the foolish dispensation of hospitality is the Akan

---

41. Schildkrout, *People of the Zongo*, 69.
42. Debrunner, *History of Christianity*, 241.
43. See Arhin, "Strangers and Hosts," 65; Nyamnjoh, *Insiders and Outsiders*.

proverb: "A visitor is a guest for two days, on the third day, put him or her to work (by giving him or her a hoe)." The logic behind these Akan proverbs is that a person cannot remain a visitor indefinitely. At some stage, they have to become members of the lineage. This change of status signifies the need to work to feed themselves and assist the community. Thus, while hospitality is a highly cherished value among the Akan, prudence must guide the practice of the value. Therefore, some native Akan cognates – including Christians, Muslims, and followers of indigenous religions – sometimes feel that the *zongo* Muslim dwellers have overstayed their welcome in their localities. They believe that hospitality is more than welcoming people and that it should also require avoiding being misused or exploited. Giulia Casentini acknowledges that misgivings of native cognates are expressed in "an enduring stereotype in Ghanaian society about zongos" and who associate high crime rates with the presence of Muslim "strangers." This is in spite of the fact that, in many cases, these Muslim outsiders or "strangers" were born and have lived in these *zongo* towns and villages for many generations. This reality challenges both the notion of "stranger" and the local discourse on Christian-Muslim relations.[44]

These misgivings are also expressed in cases where Muslim "strangers" have not only taken permanent ownership of the land allocated to them in the spirit of hospitality but have sold parts of it to others. In southern Ghana, almost all communities with *zongos* appear to have this particular problem. The constant litigation that ensues often worsens the atrocities associated with the land guards deployed by the local chiefs.

For instance, initial peaceful coexistence between Christians and Muslims in the Kasoa township has recently been greatly damaged. Over time, its original name, Odupongkpehe, has been changed to Kasoa (a Hausa term for market) due to the influx in the early 1970s of Hausa and Fulani Muslims from the Northern Region, who came to engage in commercial activities. Violent confrontations take place frequently among the native Christians and Muslim immigrants over issues related to land acquisition and ownership, as well as because of ignorance and misunderstanding of each other's role in the larger community. These are often the underlying issues embedded in non-cognate Christian-Muslim relations, which frequently lead to mistrust and communal tensions.[45]

As a result, there have been violent eruptions – not only between Christians and Muslims but also between Muslims in Kasoa as well as Agona Nyakrom,

---

44. See Casentini, "Migration Networks," 452–53.
45. See Shack and Skinner, *Strangers*, 19.

Takoradi, Kumasi, Oda, and Wenchi. According to James Anquandah, there were twenty reported cases of intrareligious and interreligious clashes in Ghana between 1987 and 1989, resulting in the loss of human lives and property. For example, riots broke out between Christians and Muslims at Sekondi, Kumasi, and Mampong in 1996. Mention could also be made of riots between Christians and Traditionalists at Half Assini, Labadi, and Korle Gonno in September 2001. Strangely, there have also been reports of intra-Muslim clashes among Muslims at Akim Oda, Atebubu, and Kwesimintsim in 1995 through to 1998.[46]

Lineage associations are also critical issues in intra-Muslim rivalries in Ghana and are the reason that "tuba" and "alien" Muslims have been unable to forge alliances to advance Islam. Growing up at Abora, a suburb of Cape Coast, I observed bitter rivalry between the members of the "tuba" Ahmadiyya Muslim Movement and the "alien" Muslims (sunni). Though the rivalry was considered doctrinal and theological, I observed that it was more a lineage conflict. Two key mosques were built close to each other, on a piece of land – and these could be described as sacred spaces not meant for all Muslims but, instead, only for those belonging to certain lineage groups. Poor relations between Christian and Muslim cognates (and non-cognate Muslims) are not only unfortunate but also go against the Akan people's communal understanding of life. As we have already seen, Akan hospitality is grounded on the fact that no one is an island unto themselves; rather, each and every one is part of the whole.

Bibliography

Anquandah, James. *Agenda Extraordinaire: 80 Years of the Christian Council of Ghana.* Accra: Asempa, 2009.

Arhin, K. "Strangers and Hosts: A study in the Political Organization and History of Atebubu Town." *Transactions of the Historical Society of Ghana* 12 (1971): 63–82.

Arthur, G. F. *Cloth as Metaphor: (Re)-reading the Adinkra Cloth Symbols of the Akan of Ghana.* Legon, Ghana: CEFIKS, 2001.

Assimeng, Max. *Religion and Social Change in West Africa.* Accra: Ghana Universities Press, 1989.

Azumah, John A. "The Ahmadiyya Concept of Jihad and Religious Tolerance in General and Christian-Muslim Relations in Particular: Ghana as a Case Study." MA diss., University of Birmingham, 1995.

Bannerman, J. Yedu. *Born to be a Pioneer: Memoir.* Accra, Ghana: CEFIKS, 2003.

---

46. See Anquandah, *Agenda Extraordinaire*, 67.

Buaben, Jabal Muhamad. "A Comparative Study of the Islamic Law of Inheritance and the Fante Customary Law of Inheritance." MA diss., University of Birmingham, 1985.
Buah, F.K. *A History of Ghana*, Revised and Updated. Malaysia: Macmillan, 1998.
Busia, Kofi Abrefa. *The Challenge of Africa*. New York: Praeger, 1962.
Casentini, Giulia. "Migration Networks and Narratives in Ghana: A Case Study from the Zongo." *Africa* 88, no. 3 (2018): 452–68.
Clarke, Peter B. *West Africa and Islam: A Study of Religious Development from the 8th to the 20th Century*. London: Edward Arnold, 1982.
Danquah, J. B. *Gold Coast: Akan Laws and Customs and the Akim Abuakwa Constitution*. London: George Routledge & Sons, 1928.
Debrunner, Hans W. *A History of Christianity in Ghana*. Accra: Waterville Publishing House, 1967.
Debrunner, H. and H. J. Fisher. "Early Fante Islam II." *The Ghana Bulletin of Theology*, vol.1, no. 8, Trinity Term, 1960: 13–29.
Eshun, Daniel Justice. "Speaking for Ourselves: The Ghanaian Encounter with European Missionaries, Sixteenth to Twenty-first Centuries." *Mission Studies* 38, no. 3 (2021): 372–97.
Fisher, H. J. "Early Muslim-Western Education in West Africa." *Muslim World* 51 (1966): 288–98.
Hagan, G. P. "An Analytical Study of Fanti Kinship," in *African Studies Research Review*, vol. 5 (1967), 59.
Healey, Joseph, and Donald Sybertz. *Towards an African Narrative Theology*. Maryknoll: Orbis Books, 1997.
Hiskett, Mervyn. *The Development of Islam in West Africa*. London: Longman, 1984.
Hutton, William. *A Voyage to Africa*. London: Longman, 1821.
Jennings, Brian K. *Leading Virtue: A Model for the Contextualisation of Christian Ethics*. Berlin; Oxford: Peter Lang, 2009.
Levtzion, Nehemia. *Muslims and Chiefs in West Africa: A Study of Islam in the Middle Volta Basin in the Pre-Colonial Period*. Oxford: Clarendon Press, 1968.
Manoukian, Madeline. *Akan and Ga-Adangme Peoples: Western Africa Part 1*. London: International African Institute, 1950, repr. 1964.
Mobley, Harris W. *The Ghanaian's Image of Missionary: An Analysis of the Published Critiques of Christian Missionaries by Ghanaians 1897–1965*. Leiden: Brill, 1970.
Nukunya, G. K. *Tradition and Change in Ghana: An Introduction to Sociology*. Accra: Ghana Universities Press, 1992.
Nyamnjoh, Francis B. *Insiders and Outsiders: Citizenship and Xenophobia in Contemporary Southern Africa*. London: Zed Books, 2006.
Samwini, Nathan. *The Muslim Resurgence in Ghana since 1950: Its Effects upon Muslims and Muslim-Christian Relations*. Berlin: Lit Verlag, 2006.
Sanneh, Lamin. "Christian Experience of Islamic Da'wah, with Particular Reference to Africa." In *The Islamic Foundation/Quran House* (ed.), Christian Mission and

Islamic Da'wah, Proceedings of the Chambesy Dialogue Consultation (Leicester/Nairobi/Kano, 1982).

Schildkrout, Enid. *People of the Zongo: The Transformation of Ethnic Identities in Ghana*. Cambridge: Cambridge University Press, 1978.

Shack, William A., and Elliot P. Skinner, eds. *Strangers in West African Societies*. Berkeley: University of California Press, 1979.

Trimingham, J. S. *The Influence of Islam upon Africa*. London: Longmans, Green, 1968.

Ward, W. E. "Problems of Gold Coast History." *Gold Coast Review* 11, no. 1 (January–June 1926): 28–44.

Wilks, Ivor. "The Position of Muslims in Metropolitan Ashanti in the Early 19th Century." In *Islam in Tropical Africa*, edited by I. M. Lewis, 19–21. 2nd edition. Cambridge: Cambridge University Press, 1980.

19

Pig Feet in Madina's Multireligious and Multi-ethnic Zongoscape, Toward Hospitality

Afterlife of Trotter Barrels

Rashida Alhassan Adum-Atta

Introduction: Stepping into Madina Market

Accra cra cra cra, last two, Accra cra cra, Legon, Okponglo, 37, Circle, cek cek cek, circle cek cek, Adenta denta denta denta, Adenta Oyibi Oyibi Oyibi, La Paz La Paz La Paz, Botwe Botwe Botwe, school junction Botwe . . . promotion, pen drive, memory card promotion, donkomii ooo, donkomi, two two cedis, mmienu three cedis, enko to nu five, two cedis oo two cedis. Madam flesh amo oo flesh oo flesh . . . flesh tilapia oo flesh, madam bag one cedis, flesh salmon tuna madam . . . piesie, odehye, kaakyire, aho, awuraa, obaapa, kostoma, piesie papabi, me nanaa, abrewa ahouf3 (when pregnant), ataa maame, med, hajia, amariya . . .

The above vignette reflects the city's soundscape,[1] congestion, and excitement as commuters travel through the busy streets of Madina Zongo junction, a

---

1. For further readings, see Lefebvre, *Production of Space*; Lefebvre, *Urban Revolution*; Smith and Hetherington, "Urban Rhythms," 4–16.

suburb of Ghana's capital city, Accra. Approaching the Madina market, one cannot overlook the cultural dynamics, diversity, and competitive nature of the location; *trotro* (public bus) *mates* yelling out their travel destinations, street vendors directing people to their goods, and traders appealing to customers with sweet persuasive titles such as "my daughter," "my son," "my love," or "good woman."

Figure 1: Madina Zongo junction on a typical business day

Interestingly, in the midst of this chaos are market preachers attempting to put across their own messages.[2] The hospitable nature of the market, welcoming of all religious practitioners, creates within itself internal boundaries for those who visit and are part of this institution. Christians, Muslims, and believers of traditional religion share a common space in which they negotiate their religious identity. In other words, believers constantly negotiate shared spaces with the religious Other. Semiotic devices such as stalls, display signs, and religious images are key for market players in experiencing both the market and its foods. For instance, Christians usually display some kind of material objects, such as a picture of Jesus Christ, a Bible, a cross, an inspirational message, and, in recent times, stickers of "Men of God."[3] My interaction with them revealed that they believe that these material objects serve as protection

---

2. See Larkin, "Techniques of Inattention," 989–1015.

3. Roland Barthes's terminology – "a system of communication" – alludes to how commodity production infiltrates the literary art realm. His term resonates as stickers found on foodware by Christians, and a verse from the Qur'an (The Chapter of the Cow, also known as the Throne Verse, in Surah-al Bakara, verse 255) are posted on the structure in which the food is sold, to establish some form of communication or knowledge that enables residents of

against "the evil eye." They also serve as identity markers for members within their religious circles, and this is used as a means of increasing sales since they would rather buy food items from their members. For instance, some Muslims buy from Muslim women who dorn the hijab.

Muslims, on the other hand, display printed Arabic texts on their wares, the most common being Qur'an 2:225, which is known as the "throne verse." For others, concrete manifestations of religious identity – such as the mark of the *sujood* on the forehead or a hijab – attract customers. Through these markers, we see "the hidden presence of the sacred"[4] in an inclusive and exclusive process that results in symbolic boundaries that "are conceptual distinctions made by social actors to categorize objects, people, practices, rituals, and even time and space."[5] Practitioners of African Traditional Religion do not often display markers of their reigious identity; however, the Kla shrine lives in the market, and offers protection to traders and their patrons according to the Queen Mother of the market.[6]

Indeed, Madina is a true reflection of a vibrant space, where interethnic and interreligious interactions are visible. Madina initially started as a *zongo*[7] and currently accommodates people with different ethnic, religious, and class backgrounds. Today, Madina's Zongoscape – a sprawling suburb in the La Nkwantanang municipality in Accra – was created in 1959 with the permission of the La Mantse (the landowners) and has often been referred to as a "settler

---

Madina Zongo and non-residents, to identify with some meals (for example as halal). Barthes, "Toward a Psychosociology," 20–27.

4. Foucault and Miskowiec, "Of Other Spaces," 23.

5. Lamont and Molnar, "Boundaries," 168.

6. This was revealed in an interview with Maa Shey, the "Queen Mother" of the new market. The interview was conducted at Madina's new market, also known as the Bokye market, on 10 August 2019.

7. *Zongo* is a Hausa term meaning the camping place of a carrier or a lodging place of travelers. It is also a term that referred to the section of a town where Muslim traders lived. As Muslim merchants and clerics moved to the south, which was considered Christian to a large extent, they isolated themselves and founded their own settler communities that helped them to maintain their identity and, in most cases, brought in food ingredients that they traded. Some of these ingredients were peculiar to their places of origin but have been misconstrued and hence associated with northern Muslims. To date, the *zongo* communities are perceived to be a hub for meals such as Waakye, Tuo Zaafi, "Burkina," Hausa beer also referred to as Tankwa Bia, Samia or Puha, Sobolo etc. There are several *zongos* scattered along major cities in Ghana, and Madina is one such settlement. For further readings, see Ntewusu, "Northern Factor"; Schildkrout, *People of the Zongo*; Ntewusu, *Settling In*; and Abdul-Razak, "Role of Muslims."

town," a "diasporian community," and "strangers' quarters."[8] Alhaji Seido Karbo, Maafio, and two other Ga women assisted in the creation of Madina market to serve Madina and its environs with food and important household items. By involving non-Muslims in its creation, Karbo employed the Rabian notion of "methodologies of inclusiveness."[9] Sixty years later, Madina Zongo has developed into one of the major residential and commercial centers in Accra. It is now a place where Muslims and Christians coexist on many levels; and as a food port, the market serves as a central hub, which is the focus here.

This essay explores interreligious encounters at the Madina market, with a focus on the presence of pig trotters that come to Ghana through a global food network and are considered haram and unclean by Muslims. I draw inspiration from Sanneh's notion of "idealized Africa" as outlined by Ammah's approach of inclusiveness[10] in the market, which permits the presence of everyone and, by extension, various food ingredients in the market. In what follows, I highlight the embodied encounters between traders in the market – which is inhabited by people of different religious traditions – and patrons who frequent the market. I focus on the religious sensitivities of market players, the negotiations involved due to the presence of pig trotters, and how this evokes strong responses among those frequenting the space – for example, market women and customers. In subsequent sections, I offer an interesting twist to the notion of haram and levels of haramness by discussing the afterlife of trotter barrels used by many Muslims.

In this essay, I make use of narratives obtained from interlocutors in connection with the Madina market, pig trotters, and religious sensibilities. Pig trotters – as an ingredient considered haram – raise issues of contamination, purity, and disgust. Therefore, methodologically, this paper gathered data from interviews, participant observation, and group discussions. I gathered this ethnographic data as part of my PhD dissertation between 2018 and 2021 –

---

8. These terms are used to reflect their migratory nature. In the words of Sanneh, "The hijrah community is the ultimate in millenarian enclaves. In hijrah they observe with unusual intensity and mindfulness the obligatory rituals of purification, prayer, fasting and dietary regulations. They peruse the code and the manuals and adhere with punctilious faithfulness to the letter and spirit of the law. With fastidious care and detail, they water the seeds of rebellion and keep the mainstream structures and institutions to which they object in view. Now and then they take a rest from these activities by maintaining ties with their world, recruiting newcomers and fitting our sympathizers to keep up the pressure." Azumah and Sanneh, *African Christian*, 5–6.

9. Ammah, "They Must Also Call," 201. Ammah proposes a conscious involvement of the "other" in dialogue in order to create a better life for humanity. She encourages dialogue for all as it epitomizes the "language of God."

10. Ammah, 201.

over a period of twenty-four months – in Hausa, English, and Twi, which are the lingua francas of Madina Zongo.

Before delving into the issue of pig trotters, it is important to give a brief background on the subject of Christian-Muslim relation in a plural setting such as the Madina market. This will be useful to understand the background of gastro-politics there.

Boundaries That Coexist: Sanneh's Intervention

Over the last few decades, there has been a significant body of literature on religious relations in West Africa. Scholars such as Lamin Sanneh have made significant academic contributions on this subject.[11] Sanneh provides insightful analysis of Christian-Muslim relations in sub-Saharan Africa. He points out that in spite of efforts to live peacefully, these relations have been challenging due to factors such as increasing fundamentalism, jihadist movements, and issues of place-claiming. Sanneh gives the historical information about these categories. I contribute to this discussion of Christian-Muslim relations by focusing on how food-matters and food sharing is an important part of everyday coexistence in an interreligious context.

Sanneh's scholarship which began in the 1970s, chronicles the interactions and relations between African Muslims and Christians. As an African Muslim convert to Christianity, Sanneh drew on his own experiences as he engaged the entangled relations and interactions between Muslims and Christians.[12] In his work *Piety and Power*, Sanneh writes:

> The fact is that Christianity and Islam in Africa for the most part enfolded within the larger setting of the old Africa, with its deep-rooted hospitality, tolerance, and generosity, and it would be surprising if nothing of that admirable heritage did not survive in the new religions. Both sides are involved in a creative

---

11. The subject of Christian-Muslim relations has received much attention from many other scholars such as John Azumah, Johnson Mbillah, Martha Frederiks, Benjamin Soares, and Kwabena Asamoah-Gyadu. These scholars have made historical, theological, and sociological contributions toward religious encounters in Africa. For further readings, see Azumah, "Evangelical Christian Views," 128–38; Azumah, "Integrity of Interfaith Dialogue," 269–80; Azumah, "Boko Haram," 33–52; Mbillah, "Interfaith Relations," 109–17; Frederiks, "Understand Our Differences," 261–74; Soares, *Muslim-Christian Encounters*; and Asamoah-Gyadu, "Christ is the Answer," 93–117.

12. Sanneh, "Christian-Muslim Encounter," 101–10, and Sanneh, *Piety and Power*.

transformation process, and it cannot be stressed enough how much Christian and Muslim Africans owe to traditional Africa.[13]

Perhaps it is not surprising that the marketplace reflects Sanneh's idealized Africa, both as a hospitable space and as one that could be marked by various kinds of tensions. This is because the market is embedded in social relations of the moral economy. Even though Sanneh – a great scholar – provides useful information regarding Christian-Muslim relations, he places much emphasis on theology and conflict but ignores the everyday encounters that shape these relations. On a deeper level, Sanneh's works offer a unique reflection on what it means to encounter religion in Africa. He points out strict religious regimes that mark boundaries and offers methodological and theoretical approaches to the subject.

Drawing inspiration from Sanneh's work and further analysis with ethnographic insights, this paper argues that in the multireligious and multiethnic neighborhood of Madina, food or food pathways open up discussions on *modes of coexistence* ranging from hospitable to hostile. This is exemplified by what Maa U, the secretary of the Madina market, said when I inquired about Christian-Muslim relations at the market:

> Ooh, we are fine, everything here is peaceful, everything here is okay, no problem at all. Eerh no problem, everyone comes to sell in order to put food on the table. Eerh everything is fine. But you see, because we are human beings and especially majority being women, things are not easy. Some of us women are very stubborn; no curses at the marketplace, yet, they would curse, we don't like curses in the market, we ask them to leave their worries to God, but . . . huh. The market is for everyone irrespective of your ethnic or religious affiliations, it should be treated as a sacred place, but you see human beings are just difficult to handle.

My interaction with Maa U raised two sensitive issues. The first is the centrality of religion in the day-to-day interactions of religious practitioners in the market and the role of food therein. The second is the fact that religion is not merely connected with doctrine and faith but extends to mundane daily interactions. More so, the market is a natural meeting place, where people negotiate their religious identity. In other words, the market functions to highlight both peaceful and conflictual interactions among customers, traders, and religious practitioners. Prior to this casual conversation, I had visited Maa

---

13. Sanneh, *Piety and Power*, 23–24.

U several times to discuss religious matters in relation to food and the market association leaders and had purchased her wares; thus, she was aware that I was a researcher. As Maa U tried to describe the marketplace as relatively peaceful, while hesitating to provide extensive details regarding the everyday tensions associated with human interactions in the marketplace, our conversations drew my attention to issues of hospitality and territoriality.

Like most markets in Ghana, the Madina market is dominated by women, and their leaders are referred to as the "queens" of commodities. Gracia Clarks describes it like this: "Many market locations are identified by a commodity name, testifying to the central importance of shared commodity ties in organizing the traders within them as well as to the visual impact of these solid ranks of repetitive displays on customers and traders from other locations."[14] For example, the butcher shop and grinding mill are exclusively male-dominated jobs, with most butchers originating predominantly from the Dagomba ethnic group.[15] These butchers process and sell halal meat. They suggest that butchery is a traditional, clan-based occupation.

Christians and Muslims are known to buy halal meat from butcher shops, with both private and state abattoirs managed by Muslims. Muslims and Christians as mentioned earlier, buy food ingredients from each other and are known to share meals as well, with some Christians even ensuring that a fowl is slaughtered in the halal way during Christmas in order to serve their Muslim guests and neighbors. While some Christians make a conscious effort to serve their Muslim guests, some Muslims in Madina confess that they are unable to eat the "other's" meal due to issues of trust. This view is also expressed by Muslims who reject food from their Christian friends or neighbors because of concerns about religious pollution. For instance, some Muslims would not like to share food with the religious "other" who is known to consume pork or alcohol.

"Pig trotter" – or simply "trotter" – is the culinary term used to refer to the feet of pigs. Pigfeet (trotters) come to Madina through a global network of multinational meat processors and merchants, mainly from Europe. Denmark, Germany, Holland, and Sweden are among several European countries that export this product, under well-known brand names such as Orange Top (formerly Miss Piggy), Rosita, and Johnny's (*Obaa Pa*).[16] Pork products in

---

14. Clarks, *Onions Are My Husband*, 9.

15. The Dagomba are an ethnic group from northern Ghana.

16. This means "good lady" in Twi, a Ghanaian local language. This brand has been indigenized to appeal to local Ghanaian consumers.

Figure 2: A market preacher in action with sound system in one hand

brine are specifically developed for export to areas with hot climates – for example, West Africa, the Caribbean, and South America. Salted pork front or hind feet is one of the most popular brine products imported from Europe. Pig feet, packaged in a barrel with a concentrate of brine as a preservative, are highly valued and described as tasty. Trotters are also used for the preparation of stews and soups because the gelatin in the trotter bones is said to have a special thickening agent. Trotters are used in soups such as palm nut soup, groundnut soup, and light soup. Trotters are fried at pubs and drinking spots and are said to be very tasty when accompanied by alcohol. Trotters are found in Madina market because of high demand. This also generates significant employment in what is a huge global market and supply chain. Pig trotters are consumed globally, since many people have developed taste for foreign imports. For that matter, food seems to always be on the move as people negotiate menus. In Madina market, Muslim traders and patrons, however, avoid places where trotters are displayed since pig feet are considered haram according to Islamic teaching.[17] My interlocutors also suggested that Muslims do not rent their stalls to people who intend to sell trotters since such income might not be considered as halal income.[18]

---

17. Pig feet and pork are generally considered prohibited (haram) according to Islamic teachings as set out in the Qur'an, and they are viewed with disgust by Muslims. For example, Qur'an 5:3 says, "Forbidden for you (for food) are: dead meat, the flesh of swine, and that on which hath been invoked the name of other than Allah." Qur'an 2:173, 6:145, and 16:115 all address the prohibition of swine.

18. Adum-Atta, "Politics of Purity," 421.

Despite these religious prohibitions, Madina market, unlike markets at other *zongos* in Accra – for example, Nima, Mamobi, Sabon, and Sukura – accommodates trotter sellers, making room for this so-called haram ingredient and permitting it to coexist with the "other." This is a reflection of the type of coexistence that is said to characterize this space. I suggest that Madina market accommodates pig feet due to their earlier arrangements of including and involving all parties in the creation of the market, as evidenced in Sanneh's "old Africa" and Ammah's notion of inclusiveness.

By employing the methodologies of inclusiveness, the market players who helped create and build Madina made room for all to coexist, thus building bridges. Sanneh also articulates that the old Africa, before the emergence of the new religions, was deep-rooted in acts of hospitality, tolerance, and generosity. Hence, he would find it surprising "if nothing of that admirable heritage did not survive in the new religions."[19] In contrast, the everyday reality is that market players create physical and invisible boundaries due to religious taboos. The presence of pig feet in Madina market provokes sensitive feeling and creates dietary boundaries that are influenced to a large extent by religious taboos.

It is against this background that I present an interaction with one of my trotter sellers, Auntie Abigail. I met her during my failed attempt to buy pig trotters from her (she refused to sell trotters to me and, instead, schooled me on how "we" Muslims abhor it). It turned out that my dress code – a long dress with a hijab – largely influenced her response toward me. In the period leading up to this encounter, I had worked to overcome my fear of pollution. My fears stemmed from my lived experiences and socialization as a Muslim. In an attempt to overcome my anxiety, I focused on the positive possibilities of this research and soon struck up acquaintances with several trotter sellers. Indeed, they confessed that they were amazed at my willingness to come close to them and, in some cases, even share food with them. According to Auntie Abigail,

> I have lived in Madina Zongo for over 2 decades now, and this is the work I do. I have learned a lot about Muslims by living with them. My landlord is a Muslim and so are most of my neighbours too. I live peacefully with them, I feel a part of them, I respect their way of life, and I join them when there is a get-together. The Hajia's, the Alhaji's and the Amaeriya's are nice when they do not know what I sell at the market, I have always attempted to keep a good relationship with them by way of greetings. Occasionally

---

19. Sanneh, *Piety and Power*, 23–24.

they would tell me, "Auntie we have a wedding oo, or some other event so please come along and help us prepare what we will serve to our guests." At times when I am not personally invited, because of my relationship with them, I feel obliged to go and assist them.[20]

Auntie Abigail, who is in her fifties, explained that offering help to her neighbors was seen as a sign of solidarity and helped maintain some social relations among them. However, this soon ceased when her neighbor spotted her selling trotters. At the individual level, however, this discourse of harmonious coexistence proves to be more complex as neighbors and market players create physical and invisible boundaries in order to respect their religious taboos, which, in turn, enable them to navigate this context of coexistence.

Douglas also asserts that prohibitions on food represents a means of creating order within the theology of the times, affirming that certain animals served as a model of the divine order, while others appeared disorderly. Religion is thus a means of figuring out humanity's place within nature. In other words, she suggests that prohibitions with regard to food inspire mediation of oneness, purity, and completeness of God.[21] We see this in the Qur'an where it addresses the prohibition of swine: "Forbidden for you (for food) are dead meat, the flesh of swine and that on which hath been invoked the name of other than Allah. The Qur'an prohibits the consumption of pork" (Q 2:173; 6:145; 16:115).

Religious food taboos are mostly characterized by the notion of disgust and pollution. Sara Ahmed writes that "through disgust, bodies 'recoil' from their proximity."[22] Some interlocutors think of the pig as filthy and are disgusted at the sight of trotters. The issue of disgust is not limited merely to the object of disgust (trotter) but extended to the actor (eater, seller, or buyer). Ironically, at the marketplace, the different geographic spaces people occupy seem to concretize this so-called disgust. It appears as if disgust becomes a "visible" space, separating people and space.[23]

Guided by the theory of pollution and taboo, Mary Douglas – in *Purity and Danger* – reveals a focused attention on the relationship between dirt, cleanliness, and the design and organization of space.[24] For this reason, market users who abhor pig or trotters, avoid places where they are displayed. Douglas explores the social and cultural systems through the evidence of the everyday,

---

20. This interview with Auntie Abigail was conducted at the Madina market on 19 July 2020.
21. Douglas, *Purity and Danger*, 174.
22. Ahmed, *Cultural Politics*, 83.
23. Ahmed, 83.
24. See Douglas, *Purity and Danger*, 100.

both the excluded and the prohibited. Douglas's ideas of pollution and taboos resonate with the notions of disgust and the anthropology of imagination proposed by Sara Ahmed and Deborah Durham.[25] They argue that the anthropology of disgust opens up ideas of the "mind-body problem, the nature of selfhood, the senses, intimacy and emotion, and the nature of imagination."[26]

Toward Hospitality: Afterlife of Trotter Barrels

To maximize their profits, trotter sellers not only sell the pig feet contained in the barrel but also the empty barrels. Trotter barrels have long been useful containers for storing a variety of liquids and are also used by *koko* (porridge) sellers for soaking ingredients such as maize, millet, and sorghum. Local artisans modify the barrel by installing a tap for easy access to liquids. Such barrels are important for domestic use, for use in schools, and as water storage for religious cleansing at the mosque. They are sold to retailers of plastic products who cleanse them with detergent and dry them out to reduce the brine stench.

Figure 3: This picture shows a customer buying pig trotter and the author in a white hijab speaking to a trotter seller (picture taken by Nabeel Adum-Atta)

---

25. See Ahmed, *Cultural Politics*; Durham, "Disgust," 132.
26. Durham, "Disgust," 132.

The afterlife of these barrels are enormous. They create food connections through their everyday usage. Foods and containers are inherently bound together, intimately connected, having the ability to influence each other's state, taste, and meaning. This offers a unique reflection on the social, material, and symbolic use of the container and the web of relations involved. I am familiar with these barrels from my own experiences growing up; and as I have noted, these containers move through various spaces and incarnations, from the market to domestic to religious to commercial to private spaces. It was this research that made me realize that the barrels initially contained pig trotters. Based on ethnographic engagements with interlocutors in Madina Zongo, it seemed that interlocutors are usually ignorant about the tabooed content.

Figure 4: Trotter barrels being used as water storage at a mosque

Focusing on the uses of the trotter barrel and concerns about pollution and contaminations led to prescriptions of cleansing. Is it acceptable to buy a trotter barrel and use this object as a storage object? Can an object that once contained an item deemed as a religious taboo be used for a religious ritual by religiously observant adherents?

According to many Muslim scholars at Madina, including the spokesperson of the National Chief Imam, Sheikh Aremeyaw, Muslims who unknowingly consume that which is not permissible – like dog or pig – are expected, when they realize their mistake, not to repeat such an act. There is no ritual cleansing for dietary trespassing. However, with regard to objects such as trotter barrels that have been in contact with a religious taboo, Sheikh Arimeyaw prescribes that it should be cleansed several times. Alternatively, Mallam Ramadan prescribes that one should abandon that object if there are alternatives. With reference to this matter, Islamic jurists prescribe that objects that have been contaminated by a religious taboo be cleaned seven times to ensure purification.[27] Due to my close proximity with trotter sellers, my family and friends associated me with pollution – perhaps "stained by studying" – and, consequently, challenged me to take a ritual bath (*ghsul*). Though Islam does not prescribe such purification rites for my act, these exchanges were opportunities for reflection that provided important insights.

For example, Iddris, one of the interlocutors whom I conversed with about his use of trotter barrels as a receptacle, said, "The pig feet is in the market, it is not here, it is not inside," and, after a long pause, added, "wai Allah what if we drink haram?" My conversation with him clearly showed that he had no idea about the original contents of the container. But what if he had been aware of this? To better appreciate my question, consider the case of Hajia Azumah, a trader at Madina market, who thinks that cleaning the barrel with soap and water is enough to make it acceptable for use by a Muslim. On some level of haramness, Hajia Azuma bemoans that "my sin will be lesser than the one who rather eats the pig." She told me that she did not commit any crime; her crime would have been to eat the pork.

Figure 5: Trotter barrel being used for water storage

---

27. "Categories of Najis and its Cleansing Method, https://www.researchgate.net/figure/Categories-of-najis-and-its-cleansing-method_tbl1_273538029/amp accessed 30 November 2021.

Many people, like me, are unaware of the content of the barrels because information about the products, including ingredients, is inscribed using the same color as the barrel – typically, white – and is, therefore, not easily noticed. While it is hard to say if this is simply part of the aesthetics or whether it is intentionally designed this way in order to slightly camouflage the original contents of the barrel, typical trotter barrels have such inscriptions on their side. For instance, on Johnny's Brand barrels, the phrase *Obaa Pa* is written beneath the brand name, beside an image of pork front or hind feet and a crowned image of a tiger lying with his right front limb almost touching the image of the pork front or hind feet and a flying or wagging tail. Beneath this image are the words "maggie's legs," "made in Germany," and "Tel. 0049-1708137930." I also chanced upon an old barrel from Miss Piggy, now rebranded as Orange Top. On the barrel is an image of a female pig in a runway pose, holding a flying flag to her right paw and with her left arm at her waist. She wears a low-necked dress, defining her rather prominent cleavage, and a skimpy skirt with a loose waist belt. She looks away from the camera, showing off round dangling earrings. These aesthetics are important brand identity pointers for the few retailers who are uneducated, allowing them to readily identify brands and products through such logos.

Figure 6: Barrel of Miss Piggy (now Orange Top)

Mary Douglas argues that "there are two distinct ways of cancelling a pollution: one is the ritual which makes no enquiry into the cause of the pollution, and does not seek to place responsibility: the other is confessional rites."[28] Religiously adherent Madina Muslims appear to follow the first approach, seemingly unaware of dietary trespassing as a result of being ignorant of the original contents of the container. On the other hand, retailers of palm oil – which is one of the more common food items stored in these barrels – argue that cleansing these objects and eliminating the contaminating ingredients avoids any transfer of contamination and, thereby, protects customers from pollution.

Conclusion

This essay has sought inspiration from Sanneh's concept of idealized Africa – that is, the elements that depict old African hospitality, tolerance, and generosity. This notion is epitomized in the Madina market, where religion and food items are plentiful and are inclusive and accessible to a variety of religious adherents. The creators of the market exemplify tolerance by allowing a variety of foods to coexist. In other words, the market space is an embodiment of everyday religious encounters in a religiously pluralistic context. Bryan Lawson notes that "this space is both that which brings us together and simultaneously that which separates us from each other";[29] and is, ironically, the starting point of meals.[30]

Second, the essay has focused on people living together in quite narrow spaces, where they cannot easily avoid each other. As pointed out earlier, Christians and Muslims are, to a large extent, willing to eat one another's food, meaning that Muslims are not disgusted by the religious "other" or the religious beliefs of Christians per se. The concern here is about pork but not only the pork itself; rather, the concern is the belief that impurity "travels" from the trotters to a wider network of people and objects who have been in contact with it. The risk of "contamination" awakens and exposes latent negative feelings toward Christians in general – feelings that might otherwise have remained dormant. Muslims in Madina may, therefore, attempt to coexist peacefully with their neighbors; however, fears of pollution from a tabooed food ingredient makes people like Auntie Abigail – who sells pig trotters – keep

---

28. Douglas, *Purity and Danger*, 138.
29. Lawson, *Language of Space*, 6.
30. Bates, *Markets and States*, 6–7.

negotiating their shared space. Finally, Iddris's question – "What if we drink haram?" – chronicles the religious sensitivities and sentiments with regards to consumption.

This essay has taken food, foodways, as well as their sociocultural context as well as its discursive realms as its central theme. I have shown that the afterlife of trotter barrels and their various subsequent uses show that people are willing to tolerate others through negotiations that fit their religious circumstance – for example, cleansing the barrel seven times as prescribed by Islam. Food, therefore, provides a lens through which to understand religions, cultures, and the embodied experiences of social relations as well as the establishment and maintenance of social networks.

Bibliography

Abdul-Razak, Issifu. "The Role of Muslims in the Socio-Economic Development of Ghana: A Case Study of Madina Zongo." MPhil thesis, University of Ghana, 2010.

Adum-Atta, Rashida Alhassan. "The Politics of Purity, Disgust, and Contamination: Communal Identity of Trotter (Pig) Sellers in Madina Zongo (Accra)." *Religions* 11, no. 8 (2020): 421–33.

Ahmed, Sara. *The Cultural Politics of Emotion*. Edinburgh: Edinburgh University Press, 2004.

Ammah, Rabiatu Deinyo. "'And They Must Also Call unto the Way of the Lord with Wisdom': The Perspective of a Muslim Woman on African Women in Inter-Faith Encounters." In *Trajectories of Religion in Africa: Essays in Honour of John S. Pobee*, edited by Cephas N. Omenyo and Eric B. Anum, 185–202. Amsterdam; New York: Editions Rodopi, 2014.

Asamoah-Gyadu, J. Kwabena. "'"Christ is the Answer": What is the Question?' A Ghana Airways Prayer Vigil and Its Implications for Religion, Evil, and Public Space." *Journal of Religion in Africa* 35, no. 1 (2005): 93–117.

Azumah, John. "Boko Haram in Retrospect." *Islam and Christian-Muslim Relations* 26, no. 1 (2015): 33–52.

———. "Evangelical Christian Views and Attitudes Towards Christian-Muslim Dialogue." *Transformation* 29, no. 2 (2012): 128–38.

———. "The Integrity of Interfaith Dialogue." *Islam and Christian-Muslim Relations* 13, no. 3 (2002): 269–80.

Azumah, John, and Lamin Sanneh, eds. *The African Christian and Islam*. Carlisle: Langham Academic, 2013.

Barthes, Roland. "Toward a Psychosociology of Contemporary Food Consumption." In *Food and Culture: A Reader*, edited by Carole Counihan and Penny Van Esterik, 20–27. Routledge: New York, 1961. Reprint, Routledge: New York,1 997.

Bates, Robert H. *Markets and States in Tropical Africa: The Political Basis of Agricultural Policies*. Berkeley: University of California Press, 1981.
Clarks, Gracia. *Onions Are My Husband*. Chicago: University of Chicago Press, 1994.
Douglas, Mary. *Purity and Danger: An Analysis of Concepts of Pollution and Taboo*. London: Routledge, 2001. First published 1966.
Durham, Deborah. "Disgust and the Anthropological Imagination." *Ethnos* 76, no. 2 (2011): 131–56.
Foucault, Michel, "Of Other Spaces." Jay Miskowiec *Diacritics* 16, no. 1 (Spring 1986): 22–27.
Frederiks, Martha. "Let Us Understand Our Differences: Current Trends in Christian-Muslim Relations in Sub-Saharan Africa." *Transformation* 27, no. 4 (2010): 261–74.
Lamont, Michele, and Virag Molnar. "The Study of Boundaries in the Social Sciences." *Annual Review of Sociology* 28 (2002): 167–95.
Larkin, Brian. "Techniques of Inattention: The Mediality of Loudspeakers in Nigeria." *Anthropological Quarterly* 87 (2014): 989–1015.
Lawson, Bryan. *The Language of Space*. Routledge, 2001.
Lefebvre, Henri. *The Production of Space*. Oxford: Blackwell, 1991.
———. *The Urban Revolution*. Minneapolis: University of Minnesota Press, 2003.
Mbillah, Johnson. "Interfaith Relations in Africa." In *African Theology on the Way: Current Conversations*, edited by Diane B. Stinton, 109–17. London: SPCK, 2010.
Ntewusu, Samuel A. "The Northern Factor in Accra: A Historical Study of Madina Zongo as a Sub-Urban Settlement 1957–2000." MPhil thesis, University of Ghana, 2005.
———. *Settling In and Holding On: A Socioeconomic History of Northern Traders and Transporters in Accra's Tudu, 1908–2008*. Leiden: African Studies Centre, 2012.
Sanneh, Lamin. "The Christian-Muslim Encounter in Africa." In *African Challenge*, edited by Kenneth Y. Best, 101–10. Nairobi: Transafrica, 1975.
———. *Piety and Power: Muslims and Christians in West Africa*. Maryknoll: Orbis Books, 1996.
Schildkrout, Enid. *People of the Zongo: The Transformation of Ethnic Identities in Ghana*. Cambridge: Cambridge University Press, 1978.
Smith, Robin James, and Kevin Hetherington. "Urban Rhythms: Mobilities, Space and Interaction in the Contemporary City." *Sociological Review* 61, no. 1 suppl (2013): 4–16.
Soares, Benjamin, ed. *Muslim-Christian Encounters in Africa*. Leiden: Brill, 2006.

Summative Note

20

Land, Grief, Justice, and the (Ir)relevance of Hospitality

A Christian's Theological Reflection on Issues Arising out of the Papers of the Conference on "Hospitality and Territoriality"

Ida Glaser

O land, land, land, hear the word of the LORD!

Jeremiah 22:29 ESV

The market is for everyone irrespective of your ethnic or religious affiliations; it should be treated as a sacred place, but you see human beings are just difficult to handle.

Maa U of the Madina Market[1]

Moses met God in the *midbar* (Exod 3:1).[2] Why did he take his sheep into this place? One ancient rabbinic answer is that Moses foresaw the significance of the *midbar* in the formation of Israel: "The ascent from Egypt was through the wilderness, the Torah was given in the wilderness; the manna and the quail were obtained in the wilderness; the Tabernacle, the Shekinah,

---

1. As quoted in Rashida Alhassan Adum-Atta's essay "'The Pig Feet Is in the Market, but What If We Drink Haram?': The Multireligious Foodscape of Madina," found in this volume, @@.
2. *Midbar* is usually translated "wilderness" or "desert" in English.

the priesthood, kingship, the well, the clouds of glory – all occurred in the wilderness" (Midrash Tanchuma, Shemot 14:1).

But there is also a more practical answer. The great commentator Rashi tells us that it was to make sure that the sheep did not graze on private property (Exodus Rabbah 2:3). The Midrash Tanchuma applies the same reasoning to explain why David led his flock into the *midbar* – namely, "to keep them from feeding from the field of others" (Shemot 7:1 or 1 Sam 17:28). Here, the *midbar* is not defined by desert conditions (it had to have enough vegetation to feed the flocks!) or by its wildness but by the fact that it is not owned by any human being. It is, if you like, the territory of God alone; and perhaps we may conclude that this is one reason the wilderness is so important as a place where humans encounter God.

Today, there is hardly an acre of the earth that is not seen as belonging to some human entity. No longer are there habitable places to which the ambitious or the disenfranchised can simply go and make a home for themselves without being deemed as encroaching on someone else's territory. Where are the places to which shepherds can take their flocks without "feeding from the field of others"? While we can think of "territory" as the home of people or the area under a particular dominion, territory can also be seen as a locus of law.[3] A key question for religious people is, then, "Where are the places in which we can faithfully follow God's law?" We will return to such questions at the end of this essay.

The papers in this volume suggest that almost all the tensions in Christian-Muslim relations can be understood in terms of territoriality and hospitality. The overall impression created is that territoriality is a fundamental problem, to which proper hospitality offers an important solution. Indeed, the title of the conference this book came from – "Territoriality and Hospitality: Christians and Muslims Sharing Common Space" – assumes that there is some truth in this idea. In particular, the organizers were interested in the notion that African understandings of hospitality could be attributed to the peaceful cohabitation of Christians and Muslims in many areas of the continent. For example, Patrick Ryan's analysis of land stewardship in the West African Sahel (chapter 12) demonstrates that indigenous communities were able to welcome foreigners and to accept a measure of foreign administration, while retaining their guardianship of the land.

---

3. See Davies, *Gospel and the Land*, 189.

In this paper, however, I argue that territoriality is not in itself the problem and that hospitality, however important it may be for Christian-Muslim relations in any context, is not in itself an answer to territorial tensions.

In the essays in this volume, territoriality is presented as a problem because people want territory and dispute territory. For example, Daniel Madigan (chapter 6) remarks that territoriality – whether referring to physical or to spiritual territory – is "deleterious" to the human condition. His solution is expressed in terms of hospitality as a recognition of God as the host of all humanity. Muslims and Christians alike see hospitality as an obligation, and positive models of engagement are evident in shared territory as well as in mutual hospitality (see, for example, chapter 19 by Adum-Atta).

Yet territoriality and hospitality are not opposing but complementary concepts and, therefore, should not be viewed as simply positive and negative or problem and solution. Indeed, one could define the territory of an entity as the space within which that entity functions as host. If we offer hospitality, this generally takes place in our own territory. If hospitality is received, this happens in someone else's territory. Thus, the very notion of hospitality implies the existence of territory, even if that territory is only a tent or a room. This means that hospitality in itself will not solve problems where territory is in dispute. On the other hand, seeing territorial rulers as hosts with responsibility for the guests in their lands could greatly reduce conflict – but only if the guests are willing to remain as guests and carry out their own responsibilities.

As a comparative theologian, my contribution is to ask what it is about the world and about human nature that makes territoriality so central and then to reflect on the implications for the situations explored in several of the conference's case studies. The following study is rooted in Genesis 1–11, which I regard as the Bible's essential analysis of the world and of humanity.

Humans Are Territorial Beings

Territoriality cannot be *the* fundamental problem because human beings, by their created nature, are territorial. By that I mean that God made human beings to live in a place and to take responsibility within that place. The Torah is not only the story of a people amid peoples but also the story of the promise of a land (*aretz*) amid lands. Indeed, we can read it as the beginning of the story of the whole earth (also *aretz*) that God created in Genesis 1:1–2:3. The repetition of the word *aretz* at the beginning and end of the section emphasizes the point that this story is about the heavens and *aretz* (1:1; 2:1). The enigmatic introduction to the next section makes a similar claim: "These are the generations [*toledoth*] of the heavens and the *aretz*" (Gen 2:4 ESV). Similar *toledoth* formulas are found at the beginning of each section of Genesis, but these *toledoth* elsewhere refer to human beings. In our current context, we can read this intriguing difference as implying that the whole of what is to come, as recorded in the later chapters of Genesis, is telling us what came out of the heavens and the *aretz*.[4] We then read that the humans came from its soil (*adamah*) and were enlivened by the heavenly breath (Gen 2:7).

The Qur'an shares the vivid illustration of the relationship between humans and the land or earth. It, too, describes God forming the first human out of the earth before breathing into him the life-giving spirit and placing him in a particular place. Both scriptures also describe the next human as being taken out of the first, thus showing their interdependence, which will be expressed in hospitality. Both picture God as the bountiful host who provides all that is needed by his creatures.

In the Bible, territory is the original blessing, and the human being is the original gift to the land. God made the earth and put humans in it. The broad description of Genesis 1 is complemented by the detailed story in Genesis 2:8–15, where God prepares the beautiful garden with its provision of food and water. The responsibility of the humans is to fill the earth with people, till the ground, eat the food, and have dominion over it all. Yet, they are not *given* the land. God is still the maker and the owner, and the humans are, as it were, his guests. They are given an amazing measure of autonomy, but they are also given limits. They step beyond the bounds of hospitality by insisting on eating the one fruit that the host asked them not to eat; as a result, they are ejected from the land (Genesis 3). From then on, loss of land would regularly be a form of judgment, while the giving of land would be a blessing. For example, Cain's punishment would be land loss. At the time of Noah, the land would disappear completely before it was restored; the Babel generation would be scattered, and the paradigmatic judgment on Israel would be exile.

Outside Eden, we read of people spreading out into new spaces, moving toward the settling of peoples in their various territories (again, the word is *aretz*) in the "Table of Nations" of chapter 10 (see Gen 9:19; 10:5, 20, 31, 32). A complementary view of the spread of peoples across the *aretz* appears in the Babel story (Gen 11:1–9), whereby Babel or Babylon would become the paradigm and the picture of an anti-God imperial territorialism, which will appear in different forms until the end of history (Revelation 18). It is from this imperial territory that Abram is called to leave his *aretz* and go to a new

---

4. A. Azad and I. Glaser, *Genesis 1–11*, 6–7.

aretz (Gen 11:28–12:1). Yet, the whole of the Torah portrays Abram and his descendants as moving and sojourning in lands that were populated by other peoples. I repeat, it is not only the story of a people among peoples but also the story of a land among lands. This is emphasized in Deuteronomy, the last book of the Torah, which is Moses's final teaching to the people as they prepare to enter the promised land. As he recounts the history of the people of Israel, Moses tells the people that other peoples, too, have their allocated land. Further, God forbade them to attack the land that he himself gave to Ammon, Moab, and Edom, the very peoples who would become their enemies (see Deuteronomy 2–3).

In short, the promised land, at whose boundary the Torah ends, may be seen as a renewal of the lost garden with which it begins. However, a chosen people and a promised land cannot be rightly understood except as part of God's dealing with all peoples in the whole *aretz*. Christian studies of land in the Bible often focus on the particular land given to the people of Israel, but they seldom ask why *any* land should be so important a theme in biblical history.[5] The overview given above answers this question in two ways. First, if human beings are territorial by their very nature, a chosen people have to have a place in which to live. Second, humans were made for the *aretz* just as much as the *aretz* was made as their home. Thus, while the creation of humans may have been the climax of creation, the creation of the *aretz* was its foundation. Therefore, it is not surprising that the New Testament describes the eschaton in terms of a "new heaven and a new earth" (Rev 21:1) since the biblical vision, from beginning to end, is of human beings with God among them in the *aretz*.

It is, therefore, striking that the chosen people are seldom portrayed as living securely in the promised land. Abraham and his family have no land. God's call to them is to leave their land, and the land of Canaan would not be given to them until it was time for the people of the land to be judged. When Israel settles the land, their continued presence would depend on their honoring their divine host. More often than not in their history, the people of Israel would be outside the land that had been promised to them. The promise of the land seems to be more significant than the occupation of the land or the possession of it.

Of course, the story of Israel and its God-given land reflects the territorial tensions of biblical times and mirrors the human condition of today's world. The rise and fall of power within lands and the expansion and contraction of

---

5. Two exceptions that have informed my own thought are Brueggemann, *Land*, and Davies, *Gospel and the Land*.

empires is the ongoing backdrop to biblical history. We might say that part of the purpose of the *Bani Isra'il* is to offer an alternative to such territorial patterns.[6]

The questions pile up as we read of how God's allocation of Canaan to Israel coincided with his judgment on its previous inhabitants, of the tensions within the land and between the people of Israel, of the rise and fall of empires, of wars between neighboring polities, and of exile and resettlement. How far does God's "giving" of land mean that it now belongs to the recipients rather than to him? Can peoples with different gods share territory? If God directed the destruction of the Canaanite inhabitants, might he direct the destruction of other people today? If living in the land depends on godliness rather than political power, is there any place at all for warfare? From his extensive study of land themes throughout the Bible, Walter Brueggemann draws this conclusions: if we grab land, we lose it; but if we let it go, God will give us what we need.[7]

It is important that the rise and fall of empires and the expansion and contraction of their territories are seen as being under God's control. While such empires are eventually punished for the injustices that they have perpetrated, they are often seen as God's instruments of punishment, and it is clear that they would have no power without God's permission. The book of Daniel – with its narratives of rulers and its visions of how earthly powers are looked on from a divine perspective – is paradigmatic. It is well-known that this book raises acute questions about the Holy Land, about the last days, and about the role of Muslim peoples, and has done so for generations.[8] It is worth noting that the biblical treatment of empire raises questions about current nation-states and the history that has brought about existing land divisions. To what extent were the British Empire and other colonial powers under God's providence? Where does one discern God's judgment in the rise and fall of these powers? Can one view Islamic expansion through a similar lens? The effect of the postcolonial setting of state borders is frequently discussed, but how should we view the notion of fixing territorial boundaries? At the very least, the Bible holds up a mirror for humanity to reflect on its own territorial dynamics – namely, the relationship between power and land.

---

6. The Arabic phrase *Bani Isra'il* (sons of Israel) describe the biblical people of Israel. It is used here to make a clear distinction between biblical Israel and the current State of Israel.

7. Brueggemann, *The Land*, 1–14.

8. Daniel features in Christian apocalypses that reflect on the Islamic conquests as early as the *Apocalypse of Pseudo-Methodius* (late seventh century); and Luther and Calvin disagreed on whether Daniel was fulfilled in Christ (Calvin) or referred to "the Turk" (Luther).

Based on the preceding sections of this book, an initial conclusion suggests that, as with so many other aspects of life, the problem is not with territory itself but with greed and abuse on the part of human beings. The Bible presents land as good and humans as territorial beings; but it also presents humans as sinful and territorial disputes as a perennial result of the human condition. It is not so much that territoriality is deleterious to the human condition as it is that the human condition produces distorted and destructive territorialities.

The statement made by Maa U of the Accra Madina market, which headlines this essay, sums it up: "The market is for everyone irrespective of your ethnic or religious affiliations, it should be treated as a sacred place, but you see human beings are just difficult to handle." It is not the place or the system that is the problem but the "difficult-to-handle" people in the place! The question then is this: How can we, on the one hand, deal with the underlying sinfulness of human beings and, on the other hand, manage or regulate individuals, groups, and nations in a way that minimizes the injustices and suffering that sin causes? There are theological questions concerning sin and salvation on which Muslims and Christians are likely to have different answers, as well as practical questions concerning law and ethics about which some agreement is more likely. I have identified two themes – which underlie many of the chapters in this book – that make the path to agreement very difficult, and to these I now turn.

The First Difficulty: The Loss of Land

One possibility is to assert that the problem is sin and that peoples and their leaders need to learn to act justly within their territories and to be content with the territories that they have. However, the territorial tensions explored in the essays in this book are much more complex in nature. In each case, there is a history. A territory is disputed not only because a greedy entity has decided to grab more land but also because, typically, there is a history that has led to more than one party believing that they have a right to the land or a need for it.

Implicit in many of the essays is the experience or the perception of territorial loss, including past or present losses, and/or of loss of control within the land itself. Perhaps the most important implication of the idea that humans are territorial by their created nature is that the loss of land is devastating. Expulsion from Eden was a terrible punishment, and Cain, the "tiller of the soil" (Gen 4:2 JPS), considered the double punishment of exile and unfruitful land unbearable (Gen 4:13).

In short, if human ties to land are so strong, it follows that loss of land is traumatic.[9] All people have rituals for mourning the loss of others, and the trauma caused by the loss of such things as security, health, and wealth is widely recognized. But to what extent is there acknowledgment of the trauma involved in the loss of land, even when such loss may actually materially benefit a community?[10] Because communal trauma passes from generation to generation, territorial conflicts are unlikely to be resolved unless both the consequent and the historical dimensions of land loss are acknowledged and dealt with.

At the front of the TSI conference hall were displayed the words of Lamin Sanneh: "It behooves us on each side to spare no effort in love and trust to believe the best in the other."

This is an inspiring starting point for The Sanneh Institute, but I have no doubt that, as a historian, Sanneh would have understood that following on from land loss, "love, trust, and believing the best in the other" are not the starting points for dialogue. John Azumah's doctoral work, too, was historical, exploring areas of African history that caused tremendous communal trauma as people lost not only ownership of their land but also ownership of themselves.[11] He describes his study as "an attempt to rake up thorny and potentially hostile bits of the past as a kind of therapy for dialogue and reconciliation."[12]

The essays in ths book demonstrate that the communal history of many West Africans, as well as peoples elsewhere, is one marked by land loss and land tension. One of the ways in which The Sanneh Institute's scholarship can fulfill its vision of bringing glory to God and transformation in society will be through building on Sanneh's and Azumah's study of that history. As the different "sides" trust each other sufficiently to study together, they may come to understand not only their own communal trauma but also the other's perception of the losses. And that understanding may, in turn, lead to "believing the best."

---

9. By trauma, I mean a severe psychological wounding caused by a situation of great danger. This can be either communal or individual, or both.

10. For example, even voluntary emigration has a dimension of loss.

11. This work was published in 2001 under the title *The Legacy of Arab Islam: A Quest for Inter-religious Dialogue*.

12. Azumah, *Legacy*, 234.

Understanding Trauma

I have argued elsewhere that the key concepts for a biblical understanding of trauma are danger and helplessness, with their corollaries being safety and control. Trauma is caused by situations where people feel danger that they are helpless to avert. Therefore, traumatized people seek safety and control over their situations. Biblically, God is the only being who can be – and, in fact, is – safely in control.[13]

In the specific context of land loss, the following three observations seem pertinent. First, it is to be expected that people who have suffered land-loss trauma will do everything in their power to regain a sense of safety and control. They may easily feel unsafe even when they are in no particular danger, and they may feel threatened when they are in situations where they perceive that others have control over them. Further, a characteristic of trauma is an expectation that the traumatizing events will be repeated. This is due to the fact that the event is stored as a present memory until it can be sufficiently processed to be experienced as a memory of the past. Indeed, it can be said that such suspended storage of the memories is at the heart of much "post-traumatic stress disorder," and this is why processing memories is so important in the treatment of this condition. There is likely, then, to be a fear that present events are going to lead to yet more land loss. In such cases, it is not surprising that people often fight to retain whatever land they have or to regain lost land. In doing so, they may feel that they are fighting for their very existence.

Second, having land does not, in fact, guarantee safety. The land can be lost through, for example, environmental disaster as well as through exile or conquest. There can be injustice and a variety of dangers within the space one thinks one controls. While human beings may need their places and their homes, regaining control of the land does not necessarily reverse the process of traumatization.

Third, safety is a very important theme in the Bible. Christians use the theological word "salvation" to describe this idea of safety. This word is usually used to refer to spiritual safety that begins in this world and is consummated in the eschaton. However, the concept can also be very relevant to trauma. Germane are the ideas that salvation has to do with a relationship with God (for example, the picture of the saved person as God's child, i.e. 1 John 3:1) and the eschatological hope is of a safe place (a new earth where there are no more dangers, i.e. Rev 21:1–4). In my own thinking, these ideas come together in the Name of God perceived in rabbinic comment on Jacob's divine encounter

---

13. See Glaser, "Trauma Observed," chapter 4.

in Genesis 28:10–16: *Ha-Maqqom*, or The Place (*Genesis Rabbah* 48:9). It is not just that the world is the place where God came to meet Jacob – and may come to meet us – but, rather, that God is "The Place" in which we all find our own places. In the midst of all our longings for land and home, God himself is the safe place where we can always live.

Dealing with Grief and Anger

One reason that it is difficult to get to that safe place whereby we can work for temporal land security is that land loss leads to grief and anger. The Bible offers some key resources here. A helpful paradigm of land loss is the exile of biblical Israel, which takes up a great deal of space in the Old Testament and is also alluded to in the Qur'an (Surah 17:2–4; 21:95–97). In both, this loss of land is interpreted as God's judgment. This understanding gives people a way forward since they can repent and, eventually, return home. However, the Bible also gives us a glimpse of how terrible the judgment was for those who experienced being torn away from their land. While Lamentations expresses the agonies of those struggling for survival in a devastated Jerusalem, Psalm 137 (ESV) is the cry of people who enjoyed material security but were now exiled from home:

> By the waters of Babylon,
>   there we sat down and wept,
> when we remembered Zion.
> On the willows there
>   we hung up our lyres.
> For there our captors
>   required of us songs,
> and our tormentors, mirth, saying,
>   "Sing us one of the songs of Zion!"
> How shall we sing the LORD's song
>   in a foreign land?
> If I forget you, O Jerusalem,
>   let my right hand forget its skill!
> Let my tongue stick to the roof of my mouth,
>   if I do not remember you,
> if I do not set Jerusalem
>   above my highest joy!
> Remember, O LORD, against the Edomites
>   the day of Jerusalem,

> how they said, "Lay it bare, lay it bare,
> down to its foundations!"
> O daughter of Babylon, doomed to be destroyed,
> blessed shall he be who repays you
> with what you have done to us!
> Blessed shall he be who takes your little ones
> and dashes them against the rock!

This Psalm mirrors for us our own reactions to loss of place, but also helps us to understand the reactions of others:

- Grief – interestingly, grief is not triggered by present discomfort, nor even by memories of past danger, but by memories of what has been lost
- Depression – loss of motivation for singing and all that goes with it
- Despair – feeling cut off from God and not seeing the way forward
- Nationalism – the determination not to forget one's own people
- Outrage – at all the destruction

There are many people who are disturbed at finding this combination of emotions in a song of worship to God. It is not uncommon to find Christian liturgies bracketing verses 7–9 as optional, implying that these words are not suitable for use in public worship. The laments in verses 1–6 are viewed as appropriate expressions of pain, in line with the therapeutic orthodoxy of facing grief. However, the imprecation of verses 7–9 is considered not only inappropriate but potentially dangerous.

Yet the very existence of this psalm invites us to acknowledge these emotions rather than to try to suppress them. Perhaps we can conclude that worship is not only an appropriate context for expressing such emotions but that it is also the most appropriate place for doing so. If God is indeed the Safe Place, he is the one to whom we can admit all our dangerous emotions. I do not have space here to explore this psalm in the context of other biblical material about the exile, but I want to suggest that, if we do so, we can see a crucial place for the acknowledgment of traumatic anger and pain in dealing with land issues. The psalm functions as a mirror that helps us to normalize our situations and to feel our common human condition.[14]

The more significant question raised by verses 7–9 is this: What do we do with the past in order to be able to live well in the present and in the future? Lament over loss was not sufficient for the psalmist; something had to be done

---

14. See Glaser, "We Sat Down," 641–52.

about the outrageous actions that had caused the loss. The following four observations help to unpack these verses.

First, the appeal is being made to God. It is God who is asked to "remember" the evil that has been done, with the implication that it is God – and not the psalmist or his kin – who will deal with that evil. And prophetic passages elsewhere – for example, in Obadiah – affirm that God has seen and does indeed judge evil.

Second, this is not so much a cry for *vengeance* as a cry for *justice*. Vengeance returns the offense and more, as in the sevenfold divine vengeance that protects Cain and the escalation of it by Lamech to seventy-sevenfold (Gen 4:15, 23–24). In Torah law, human beings are constrained to a justice that stops at "eye for eye, tooth for tooth" (Exod 21:24; Lev 24:20; Deut 19:21). Justice requires that we do to them as they did to us. That might work in the cases mentioned in the Torah, such as a small-scale dispute that has caused damage, or false witness in court. But, in the case of long-standing land disputes between whole groups of people, can justice for all be realistically attained? This is particularly the case where there are differing views regarding the nature of territory.

In their different contexts, both the Qur'an and the New Testament quote "eye for eye" and suggest alternatives to it. In its legal context, the Qur'an asserts that refraining is better than exacting justice (Surah 5:45). Jesus's Sermon on the Mount, exploring the underlying roots of the law and the character of God in the context of Roman occupation, goes further and recommends that the victim should offer to take on the punishment due to the perpetrator – a cheek for a cheek, a garment for a garment, a mile for a mile (Matt 5:38–41)! Could we see this as opening a new kind of hospitality? A welcome for the enemy that could, as Surah 41:34 suggests, turn the person into a friend? Either way, it is implied that a person must first acknowledge that injustice has been done and then that justice should redress the balance by choosing to somehow absorb the injustice rather than retaliate against it.

Third, the psalmist's people may have been victims in this case, but they were not themselves innocent. The prophets insist that the exile was God's judgment on the injustices committed by Israel (see Jeremiah 22). One cannot but remember that they had themselves been the instruments of God's terrible judgment when they settled in their promised land.[15] One might read Jesus's

---

15. They had killed Canaanite children at God's command (Josh 6:21; see also Deut 7:1–2). I do not have the space to elaborate on the possible implications of this observation, but it emphasizes the commonality of human suffering that accompanies territorial change and the sinfulness of the executioners of judgment.

teaching on "eye for eye" in the context of his summarizing statement later in the Sermon on the Mount: "Judge not, that you be not judged. For with the judgment you pronounce you will be judged" (Matt 7:1–2 ESV; compare Surah 5:44).

Fourth, the Hebrew Bible suggests elsewhere that God shares his people's lament. The verse from Jeremiah that was cited at the start of this essay is taken from a chapter that warns the king against injustice, declares woe on the unjust king, and then predicts the punishment of exile. The chapter finishes with a short poem:

> Is this man Coniah a despised, broken pot,
>   a vessel no one cares for?
> Why are he and his children hurled and cast
>   into a land that they do not know?
> O land, land, land,
>   hear the word of the LORD!
> Thus says the LORD:
>   "Write this man down as childless,
> a man who shall not succeed in his days,
>   for none of his offspring shall succeed
> in sitting on the throne of David
>   and ruling again in Judah." (Jer 22:28–30 ESV)

The imagery of child loss alongside land loss offers a striking parallel to Psalm 137. The peak of the lament comes at the center: "O land, land, land!" Brueggemann describes this as Yahweh's "lean cry of grief" as he laments over the land and the king.[16] Rabbinic commentary also hears the divine voice as a reading of the center of our psalm: "'If I forget you, O Jerusalem . . .' is God's own response to His peoples' despair."[17] The traumatized who call on God to remember are assured that he will not forget because their pain and their injustice is his concern, and they can trust him to do right.

The Second Difficulty: Views of Land

If – and it is a big *if* – humans manage to deal with the trauma of land loss and work toward justice and forgiveness, what are the possible ways forward into peaceful and just futures within our respective lands? If the case studies

---

16. Brueggemann, *Jeremiah*, 204–5.
17. *Pesiqta Rabbati* 28:1.

in this volume are anything to go by, the answers will not be easy. We may be able to trust God to do right, but we will need a great deal of wisdom if we are to do right ourselves!

Throughout this essay, there is a largely shared understanding that all land ultimately belongs to God and that humans are guests within his land. As Maa U observes, this means that each place should be a sacred space in which people can live and work together. However, there remains a huge problem in putting this excellent ideal into practice: the different parties have different views of the nature of territory; consequently, a misunderstanding of each other's perspectives can have fatal consequences. Here are some of the varying, and sometimes incompatible, views:

Bounded and unbounded territory. Tensions between herders and farmers underlie some of the current West African disputes. These disputes are exacerbated by the farmers' views of territory as bounded – "this is the edge of my field" – and the herders' view of territory as unbounded – "this is the space in which people move and find the pasture they need."[18]

Indigenes and incomers. The idea that the original peoples of a land – if they can be identified – have a status different from that of incomers appears in different ways in various contexts. On the one hand, papers from Africa express the hope that the autochthonous peoples can welcome incomers as guests. On the other hand, one can note that such innovations as the nation-state and democracy raise the expectation that incomers become equal citizens. Sometimes, the incomers may supplant the indigenes; that is, conversely, the guests supplant the hosts.

The nation-state and religious territory. In today's international world, the concept of the nation-state is used to categorize all territory. As observed at the beginning of this paper, there is no longer a "wilderness" that is under the sole ownership of God. How then does the concept of the nation-state relate to the concepts of the Muslim *umma* and the Christian "community"?

One of the hopes of the organizers of the inaugural conference and of this festschrift was that African views of territory might offer hope for hospitable coexistence of Muslims and Christians. Of particular importance is Azumah's idea – explained in *The Legacy of Faith* – that land is a "sacred trust" from the gods or ancestors over which the first settlers have guardianship.[19] All future settlers are seen as non-kin guests, with the autochthonous people as their

---

18. For a relevant case study from a conference attendee who did not offer a paper, see Baidoo "Farmer-Herder Conflict."

19. Azumah, *Legacy of Faith*, 40–42.

hosts and patrons. Incomers are allocated their own living space – known as a *zongo* – and it was as such non-kin guests that Muslims were welcomed into African lands. Ryan's case study (chapter 12) demonstrates how this enabled societies to develop in which there could be Muslims ruling society at the same time as autochthonous guardianship of the land.

Azumah correlates this view of land with African religious openness, in which "religion" is not bounded. Thus, while aspects of Islam can be adopted, "conversion" from one religion to the other is not an appropriate concept. Two decades earlier, a Sanneh paper correlated the *zongo* idea with what he called "the domestication of Islam and Christianity in Africa," employing spatial language to map subsequent religious development.[20] The "host" status of the autochthonous people resulted in hospitality toward Christian missionaries and Muslim settlers. And it was Africans who decided what they wished to accept from the incoming religions rather than the missionaries who decided what they wanted to give.

However, both Sanneh and Azumah go on to examine the development of Islamic jihad or reform movements that challenged and sought to destroy traditional models. Sanneh comments on the irony of the reformers fighting the very system that had enabled them to settle,[21] underlining what happens when guests become so comfortably settled that they wish to become hosts. In *The Crown and the Turban* – a later work – Sanneh examines both Christian and Muslim territorialism, and it is very clear that neither is compatible with traditional African views of land. This latter discussion is situated within the conceptual notion of the nation-state, which, he says, can be "the opiate of the people, an intoxicating infusion of sentiments of national transcendence in defiance of logic and history."[22] Sanneh was thoroughly aware of the tensions with regard to the varying views of territory that I have identified!

The past two decades have demonstrated that while, on the one hand, traditional African religious openness persists, on the other hand, competing ideas of power-linked Islam, Christian-linked Western power, and nation-states also persist. We might also note that while the *zongo* concept offers an attractive model of hospitality, it is unlikely to be compatible with the idea of citizenship in a democratic nation-state. The view of land whereby the "strangers" can settle, farm, and own all the fruits of the land but can never own the land itself

---

20. Sanneh, "Domestication," 3.
21. Sanneh, "Domestication," 5; see also Sanneh, *Crown and the Turban*, 213–14.
22. Sanneh, *Crown and the Turban*, 187.

implies that the descendants of new incomers can never be equal citizens with the indigenes.

What resources might the Bible offer for dealing with such competing views of territory? Is there a biblical way of adjudicating between open and bounded models or between traditional African and modern nation-state models? Or is there another way of negotiating toward the coexistence of different models? What follows here are a few pointers toward further study.

It seems that the variety of contexts reflected in the Bible represent a range of territorial models that display varying strengths and weaknesses. The peoples of the ancient world, with their myths of their own gods establishing the people in the land, were nearer to traditional African views of land than to modern Western ideas. At the same time, there were always empires expanding their territories and migrations of peoples for various reasons.

Biblical Israel had the challenge of living under God in the midst of this territorial world. The patriarchs functioned with an unbounded view of territory as they moved freely around and beyond the "promised land." The Egypt generations functioned as incomers within the bounded territory of the Pharaoh and the designated *zongo* of Goshen. The wilderness generation was again in unbounded territory, constituted into a people under God's laws. The generations of the exile would again be incomers in a foreign land but, this time, coming under duress rather than voluntarily.

This is the context for the enduring theme of the land promised to Abraham's descendants, in which they would live from the time of the conquest to the exile and to which some of them would return after the exile. It was also where, at the time of Jesus, they lived under foreign rule and the place from which they would again be exiled from 70 CE until the mid-twentieth century. This land is also an area that continues to be a focus of local as well as international dispute. It is in this wider context that one must return to the question, why *a land*? Since a people, by its very nature, needs a home, the allocation of a land is not surprising. But going beyond this obvious point, the people are the locus of God's special presence and also the recipients and enactors of God's law. The land, then, is the territory that contains the temple, which is under God's law.

This is a clue to understanding the exceedingly difficult question of the conquest. The horrifying destruction of the Canaanites and their property, as well as their religion, is described in terms of God's holiness – just as the Israelites had experienced terrible cleansing judgments in the wilderness, so the land had to be cleansed in order to be the holy place. The picture is one in which God's holiness destroys all that is unholy; in other words, the presence of God is simply not compatible with the presence of anything unholy. In short, the fundamental question is not about the conquest of territory but about dealing with sin and with human sinfulness. If the promised land is to be a new Eden in the midst of the extra-Eden world, it can no more tolerate either Canaanite or Israelite sin than the original Eden could tolerate the original sin.

Sadly, as the subsequent history of Israel demonstrates, the conquest certainly did not deal with Israel's sinfulness, let alone the sinfulness of others. Moreover, the hope of a new Eden still lies in the future.[23] Unfortunately, Christian people have not always recognized that Joshua's conquest was a unique event, with no scriptural warrant for its emulation in any other context. The territorial model was strictly bounded in that the Israelites were given this territory and no other and that tribes and families were given boundaries within this territory. The Israelites were not the autochthonous people: as the indigenes had forfeited their land because of their injustice and wrong worship, and the Israelites would, albeit temporarily, forfeit the land for the same reasons. The model of biblical Israel offers resources for reflection on territorial issues, but it also presents ongoing challenges in considering how far it sets a precedent that other peoples may follow.

Islamic history has its own territorial expansions, beginning with the establishment of God's law under the prophethood of Muhammad in Medina as well as the conquest of Mecca. This presents its own interpretative challenges. In the context of Christian-Muslim relations, the ongoing implications of our histories of religious territory are crucial to negotiating between the various territorial models.

A key issue is what I have called "control." I have argued that, given histories and current fears of land loss, people and peoples are likely to feel in need of control of their situations. If one considers the perennial human desire for power, it is no surprise to find all parties wanting to follow their own territorial model and to have a measure of power within it. The religious dimension adds the questions of what divine law should be followed as well as which human agency should be in charge.

But I have also argued that people and peoples feel the need for safety. In our plural world, I want to further suggest that everyone cannot be safe if everyone is seeking control. We can only achieve safety for everyone if someone

---

23. See, for example, Isa 11:1–9; 35:1–10; 2 Pet 3:13; Rev 21:1–8. In each case, note the references to dealing with sin and establishing righteousness.

is in control and if everyone agrees on who that is.[24] Perhaps the ideal is an agreed territorial model and shared leadership. However, if each party has incompatible views of land and no compromise is possible, the safest option for all may be the dominance of some. Perhaps the best-case scenario can be described in terms of hospitality, whereby the controlling group has the responsibility of host and other groups have the responsibility of guest. Here, it is relevant to note that God is the Safe Place. We can only risk not being in control if we recognize that the whole *aretz* belongs to God, who is himself the place in which we can find our ultimate safety.

Living with Difficulty: Do We Have to Be the Host?

The Hebrew Bible has the promise of land at its heart, yet its promise remains unrealized. In the New Testament, although the Israelites had returned from exile, they were under yet another imperial power and, therefore, not in control of the land. Indeed, there is a great deal of evidence pointing to the fact that the Jewish people saw themselves as in "exile," and the New Testament sees Jesus as the one who brings this exile to an end. The people's concern was less about how they could worship outside the land and more about how they could keep God's covenant while under foreign domination. Both concerns can be expressed in the phrase "How shall we sing the LORD's song in a foreign land?"(Ps 137:4 ESV).

It is commonly said that the New Testament itself says little or nothing about the land or that the concept of the promised land moves to the eschaton – namely, to the new heaven and the new earth of Revelation 21. However, if one assumes Old Testament views of the land and takes seriously the parables that view the Messiah as one coming into his inheritance, we can perceive that the gospels present Jesus as coming to his land, traveling through his land, inspecting his tenants, and correcting wrongs in his land.

The place at the heart of the land is the temple, and the place at the heart of the temple is the "Holy Place" that symbolizes the dwelling place of God. It is in the Holy Place that Luke's narrative begins, and this is where we see people waiting for the Messiah (Luke 1:8–10; 2:22–38). Yet it is in the wilderness that John the Baptist prepares people to receive the Messiah, it is in the wilderness

---

24. I wrote this statement on 20 January 2021 – which was also the inauguration of Joe Biden, the forty-sixth president of the United States of America – reflecting on how recent events had demonstrated to the world that a country is unsafe for everyone if there is no agreement as to who is leading it!

that the Messiah defeats the devil, and it is in Galilee that he does most of his healing and preaching. When the Messiah comes to the temple, it is in judgment and in dispute with the temple leaders; and as he leaves the temple with his disciples, he tells them that the temple would soon be destroyed – and so it was, just four decades later. From then on, the Jewish people were again scattered in lands not their own, and Christians, similarly, have had no physical promised land.

Of course, history frequently recounts cases where Christians have taken control of lands. Recently, Jewish people have also again taken control of the promised land. The point here is simply that the Messiah's coming, far from giving the Israelites control of their land, led to further land loss and to the loss of the temple. Normality for God's people became living as guests in others' lands rather than as hosts in their own. One of the implications of this paper is that this normality is not an easy one; on the contrary, it is an existence marked by ongoing grief and desire for land. Observant Jews continue to lament the loss of the temple on the annual day of Tisha B'av, while expressing the hope for "next year in Jerusalem!" as they celebrate the Passover. The New Testament describes Christians as "exiles" on earth, looking forward to "a new heaven and a new earth" (1 Pet 2:11; 2 Pet 3:11–14 NIV). However, I am not aware of any regular communal recognition of the pain of exile or any reminder of what it means to be guests rather than hosts.

The gospels present the Messiah himself, the rightful owner of the land, as a guest with no home of his own, who is dependent on the hospitality of others (see Matt 8:19–20; Luke 8:3). He is the ultimate host (Luke 14:7–24), but he is also a rejected guest, for whom there is "no room . . . in the inn" (Luke 2:7 KJV; see also Matt 13:54–58; Luke 9:51–53, 58; 20:9–18). As John summarizes, "He came to his own, and his own people did not receive him" (John 1:11 ESV). To follow the Messiah is, then, to accept guest status and to risk rejection.

It is striking that one of the first miracles recorded in all three Synoptic Gospels is the healing of Simon Peter's mother-in-law (Matt 8:14–17; Mark 1:29–31; Luke 4:38–39). Jesus comes as the guest and heals the host so that she can welcome him. We are reminded of the visit of the Shekinah (manifestation of God's presence) to Abraham in Genesis 18. This is one of the few incidents in Abraham's life that is common to the Qur'an and the Bible and which Jews, Christians, and Muslims alike see as a paradigm of hospitality. The Jewish tradition not only sees Abraham as the paradigmatic host but also the Shekinah as the paradigmatic guest, visiting the sick man recovering from circumcision and healing him so that he could welcome his guest.[25]

Recall Maa U's words: ". . . it should be treated as a sacred place, but you see, human beings are just difficult to handle."

It took miracles to enable Abraham and Peter's mother-in-law to be good hosts, but when it comes to territory, peoples do not enjoy having guest status. Would guests be less "difficult to handle" if their hosts were good hosts? And would hosts be less "difficult to handle" if their guests were good guests? And what would happen if, instead of disputing over who is the host, we followed the examples of the Shekinah and Abraham, and the Messiah and Peter's mother-in-law, with the guest working for the welfare of the host and the host awed by the honor of welcoming the guest? Maybe we can aspire to this and work toward it in small ways. Having said that, however, from a Christian theological perspective, it sounds a bit like the "wolf will live with the lamb" (Isa 11:6), which will not be achieved until the eschatological vision is fulfilled. Humanity is "fallen" and will continue to be "difficult." If the Messiah himself was not accepted – either as host or guest – by most of the leaders of his own people, we can expect territorial tensions to persist.

In conclusion, we will continue to ask, with the psalmist, "How shall we sing the LORD's song in a strange land?" (Ps 137:4 KJV). The reflections in this paper indicate that we can indeed "sing the LORD's song" and faithfully follow the Lord's requirements in a strange land as we welcome the Lord, our rightful host, as the guest among us. But the more acute question is how we can faithfully "sing the LORD's song" in a land that we share with others or in one that we regard as our own. That is a challenge for Muslims and Christians alike, and it is the task of The Sanneh Institute to help us to face this challenge together.

Bibliography

Azad, A., and I. Glaser, *Genesis 1–11: Bible Commentaries from Muslim Contexts*. Carlisle: Langham Global Library, 2022.

Azumah, John Alembillah. *The Legacy of Arab Islam: A Quest for Inter-religious Dialogue*. Oxford: Oneworld, 2001.

———. "'We Sat Down and Wept': Biblical Babylon and Israel as Resources for Conflict Situations." *The Round Table: The Commonwealth Journal of International Affairs* 94, no. 382 (2005): 641–52.

---

25. *Bava Metzia* 86B; *Sotah* 14:4.

Baidoo, Ibrahim. "Farmer-Herder Conflict: A Case Study of Fulani Herdsmen and Farmers in the Agogo Traditional Area of the Ashanti Region." MA diss., University of Ghana, 2014.

Brueggemann, Walter. *A Commentary on Jeremiah: Exile and Homecoming*. Grand Rapids: Eerdmans, 1998.

———. *The Land: Place as Gift, Promise, and Challenge in Biblical Faith*. Minneapolis: Fortress, 2002.

Davies, William David. *The Gospel and the Land: Early Christianity and Jewish Territorial Doctrine*. London: Darton, 1964; Berkeley: University of California Press, 1974.

Glaser, Ida. "A Trauma Observed: Biblical Reflections on Safety, Control and Fragmentation." In *Tackling Trauma: Global, Biblical, and Pastoral Perspectives*, edited by Paul A. Barker, 51–82. Carlisle: Langham Global Library, 2019.

Sanneh, Lamin. *The Crown and the Turban: Muslims and West African Pluralism*. Boulder: Westview, 1997.

———. "The Domestication of Islam and Christianity in African Societies: A Methodological Exploration." *Journal of Religion in Africa* 11, no. 1 (1980): 1–12.

Contributors

John Azumah is the founding executive director of The Sanneh Institute in Accra, Ghana. Azumah obtained a PhD in Islam and Christian-Muslim Relations in Africa from the University of Birmingham, UK, and has taught in Ghana, South Africa, India, the UK, and the USA. He served as presidential visiting fellow at Yale University and as a visiting professor at the Yale Divinity School. Among Azumah's numerous publications are *The Legacy of Arab-Islam in Africa: A Quest for Inter-Religious Dialogue* (Oneworld Publications, 2001).

Martin Accad is the 11th president of the Near East School of Theology in Lebanon. Accad is a professor of Islam and Middle Eastern Christianity, also teaching hermeneutics, Christian-Muslim relations, and peacebuilding. He is the author of *Sacred Misinterpretation: Reaching Across the Christian-Muslim Divide* (Eerdmans, 2019), and co-editor, with Jonathan Andrews, of *The Religious Other: A Biblical Understanding of Islam, the Qur'an and Muhammad* (Langham Global Library, 2020).

Rashida Alhassan Adum-Atta is a PhD researcher on the Madina Project at Utrecht University, the Netherlands, focusing on "Food as Entry Point to the Material Study of Religion in Plural Settings." Her research investigates how food acts to include and exclude in everyday social relations and the implications for coexistence in Madina Zongo, a diverse neighborhood in Accra, Ghana. Among her publications is "The Politics of Purity, Disgust, and Contamination: Communal Identity of Trotter (Pig) Sellers in Madina Zongo (Accra)."

J. Kwabena Asamoah-Gyadu is Baeta-Grau Professor of Contemporary African Christianity and Pentecostalism at the Trinity Theological Seminary, Legon, Ghana. He is a past president of the Seminary. Kwabena has a PhD in theology from the University of Birmingham, UK. Kwabena is a Fellow of the Ghana Academy of Arts and Sciences and has published extensively in his fields of research interest in Pentecostalism, World Christianity, and Christianity and Media in Africa including *African Charismatics: Current Developments Within Independent Indigenous Pentecostalism in Ghana* (Brill Academic Publishers, 2004).

Akintunde E. Akinade is a professor of theology at Georgetown University's Edmund E. Walsh School of Foreign Service in Qatar. Before joining

Georgetown, he was professor of religion at High Point University in High Point, North Carolina. He has also taught at Wesleyan University, USA, College of New Rochelle, New York, Union Theological Seminary in New York, New York Theological Seminary, and Adeyemi College of Education, Nigeria. He is the author of *Christian Responses to Islam in Nigeria: A Contextual Study of Ambivalent Encounters* (Palgrave Macmillan, 2014).

Cheikh Anta Babou is a historian of Islam and the modern West African Muslim diaspora at the University of Pennsylvania, USA. Educated at University Cheikh Anta Diop of Dakar and Michigan State University, Dr. Babou is the author of *Fighting the Greater Jihad: Amadu Bamba and the Founding the Muridiyya of Senegal, 1853–1913* (Ohio University Press, 2007), a French translation of the book was released by Karthala under the title *Le Jihad de l'Ame* in (Karthala, 2011). His latest book, *Amadou Bamba, le fondateur de la Mouridiyya* (Histoire Générale du Sénégal, 2021), is an intellectual biography of the founder of the Muridiyya order.

Elias Kifon Bongmba has a PhD from the University of Denver, USA, and holds the Harry and Hazel Chavanne Chair in Christian Theology at Rice University, USA, where he teaches African Religions and World Christianity. Bongmba is the former president of the African Association for the Study of Religion and associate editor of Religion and Theology. Bongmba is co-editor of *Philosophy and its Others: Contemporary Legacies of German Idealism* (Bloomsbury Academic, 2023).

Joel A. Carpenter has a PhD from John Hopkins University, USA, and is professor and provost emeritus of Calvin University in Grand Rapids, USA, where he was also the founding director of the Nagel Institute for the Study of World Christianity. His current work includes consulting on research and faculty development projects in world Christianity, chairing the board of Langham Partnership USA, and editing a book series, Studies in World Christianity, with Baylor University Press. His most recent publications include are *Christianity and Social Change in Contemporary Africa* (Langaa, 2020), co-edited with Francis Nyamnjoh.

Farid Esack is a leading Muslim liberation theologian who cut his teeth in the South African struggle for liberation. He is an emeritus professor in the Department of Religion Studies at the University of Johannesburg, South Africa. In 2018 he was awarded the Order of Luthuli, South Africa's highest national award, for "his brilliant contribution to academic research and the fight against race, gender, class, and religious oppression". Among Esack's major publications is *Qur'an, Liberation and Pluralism: An Islamic Perspective of Interreligious Solidarity Against Oppression* (Oneworld Publications, 1996).

F. Peter Ford, Jr. is a retired missionary professor of Islam and Christian-Muslim relations. He served under the Reformed Church in America and taught in theological institutions in Sudan, Ethiopia, Kenya, and Lebanon. He holds theology degrees from Gordon-Conwell Theological Seminary, USA, Western Theological Seminary, USA, and a PhD in religion (Islamic studies) from Temple University, USA. His published works include his dissertation (a translation and analysis of an Arab Muslim work about Jesus) and several professional book chapters and articles in academic journals.

Ida Glaser has a PhD from the University of Durham, UK, and is director of the Center for Muslim & Christian Studies, Houston, USA, and international academic coordinator for the Centre for Muslim-Christian Studies, Oxford. Her research interests are in biblical interpretation in Islamic contexts, and she is series editor of the "Routledge Reading the Bible in Islamic Context" series and the Langham "Windows on the Text" series. Her publications include *The Bible and Other Faiths* (Langham Global Library, 2005) and *Thinking Biblically about Islam* (Langham Global Library, 2016).

Kauthar Khamis is a lecturer at Islamic University College of Ghana, and currently a PhD student on the Madina project at Utrecht University, the Netherlands. Khamis's chapter is part of her PhD thesis on women's beauty practices in the multi-ethnic and multi-religious community called Madina.

Daniel A. Madigan, SJ, is Jeanette W. and Otto J. Ruesch Family associate professor and director of Graduate Studies in the Department of Theology and Religious Studies, senior fellow of the Al-Waleed Center for Muslim-Christian Understanding, and faculty fellow of the Berkley Center for Religion, Peace and World Affairs at Georgetown University. He is also an honorary professorial fellow of Australian Catholic University. He is the author of *The Qur'ân's Self-Image: Writing and Authority in Islam's Scripture* (Princeton University Press, 2001) and a co-editor of *The Routledge Companion to the Qur'an* (Routledge, 2021).

Ferry Mamahit has a PhD in Old Testament studies from the University of Pretoria, South Africa. He is currently a faculty member at Southeast Asia Bible Seminary in Malang, Indonesia, a research associate at the Centre for Muslim-Christian Studies, Oxford, UK, and serves as the executive director of the Center for Interdisciplinary Studies on Religion and Culture in Semarang, Indonesia.

His notable publications include "Abangan Muslim, Javanese Worldview, and Muslim-Christian Relations in Indonesia" and "Reality, Theology, and Praxis of Difference: Building Cross-Cultural Religious Literacy Competencies for Christian Educators."

David Marshall has a PhD from the University of Birmingham, UK, and is the academic director of the Building Bridges Seminar at Georgetown University, USA, guest editor of Islamochristiana, the journal of the Pontifical Institute for Arabic and Islamic Studies (PISAI), and assistant chaplain of St. Ursula's Church, Bern, Switzerland. He has taught at many universities and seminaries including St Paul's, Limuru, Kenya, the University of Edinburgh, and Duke Divinity School. He is the author of *God, Muhammad and the Unbelievers: A Qur'anic Study* (Routledge, 1999).

Haruna Y. Mogtari is a PhD candidate and the executive director of Step Missions International (SMI), an indigenous mission organization, based in Ghana. Mogtari's research interest includes Islam, interfaith, chieftaincy and Fulani studies. His most recent publications are as follows: *Pulaaku: Towards a Holistic View of the Fulani* (SonLife Ghana Limited, 2020) "Fulani herdsmen Traditions and Care for the Land," among others.

Joshua Ralston has a PhD from Emory University and is a reader in Christian-Muslim Relations at the University of Edinburgh. He previously taught theology at Union Presbyterian Seminary in Richmond, USA, and has been a visiting professor in Egypt, Nigeria, and Australia. He is the author of *Law and the Rule of God: A Christian Engagement with Shari'a* (Cambridge University Press, 2020) and co-editor of three books, most recently *Beyond Binaries: Religious Diversity in Europe* (Brill, 2023).

Patrick J. Ryan, SJ, is the Laurence J. McGinley Professor of Religion and Society at Fordham University. He earned a PhD from Harvard University and for about half of his life, as a Jesuit priest, Fr. Ryan worked in West Africa, mostly in Nigeria and Ghana. He served as the first President of Loyola Jesuit College, a secondary school in Abuja, Nigeria. The author of numerous articles, scholarly and popular, Fr. Ryan's major publications include: *Imale: Yoruba Participation in the Muslim Tradition: A Study of Clerical Piety* (Scholars Press, 1978) and *The Coming of Our God: Scriptural Reflections for Advent, Christmas, and Epiphany* (Paulist Press, 1999).

Kelefa Sanneh is a staff writer at *The New Yorker* and a contributor to "CBS Sunday Morning." He is also the author of *Major Labels: A History of Popular*

Music in Seven Genres (Canongate, 2021). He lives in New York City with his family.

Fr. Cosmas Ebo Sarbah (Catholic) has a PhD from the Centre for Christian-Muslim Relations at the University of Birmingham, UK. He also holds a licentiate from the Pontifical Institute for the Study of Arabic and Islamic Studies, Rome. He is director of Interreligious Dialogue for the Catholic Archdiocese of Cape Coast, Ghana, and senior lecturer of Comparative Religion and Interreligious Relations at the University of Ghana. His research interests include comparative religion, interreligious dialogue, and ecumenism in Christianity and Islam in sub-Saharan Africa.

Caroline Seed has a PhD from the Greenwich School of Theology, UK, is a mission partner with Church Mission Society (CMS), and is on faculty at George Whitefield College, South Africa, as part of the Theological Education Development Services (TEDS) team. She coordinates training for theological institutions in the areas of theological research and academic administration. Her publications include "Monotheism, messianism and Children of Israel: Reception of the Gospel of John among the *Isawa* of Northern Nigeria and the *Qiang* of Western China, 1913-1935."

Rt. Rev. Rowan Williams was born in Wales and has a PhD in philosophy from the University of Oxford. He was the bishop of Monmouth in Wales before becoimg archbishop of Canterbury in 2002, and then master of Magdalene College, Cambridge, from 2013 to 2020. He now lives in Cardiff. He has written widely on theology and culture, and is the author of *Christ the Heart of Creation* (Bloomsbury Continuum, 2018) and many other books.

Langham Literature and its imprints are a ministry of Langham Partnership.

Langham Partnership is a global fellowship working in pursuit of the vision God entrusted to its founder John Stott –

> *to facilitate the growth of the church in maturity and Christ-likeness through raising the standards of biblical preaching and teaching.*

Our vision is to see churches in the Majority World equipped for mission and growing to maturity in Christ through the ministry of pastors and leaders who believe, teach and live by the word of God.

Our mission is to strengthen the ministry of the word of God through:
- nurturing national movements for biblical preaching
- fostering the creation and distribution of evangelical literature
- enhancing evangelical theological education

especially in countries where churches are under-resourced.

Our ministry

Langham Preaching partners with national leaders to nurture indigenous biblical preaching movements for pastors and lay preachers all around the world. With the support of a team of trainers from many countries, a multi-level programme of seminars provides practical training, and is followed by a programme for training local facilitators. Local preachers' groups and national and regional networks ensure continuity and ongoing development, seeking to build vigorous movements committed to Bible exposition.

Langham Literature provides Majority World preachers, scholars and seminary libraries with evangelical books and electronic resources through publishing and distribution, grants and discounts. The programme also fosters the creation of indigenous evangelical books in many languages, through writer's grants, strengthening local evangelical publishing houses, and investment in major regional literature projects, such as one volume Bible commentaries like *The Africa Bible Commentary* and *The South Asia Bible Commentary*.

Langham Scholars provides financial support for evangelical doctoral students from the Majority World so that, when they return home, they may train pastors and other Christian leaders with sound, biblical and theological teaching. This programme equips those who equip others. Langham Scholars also works in partnership with Majority World seminaries in strengthening evangelical theological education. A growing number of Langham Scholars study in high quality doctoral programmes in the Majority World itself. As well as teaching the next generation of pastors, graduated Langham Scholars exercise significant influence through their writing and leadership.

To learn more about Langham Partnership and the work we do visit **langham.org**